NEW EVERY MORNING

D. James Kennedy

MULTNOMAH BOOKS
SISTERS, OREGON

232

This book is dedicated to Mary Anne Bunker and Ruth Rohm,
my efficient secretaries who have faithfully served me through the years.

There are a few people I would like to thank for their help with this book.
First of all, I thank Kirsti Newcombe for her invaluable help with much of the editing of this volume.
Also, I need to thank Mary K. Moore and R. Matthew Ray for their editing help as well.
Finally, I am also most appreciative of Greg Johnson and the staff of Alive Communications,
who made this book possible in the first place.

NEW EVERY MORNING

published by Multnomah Books
a part of the Questar publishing family

and published in association with the literary agency of Alive Communications, Inc.,
1465 Kelly Johnson Blvd., Suite 320, Colorado Springs, CO 80920

© 1996 by D. James Kennedy and Jerry Newcombe

International Standard Book Number: 1-57673-068-9

Cover photo by Pat O'Hara
Cover design by Kevin Keller
Edited by Lisa Baba Lauffer
Copyedited by Candace McMahan

Printed in the United States of America

Most Scripture quotations are from:

The New King James Version (NKJV) © 1984 by Thomas Nelson, Inc.

Also quoted:

The King James Version (KJV)

The Holy Bible, New International Version (NIV) © 1973, 1984 by International Bible Society,
used by permission of Zondervan Publishing House.

For information:
QUESTAR PUBLISHERS, INC.
POST OFFICE BOX 1720
SISTERS, OREGON 97759

96 97 98 99 00 01 02 03 — 10 9 8 7 6 5 4 3 2 1

A GREAT NEW YEAR

Surely goodness and mercy shall follow me…

PSALM 23:6

Happy new year!

Do you have bright hopes and ambitious plans for the year ahead? I think we should purpose to make this year a great one for God's glory! But how can we do that? We lay our plans and make our resolutions, and yet, sometimes what we deemed the year of great prospects turns out to be a year of disaster. One recent study found that seventy percent of people couldn't keep their new year resolutions even through the month of January, much less the whole year.

So how can you and I make this new year great? Let me offer a prescription of five elements that can contribute to an excellent year…even to a successful life! You can find these elements in Proverbs 3:1–10, wherein God promises that if we obey His commands, we will experience "long life and peace." As you read through the passage, you'll find these themes:

1. Keep God's commands for a long and happy life.
2. Live by mercy and truth for popularity and a good reputation.
3. Trust in and acknowledge the Lord for direction and guidance.
4. Fear the Lord, and forsake evil for good health.
5. Honor and give to the Lord your possessions for financial well-being.

Generally speaking, if you follow each command, you'll receive each corresponding reward. But keep in mind that these are general principles, not guarantees. Many people who live good and godly lives do not experience all five consequences.

Neither are these "five easy steps" to Paradise. We don't achieve admittance to heaven by following *any* set of rules or living a good life. The Bible makes it abundantly clear that we receive salvation by God's grace only, never by human works. But if we love Jesus, we want to show Him that love by obeying His Word.

This year ask God to show you what goals He has for you. Then ask Him how you can achieve those goals. Submit yourself to Him and purpose to love Him in all you do, and you'll most definitely have a happy and spiritually prosperous year!

A year of self-surrender will bring larger blessings than fourscore years of selfishness.

ANONYMOUS

TIME WILL BE NO MORE

*The days of our lives are seventy years; and if by reason
of strength they are eighty years…it is soon cut off, and we fly away.*

PSALM 90:10

Each morning we receive one brand-new, shiny, golden day, set with twenty-four jeweled hours. Every one of us receives precisely the same amount of time each day. Today some of us will use our twenty-four hours to God's glory and the betterment of humankind, others will waste them, and still others will use them for evil. Each of us has the same amount, and what we do with this day will have eternal consequences.

How will you invest this day?

Time is an irreplaceable asset. Once it's gone, we can never get it back. Scripture tells us that one day time will cease and eternity will begin. When that happens, we will have to account for how we spent the time God gave us. So we must choose wisely the ways we invest it.

When we speak of investing, we usually speak of investing *money*. People invest money because they realize that they must prepare for their future, for later years in this life. As believers in God, we must realize that we have an eternal future to prepare for and that we need to invest our *time* wisely that we might have dividends, not only in this life, but forever.

So what are wise investments of our time? We invest our time wisely when we concern ourselves with the things that concern God—when our hearts break with the sorrows that break God's heart. And what breaks God's heart more than lost people? Jesus came to seek and save the lost. He gave His life looking for us. He died to redeem us. This was His joy. Christ finished the work God gave Him, and He sends us into the world to do the same.

So today, invest yourself in people as much as possible. As you invest your time in people and the great work of Christ's kingdom, you invest in eternity!

*There are no ordinary people. You have never talked with a mere mortal.
Nations, cultures, arts, civilizations—these are mortal, and their life is to ours
as the life of a gnat. But it is immortals whom we joke with, work with, marry, snub and
exploit—immortal horrors or everlasting splendours.*

C. S. LEWIS

STAY FOCUSED

...one thing I do...

PHILIPPIANS 3:13

Have you ever watched interviews of athletes who have won come-from-behind victories? What do these people almost invariably credit for their ability to win games? Focus. Concentration. Fixing their eyes on the goal, then playing their best to achieve it.

As Christians, we, too, need to focus our attention on our goal—to glorify God and enjoy Him forever. The apostle Paul knew his goal. He pressed toward the mark, keeping "one thing" in mind, just as Jesus set His face toward Jerusalem. Paul was not distracted by past failures. Instead, he persistently reached forward, toward things ahead. He wanted to share the gospel with as many Gentiles as he could. Though beaten, imprisoned, and shipwrecked, he never gave up; he pressed on with the "one thing" he had to do.

Think of the impact we could make if we imitated Paul just as he imitated Christ!

Unfortunately, we often lack this kind of concentration. We begin something but get sidetracked and go on to something else. Then something new further distracts us, and off we go in that direction. In this way we hop from one distraction to another.

Does this sound familiar?

For those of us who feel this scenario hits a little too close to home, I believe we need to pursue the same thing pursued by athletes, the apostle Paul, and our Lord and Savior Jesus Christ: self-discipline. How? By engaging in three actions that will contribute to our success. First, we need to carefully select definite and clear-cut goals, both long- and short-range, that lead to our ultimate goal—to glorify God and enjoy him forever. We must choose these goals with the intention of glorifying God and advancing His kingdom. Second, we need to stay focused. We must maintain a burning desire to reach our goals. If something distracts us, we need to return our focus to our ultimate goal. And third, we need to create workable plans. We cannot reach a goal without charting a course to meet it. I agree with the maxim "People do not plan to fail; they just fail to plan."

Today take some time to evaluate your ability to maintain your focus. If you think you've fallen short, read through the three actions that lead to self-discipline, and prayerfully commit to one way you can cultivate focus in your life. Then put it into action, and wait for God to show you the results of focusing on that "one thing" in your life!

Plan your work, and work your plan.

DIRECTION AND GUIDANCE

Trust in the LORD with all your heart, and lean not on your own understanding; in all your ways acknowledge Him, and He shall direct your paths.

PROVERBS 3:5–6

You're at the beginning of a new year. What plans do you have for yourself in the year to come? And how do you choose your goals for each new year?

As we stand at the beginning of another year, Proverbs 3:5–6 offers us direction and guidance. You and I desperately need God's direction in our lives. How do we receive it? By trusting in the Lord with all of our hearts and not leaning on our own understanding. God doesn't ask us to stop using our brains, but He does want us to avoid relying on our own self-confidence, despite the world's affirmation of that trait. Often what the world affirms, the Lord abhors. God wants us to rely on Him and Him alone. So as you choose goals for the year, trust God to guide you. Don't use your own reasoning to back up your plans; ask God to guide you, then listen for His answer.

The Proverbs passage promises us that if we acknowledge God, He'll direct our paths. So how do we acknowledge God? We acknowledge our Lord by seeing Him in every aspect of our lives, by having a vision of Him and His providential workings in and through us. We acknowledge Him by seeking Him first in all we do and by obeying His commandments. What has God done in your life recently? And how can you remain obedient to His call on your life?

As we acknowledge God's rightful place in our lives, He'll direct us along the pathways of our lives. He does this in three main ways. First, God directs us through His Word. As long as we follow Scripture, we can be certain we're traveling the right path. Second, God directs us through circumstances in our lives. Sometimes He guides us by opening doors, sometimes by closing them. Sometimes He makes our paths smooth; sometimes He allows us to fall flat on our faces. Sometimes He removes obstacles; sometimes He throws them in our way. Third, God guides us through His Holy Spirit. Sometimes the Spirit's "still small voice" pulls us back from a venture we've planned, and only much later we discover that He has spared us from disaster!

Although we may not always see God's hand immediately, He does guide us when we trust Him. Often we only see His guidance in retrospect. But we can rely on His promise to provide direction if we trust Him in every aspect of our lives—in our home lives, at work, at school, as we drive our car, as we eat our meals, as we conduct business. As you ponder your goals for the year, invite God to guide you. As you acknowledge Him, He'll direct you down the right path for your life.

Jesus, Savior, pilot me, over life's tempestuous sea.

EDWARD HOPPER

January 5

GOOD HEALTH

Do not be wise in your own eyes; fear the LORD and depart from evil.
It will be health to your flesh, and strength to your bones.

PROVERBS 3:7–8

When did you last hear a health news update about another food to avoid or another theory on exercise? We live in such a health-conscious society, and we seem to constantly hear ways to promote our health through proper diet, exercise, and annual checkups. No doubt these precautions are of value. But underlying our physical health is our spiritual health. In reality, God controls every germ, every virus, and every bacterium. He's ultimately in control of our health, just as He controls life and death.

If you would have "health to your flesh, and strength to your bones," then fear the Lord and depart from evil. If we want true health, we need to pursue good. We need to reject the idea that we can find happiness or fulfillment by compromising with the world and engaging in sinful amusements. After all, many sinful and evil practices, such as substance abuse and promiscuity, result in bad health. Instead, we need to find our joy by following God.

As long as we live in this fallen world, we'll experience sickness and sorrow. Many godly people live with pain every minute of their lives, and good health is no measure of spirituality. Only in heaven will we be totally free from sickness and pain. And yet, generally speaking, we'll gain life and health if we follow God's ways. Recent studies have shown the link between being spiritually committed and having good health. One recent article documented the link between mental and physical health and being a committed Christian; it was appropriately entitled "For good health, go to church."

How can you walk in God's ways today to gain "health to your flesh, and strength to your bones"?

God helps the sick in two ways, through the science of medicine and surgery and
through the science of faith and prayer.

NORMAN VINCENT PEALE

January 6

MARK AND DEMAS

*…for Demas has forsaken me, having loved this present world, and
has departed for Thessalonica…*

2 TIMOTHY 4:10

Do you have the courage and stamina to fight the good fight to the end? When faced with seemingly overwhelming obstacles, will you give up, or will you stand firm?

Mark and Demas, colleagues of the apostle Paul, clearly illustrate the startling contrast between faithful and faithless soldiers in God's army. In the beginning, Demas seemed a better soldier for Christ than Mark. Demas had served as Paul's right-hand man, traveling with him on all four missionary journeys and experiencing shipwrecks, trials, and beatings. Mark, on the other hand, had "chickened out" on Paul's first trip. Mark had quit and gone home, and when Mark felt ready to serve again, Paul refused to let Mark travel with him.

But years later, in his prison cell awaiting death, Paul realized which man was the real soldier for Christ. Demas had now forsaken him, "having loved this present world," and Paul eagerly awaited Mark's arrival. By this time, Mark had matured, having had Barnabas as a mentor, and Paul considered him "profitable" in the ministry. In fact, Mark authored the Gospel of Mark!

This story of Mark reminds me of three young men who joined the British army and became lieutenants. When World War I broke out, one of the young lieutenants, who was rich and spoiled, panicked at the thought of fighting and managed to get a discharge. The others sent him two white feathers, signifying that they viewed him as a coward. When his fiancée discovered that he had quit, she broke their engagement and gave him a white feather from her hat.

Ashamed, this young man enlisted as a private under an assumed name. He fought on the front lines, and there he rescued both of his buddies. Afterward, he returned their feathers to them. When wounded, this young man found his fiancée, who had become an army nurse, and returned her feather, too. At that point, she knew her quitter had tried again; her coward had become a hero.

When the struggles come, will you be a hero? Commit today to enter the discipline of a soldier, preparing yourself by God's power to endure and win any battles you may face.

Finish what you start.

ANONYMOUS

ALL THINGS THROUGH CHRIST

I can do all things through Christ who strengthens me.

PHILIPPIANS 4:13

We all have tapes playing in our minds, the tapes of parents, teachers, coaches, and others telling us how inadequate we are. You probably have a phrase or two that come to mind—comments someone once made to you, comments devastating and character-forming all at the same time. You could quote them verbatim, right?

"You're a dunce!" That's what she said. "You're a dunce, and I am going to fail you." And the teacher failed Einstein in mathematics.

"I'm sorry; we don't want you in our choir. You can't sing, so don't come back." But Jerome Hines became the greatest basso profundo the Metropolitan Opera has ever known.

Many of us have horrible self-images because we believe lies rather than the truth of God. Often we've heard from parents or misguided authorities that we have no worth, and we buy it. We believe the lies of our past. Even our own failures mock us: "You can't do it. Don't you remember? You tried before, and you blew it. You even tried twice, three times, and you failed. You can't do it."

But those are lies. As the old maxim puts it, "God don't make no junk."

Inspirational speaker and writer Zig Ziglar reminds us that we should learn from what he calls the "successful failures." Walt Disney went broke seven times before he succeeded. Thomas Edison made fourteen thousand experiments that failed before he developed the incandescent light. Babe Ruth recorded the most strikeouts in the history of baseball, yet he became one of the greatest hitters of all time. Nobody remembers these men's failures, but everybody remembers their successes. Ziglar says that a big shot is just a little shot that kept on shooting—when people or past experiences told that person that he or she couldn't hit the mark, that person kept on shooting.

"I can do all things through Christ." Who made that claim? Paul the Apostle—with his thorn in the flesh and his weak eyes, who was "contemptuous in his speech" and "contemptible in his talk." The same Paul who turned the world upside down for Christ!

When you have doubts about your abilities to accomplish something, ask God to tell you the truth about who you are, about Whose you are. Then invite Him to do a great work in you and through you. Make this your motto: "I can do all things through Christ who strengthens me."

What a man accomplishes depends on what he believes.

BANKERS BULLETIN

January 8

WHATSOEVER IS LOVELY

Finally, brethren, whatever things are true, whatever things are noble, whatever things are just, whatever things are pure, whatever things are lovely, whatever things are of good report, if there is any virtue and if there is anything praiseworthy—meditate on these things.

PHILIPPIANS 4:8

Philippians 4:8 is probably the original proclamation of positive thinking! In this passage lies the secret of a happy life, a positive attitude, a winsome personality, advancement in life, and acceptance by others. Certainly we all desire these things. As we fill our minds and hearts with the true, the noble, the just, the pure, the lovely, and the good, then God will lift us up and grant us peace.

What do you spend time thinking about? Do you meditate on virtuous things?

Keeping our minds and hearts trained on the praiseworthy is difficult. Because of their separation from God, many media producers create material that is the opposite of all these wonderful things. They show us the false, the ignoble, the unjust, the ungodly, the unkind, the crass, and the ghastly. All of this pours out of television sets, movie screens, novels, and magazines of modern times.

Television and movie producers defend their creations by saying, "We're only reflecting reality." Well, I want to say back to them, "Yes, but life is more than the gutter, the toilet, and the brothel!" We can't deny the reality of the gutter. But roses are just as real and much more worthy of our devoted attention.

Today and every day, set your thoughts on things above. Surround yourself with everything praiseworthy. Drink in the true, noble, pure, and lovely, and allow God to grant you His peace as you do so, for He is the source of it all.

Where there is beauty, there is the Spirit of God.

R. C. SPROUL

THE PROMISES OF GOD

'God is not a man, that He should lie, nor a son of man, that He should repent.
Has he said, and will He not do it? Or has He spoken, and will He not make it good?'

NUMBERS 23:19

Think of a time when someone broke a promise he or she made to you. How did you feel? How did that broken promise affect your relationship?

We live in a world of broken promises. Our courts are clogged with lawsuits because of them. But our Father in heaven makes thousands of promises in His Word (How many? Approximately eight thousand!), and He keeps *each one*. When God promises something, we can count on the fact that He will come through for us.

The most important promise God has made is His promise to save us from our sins. "Believe on the Lord Jesus Christ and thou shalt be saved," says the promise. And faith responds: "Lord, I believe in you. I believe that that promise is true." God changes your life and stamps your passport to Paradise simply because you believe His promise.

When we claim God's promises, we experience tremendous blessings. A delightful member of our church, who has now gone home to the Lord, witnessed to prison inmates six days a week for more than forty years. This man was quite enthusiastic about the promises of God. He would have the prisoners memorize 1 John 1:9: "If we confess our sins, He is faithful and just to forgive us our sins and to cleanse us from all unrighteousness." He called this promise "the Christian's bar of soap," and he encouraged his inmate friends to bank their lives on it.

But while God yearns to fulfill His promises to us, we often fail to claim them. Think of the blessings you've received in your lifetime. Did you not receive those blessings because you claimed certain promises God made to you? In the same way, we *miss* certain blessings because we never claim God's promises. God is prepared to fulfill His promises. He has written and signed checks from His account in the Bank of Heaven—He is ready to bless us—but those checks lay on a shelf in a closed Bible, unclaimed, uncashed.

God wants to bless your life. Are you ready to claim His promises?

What God has promised, you can take to the bank.

AQUIRING HUMILITY

*Therefore humble yourselves under the mighty hand of God, that
He may exalt you in due time...*

1 PETER 5:6

Pride, says the Bible, goes before destruction, and a haughty spirit before a fall. Pride lay at the root of Adam and Eve's downfall and thus of our own. It threatens our families, our friendships, even our salvation. Pride has become entrenched in our human nature; we think we can make it through life on our own power.

Yet everything we have comes from God. Ask yourself the question Paul asked the Corinthian Christians: What do you have that you did not receive? God is the source of *everything*. Thus, none of us has reason to be proud.

So how can we acquire humility? We begin by putting ourselves into proper perspective, seeing ourselves in relationship to God. When we look to God, we grasp our unworthiness. Yet humility doesn't come from abasing ourselves. It comes from glorifying God, seeing Him as the source of all we are and all we have. In His love, God accepts us unconditionally and lifts us to higher ground. He shows us that we are His children, made in His image, adopted into His family as sons and daughters of a glorious and victorious King!

Another antidote to pride is gratitude. Whenever we accomplish anything in life, we can choose to be proud or grateful. As we realize that we accomplish nothing without God, we must choose gratitude, giving the glory to Him for all He does for us.

We can't have prideful hearts and maintain a right relationship with God. God doesn't need our accomplishments, nor is He interested in our vainglory. He wants *us!* Christ wants us to cultivate humble hearts that bow before His grace and His cross—the ultimate example of humility.

Today view yourself in relationship with God and thank Him for all He has accomplished in your life. Lay your achievements at His feet, blessing Him for His goodness to you.

It was through pride that the devil became the devil.

C. S. LEWIS

JUSTIFICATION BY FAITH

Therefore we conclude that a man is justified by faith apart from the deeds of the law.

ROMANS 3:28

The most crucial question anyone could ever ask is: "How can I be right with God?" We all need to know how we—sinful human beings—can ever secure right relationships with a holy, sin-hating God.

Do you want to know the answer? Here it is: You and I can gain right relationships with God through justification by faith.

Justification by faith is one of the central doctrines of Christianity. But what does it mean? Justification is a judicial term. If an accused person goes before the bar of justice, the judge can only justify that person if the judge or jury finds the person innocent. If a judge or jury finds the accused guilty, the judge may condemn that person, sending him or her to prison. A governor or king may pardon the prisoner, but even so, the person is still a pardoned criminal, and that is vastly different from being justified. To be justified is to be made "just as if I'd never sinned." No human judge can ever proclaim that, but God can! When we repent of our sins and trust in Christ alone for our salvation, the miracle of justification takes place.

How well I remember that day when I first discovered the truth about myself. I went before the bar of God's judgment. Justice accused me, and the scales tipped against me. The Judge looked me sternly in the face and said, "I pronounce that you shall die. Do you have anything to say for yourself?" For the first time in all my self-righteous life, I was speechless! The Judge brought down his gavel and pronounced the sentence: eternal death.

But as death descended upon me, Jesus suddenly intervened, declaring, "Surely he deserves to die, but the spear pierced My side instead. I went to hell for him so he wouldn't have to. Now let him go free." That day, Christ transformed my life, and I have not been the same since.

Have you been justified by faith? Jesus has already served your sentence, and He waits for you to turn to Him, trusting Him with your life. Because He died in your place, your slate can be clean. If you haven't already, make today the day you accept His free gift of eternal life.

All of the religions of this world are simply good advice. Only Christianity is good news.

SANCTIFICATION AND GLORIFICATION

*'Sanctify them by Your truth. Your word is truth. And for their sakes I sanctify Myself,
that they also may be sanctified by the truth.'*

JOHN 17:17, 19

If we ever want to enter heaven, we need to be holy, totally free from sin, absolutely perfect. But, of course, we fall far short of that standard. And so our salvation depends on divine intervention which God has made possible through Christ's death and resurrection.

Salvation is a three-step process. The first step is *justification,* which we discussed yesterday. Justification is a one-time act which starts our Christian life. When we give our lives to Christ, He cleanses us through His blood by His grace. He makes us pure, fit for eternity in heaven. The second step in our salvation is *sanctification.* Sanctification takes a lifetime as God gradually changes us into the image of His Son. We don't become divine in any way, but God subdues our fallen nature so that His nature may shine through us. The third and last step in salvation, *glorification,* doesn't happen until we are finally in heaven. God will completely set us free from all sin and imperfection, and we will finally realize our true selves. We will be glorified, exactly the way God meant us to be—holy, perfect, and acceptable to Him.

But until we reach heaven, we must allow God to sanctify us in preparation for eternity with Him. To sanctify means "to cleanse, to set apart from sin, to make holy." Sanctification comes about as we draw closer to Christ. As the branches are linked to the vine, so we are linked to Jesus Christ through His Word, the sacraments, prayer, and worship. As we apply these disciplines, we appropriate more of His grace and His fruit becomes evident in our lives. This process requires partnership between us and God. Sanctification, on the one hand, is *God's* work, as all of salvation is; on the other hand, *we* run the race, press on toward the goal, struggle against sin, and work out our salvation with fear and trembling.

So today and every day, draw near to God. Spend time with Him. Reach out in faith to Him. And you will come to know the blessing of God's holiness and the meaning of His sanctification.

*Awake my soul, stretch every nerve, and press with vigor on.
A heav'nly race demands thy zeal, and an immortal crown.*

PHILIP DODDRIDGE

January 13

SELF-DISCIPLINE

But the fruit of the Spirit is…self-control…

GALATIANS 5:22–23

Here's a tough question for you: How much self-discipline do you have? Do you make goals for yourself and regularly meet them, or do you find yourself side-tracked by diversions more often than not?

The Scripture says that the one who rules his or her spirit is better than the one who takes a city. Great men and women have always had an extraordinary amount of self-discipline. Stop and consider the discipline it took for William Carey, that great pioneer missionary, to translate the Scriptures into forty or so languages. David Livingstone needed discipline to continue for twenty-nine thousand miles across the continent of Africa, even when the natives begged for time to rest. George Washington led a successful life. Did he owe his success to coincidence? Was it due to being in the right place at the right time? Some might pass it off that way, but if you look more closely, you'll see that Washington had an amazing amount of self-discipline. He arose promptly at four in the morning. He led a disciplined devotional life. By half past eight in the morning, he had already completed most of the day's work. He went to sleep early each night. He allowed the Spirit to control his mind.

If we want to accomplish all that God has called us to do, we need to pursue self-discipline. And since we tend to make resolutions for self-discipline at the dawn of each new year, let me suggest one: Watch very little television this year. While some programs are downright anti-Christian in their morality, much of television is simply a waste of time. Recently I heard about a talented Christian speaker and writer. Though he was relatively young, he was writing his forty-first book! One of the keys to his prolific achievements was that he didn't spend *any* time watching television. A recent study of many CEOs from Fortune 500 companies found that eighty-one percent of them watch less than one hour of television per day. That's far less than the average viewer. Think of how much you could accomplish if you acquired this discipline!

Today, ask God to show you how He'd like to develop self-discipline in you. Then allow God to work in your life in whatever way He desires so that you might glorify Him with the fruit of self-control.

Early to bed, early to rise makes a man healthy, wealthy, and wise.

BENJAMIN FRANKLIN

WHAT IN THE WORLD ARE WE DOING?

…'These who have turned the world upside down have come here too.'

ACTS 17:6

Do you ever sit back and wonder about your purpose in life? Do you wish to know at the end of your life that you didn't live in vain? Socrates said that an unexamined life is not worth living. I think it behooves us from time to time to ask, "What in the world am I doing? What is my life really amounting to?"

I believe we should "be about our Father's business"—advancing the kingdom of our Lord Jesus Christ. What could be more important—and more meaningful?

In the book of Acts, we read that the early Christians were "turning the world upside down." The world had been turned upon its head in the fall and rebellion of humankind, and it desperately needed to be turned right side up. Though the early Christians faithfully pursued this goal, our world still needs to be turned right side up so that individuals might see God as He really is. Men and women need to turn their eyes from the material mud flats beneath—even if those "flats" are breathtaking mansions on waterfront property—and lift their eyes to the stars and know that God has created humanity for eternal life with Him.

My friends, our world still needs a spiritual revolution that turns the world upside down! But I am afraid that many Christians are like Edith. Edith is described in a certain novel as a small country bounded on the north, the south, the east, and the west by Edith itself. So many of us seem like that country, self-absorbed in our little circumscribed worlds. We don't pay attention to anything outside our spheres of concern.

Are you a world revolutionary? Have you determined in your heart to change the world, to turn it upside down for Christ? Have you hitched your life to this grand cause? Or are you meandering around in some small eddy out of the main current of human events? If you haven't already, join in the grand plan to win as many people for Christ as you can. Determine today to touch one life with Christ's love. This is "what in the world" we should be doing.

I look upon the world as my parish.

JOHN WESLEY

January 15

EVERY REALM OF THE WORLD

*…and God said to them, 'Be fruitful, and multiply; fill the earth and subdue it;
have dominion over the fish of the sea, over the birds of the air, and
over every living thing that moves on the earth.'*

GENESIS 1:28

Yesterday we learned that the early Christians "turned the world upside down." We addressed the need to proclaim the gospel, which has the potential to change individual lives. Today I want to deal with the social impact of the gospel.

When you look at the impact of the Church in history, you can see the incredible ways Christianity has transformed the world for the better. Although these changes didn't happen overnight, we see the gospel's influence in abolishing slavery in the United States, bringing about university education, inspiring some of the greatest art in the world, causing hospitals to be built all over the world, and spreading a higher morality the world over. These changes occurred as Christians spread the gospel to the world around them. These powerful results reflect obedience to what I call "the cultural mandate" that God gave to humankind in Genesis 1—that we should subdue the earth for God's glory.

God has commissioned us to transform the world. Unfortunately, it's easy to put our blinders on and ignore the impact of worldwide events. Too many professing Christians have developed a certain pietistic, self-centered view, pursuing only that which makes them feel good rather than the revolution Christ desires.

I thank God for men and women who are genuinely concerned that the gospel of Christ has its application in every realm of the world. What part are you playing in making this dream a reality? Will you join me and the rest of God's devoted servants as we endeavor to change the world for the better?

Jesus Christ is 'the Man who changed the world.'

HERBERT LOCKYER

ASTROLOGY AND YOUR FUTURE

All the counsel you have received has only worn you out!
Let your astrologers come forward, those stargazers who make predictions month by month,
let them save you from what is coming upon you.

ISAIAH 47:13, NIV

Have you ever wished you could see into the future and know every detail of the rest of your life? Wouldn't that knowledge make things easier? It seems that many people today desire that kind of enlightenment. In fact, astrology, one of the most ancient methods of foretelling the future, has become quite popular again. Do you know who helped make it popular? Adolf Hitler. Hitler had five full-time, paid astrologers on his staff, helping him run the Third Reich. But although he had some remarkable successes, his life ended in disaster, burned up in flames.

Astrology holds a strange attraction for humans, and many people don't see anything wrong with it. But reliance on astrology, a tool of the devil, can be extremely dangerous. Astrology is harmful because it makes us dependent. It weakens our character by depriving us of the ability to make intelligent, rational choices. Many people find its false power addictive, and if they allow it to take them over, it will destroy their lives. Listen to this story. A man once had an astrologer tell him his future. The astrologer said that this man would marry young, but his first wife would not be the wife who would bring him satisfaction. He would marry again, and this second wife would bring him a lifetime of happiness. This man eventually married a lovely girl who made a delightful wife, but he felt so impressed by the fatalistic claim of the astrologer that he deserted this woman after a year and a half. He divorced his first wife and remarried. But the second wife, supposedly the wife of his dreams, became a fanatical cultist and drove him out of his mind.

A young lady once asked me, "Do you know what my sign is?" I said, "No, what is it?" She said, "My sign is the sign of the cross." What a wonderful perspective! The cross is the proper sign for all Christians, for we can entrust our future to God because of it. Don't be afraid if you don't know all the details of your life, and don't seek to know them through dubious means such as astrology. Instead, trust God day by day. He has *all* the answers. And remember that because He has redeemed you, you already know the two most important things about your future: (1) Heaven will be your eternal home, and (2) while you are on earth, God will work all things together for your good.

Satan doesn't care if you worship him or the stars, as long as you turn away from God.

THE NEED FOR HOPE

...at that time you were without Christ, being aliens from the commonwealth of Israel and strangers from the covenants of promise, having no hope and without God in the world.

EPHESIANS 2:12

Have you ever felt utterly hopeless? Maybe even today you face a struggle that has sapped you of all expectation.

Hope seems a rare commodity these days. Our society has gotten rid of God, banning Him from schools by banning the Bible and prayer and seeking to do so in every other possible area. Meanwhile, the gloom grows deeper and the darkness more impenetrable. Hopelessness settles in about us. In increasing numbers people flee from this world of hopelessness in whatever ways they can—fleeing into a world of drugs, into a world of alcohol, into a world of escapism of some sort. Some even escape their hopelessness in the ultimate way—by committing suicide.

But as Christians, we can have hope based on the objective standard of God's Word. Through Christ, we've been born again unto a living hope. What is that hope? That we shall live in God's presence forever as His eternal children. When the galaxies have long ago burned out, we shall still live with Christ. When this world gets us down, we have the hope that this life is just the slightest, quickest movement of the shuttle in the eternity which lies before us. Because of that truth, our source of hope will never run dry.

We can have this hope only when we answer God's call to come to Him and live our lives with and for Him, trusting in Jesus Christ as our Savior. Do you have this hope in the midst of a hopeless world? If you build your hope on anything other than Christ, His blood, and His righteousness, you hope in vain. Trust in the Lord, and you will have a glorious, everlasting hope, one that will carry you from now into eternity.

There is no medicine like hope.

O. S. MARDEN

ABRAHAM

After these things the word of the Lord came to Abram in a vision, saying,
'Do not be afraid, Abram. I am your shield, your exceedingly great reward.'

GENESIS 15:1

Today, do you face something that you fear? Then let Abram's example in Genesis 14 encourage you to endure and to trust God.

Four kings had traveled all the way from the Mesopotamia area and had invaded Israel, taking captive the kings of Zoar, Sodom, Gomorrah, and other cities. In addition, these kings had plundered a lot of the goods belonging to these cities.

When Abram heard that the kings had taken captive his nephew Lot, he gathered together a few hundred menservants, armed them, and took off in pursuit. After traveling some distance, Abram overtook the kings' forces, freed all the captives, and returned all the goods. Despite his heroic feat, Abram refused to take any reward, saying that he would not have it spread abroad that he had become rich by the kings of Sodom and Gomorrah.

In Genesis 15 we read, "After these things the word of the Lord came to Abram in a vision, saying, 'Do not be afraid, Abram. I am your shield, your exceedingly great reward.'" After rescuing the captives, Abram had a great deal to fear. Four kings of good-sized nations were angry with him and could have come to exact retribution from him. But God, stronger and more powerful than those kings (and any tyrant on earth), told Abram not to fear, for God was his shield.

Like Abram, we face many fears—the trials and difficulties that come into our lives, our mortality, evil. This world is full of dangers, and so often we feel fear clutch at our hearts. Yet God comes to us again and again, saying, "Do not be afraid."

The next time you feel fear creeping in, trust your Father who holds the future. He will bring you victory over every challenge you face.

The fear of God kills all other fears.

HUGH BLACK

January 19

SEEK FIRST THE KINGDOM

'…seek first the kingdom of God and His righteousness…'

MATTHEW 6:33

Whether or not we're aware of it, we all have pursuits in life, ultimate goals we want to achieve. Whatever our pursuits are, they drive the rest of our lives. Wittingly or unwittingly, we choose our daily actions to help us reach our ultimate goals. And Jesus Christ told us exactly what we should wholeheartedly pursue first and foremost—God's kingdom and His righteousness.

If we want to seek God's kingdom first, we must examine our priorities. As we do, we often find we're far off the mark. Many people set moneymaking as their primary goal in life. They choose this goal in the most uncritical fashion, without ever asking if they should spend their time, effort, and energy on it. Other people adopt pleasure as their ultimate goal. They want only enough money to enjoy their pleasures. Such people are little different from the ancient pagan hedonists who openly declared pleasure as their god. Yet others spend their lives building their own kingdoms where they can rule over others. They amass as much power as they can so they can have control.

But God asks, "Should you then seek great things for yourself? Seek them not." Jesus continues centuries later, "But seek first the kingdom of God and His righteousness; and all these things shall be added to you." Clearly, God wants His kingdom to be our ultimate pursuit in life. What does it mean to seek the kingdom of God? First, we seek the extension of His kingdom by sharing the gospel of Christ with those who don't know it. Second, it means discipling, teaching, and building up people in the faith. The kingdom should extend until every phase of our lives is under His dominion. Then we will be at peace with Him and ourselves.

Have you evaluated your priorities recently? Have you made seeking God's kingdom your ultimate pursuit? If not, do so today. Invite God to use you however He desires to draw people to Him.

Only one life, 'twill soon be past.
Only what's done for Christ will last.

ANONYMOUS

LOYALTY IN A DISLOYAL WORLD

Then Jesus said to the twelve, 'Do you also want to go away?' Then Simon Peter answered Him, 'Lord, to whom shall we go? You have the words of eternal life.'

JOHN 6:67–68

Orson Welles once complained, "When you're down and out, something always turns up—and it's usually the noses of your friends."

How loyal are you to the people in your life?

Loyalty is a noble trait, but often people are more committed to themselves than to anyone or anything else. In view of so many dissolved marriages, you'd almost think the marriage vow states, "Till *inconvenience* do us part." Most definitely, loyalty in our time seems rare, as evidenced by the alacrity with which people change friends, jobs, communities, and churches.

Jesus knew the sting of betrayal. One time, after a large crowd abandoned Jesus, refusing to follow Him anymore, He turned to the twelve disciples and asked them if they were going to leave Him too. Peter answered so well for all of us who follow Christ: "Lord, to whom shall we go? You have the words of eternal life." Jesus then lamented that even one of those remaining twelve was a devil (referring to Judas—the ultimate example of disloyalty—who would betray Christ for money).

But the Bible also has some positive examples of loyalty. Consider King Saul's son Jonathan, who made tremendous sacrifices for David. He even gave up his throne for David's sake. Or think of Ruth, who said to her mother-in-law, "Entreat me not to leave you, or to turn back from following after you; for wherever you go, I will go…Your people shall be my people, and your God, my God." (Ruth 1:16). What a tremendous testimony of loyalty!

Loyalty is such a rare trait that those who exhibit it distinguish themselves from the rest of the world. I encourage you today to stay loyal and faithful to your spouse, your family, your church, your boss, and your friends. You will reap wonderful benefits for doing so. And if you need an example of loyalty, look to our Lord and Savior. Jesus Christ has promised that He will never leave us or forsake us. He gave His very life for us. No one is more loyal than He!

God does not hold me responsible for success but for faithfulness.

ANONYMOUS

PRESSING TOWARD THE MARK

...forgetting those things which are behind and reaching forward to those things which are ahead, I press toward the goal for the prize of the upward call of God in Christ Jesus.

PHILIPPIANS 3:13–14

Have you ever wondered why some people succeed while others fail? Do successful people have heredity, environment, luck, money, or education on their side? Those factors have probably contributed toward the success of some, yet we all know people who have enjoyed these benefits and have amounted to little. On the other hand, history is replete with examples of those who had none of those advantages yet succeeded magnificently.

So what are the secrets of success? I believe that Paul tells us some of those secrets in Philippians 3:13–14. First, Paul says, "...reaching forward to those things which are ahead." How important that is! This picture alludes to a runner who stretches his or her hand way in front of the body. Through this picture, Paul tells us that we need that eager aspiration, that enthusiasm that comes from God within us, causing us to reach out toward greater things. We need that eagerness of heart if we're to succeed. Too often we go through our jobs, our devotions, our worship, and our service for Christ with perfunctory attitudes. But when we have eager anticipation, God can do great things through us.

Second, Paul says, "I press toward the goal for the prize." The phrase "press toward the goal" means to pursue, to go after something in an intense way. In addition to eagerness of spirit, we need to exert great effort to reach our goals. We need to clearly define worthy pursuits and forget about all of our failures. We need to exert energy to meet our goals and not let anything get in the way of reaching them.

Today ask the Lord to show you a goal worthy of your effort. Then ask Him to give you the enthusiasm and energy to press toward it. As you do so each day, you'll get closer to "the prize of the upward call of God in Christ Jesus."

Persistent people begin their success where others end in failure.

EDWARD EGGLESTON

LIFE: AN INALIENABLE RIGHT

'For indeed, as soon as the voice of your greeting sounded in my ears,
the babe leaped in my womb for joy.'

LUKE 1:44

For You have formed my inward parts; You have covered me in my mother's womb.

PSALM 139:13

Close your eyes for a moment, and pay attention to some things you probably take for granted most days: the beating of your heart, your lungs filling with oxygen, your muscles supporting and moving your body. These are gifts life gives us.

Today is the anniversary of the Supreme Court decision *Roe v. Wade*, which has resulted in the death of tens of millions of unborn babies in this nation. "Abortion stops a beating heart," says the National Right to Life Committee. Aborted babies never get to enjoy the life-giving gifts that you and I take for granted every day.

The late Dr. Francis Schaeffer said in one of his last messages that the right to life is more basic than the right to liberty, the right to the pursuit of happiness, or any other right. Indeed, if you lie dead in your coffin, you don't care how many shackles and chains have been wrapped around you, nor do you care how much money you have in your bank account. If you don't have life, you don't have anything.

But the right to life is challenged by those who assert an inherent right to choose. People in favor of abortion call themselves "pro-choice." But I don't agree with that term. After all, the unborn baby has no choice at all in the matter. (I'm reminded of the bumper sticker "Equal rights for unborn women.") To those who are pro-choice, I can only encourage you to seek God's heart in this matter.

Maybe someone you know has had an abortion. Maybe you yourself have had one. In either case, remember that the God who gives life also grants mercy. God offers grace and forgiveness to all who flee to the Cross, confess their sins, and ask Him to forgive their sins. You can be sure of that.

Meanwhile, we should all pray that this horrible practice will end. Today, every time you're aware of your heart beating, ask God to reestablish the right to life in our nation.

*And if we accept that a mother can kill even her own child, how
can we tell other people not to kill one another?*

MOTHER TERESA

IF GOD IS LOVE, THEN WHY...?

Then Job answered the Lord and said: 'I know that You can do everything, and that no purpose of Yours can be withheld from You...I have heard of You by the hearing of the ear, but now my eye sees You. Therefore I abhor myself, and repent in dust and ashes.'

JOB 42:1–2, 5–6

Have you ever said, "Why me, Lord?" when something bad happened to you? Rabbi Harold Kushner, in his book *When Bad Things Happen to Good People,* tried to answer this question. Unfortunately, Rabbi Kushner's conclusions were not biblical. Kushner says, "God would like people to get what they deserve in life, but he cannot always arrange it." He says that God does not really control the events of this world but helps us respond to them in more positive ways. But the Bible says that God is all-powerful and all-good, able to do anything and wanting to bless us.

Another example of Kushner's unbiblical assertions is that Job, a man who endured tremendous tribulation, thought of himself as a good man. But notice what Job actually says in Job 42:5–6 after God confronts him: "I have heard of You by the hearing of the ear, but now my eye sees You. Therefore I abhor myself, and repent in dust and ashes." When Job asked God, "What have I done wrong?" God did not answer his question. Instead, God just showed Himself. Through this revelation, Job came to see that God has no limitations and imperfections whatsoever, and that by comparison, he himself was vile.

None of us is good; none of us deserves unending blessing. The Bible says so. So the question is not "Why do bad things happen to good people?" but "Why do good things happen to bad people?" Peter tells us that we should not be amazed when fiery trials come upon us. We should expect that God will try our faith with fire, so that we might come out as pure gold. For He is in the process of forging our character, drawing us nearer to Him for now and for eternity.

Have you been experiencing a severe trial in your life? Don't despair. Instead, thank God for the trial, no matter how difficult, and keep trusting Him. God will never disappoint you. Our false, unbiblical perceptions of Him might, but He Himself never will.

If it is true that all of us deserve hell, then anything we get in this life, less than that, is gracious.

FAITH WITHOUT WORKS

But someone will say, 'You have faith, and I have works.' Show me your faith without your works, and I will show you my faith by my works.

JAMES 2:18

Do you ever get confused by all the different religions in the world? Many do. So let's reduce this complex subject to its simplest components. Ultimately, only three types of religions exist. The first type of religion ("Christian" or otherwise) teaches that people become acceptable to God by their own works, such as keeping commandments and following certain rules of morality, piety, and benevolence. Another type of religion teaches simply that people are saved by faith in Christ. And the third type of religion teaches that people are saved by a combination of faith and works.

The Bible makes it clear that only by faith in Christ can we be saved. We can't add good works to the equation. However, the Bible also says that true faith in Christ manifests itself in good works. Faith is invisible. Someone may *say* that he or she has faith, but you cannot see it, nor can a person show it apart from works. And that is precisely why, at the Judgment, God judges people by their works. Though only Jesus can save us, we demonstrate the genuineness of our faith in Jesus to the world by the works we do. In the second chapter of his letter, James denounces the barren orthodox, those who believe that they save themselves by the correctness of their creed, those who may confess expertly, may argue their faith with great eloquence, and believe it in all of its details; yet they have no fruit: joy, love, peace, works, or service for Christ. They may *profess* religious faith, but their actions show they don't *possess* it.

Do people know what you believe by how you live? Today, choose to honor God in all you do, so that those around you may know the truth.

The first good work you will ever perform is to believe on the Lord Jesus Christ.

ANONYMOUS

FORGIVING OUR ENEMIES

'But I say to you, love your enemies, bless those who curse you…'

MATTHEW 5:44

I want to talk to you today about the incredible importance of forgiveness in our lives. Without it, we'll never make it in this world or the next. Doctors now know that we don't get ulcers as much from what we eat; we get them from what's eating us. If you want to have a miserable existence and risk contracting one or more diseases, then hold resentment and unforgiveness in your heart. They can destroy the body.

Would you prefer to cultivate a forgiving heart? Then learn from Joseph's example. He had much to forgive…

•He had to forgive his father, Jacob, because of Jacob's folly in preferring him over his brothers.

•He had to forgive his brothers for throwing him into a pit then selling him into slavery as a mere alternative to killing him. He had to forgive his brothers for all his years of slavery in Egypt and for the long, arduous tasks he had to perform until finally he was accepted into Potiphar's household.

•He had to forgive Potiphar's wife, who took hold of his garment, bringing his integrity into question.

•He had to forgive Potiphar, who never even looked into the matter between Joseph and his wife but condemned Joseph out of hand, sending him to prison to languish for years.

Joseph could well have said he had much to set right, but he never did. Instead he freely forgave them all.

Abraham Lincoln is also a wonderful example of forgiveness. He regularly forgave his enemies. On the very afternoon before he was shot, Lincoln gave instructions to his cabinet, many members of which were bent on stepping on the face of the South now that the Civil War had ended. Lincoln told his cabinet, "There will be no reparations." He had a heart as big as the whole world and yet not big enough to hold a grudge.

Do you have an enemy whom you have not forgiven from your heart? Then ask God for the grace to forgive; after all, Jesus has forgiven us for so much more—who are we to hold grudges?

I shall never permit myself to stoop so low as to hate any man.

BOOKER T. WASHINGTON

THE FOLLY OF SHORTSIGHTEDNESS

For we walk by faith, not by sight.

2 CORINTHIANS 5:7

Is your spiritual vision 20/20? Sadly, many of us suffer from spiritual short-sightedness. For example, Adam and Eve exhibited shortsightedness as they contemplated only the immediate delight and satisfaction that would come from eating the forbidden fruit. They didn't consider the long-term, disastrous results.

Abraham, on the other hand, was a man of great vision. The Bible says that Abraham sought a city whose builder and maker was God. Though he passed through many of the cities of this world, he knew his long-term search would be worthwhile.

Moses is also a prime example of a man with farsighted vision. He endured seeing Him who is invisible. That takes very long vision, and God calls us to the same effort. We must look not merely upon the things we can see—short-lived, temporal things—but upon the things we cannot see—the long-term, the eternal. Yet most people spend more time planning a party than they do planning where they'll spend eternity! How many people have told me that they're ready to die because they've made out their wills and have bought their burial plots. How utterly deceived people can be! No wonder the Bible calls sin folly and the sinner a fool, because our shortsightedness is foolishness.

If God had called us to climb Mount Everest in order to gain eternal life, millions would line up to try it. But He calls us to no such arduous task as that but instead to simple trust in Christ as our Savior. Doing that humbles us because we must acknowledge our sin and our unworthiness, casting ourselves upon Him and His mercy.

Sometimes people criticize Christians for not living in "the real world." And yet ultimately two real worlds exist: heaven and hell! We must focus on eternity, cultivating a long-range view on life.

A little faith will bring your soul to heaven; a great faith will bring heaven to your soul.

CHARLES SPURGEON

January 27

TWO OPTIONS

'Today, if you will hear His voice, do not harden your hearts…'

HEBREWS 3:15

There are two groups of people: those who are on their way to heaven and those who are not. The first group comprises people who have trusted in Christ alone for their salvation, gaining eternal life for their souls through Christ's death on the cross. The second group consists of people who haven't committed their lives to Christ, including (ironically) those who may be *trying* to work their way into heaven, hoping to gain entrance by their own merits.

Which group are you in today? Have you made the decision to give your life to Christ?

Many decisions in life offer only two options. And often we find that while we're deciding which option to choose, we've already chosen one by default. For example, suppose your car is stalled on a railroad track, and before you've restarted it, a train approaches at high speed. Two options now loom before you. You can leap from your car and save your life, or you can stay in your car and try to save both your life and your auto. As you weigh the dangers and gains of both options, you've made a choice with life-impacting consequences: You're still in your car, and the train is still coming!

Likewise, you have two options today: life or death. But while you consider your options, you've already made a choice, for if you've never accepted Christ, you're still in that state of death into which every soul was born. And every second you put off that decision, the judgment train of God continues to roll.

Christ's gift of salvation is the greatest offer ever made. Someday God will rescind His offer, and this period of grace will end forever. But now, the sun of His grace shines, and the offer of His free gift is still available. I urge you this day, at the dawn of this new year (if you have not already), to repent of your sins, to place your faith in Jesus, and to accept Him as your Savior and Lord. Your life will never be the same again!

Salvation is free for you because someone else paid.

ANONYMOUS

OUR FOOTPRINTS

'Those who are wise shall shine like the brightness of the firmament, and those who turn many to righteousness like the stars forever and ever.'

DANIEL 12:3

When your time comes to leave this earth, what would you like others to remember about you? Have you thought of how you could make a lasting impact on this world? Most of us would like to know that we've made some enduring contribution and that people will never forget us. We hope that our lives will not have been just footprints in the sand along the edge of the water, washed away by the next wave to hit the shore.

Ever since the beginning of humankind, people have desired to make a memorable stamp on the world. Some people have attempted to leave great monuments to secure their names in the annals of history. Have they succeeded? Consider the Great Pyramid of Giza, no doubt one of the most massive structures in the world. Someone built that pyramid as a memorial to himself. "Who?" you ask. He was King Kufoo, not exactly a household name. The Shah of India had a similar wish, desiring that his wife would be remembered by others for centuries. So the shah built the Taj Mahal. Yet he, too, built in vain; after all, who knows the name of Arjumand? How about the Great Wall of China? The Wall is the largest man-made structure in the world. Astronauts say you can even see it from outer space. Yet no one remembers the name of Chin She Whon Tea, the man initially responsible for this incredible structure.

While these people are forgotten by the masses, we *can* make a permanent imprint on the world. In fact, God placed the desire in our hearts for significance and permanence. Why? Because we're bound for eternal life. So how can we make a name for ourselves for eternity? By bringing others to a saving knowledge of Christ's grace that they may have eternal life.

Do you know someone who needs to discover God's gift of grace? Those saved through you will be ever grateful that you took the time and made the effort to bring them into God's presence. If you bring others to Christ, you shall shine like the stars of the firmament forever.

He who has no vision of eternity has no hold on time.

THOMAS CARLYLE

TO OBEY IS BETTER THAN SACRIFICE

'…Behold, to obey is better than sacrifice…'

1 SAMUEL 15:22

Do you ever dread going to the doctor or dentist, fearing what he or she might find in the exam? Well, every once in a while, we need to have a spiritual check-up, as painful as it may seem. Let's search our hearts today.

Have you neglected any duty in your life that God has called you to perform? God wants us to obey Him. To obey (follow Him in whatever He asks) is better than sacrifice (the confessions we offer to Him). Husbands and wives, have you neglected duties to each other? Do you have that tender relationship of love and intimacy that Christ calls us to? Or have you let it sit on the back burner for a while? As children, do you honor your parents? Do you fully obey that commandment, or do you do it only when it's convenient? What about the other commandments in the Bible and the whisperings of God to your heart, calling you to some great work—have you obeyed?

We also need to search our hearts for any evil. Have you persisted in evil habits contrary to God's will? We need to allow God's Word to convict us so that we might obey Him in all He asks. One of our church members told me that a few years ago I really convicted him when I talked about his addiction to cigarettes. This man was absolutely bound to smoking despite Scripture's admonition against bondage to anything. I wonder how many condemn drug addiction in the young yet themselves nurture an addiction to cigarettes? Some four hundred thousand Americans will die this year from smoking-related diseases! Others are in bondage to the bottle and refuse to obey the Lord, refuse to see their bodies as the temple of the Holy Spirit. Yet others habitually look at pornography in magazines, movies, television, or videos, all of which surround us like a polluted swamp.

Consider your life today. Have you avoided a duty God has called you to? Do you not want to hear some passage of Scripture because you know you are disobeying it? Then face it today. Ask God to forgive you, then purpose in your heart to obey. Remember: "To obey is better than sacrifice."

Yes, Lord.

MOTTO SPOTTED ABOVE THE SINK OF A JOYFUL,
WELL-RESPECTED, ACTIVE CHRISTIAN

DEBTORS

I am a debtor both to Greeks and to barbarians, both to wise and to unwise.

ROMANS 1:14

Are you in debt? These days, it seems, who isn't? But financial obligations are one thing. We also incur spiritual debts. Paul claimed he was a debtor to the Gentiles, the barbarians, the wise, and the unwise. Yet how could this be? What had those people done for him? Nothing at all! At least, nothing good. In fact five times they beat him with forty stripes minus one. Three times they beat him with rods, and once they stoned him and left him for dead. So what debt did he owe?

Just the same debt that pertains to every single person who claims to believe in Jesus Christ. Everyone who has received the gospel of Christ has received it as a steward, responsible to God, who gave it, and to the rest of humankind, for whom it's intended.

"I am a debtor," cried William Carey as he launched the modern missionary movement, setting sail for India to bring the gospel to the Hindus.

"I am a debtor," cried David Livingstone as he plunged for the first time into the interior of Africa to open the dark continent to the light of Christ's gospel.

"I am a debtor," cried William Wilberforce as he devoted his entire life to ridding Great Britain of the onerous slave trade. On his deathbed he received word that he had finally succeeded.

"I am a debtor," cried Florence Nightingale as she went to far-flung battlefields to begin the noble profession of nursing, to bind up the wounded, and to care for the dying.

"I am a debtor," cried William Booth as he started the Salvation Army to reach the downtrodden of the world.

And how about you, my friend? Are you a debtor? Does the realization of what Jesus Christ has done for you compel you to serve Him and others? Today ask God to use you to share the good news.

That land is henceforth my country which most needs the gospel.

COUNT ZINZENDORF

YOUR THOUGHT LIFE

For as he thinks in his heart, so is he…

PROVERBS 23:7

Many people constantly dwell on negative thoughts. They dwell on their fears, hurts, and problems. They focus on the fly in the ointment, never seeing the ointment but only the fly. With their negativity and destructiveness, these people can ruin the lives of those who have the misfortune of living with them and around them. Most of all, these pessimistic people destroy their own bodies and souls with their negative thoughts. And so their lives shrivel.

What kind of thoughts do you dwell on? Are you a positive thinker, or do you most often find yourself dwelling in the pit of despair?

Echoing a biblical truth, Marcus Aurelius once said, "The most important things in life are the thoughts you choose to think." The Bible says, "For as he thinks in his heart, so is he." Many people believe that they don't choose their thoughts at all, that instead their thoughts choose them. Thoughts rush at them in a stream, like a rolling script going across a TV screen, and no one can control them. But this is not so.

We *do* choose our thoughts. We choose what we think, and what we choose to think impacts our lives. Our thoughts determine what we say and how we say it. They determine what we are and what we become. "For as he thinks in his heart, so is he." We are the outward embodiments, the incarnations, of our thoughts, and because of this, we need to choose well what we think.

Take notes from the apostle Paul. He was beaten and imprisoned for the gospel's sake. Because of all his trials, he could easily have had a gloomy outlook. Instead he chose to think good and positive thoughts, beginning with thoughts of the Lord. We should heed Paul's instruction: "Whatever things are true, whatever things are noble, whatever things are just, whatever things are pure, whatever things are lovely, whatever things are of good report, if there is any virtue and if there is anything praiseworthy—meditate on these things" (Philippians 4:8).

Do you need to make a thought adjustment today? Let me encourage you to counteract your negative thoughts with positive ones. And as you do this, watch how you and your life change.

Every act of a man springs from the hidden seeds of thought.

JAMES ALLEN

TRANSFORMING YOUR PRAYER LIFE

You ask and do not receive, because you ask amiss...

JAMES 4:3

What do the following bestseller titles communicate to you about our society: *The Virtue of Selfishness* and *Looking Out for Number One*? What does it mean to you that we buy books like these in droves?

Tragically, selfishness characterizes our age. Our society has hurled God from the throne and crowned self as monarch. Then we've turned around and treated God as the conduit to all our desires. We "conjure up" God as if He were a genie in a bottle, commanding Him to manipulate the world to our liking.

But we shouldn't treat God as a means to whatever we want. He isn't a means to our own ends; He Himself is the end we should seek. If we think otherwise, we should ask the Lord to change our selfish hearts.

Selfishness is at the root of many an unanswered prayer. When we "ask amiss," we ask for fulfillment of our selfish desires, not for the furtherance of God's kingdom. But Christ showed us, through the Lord's Prayer (found in Matthew 6), that we must seek God's kingdom first, not our own. The first petition in the Lord's Prayer is "Hallowed be thy name." We should make it our priority to praise and honor God when we pray. The second petition reads, "Thy kingdom come." We should diligently beseech Jesus Christ to bring His kingdom into this world and into our lives. The third petition is "Thy will be done." We need to lay our will at Jesus' feet and ask Him to fulfill His purposes through our lives.

Today pray, "Lord, what would you have me do this day?" Then make yourself available to do His will and further His kingdom in whatever way He desires. Pray every day, focusing your petitions not on yourself but on your King.

Seven days without prayer makes one weak.

ALLEN E. BARTLETT

TRANSFORMING PRAYERS

You ask and do not receive, because you ask amiss, that you may spend it on your pleasures.

JAMES 4:3

Unanswered prayers are a stumbling block. Often when people pray but don't hear answers from God, they believe that God doesn't listen, that He doesn't care, or even that He doesn't exist.

But God is most definitely there, and He wants to answer our prayers. However, we often get in His way. God doesn't answer some of our prayers because we ask "amiss," as James puts it. In other words, there's something wrong with the sender (us), not the hearer (God), of the prayers.

If you've persistently asked God to answer a prayer, yet you haven't heard an answer from Him, you might have "static on the line," an obstruction in communication with your heavenly Father. I'd like to share with you five prayers that can put you back on course to an effective prayer life:

1. "O God, slay me." As new creatures in Christ we constantly wrestle with our old wretched selves. As long as the old nature prevails, God will not answer our prayers. Thus, we should ask God to slay our old nature.

2. "O God, cleanse me by Thy blood." If we expect God to answer our prayers, we should not come into His presence stained in sin. Instead we must confess and turn away from our sins.

3. "Fill me with the Holy Spirit." We need to pray that the Spirit will fill us and empower us to live for God daily and to overcome temptation.

4. "God, lead me this day." God has a perfect plan, a far better plan for our lives than we can create. We must allow Him to lead us in His will daily.

5. "Dear Lord, use me this day for your glory." We must make ourselves available to God as His bond servants, willing to do whatever He asks of us.

I encourage you to sincerely pray these prayers, meditate upon them, and use them to present yourself to God as a clean and willing servant. As you pray this way, Christ will surprise you with joy as He makes Himself known more fully in your daily walk. You'll no doubt find that as you pray according to His will, you'll experience some incredible answers beyond your wildest dreams!

Heaven is never deaf but when man's heart is dumb.

FRANCIS QUARLES

THE MIRROR OF THE WORLD

Finally, brethren, whatever things are true, whatever things are noble, whatever things are just, whatever things are pure, whatever things are lovely, whatever things are of good report, if there is any virtue and if there is anything praiseworthy—meditate on these things.

PHILIPPIANS 4:8

Whatever we hide in our hearts reflects in our behavior, and our behavior reflects our hearts to the world. If you could see your heart in a mirror, what characteristics would that mirror reflect?

A family decided to move to a town across the river from where they lived. They could only cross the river by sailing on a large raft. The family members asked the man who operated the raft, "What kind of people live in our new town?" He said, "Well, what kind of people did you find in your old town?" They said, "Oh, these were the most wonderful people—loving, caring, kind, and thoughtful. We really hate to lose them." The man replied, "Well, I think you'll find that the people in your new town are the same kind of folks."

A week or so later, another family sailed across the same river on the same raft. The family members asked the man the *same* question as the first family, and they received a similar response: "What kind of people did you find in your old town?" This family said, "Oh, those folks! What a bunch of no-good, low-down cutthroats! They would lie about you, talk about you behind your back, and gossip. They're malicious and vile. We couldn't wait to get away from them."

Each family had attracted people who mirrored their own behavior and would continue to do so no matter where they moved. In the same way, what we reflect to the world affects the environment around us. If we want to impact people to become loving, truthful, noble, pure, and virtuous, then we need to reflect those characteristics from our hearts.

Here are some Scriptures to hide in your heart that will reflect well in the world. "Judge not, that you be not judged" (Matthew 7:1). "Therefore, whatever you want men to do to you, do also to them, for this is the Law and the Prophets" (Matthew 7:12). "For all who take the sword will perish by the sword" (Matthew 26:52). "A soft answer turns away wrath" (Proverbs 15:1). "A man who has friends must himself be friendly" (Proverbs 18:24).

Today ask God to show you how you can better reflect godly characteristics to those around you. Then put into practice anything He asks of you. As you obey, God will use you to impact your world.

The world is a looking glass and gives back to every man the reflection of his own face.

WILLIAM THACKERAY

February 4

PEACE!

…Seek peace and pursue it.

PSALM 34:14

What creates stress? Nowadays there are many situations that produce stress within us. We have stressful jobs, stressful relationships, stressful responsibilities. But listen to what one doctor says: "Since stress comes from the way in which you think, and not from the situation or people involved in your stress, you can begin to practice mind control." Well, now, isn't that news! Three thousand years after King David told us to "Seek peace and pursue it," we discover that we can find the antidote for stress in our own minds.

The apostle Paul knew the importance of peace. He began many of his epistles with the words "Peace be unto you." He ended many of them with "Grace, mercy and peace be yours." Peace is the alpha and omega of the Christian's well-being. As children of God, peace should be our normal state, and it *will* be the totality of our mental state in heaven. But right now, unfortunately, many people fail to find it.

How sad it is to see unbelievers struggle—in vain—to find peace by turning to Eastern religious practices such as transcendental meditation or yoga. But even many believers don't seem to find the peace they need. Instead, we all experience anxiety, stress, and a lack of serenity to some degree.

We need to seek the peace of God and pursue it in the morning, at night, throughout each day, in the midst of stressful situations. We need to recover weekly so that we don't build up an accumulation of ever-growing stress in our lives. Do you feel stressed out, as if you can't take any more? Then take time to lie "beside the still waters." Take time out once a week for a restful, worshipful Sabbath. Above all, take time to really hear God's words: "Be still and know that I am God."

It is not adversity that kills, but the impatience with which we bear adversity.

ANONYMOUS

THE BEGINNING OF WISDOM

The fear of the LORD is the beginning of knowledge, but fools despise wisdom...

PROVERBS 1:7

Do you face a tough decision in your life, maybe one that makes you wish for some writing across the sky to indicate which way to go? Then you could probably use a good dose of wisdom. I don't mean knowledge per se—information for information's sake. I mean wisdom: the ability to rightly apply knowledge to your life. There *is* a difference. For example, a young person might have enough knowledge to rattle off a dozen ways that smoking endangers one's health yet lack the wisdom to "just say no" when that person's peers want him or her to light up.

So how do we acquire the wisdom to help us make good decisions? By asking God for it. In James 1:5, God promises that if we ask in faith for wisdom, He will give it to us.

We also acquire wisdom by fearing the Lord. The books of Psalms and Proverbs talk a lot about the "fear of the LORD." In these instances, the term "fear" does not mean a slavish dread of Him; rather, it refers to that reverential awe of God that we should all have.

Without such fear of the Lord, we cannot acquire true knowledge or wisdom. I'm sure that many would mock that statement and set forth numerous examples of supposedly wise people who demonstrate no fear of the Lord whatsoever. But we can't make hasty judgments. We don't know how a story ends until we read the last page of a book, and that same principle applies to life. A person may gather much of the world's knowledge, yet that individual will eventually have to face the Lord God and give an account of his or her life. The Bible writes this epitaph of all ungodly people (however vast their knowledge of this world): "Thou fool!" It is impossible to gain wisdom until one first fears the Lord.

Do you desire wisdom? Then place the Lord in His right and proper place in your life—as your Lord, worthy of reverential awe.

The greatest good is wisdom.

ST. AUGUSTINE

IDOLATRY

'…you shall not bow down to them nor serve them…'

EXODUS 20:5

Two sailors squirmed in church as they heard the reading of the Ten Commandments. One of them whispered to the other, "Well, at least we didn't worship any idols." Do you also feel certain you've kept this commandment? We often seem to think we don't have to worry about this one, but if this is true, why do the Scriptures often warn against idolatry? God knew that we are religious beings who need to worship something. And when we cease to worship the one true God, we replace Him with idolatry.

God knows our weak nature, our need to follow and worship something that transcends ourselves. In fact, even before the words of the Ten Commandments had settled in stone, the people of Israel had broken them, committing spiritual adultery in Horeb by worshiping a golden calf beneath the Lord's presence while Moses was on Mount Sinai. Jeroboam doubled the sin in Bethel and in Dan, creating two calves for the people to worship. Throughout the Old Testament, from Solomon to Zedekiah, the people of Israel pursued their idols to the high places and brought God's wrath upon themselves, until Nebuchadnezzar and the Babylonian hordes came, tore down the walls of Jerusalem, and carried the people captive into Babylon. In the furnace of Babylon, the last debris of idolatry was burned away.

Idolatry is an illegitimate way to fill a legitimate need. People have quested after a tangible God—one who can be felt, seen, and heard. Within the human heart exists the desire to see and know God personally. That need does not have to remain unmet. Jesus, who was fully God and fully man, satisfies that need, revealing God's nature to us.

Have you set something or someone above God? Make sure you give God His proper place in your life as your Lord who deserves all your praise.

I will worship God, for He abides forever.

ABRAHAM (ACCORDING TO JEWISH LEGEND)

PROBLEM SOLVING IN RELATIONSHIPS

A gentle answer turns away wrath, but a harsh word stirs up anger.

PROVERBS 15:1, NIV

How are your relationships going these days? As you evaluate them, maybe you realize you've hit a snag with a close friend, spouse, co-worker, or neighbor. If so, what will you do about it?

Whether you're single or married, a child or an elderly person, solving problems in relationships is one of the most important skills you will ever learn. It not only makes for a successful family life, it also makes for a successful career, a successful education, and a successful social life. Unless we have these skills, we'll never be truly happy.

When we have a problem with someone, we have to learn to state that problem in a gentle, positive way. A simple and positive problem statement is important because if you don't start right, you'll have little hope of ending right. If in a *kind* voice, you say something like "I feel this way when you do such-and-such," the other person can discover how you react to certain statements and actions (regardless of what that person may have intended). Instead of responding angrily, respond in kindness—"a gentle answer turns away wrath."

We also need to listen actively and not interrupt. Summarize what you heard, and allow the other person to rephrase things if you didn't quite under-stand. Listening in this way is really just applying the golden rule.

Next, brainstorm with the other person a mutually agreeable solution. Offer suggestions: "Well, we could do this, or we could do that." Don't criticize any-one's suggestions (for example, avoid saying, "That's the dumbest idea I've ever heard!"). Criticism freezes the brain and destroys our ability to develop creative solutions.

Once you've brainstormed some options, weigh the pros and cons of these potential solutions, and agree on one that is mutually acceptable. Implement it, and later evaluate its effectiveness.

Perhaps you desire reconciliation with someone who matters to you. Can you take the first step and give that person a "gentle answer" today?

God gave us the ultimate soft answer. He sent His Son to die in our place upon the Cross.

HELP FOR HURTING FAMILIES

Therefore a man shall leave his father and mother and be joined to his wife,
and they shall become one flesh.

GENESIS 2:24

A patient once told a doctor, "I am in so much pain." The doctor replied, "You will get better if you follow my instructions. Number one: Don't kill yourself."

Many people who are in great pain would never think of killing themselves. But when people experience pain in their marital relationships, they often think of "killing" their marriages. Do you have a marriage in trouble or know someone else who does? Then before doing anything else, follow (or encourage your friend to follow) this first rule for a successful marriage: "Don't even consider ending it." Marriage counselors report that ninety to ninety-five percent of troubled marriages can be healed. But that can only happen if you stick with it. Think only about doing what you can to save and heal your marriage, not about the other options the world offers.

The second rule for a successful marriage is: "Maintain a vital spiritual life." Day by day draw closer to Christ, praying and reading His Word by yourself and with your spouse. We all need to know God's Word so we can avoid worldly pitfalls that can chip away at our marriages. Therefore, search God's Word, and obey it so that it may change your life and your marriage.

The third rule is: "Develop communication." The marriage encounter program begins by sending couples to their rooms, where each person writes a letter listing all the positive things about his or her spouse. Then spouses exchange letters and read them out loud. When husbands and wives go to the next general meeting, they're changed people! Tell your spouse what you like about him or her, and it will revolutionize your marriage.

The fourth rule is: "Turn up the thermostat in your marriage." Show warmth and affection and intimacy. Hold hands the way you did when you were courting. Walk with your arms around each other. As you do, you'll find that a touch can work magic.

Whether or not you have a marriage in trouble, I encourage you to apply these "rules" in your home today. As you seek to obey God's will for your marriage, He will bless it, making it healthy and vital. And remember, don't ever give up!

When a man and woman get married, they become one.
The problems start when they try to figure out which one.

PREPARATION FOR ETERNITY

As iron sharpens iron, so one man sharpens another.

PROVERBS 27:17, NIV

Have you ever noticed that the years seem to fly by at breakneck speed? A child is born, and before you know it, he or she is walking. For months, you plan a big party, and before you know it, it seems as if the party took place six months ago. You lay out the perfect vacation getaway, and soon you're wistfully poring through a photo album of the trip. It just seems as if life runs on fast forward.

Well, in one sense life *does* fly by, because from an eternal perspective, life is short. Before long, your family will grow and move away. Even your career will fade into retirement. But for those of us who are married, God has placed us on this temporal earth in part to develop our relationships with our spouses, relationships that mirror the eternal relationship between Christ and His Church.

Marriage prepares us for eternity by teaching us the process of sanctification. Sometimes we wonder why our husbands or wives rub us the wrong way, and yet, that process is part of God's design. As iron sharpens iron, so one person can sharpen the other. We have rough edges that need to be rubbed off, and many a person has found that marriage grinds off all sorts of undesirable characteristics. (Not that marriage is a grind; it's often anything but!)

Marriage is a school in which we daily learn forgiveness, patience, and love. In marriage, we learn to develop an intimate relationship, and that process teaches us how to pursue an intimate relationship with Christ. The three main ingredients in both of these relationships are commitment, love, and trust.

I hope that today you find joy in your relationship with your spouse—someone who will encourage you, even if that means helping to smooth away some rough edges. Welcome this process, because before you know it, life will be over. Then you'll experience the eternity you've prepared for, and you'll find yourself face to face with Jesus Christ as His bride.

Home—the nursery of the infinite.

WILLIAM ELLERY CHANNING

FORGIVE AND FORGET

'And forgive us our debts, as we forgive our debtors.'

MATTHEW 6:12

Christianity is a religion of forgiveness. Christ has paid the price for *all* our millions of sins; He forgives and forgets each one we confess. And He expects us to do the same with those around us, forgiving and forgetting their sins against us.

We especially need to extend forgiveness to our family members. Often we are less willing to forgive a parent, sibling, spouse, or child than we are to forgive a friend or guest in our homes. For example, how would you react if a friend spilled a cup of coffee on your favorite couch? Would you react differently if a son or daughter did the very same thing? Suppose you have company and a guest picks up a beautiful vase from the table and says, "My, this is beautiful. Where did you...Oh, my gracious! I broke it!" You'd probably reply, "Oh, don't worry about it. It's nothing. I know where I can get another one." (Never mind that you bought the vase in a little shop in Istanbul, Turkey, a place you'll never visit again!) But would you be so tenderhearted if your spouse or even a roommate broke it?

If we want to foster healthy Christian homes, we need to extend forgiveness to those who live with us. No matter how great the offense, we need to forgive, remembering that our offenses against our forgiving God are much greater. So keep short accounts with God and with your family.

Not only must we forgive others, we must also forget their offenses against us, a much-neglected aspect of forgiveness. How many times have you heard people say, "Oh, I forgive him (or her) all right, but I'll *never* forget"? But true forgiving *is* forgetting. God says that He will forgive our sins and will remember them against us *no more.* In His action He models for us how we should respond when people hurt us. Forgiveness means that you don't say, "You always do that" or "There you go again!" Forgiveness means that we don't rehash old trespasses again and again like a cow chewing its cud. If we do, we haven't truly forgiven.

If we choose not to forgive those who sin against us, neither will our heavenly Father forgive us. Do you need to forgive someone today, forgetting that person's trespass against you?

> *Every person should have a special cemetery lot in which to bury*
> *the faults of friends and loved ones.*

ANONYMOUS

JUDGE NOT

'Judge not, that you be not judged. For with what judgment you judge, you will be judged; and with the same measure you use, it will be measured back to you.'

MATTHEW 7:1–2

Which describes you better: "the swift hand of judgment" or "the patient heart of grace"? If you're like most of us, you relate better to the former. For some reason, we feel better about ourselves when we see something wrong in others.

But Jesus said, "Judge not." Does that mean that we should *never* find fault with anyone? We need to see others with clear eyes, and if someone does wrong, we should lovingly identify it to help that person get back on track. But we shouldn't make a habit of finding fault. The tense of the Greek verb used in the passage above means "do not be always, continually finding fault and judging one another." That type of continual judgment reaps its own consequences. Take, for example, the wife who constantly reminds her husband to wipe off his shoes before entering the house or the husband who over and over harps on his wife's driving skills. While each may succeed in getting his or her spouse to change behavior, the harsh comments will come back in a thousand different ways. "With the same measure you use, it will be measured back to you." That is a divine guarantee. No one is more miserable than a henpecked spouse, except for the person heaping such harsh judgment upon him or her. People who judge like this don't even know why they feel so miserable, but it's because their judgment comes back to them with the same measure they used.

In his classic book *How to Win Friends and Influence People,* Dale Carnegie writes: "Don't criticize, condemn, or complain." Although we might not live out this philosophy on a daily basis, we can still strive for such a positive ideal.

We all make mistakes, and we all deserve judgment. But fortunately for us, Christ doesn't judge us as harshly as we often judge each other. Christ is the friend of sinners. Instead of pointing out our faults, He took them upon Himself once and for all. He who has the right to judge says, "Neither do I condemn you; go and sin no more." He offers to take us into His family and to make us His own just as we are.

Let that truth sustain and inspire you. Remember that Christ has chosen to forgive you, not to judge you. And because of His sacrifice and example, extend the same grace to those you interact with today.

Love is the thing that enables a woman to sing while she mops up the floor after her husband has walked across it in his barn boots.

HOOSIER FARMER

ABRAHAM LINCOLN

Blessed is the nation whose God is the LORD...

PSALM 33:12

Today is Abraham Lincoln's birthday. This sixteenth president of the United States did tremendous things for our country, and he earned the lasting respect and loyalty of American citizens. But was he a Christian? A clergyman once asked Lincoln, "Do you love Jesus?" Lincoln responded, "When I left Springfield, I asked the people to pray for me. I was not a Christian. But when I went to Gettysburg and saw the graves of thousands of our soldiers, I then and there consecrated myself to Christ. Yes, I do love Jesus."

Lincoln was a humble and forgiving person, and he exemplifies our need as a nation to humble ourselves before God. During the dark days of the Civil War, he declared national days of fasting and prayer (not a unique practice in that time). In one of those proclamations, he said:

> It is the duty of nations as well as of men to own their dependence upon the overruling power of God; to confess their sins and transgressions in humble sorrow, yet with assured hope that genuine repentance will lead to mercy and pardon; and to recognize the sublime truth, announced in the Holy Scriptures and proven by all history, that those nations only are blessed whose God is the Lord.
>
> ...We have been the recipients of the choicest bounties of Heaven. We have been preserved, these many years, in peace and prosperity. We have grown in numbers, wealth, and power as no other nation has ever grown; but we have forgotten God.
>
> ...It behooves us, then, to humble ourselves before the offended Power, to confess our national sins, and to pray for clemency and forgiveness. (March 30, 1863)

In our day, with terrible crime rates and immorality of every kind, we would do well to heed Lincoln's words. Today, humble yourself before God, and ask Him to grant His mercy on this nation.

...with malice toward none; with charity for all...

ABRAHAM LINCOLN

SAND IN THE SHOES

…a quarrelsome wife is like a constant dripping.

PROVERBS 19:13, NIV

Remember the last time you took a walk and had to stop because something had worked its way inside your shoe? Isn't it amazing how something so small can be so aggravating?

Peter Jenkins, in his book *Walk Across America,* chronicled his experiences traveling on foot across this continent. In his book, Jenkins explained that he never felt overwhelmed or defeated by the big things. Instead, he said, "What almost defeated me over and over again was the sand in my shoes."

I believe many marriages suffer from the same principle. Unheralded, seldom-discussed "sand in the shoes" underlies many of the marital failures that scar this land. What do I mean by "sand in the shoes of marriage"? I refer to the abrasive sand of criticism.

When people get married, they often make the colossal mistake of supposing they can improve their spouses. Husbands and wives alike think they can achieve this goal by simply telling their spouses about their bad points. People seem quite confident that if they simply point out their spouses' bad points often enough, their spouses will correct their faults and again become the perfect angels they were when they were first married. In other words, the marriage license becomes a hunting license for faults. But contrary to the critic's intentions, this daily faultfinding becomes like "sand in the shoes" or a constant dripping on a rainy day.

Does this sound familiar? Perhaps you've recently been quick to point out your spouse's faults. Consider this: If you emphasize your spouse's good points, you might find that praise will take care of the bad points as nothing else will. Use your marriage license as a hunting license for good, to find virtue and not fault.

Love looks through a telescope; envy through a microscope.

JOSH BILLINGS

LOVE IN THE HOME

Husbands, love your wives, just as Christ also loved the Church…

EPHESIANS 5:25

Since today is Valentine's Day, let me take this opportunity to focus on marriage. Whether you're married or hope to be married someday, I hope you'll benefit from what I share.

If there's one thing we all need today, it's love in our homes. The Scriptures teach that the husband must love the wife (Ephesians 5:25) and that the wife must love the husband (Titus 2:4). But how must husbands and wives love each other? Unlike the message of many pop psychologists today, love is not a warm, fuzzy feeling, although warm feelings may grow out of true love. Instead, love is a commitment shown in acts of kindness and patience. The feelings will then follow, but by themselves, feelings provide a poor foundation for marriage.

We need to actively choose to love our spouses. We should do all we can to bring joy to their days, just as we did when we courted. Do you remember all you did when you were dating? Remember writing affectionate notes and planning romantic outings? Let's regain some of that enthusiasm and apply it to our marriages, if we haven't already. We can show our love in many different ways, even when we don't feel like it. We should hunt for things that will please our spouses and put some sparkle and fizz into the relationship. If our spouses like or enjoy something, we should try to develop an interest in that area too. Even if we don't feel the same level of interest, our spouses will feel loved just knowing that we want to please them.

Remember how, when you were first married, you placed your hopes and your dreams in the hands of your beloved? If any of that enthusiasm has fizzled, try to recapture it. Above all, strive to be the spouse that your beloved would like you to be. When both of you do that, you will have made this world a little bit of heaven.

Domestic Happiness, thou only bliss of paradise that hast survived the fall.

WILLIAM COWPER

THE SINGLE LIFE: HEAVEN OR HELL?

And the LORD God said, 'It is not good that man should be alone;
I will make him a helper comparable to him.'

GENESIS 2:18

When God designed the human race, He made us male and female. He recognized that it was not good for Adam to be alone, that Adam needed a companion. (If Adam had been alone, you and I wouldn't be here!)

But God's provision of a mate to Adam doesn't mean that every mature Christian should marry. Unfortunately, our society views singleness as a sign of immaturity and incompleteness. As our culture sees it, if a person is truly mature, he or she will find a suitable partner and marry.

But let's consider Jesus. Jesus never had a date. He never kissed a girl (in the romantic sense). He was never engaged. He never got married. He never had any children or any grandchildren. Yet the whole world proclaims that He is the wisest, most mature, well-balanced person to ever live, maintaining positive relationships with people of both sexes. Jesus is a model for both married and single people.

I once asked a group to tell me the names of all the married couples in the New Testament who served the Lord. The group could think of only two: Aquila and Priscilla, and Joseph and Mary. Then I asked the group to name the single people who served the Lord, and the group brainstormed quite a list: Paul, John the Baptist, Titus, Timothy, Mark, Epaphroditus, Apollos, Phoebe, and Mary Magdalene. And really, the list could go on.

Are you single? Then first of all, thank God and praise Him for your gift of singleness. Second, use your singleness as a special opportunity to serve Him, perhaps embarking on an adventure you could never experience if you were married. Third, develop your own particular gifts, skills, and interpersonal relationships. Finally, trust the Lord to accomplish His will for you in this matter, and praise Him for whatever His will may be. Whatever path God chooses for you, He will enable you to walk it well and with contentment.

I realize now there would have been no way I could have read the books I've read, written the
words I've written, gone the places I've gone, studied the courses I have studied, learned the
languages I have learned, maintained the schedule I have maintained, mended the people
I have mended—if I had been encumbered by a husband and family.

EVELYN RAMSEY, MISSIONARY, DOCTOR, AND LINGUIST
TO THE PEOPLE OF PAPUA NEW GUINEA

WHEN TEMPTED TO QUIT

*And let us not grow weary while doing good, for in due season
we shall reap if we do not lose heart.*

GALATIANS 6:9

When you think of Abraham Lincoln, what qualities come to your mind? Compassion? Concern for the disenfranchised? Humor? While all those characteristics apply, I think if we really knew Lincoln, we'd find that the overriding quality of his character was perseverance.

Believe it or not, Abraham Lincoln was a *failure*. In almost every area of his life, he experienced defeat. As a young man, Lincoln ran for the state legislature and lost overwhelmingly. He went into business and failed completely. He became engaged to a beautiful, loving girl, but she died. Lincoln then married a woman who was a continual burden to him, a thorn in his flesh. Soon thereafter he decided to run for Congress but lost decidedly. After that, he tried to get an appointment to the U.S. Land Office, but he was turned down. He then decided to run for the United States Senate, but his competition pounded him into the ground. After all these defeats, he decided to become vice president of the United States! He was, as we know, defeated once again.

Abraham Lincoln lost at nearly everything he tried until he ran for and won the presidency of the United States. He persevered despite overwhelming discouragement and defeat, and because he persisted, he became one of the greatest leaders this world has ever known. Despite all the losses he suffered, Lincoln was never a loser because he never quit.

When we hear that litany of the losses endured by such an upstanding man and respectable leader, how can we not feel just a little ashamed at the number of times we've thrown in the towel? What a great reminder that we need never give up, because God has already promised we will triumph if we've entrusted our lives to Him.

Have you experienced defeat recently? My friend, keep persevering. Never give up, but instead rely on God's promise to achieve victory in your life.

A quitter never wins, and a winner never quits.

ANONYMOUS

OVERCOME EVIL WITH GOOD

Do not be overcome by evil, but overcome evil with good.

ROMANS 12:21

Have you ever felt so mad at someone that you couldn't see straight? In the midst of many conflicts, you can't talk with the person who angered you, or else you'd end up saying something you know you shouldn't. On the other hand, you can't stop thinking about that person's offense against you. So you end up replaying the situation over and over in your mind like a broken record.

I know the feeling, but I've learned through God's Word a great truth that transforms such feelings into opportunities to share God's love. This truth is to turn the other cheek. Jesus told us to return good for evil. When we first hear that, we think, "What? Did I miss something?" because we naturally respond to an offense by returning evil for evil—an eye for an eye, a tooth for a tooth. In our humanness, we can't fathom going the second mile, turning the other cheek, or doing good to those who hurt us. Yet doing such is the art of Christian forgiveness carried through to the end.

When you overcome evil with good, forgiving your enemy and even offering kindness in return, you will experience tremendous freedom. When we respond with good, we can't help but win the battle. And we find ourselves invulnerable to evil.

Jesus is our perfect example of overcoming evil with good. When we were still sinners, having rebelled against Him, Christ showed His love to us. He went to the cross for us, taking our wrongs upon Himself. Christ asked His Father to forgive those who crucified Him. Then Jesus descended into hell, conquered it, and rose victorious. When we respond with kindness and love, we triumph in grace and give glory to Jesus.

Do you need to forgive someone today? Overcome evil with good by offering forgiveness, love, and kindness to that person. Then watch as Jesus brings freedom and victory to you because of your obedience.

He who has mastered the grace of forgiveness is far more triumphant than he
who has managed to see that no wrong to him is gone unavenged.

LLOYD D. MATTSON

PROCRASTINATION

Now as he reasoned about righteousness, self-control, and the judgment to come, Felix was afraid and answered, 'Go away for now; when I have a convenient time I will call for you [Paul].'

ACTS 24:25

Do you ever put off things until tomorrow? Do you wait for the perfect time and conditions before undertaking a challenge?

Many people procrastinate. The word "procrastination" comes from two Latin words that, combined, mean "toward tomorrow." When we procrastinate, we look toward tomorrow, counting on it as a better day to face problems and difficult situations. Mark Twain once quipped, "Never put off till tomorrow what you can do the day after tomorrow."

Although we joke about it, procrastination can be a harmful habit with disastrous consequences. In fact, George Washington unwittingly capitalized on a British officer's procrastination to free America from British rule. During the American Revolution, when General Washington decided to cross the Delaware River on Christmas Eve to make a surprise attack on the Hessian army at Trenton, one of the British sympathizers discovered Washington's plan and sent a warning note to the Hessian commander, Colonel Rahl. But when Rahl received the note, he was in his tent, playing cards with his officers. So instead of opening the letter, he put it in his pocket. Rahl finished his game just as the Americans surprised his army. Rahl's procrastination cost him his honor, his command, and his life.

But the worst effects of procrastination are in the spiritual world. Someone once said that Satan had a meeting to discuss the best way to deceive humankind. The first demon said, "I'll tell them the Bible is a fairy tale." Satan rejected this plan. The second demon said, "I'll tell them there is no God, no Christ, no heaven or hell." Satan rejected this plan, too. The third demon said, "I'll tell them everything is true. However, I'll tell them there is no hurry." Satan chose this plan.

Do you procrastinate? If so, would you like to stop? Then take some advice from Dr. Neil Fiore, author of *The Now Habit*. Fiore says procrastinators can overcome the habit by breaking down large tasks into thirty-minute segments and handling one segment a day. This procedure helps improve a person's self-image and gives that person fresh excitement about his or her work. Choose a task you'd like to tackle, and ask God to show you the first step toward reaching your goal. Then take that step today, and watch how God works through and in you!

Procrastination is wasting today's time to clutter up
tomorrow's opportunities with yesterday's troubles.

ANONYMOUS

AMAZING GRACE

For by grace you have been saved through faith, and that not of yourselves;
it is the gift of God, not of works, lest anyone should boast.

EPHESIANS 2:8–9

If we likened Scripture passages to mountain ranges, I think "by grace are you saved" would be the Himalayas. This passage towers above all others because it contains the highest biblical truth—by God's grace we are saved. The apostle Paul said that among faith, hope, and love, the greatest is love. If Paul had included grace in the list, I have a feeling grace would have topped the list. But Paul didn't include grace because he was comparing things which "abide." Grace does not abide. It did not exist before Adam's fall because it was not necessary, and it will not exist after the Final Judgment. There will be no grace for those in hell, and those in glory will have no more need of it. Today is the "age of grace."

We can best understand the concept of grace through illustration. This one, limited as it is, still brings part of the point home. About 125 years ago in czarist Russia, a Russian nobleman and his faithful servant traveled by dog sled across a vast expanse of frozen wasteland. They had traveled for several hundred miles, and their home lay only twenty miles ahead. After such a long and treacherous journey, they looked forward to a warm bed and hot food. Suddenly a pack of hungry wolves appeared behind them, apparently having caught their scent. Despite the dogs' efforts to pull the dog sled as fast as they could, the wolves started closing in. The situation was hopeless—they had no place to hide and no chance of outrunning the wolves. Suddenly, the old servant threw himself backward, off the dog sled. The wolf pack stopped and attacked the servant, sparing the nobleman's life.

Grace involves sacrifice. The greatest grace of all was God's sacrifice of His own Son on the cross. Have you accepted His grace so that you may live with Him eternally?

Amazing grace, how sweet the sound that saved a wretch like me!
I once was lost, but now am found, was blind but now I see.

JOHN NEWTON, FORMER SLAVE TRADER

SAFETY IN THE MIDST OF DANGER

But the day of the Lord will come…and the elements will melt with fervent heat;
both the earth and the works that are in it will be burned up.

2 PETER 3:10

When life hands us difficult circumstances and dangerous situations, we all need safe hiding places. When you face the fire, where do you go to seek rescue?

A whole host of dangers lie in life's path, and at any time those dangers can threaten to overtake us. Many say we have a *multitude* of places to seek safety from life's challenges, but truly we have only one—Jesus Christ.

Consider the early pioneers who traveled across the vast plains of America. As they crossed the country, they often found themselves in a sea of grass for miles on end. In autumn, the grass turned brown and dry from exposure to the sun and lack of water. This condition caused a huge fire hazard, and the pioneers greatly feared seeing a wall of fire coming their way! They feared that they would have no escape as the wind blew the fire toward them faster than they could run. But the pioneers devised a way to survive this hazard. When they saw a wall of fire coming toward them, they ignited the grass behind them. The wind bringing the fire toward them also blew out the fire behind them, leaving a safe firebreak. The pioneers simply moved into the center of the blackened area, and when the larger wall of fire approached them, it went around them, leaving them unscathed. The pioneers' only safe haven in the midst of the fire was where the fire had already been.

We read in 2 Peter that "the day of the Lord will come…and the elements will melt with fervent heat; both the earth and the works that are in it will be burned up." Even as we read, the fire of God's wrath comes upon this world, and we have only one safe hiding place. When that fire comes, we need to run to the place where the fire has already been—the cross of Christ. Through faith in Christ we realize that the fire that fell upon Him should have fallen upon us, and we find the one place of escape.

Perhaps you face a wall of fire today. If so, seek the One who has endured the fire, for you'll find safety only in His presence.

God's will is our hiding place.

CORRIE TEN BOOM

CALL ON ME

'Call to Me, and I will answer you, and show you great and mighty things,
which you do not know.'

JEREMIAH 33:3

We all go through our share of difficult times. Perhaps you're in the midst of one even now, wondering if God knows and cares about your pain. But He does. He hears your cries and wants you to know He is there for you. When we endure afflictions, when our souls despair of hope or help, when the skies turn ominously black and the green valleys wither into wastelands, then the Word of the Lord shines through like a ray of hope: "Call to Me!"

The prophet Jeremiah knew despair and darkness. Jeremiah found himself in prison, confined in the courtyard of the guard, when the word of the Lord came to him a *second* time. The first time God spoke to Jeremiah, he did not hear the Lord. But now in prison, Jeremiah's hearing was greatly improved. So often we operate the same way. When things go well for us, we allow the things of the world to distract us. But when we suffer, God's Word resounds like a thundering voice echoing off cold prison walls. Through our pain, God commands our attention in ways we never heed when things are going well for us.

Why was Jeremiah thrown into prison? In fact, why do so many of God's servants end up in prison? From Jeremiah to Paul to John Bunyan to saints of our own time, many godly people find themselves unjustly imprisoned. Sometimes those closest to God seem to suffer more than others. Why? Because in the long run, God has our eternal good in mind. He tests us and refines us. He molds us until we become what He wants us to be, even if it takes imprisonment to do it.

As Jeremiah despaired in prison, facing a tremendous, life-refining difficulty, God came to him in great grace and said, "Call to me and I will answer you." He says the same to us. Not only will He answer our requests, but He will do great and mighty things beyond what we ask or imagine. When we can do nothing else, we can "call to God."

Do you feel alone, emotionally imprisoned by the trials you face? Then call to God today, and listen for His voice. He will speak to you as you trust in His goodness, love, and provision.

God washes the eyes by tears until they can behold the invisible land
where tears shall come no more.

HENRY WARD BEECHER

THE FAITH OF WASHINGTON

If we confess our sins, He is faithful and just to forgive us our sins...

1 JOHN 1:9

How would you define the word "hero"? Do you know anyone who fulfills that definition, anyone whom you hold in such high esteem?

These days we desperately need heroes, people we can look up to and emulate. I think that George Washington fills the bill in a remarkable way. In his own day, George Washington's character was the wonder of the world. Not even his most relentless British foes of the Revolutionary War could denigrate his character.

But what gave rise to such amazing character? For starters, his parents, both dedicated Christians, raised him in a godly home. His father taught him to be unselfish, to love the truth, and to worship God. His mother helped him develop his prayer life. As an adult he carried on these good disciplines. Through his own writings, Washington has left us a legacy of his fervent prayers, such as "O most glorious God, in Jesus Christ my merciful and loving father, I acknowledge and confess my guilt, in the weak and imperfect performance of the duties of this day." Almost without fail, Washington spent his mornings and evenings reading Scripture and in prayer. Every day he maintained a consistent devotional life, seeking God's guidance. As Washington led our country, he never once trusted in his character to guide him; he trusted in Jesus Christ, the only perfect person who ever lived. Washington prayed that Christ's blood would cleanse him of all his sins, that God would accept him because of the merits and perfect character of Jesus Christ, not his own.

As good heroes do, Washington provided us a good example of a faithful Christian. He trusted Jesus with his life and maintained discipline in his devotional life. His steadfastness contributed to his greatness. How can you follow this great hero's example today?

We are what we repeatedly do. Excellence, then, is not an act, but a habit.

ARISTOTLE

CALEB

'Now, therefore, give me this mountain...'

JOSHUA 14:12

Have you ever made an outrageous request of God then stood back in amazement as He granted it? Caleb made such a request in Joshua 14: "Give me this mountain." At the age of eighty-five, Caleb requested a mountain, hill country filled with pagans. Why would he ask for a hillside full of hostile heathens? Even if he received the land, Caleb would have to face the sons of Anak, a whole family, generation, and tribe of giants who inhabited the hill.

How could Caleb possibly fight the Anakim and win this land? Though he was as strong as he was on the day forty years earlier when Moses sent him and the other spies to scope out the Promised Land, he surely didn't have the strength to overcome a family of giants twice his size. Caleb's strength doesn't fully explain his request. We have to read a bit further in the book of Joshua to find the secret. In Joshua 14:12–13, Caleb says, "Give me this mountain of which *the Lord* spoke in that day...*the Lord* will be with me, and I shall be able to drive them out as *the Lord* said" (emphasis mine). Caleb based his life upon his faith and trust in the Lord. He followed the Lord wholeheartedly, and therein lies the great lesson. Out of Caleb's trust in the Lord came the strength and courage that made this man a hero for God.

Do you have a big request to make of God today? Then follow Caleb's example. Ask for God to give you what you need according to His will. Never mind the obstacles, but trust in Him to overcome them. Our Lord delights in rewarding those who trust Him!

Prayer is not overcoming God's reluctance; it is laying hold of His highest willingness.

RICHARD CHENEVIX TRENCH

JOHN BUNYAN

'…and the one who comes to Me I will by no means cast out.'

JOHN 6:37

As you've walked along your life's path, have you ever felt you've gone astray, entirely unable to find your way back? Perhaps even today you feel a bit lost, fearing you've taken a wrong turn because of a choice you've made…

John Bunyan, the seventeenth-century author who wrote *Pilgrim's Progress*, a great Christian classic, wandered off the path leading to Christ. According to his own testimony, Bunyan was a very ungodly young man. During this period of his life, he wrote, "Then I said unto God, 'Depart from me, for I desire not the knowledge of Thy ways.'" Because he rejected God, Bunyan had no peace in his heart. He felt greatly troubled by thoughts of the future, believing he had sinned beyond the possibility of hope. But at last he read John 6:37: "And the one who comes to Me I will by no means cast out." As Bunyan came to God, God granted him mercy, and Bunyan began to see the light of salvation dawn upon him. He had come to know eternal life.

Bunyan later described his journey from despair to hope, from sinner to saint, in *Pilgrim's Progress,* one of the greatest allegories of all time. The book chronicles a journey from the City of Destruction through the Doubting Castle and other dangers to the Celestial City. In it, Bunyan describes how anyone who desires the pilgrim way may find it, and he warns of the dangers one will encounter along the way.

Bunyan had learned a great lesson: We are saved only by grace, free and unmerited. Bunyan reminds us that we are only passing through this life en route to a greater destination. Therefore, we must take care to not get side-tracked from the straight and narrow path. Where are you along this journey? Do you allow Christ to guide you? As you trust in God's grace, you can persevere to the end, for Christ gives you safe passage.

He [Jesus] hath given me a rest by His sorrow, and life by His death.

JOHN BUNYAN

A CHECKLIST FOR YOUR PRAYER LIFE

Be joyful always; pray continually; give thanks in all circumstances...

1 THESSALONIANS 5:16–18, NIV

How is your prayer life going these days? As Christians, we should pray unceasingly, lifting praises and intercessions to God as constantly as our lungs rise and fall with each breath. Our hearts should be so in tune with God that every occasion calls forth a petition for a need, an intercession for someone else, a confession of a sin, a word of thanksgiving, or an article of praise.

So often we pray narrowly, attending only to our own needs. Instead, we should pray broadly for everyone. We should pray for the lost that they might be saved and for the saved that they might win the lost. And if we know that someone is in need, we should lift that person before God's throne, asking Him for help!

We also need to regularly confess our sins. Do you keep short accounts with God or store up great debts of sin? Do you forget to confess many of your sins? Do you confess your sins of commission but forget your sins of omission? Do you confess wrong deeds but forget the thoughts that breed them? Do you confess sins of the tongue such as gossip and unkind words? Do you confess sins of poor attitudes such as coldness, lack of love, thoughtlessness, and unconcern?

And what about thanksgiving? When was the last time you counted your blessings and thanked God for each one: family, friends, shelter, daily bread, liberty, salvation?

How about praise and adoration, the graduate school of prayer? Do you praise God not only for what He has done for you but also for who He is? Do you tell God how much you appreciate His wisdom and power, His justice and mercy, His omnipotence and omniscience, all that He is and ever shall be?

I hope this little reminder will help you to pray more effectively. Start today by praying in a way you haven't prayed for a long while. Perhaps you need to clear your slate with God through confession, or maybe you need to spend time thanking Him for bestowing blessings on you. Prayer is such a great privilege, and I hope you'll engage in it wholeheartedly with every breath you take!

Pray hardest when it is hardest to pray.

CHARLES H. BRENT

ESCAPE FROM SELFISHNESS

…and He died for all, that those who live should live no longer for themselves,
but for Him who died for them and rose again.

2 CORINTHIANS 5:15

Have you ever pondered what gives us the impulse to sin? Have you ever wondered what makes us go against God's commands despite our good intentions?

I believe that selfishness lies at the root of all sin. I have thought long and hard about this, and I cannot think of any sin that doesn't originate from selfishness, from placing self rather than God at the center of our lives. Some have suggested that perhaps a person who steals or lies for his child does not act from selfishness, yet our family is bone of our bone and flesh of our flesh, merely an extension of ourselves. So I believe that whatever the sin—lust, hate, pride, theft, murder—at its core, it stems from selfishness. Even good actions are tarnished by selfish motives. A person may study how to win friends and influence people, work hard at self-improvement, and join a church and become active in it, yet all of these acts may spring from purely selfish motives.

Paul exhorts us to something higher. He says, "I am crucified with Christ." Not only is the cross a substitution, it is a representation—we must identify ourselves with Christ in His death, crucifying our selfish nature and desires with Him. When we die with Christ, we put to death all our hopes, ambitions, agendas, priorities, and plans. We nail all we desire to the cross, becoming dead to our selves.

Paul tells us in Romans 6 that we are to reckon ourselves dead with Christ. We must become dead to the flesh and alive in Christ. The next time temptation pulls at you, remember that you have died to sin and become alive in Christ. You have no obligation to your old nature, except to reckon it as dead. This is how we escape from selfishness, the fountainhead of all sin.

One can be a miser or a savage and be selfish, but not a Christian.

ANONYMOUS

PUTTING ON THE ARMOR OF GOD

*Therefore take up the whole armor of God, that you may be able to withstand
in the evil day, and having done all, to stand.*

EPHESIANS 6:13

Do you ever feel that life is a battle for which you are ill-prepared, defenseless
against the enemy's attacks?

In Ephesians, Paul tells us that we fight spiritual battles daily and that we
can win only by calling upon a strength beyond our own. So Paul exhorts us to
put on the whole armor of God every day. Each piece of armor has a special purpose to protect us from Satan's blows. The first piece is the *belt of truth*. Satan's
first line of attack is against the truth, confusing us with lies so that we give in.
Look at Eve. Satan confused her about what God said regarding the tree of the
knowledge of good and evil. But when we trust in absolute truth, Satan can
never defeat us. Over our hearts we place the *breastplate of righteousness*. We put
on Christ's righteousness to guard our hearts and keep them pure. Our own
righteousness would be but a rusty breastplate full of gaping holes. Feeble and
decaying, it would allow the enemy to penetrate and corrupt our good intentions. On our feet, we wear sturdy *shoes made of the gospel of peace*. These shoes
enable us to march forward comfortably and at a steady pace. They keep our
footing sure on any kind of rough or shaky ground. We also take up the *shield
of faith*. This shield wards off Satan's fiery darts of lust and doubt before they get
close enough to destroy and consume us. To protect our heads, we wear the *hel-
met of salvation*. It keeps us rejoicing in the hope of our salvation and gives us
additional strength when we feel weak. Last but definitely not least, we pick up
the Word of God, the *sword of the Spirit,* which we use offensively in hand-to-
hand combat with Satan. We can attack Satan with Scriptures that overpower
him.

Notice that none of these pieces protect our backs. We don't need that protection because, with God's armor on, we need never and should never retreat.

Every day we must prayerfully put on each piece of armor and "stand"
ready for whatever comes. We face spiritual battle daily, and on some days it can
be intense. None of us can face today's spiritual battles without the protection
of God's armor.

You can anticipate spiritual battle today. Ask God to prepare you, dressing you
in His armor so that He may use you and so that you may live victoriously.

We are called to be clothed in the armor of light, every piece of which is Jesus Christ Himself.

ACHAN'S SINS

*'When I saw among the spoils a beautiful Babylonian garment, two hundred shekels of silver,
and a wedge of gold weighing fifty shekels, I coveted them and took them…'*

JOSHUA 7:21

Have you ever looked at a glossy home-decorating magazine and found that the home you felt thankful for an hour ago now seems junky? Or perhaps you saw a television ad for a slick car, and suddenly the car in your driveway now seems like a jalopy.

Advertisements often lead us into covetousness. Of course, we need to provide for our families; and we don't sin when we seek to care for our needs. But we do sin when we desire the things of this world, desire them so strongly that we dwell on how we can obtain them. Sometimes we want something so dearly that we're even willing to break one or more of God's commandments to get it.

Achan, an Israelite at the time of Joshua's conquest, exemplifies the seductive power of covetousness. Before the Israelites stormed Jericho, Joshua told everyone that everything in that city was devoted to destruction, that the wrath of God would fall upon the city because of the inhabitants' sins. Later the Israelites attacked the little town of Ai, but the inhabitants of this small town defeated the Israelites, killing many of them. Joshua sought the Lord to find out why Israel had lost, and God told him that there was sin in the camp. Joshua then sought out the sin, and Achan confessed that in Jericho he had coveted some riches, so he took them and buried them under his tent. Achan's covetousness cost him dearly—it cost him his family and his life.

When we covet, we actually rebel against God's provision for us. God has given us so much already, and if we ever have a need, He fulfills it. As we trust God, we see His hand at work in our lives, providing so richly for us. The antidote for covetousness is contentment with God's blessings.

How are you doing in the area of covetousness? If you find that you want something, submit it to God. Trust Him to provide it for you if you need it and be content with all He has given you now.

Content[ment] makes poor men rich; discontent[ment] makes rich men poor.

BENJAMIN FRANKLIN

ON LEAPING OVER A WALL

For by You I can run against a troop; by my God I can leap over a wall.

2 SAMUEL 22:30

Do you ever feel surrounded by the enemy and backed up against a wall? that no matter which direction you turn, you have an obstacle in your way? Perhaps you're in such a situation today, feeling cornered by some circumstances that seem beyond your control.

We all encounter "walls" in life, things that block our paths on life's journey. For example, as Christians we all have temptations coming at us like yapping dogs, attempting to drain our spiritual resources. We also experience personal problems in our lives, in our families, and at work. As we face each of these challenges, it seems that an insurmountable wall has been erected.

But it's not impossible to leap over those walls. God can give us the ability to leap over anything this world puts in front of us.

So, you may ask, *"How* do we leap over the walls that life puts in our way?" By faith! Consider how you entered into eternal life. Did you not come to the place where you rested your hopes on God's promise that Christ had paid for your salvation and was offering it freely to those who would trust in Him? And the very moment you trusted that promise, it was fulfilled!

We can also surmount those walls by taking action. Just look at King David's life to learn a lesson or two about hurdling obstacles. In 2 Samuel 22 David recounts the many times God had helped him in battle: "I have run. I have leaped." He did not just sit there and tremble in the face of the troop confronting him. He did not just walk along the wall, feeling it, examining its height. He did not just wait for God to make his problems disappear. David took his sword in his hand and rushed into the fray. He gathered himself together and rushed toward the wall. Then, and only then, was he able to leap over it. David's life proves that faith and action are a mighty combination.

Are you facing a wall today? You can leap over it if you arise in faith, press forward, and take action. By doing so you'll experience the empowerment of the God who promised us, "Call to Me, and I will answer you, and show you great and mighty things, which you do not know." You'll then see the enemy host scatter, and you'll find yourself being transported over the wall.

Faith will beget in us three things: Vision, Venture, Victory.

GEORGE W. RIDOUT

THE USES OF ADVERSITY

...Yet their boast is only labor and sorrow...

PSALM 90:10

Perhaps nothing causes more people to stumble in their faith than the problem of suffering. None of us is exempt from tribulation. We all face it at one time or another. And in our pain and desperation, we often ask, "Why, Lord?"

Have those words ever echoed through the chambers of your soul in the middle of some dark and starless night?

We can't get rid of all pain, trouble, hurt, injury, and sorrow. People fall off things and hurt themselves. Shall we then do away with the law of gravity? People have accidents in cars, planes, trains, and boats. Shall we then get rid of all forms of transportation? Suffering is a part of our world, and if Christians were exempt from all trouble and pain, everyone would immediately recognize the payoffs. If all Christians had an abundance of money, health, and happiness, our characters would never develop. Christianity would degenerate to a mere commercial venture.

So while we would avoid adversity if we could, it serves important purposes in our lives. First, trouble and sorrow equip us to help others by making us compassionate and willing to reach out to those in need. Second, trouble and sorrow draw us to God and drive us to our knees; they make us long for our real home, heaven. The third and the greatest purpose of trouble is to make us Christlike. If we are to become like Jesus, we will, like Him, have to pass through the valley of the shadows. Although unpleasant at the moment, often out of the greatest suffering comes the greatest love and beauty.

Do you face adversity today? If so, ask the Lord to show you the purpose of it in your life. Then, if you can, look past your pain to the way God is using it to draw you closer to Him and to His kingdom.

Beyond the cross there is the glory of Easter morning;
beyond the agony of the Crucifixion there is the blessedness of Paradise.

DANGERS IN THE DARK

The true light that gives light to every man was coming into the world.

JOHN 1:9, NIV

Have you ever been afraid of the dark? Perhaps as a child you feared that monsters lurked in your bedroom, just waiting for the lights to go out. Or maybe as an adult you fear that people with evil intentions hide in the shadows, ready to attack.

Dangers *do* lurk in darkness. I refer not to "things that go bump in the night," but to very real dangers which exist in the dark. After all, darkness is the domain of the "prince of darkness," who hates the light and does all he can to keep people from coming to the light.

Many of the most dramatic, compelling, and illuminating stories found in the Bible took place at night. It was night when the Sodomites beat upon Lot's doors and demanded his two angelic visitors to molest. It was night when David looked upon the form of Bathsheba bathing upon the rooftop below, then called her to his presence and committed the sin of adultery.

But the darkest "night" this world has ever seen took place at *midday* on Calvary. In that darkness, the noon that became midnight, humankind's sin extinguished the Light of the world. Christ endured in body and soul the penalty, pain, and anguish which we so rightly deserve for our sinfulness.

But darkness couldn't extinguish the Light forever. Isaiah foretold the day when the "people who walked in darkness [would see] a great light." That great light is Jesus Christ, whom the Bible calls the Light of the world. He promises to give us the light of everlasting day if we will yield our hearts to Him. Jesus Christ is the sun of our souls, and when He comes into the darkness of our hearts, He brings a light which forever lightens our lives and gives us purpose. And when our time comes, Christ will take us to our everlasting home, and in that great day, we will discover there is *no* night there!

Because of Christ's sacrifice, you need not fear the darkness. Today rejoice in Christ's everlasting light, the light that extinguishes darkness this day and for eternity.

When He came, there was no light. When He left, there was no darkness.

ANONYMOUS

THE IMPORTANCE OF COURAGE

'...Be strong and of good courage; do not be afraid, nor be dismayed, for the LORD your God is with you wherever you go.'

JOSHUA 1:9

If someone just left thousands of people in your care with the command to lead those people through wilderness toward a promised land, how would you feel?

Joshua had that exact experience. After Moses, the Israelites' leader, died, God handed Joshua the leadership baton, and with it came the responsibility to lead the people safely to Canaan. God had created Joshua for this role; even Joshua's name, which means "the Lord saves," set Joshua apart to lead the people into the Promised Land. As you might imagine, if Joshua was going to fill Moses' shoes, he needed a little encouragement. At the beginning of Joshua's new ministry, God exhorted Joshua to have courage. *Four* times in Joshua 1, God commands Joshua to be strong and of good courage. God obviously wanted to get His message across!

You and I also need courage. If we want to fulfill the destiny God has planned for us, we need to step out in courage, knowing that God will blaze our trail for us. To receive our inheritance, to successfully fulfill our life purpose, to bring glory to God, we must have a courageous character. Following Christ isn't an easy task. It requires great strength and courage because we never know what God will call His people to do.

But we can't muster up courage on our own. Any courage we manufacture within ourselves will vanish in the face of our first trial. We need to get our courage from the Lord. When God told Joshua to have courage, He followed that exhortation with the promise that He would go with Joshua wherever Joshua went. In the same way, God gives us courage for whatever He calls us to do. How? Through our reconciliation with God. When we come to Christ and find in Him our redemption, we gain courage to fulfill God's purposes for us. We get our courage from knowing that God is our Father who has accepted us unto Himself and whose providence watches over us.

Since nothing can separate you from God's love, go forth boldly into whatever He has for you this day. "Be strong and of good courage...for the Lord your God is with you wherever you go."

Cowards die many times...The valiant never taste of death but once.

WILLIAM SHAKESPEARE

MAKE THE MOST OUT OF LIFE

So teach us to number our days, that we may gain a heart of wisdom.

PSALM 90:12

Are you getting everything you want from life? Or do the days slip by too quickly for you to meet your responsibilities, let alone reach for your dreams?

If we're going to make the most of our lives, we have to get the whole concept of life into the proper focus and perspective. We need to view life as God does, because as humans, our perspective on life is upside down!

The Bible tells us two things about life. A number of biblical texts deal with life's brevity, and others address its longevity. To make sense of these seemingly contradictory assertions, we must understand that the first group of texts discusses this present life and the second group describes the life to come. The Bible makes it clear that eternal life is the *real* life—that in eternity we wake up, as it were, from a dream, out of a deep sleep. Although this present life seems so real, it is but a shadow, a vapor that passes away. In Psalm 90, Moses says this life is like grass that grows in the morning and in the evening is cut down. Job said, "My days are swifter than a weaver's shuttle." A weaver's shuttle goes up and down so fast, yet faster than that fly the days of our lives. The moment we reach eternity, the morning that people call death, is the beginning of real and everlasting life.

But we also need to focus on today. Yesterday is gone—irretrievably, forever, completely gone! We can never bring it back. Tomorrow may never come. We never have anything but today. And so the Bible teaches us to live in the moment, making each one count.

Live this life one day at a time, and make the most of each day for God's glory. And the next time you look up at a clock and wonder where the day has gone, remember that you're one day closer to eternity!

Today is the first day of the rest of your life.

ANONYMOUS

THY WILL BE DONE

'…Behold, I have come to do Your will, O God…'

HEBREWS 10:9

Many people today seem to live in frustration, anxiety, fear, and disappointment. They endure a wearying struggle, often in vain, leading to dissatisfaction. Does this sound like your life? If so, maybe you need to discover the joy of praying to God, "Thy will be done."

These words crossed Jesus' lips often. He said, "For I came down from heaven, not to do mine own will, but the will of Him that sent me." And remember how, on that night in Gethsemane, He uttered those words over and over: "O my Father, if it be possible, let this cup pass from me: nevertheless not as I will, but as Thou wilt."

We must believe that God is good and that He has great plans for our lives. We can place ourselves in Christ's hands, remembering that those hands have been pierced for us! But so often, we shrink back in horror from Jesus' words "Not my will but thine be done." We think that if we say them, maybe something like the cross awaits us. But God has not called us to save the world! Jesus took that hell in order that we might be spared. He loves us with an everlasting love! How many people do you know who would send their children to die for you? Can Someone who would give His only begotten Son not also freely give you all things?

Oh, that we would cease struggling and rebelling against God's will for us. I believe that as we stop viewing God through our distorted, human lenses and seek His true nature as described in Scripture—that His banner over us is love, that the hands extended before us have been pierced for us—we will eagerly cast ourselves wholeheartedly and unreservedly into His hands and say with all that is in us, "Lord, Thy will be done in me."

Cast yourself in God's hands today. Say to the Lord, "Thy will be done," laying before Him all that stands in your way of following and trusting Him wholeheartedly. And when He tells you where to go and what to do, obediently follow, and watch what God can do in and through your life.

Oh, the deep, deep love of Jesus, vast, unmeasured, boundless free…

HYMN

MANY TIMES MORE

'Assuredly, I say to you, there is no one who has left house or parents or brothers or wife or children, for the sake of the kingdom of God, who shall not receive many times more in this present time, and in the age to come everlasting life.'

LUKE 18:29–30

When the Lord asks us to follow Him, He doesn't promise an easy nor simple life. In fact, He often calls us to give up something or someone for the sake of the gospel. Perhaps you've had to let go of a cherished dream or a relationship to follow Christ.

Whatever God asks us to give up, we never make those sacrifices in vain. God always repays us "many times more," not because He owes us anything, but because of His kindness and mercy. Though our sacrifices may cause us pain that we may live with for the rest of our lives, Jesus promises the blessings will be worth the sacrifices. When we look back on our lives, we'll see that whatever we gave up for His sake, He gave back to us in other ways, and then some. For example, some choose to follow Jesus even though their families reject them, but suddenly they find they have a worldwide family in the body of Christ.

As humans, we never find these sacrifices easy, but the difficulty is part of God's grand design. God tries us in order to strengthen us. A father tries to get his little son to learn to walk, not so that he will fall down and knock out a tooth, but so that he will know the joy of walking. God tries us through our sacrifices so He can test our faith, purifying and strengthening us. It is sad that many people never experience God's incredible blessings because they don't want to make sacrifices. Instead of putting their all on the altar, they stand far off and debate about the reasonableness of God's request. But God never asks us to make sacrifices until He has prepared us for them. He makes us ready to stretch and grow into stronger people. And when we undergo the trials, God blesses us tremendously.

Is God asking you to make a sacrifice that seems humanly impossible? Don't stand by and miss the blessing He has in store for you. Say "yes," obey Him, and watch Him do great and mighty things in your life.

In this world it is not what we take up, but what we give up, that makes us rich.

HENRY WARD BEECHER

THE TRIUMPHS OF FAITH

...And this is the victory that has overcome the world—our faith.

1 JOHN 5:4

Everyone wants to win in the game of life. Yet, as we look about this world, we see many losers, people who lose more often then they win, many who are victims and not conquerors. Many fall vastly short of any and all hopes they had for life. Perhaps you know someone who has reached for his or her dreams but fallen on hard times in the process.

What is the secret to victory in life? There are varying theories. Some believe that education is the great panacea, the key which unlocks all the doors of success. Others say that a positive attitude can help anyone live life victoriously. With PMA—Positive Mental Attitude—the whole world will fall in line. Yet others extol the virtues of meditation. Place your hands on your knees, squat on the floor, close your eyes, and chant your mantra; soon life will be a bowl of cherries.

We could add to this list almost indefinitely, and no doubt some of these ideas have value. But if we want the true key to victory in life, we need look no further than the Bible. Scripture describes a key that inevitably brings triumph: the key of faith. "Faith," declared the apostle John, "is the victory that overcomes the world."

Yet how can we rejoice in victory when we are constantly beset with trials, problems, troubles, and evils of every sort that threaten to overwhelm us? God promises that no evil can overcome those who believe in His Son. We can claim victory because we have faith that God will transform any trials into victories. We can rest in that confidence, and thus faith changes all things in a magnificent way. Isn't it wonderful to know beyond the shadow of a doubt that God works good in all things?

Do you feel headed for defeat today? Trust God—He can turn any loss into victory. Have faith in Him today, and look toward your situation with confidence that He works all things for good.

God and I can do anything that God can do alone!

ANONYMOUS

PURITY

Pursue…holiness, without which no one will see the Lord.

HEBREWS 12:14

Do you ever wonder how historians of the future will characterize the age in which we live? Will they call it the information age? the nuclear age? the technological age? the space age?

I'd like to suggest a term, but you probably won't feel proud of it. I think we live in a *dirty* age. Despite the ways agencies fight the air and water pollution that threaten our environment, we live in a dirty world. But I'm not talking about environmental blight—I'm talking about the moral impurities that pollute our society, affecting us far more than we realize.

I do not know when in the history of civilization society has degenerated to such an unclean state as that which we experience today. To see what I'm talking about, just peruse almost any contemporary novel, take a peek at some of the recently produced movies, or view today's television programs. Or just listen to everyday conversations!

But God calls us to holiness and purity, wanting us to counteract moral pollution. So how do we become pure and stay pure in the midst of our society's depravity? We can do so only through the pure and spotless Lamb of God.

To pursue holiness and purity, we need to understand what sin really is. Instead of enjoying the forbidden, we need to see sin as devilish and destructive, an evil force that pulls us down. As the psalmist said, "You that love the Lord, hate evil." Guard your heart from the evil that surrounds you daily. Forsake the depraved, and feed your mind on the things of God.

We also must seek accountability. Do you know a mature and trustworthy Christian who can hold you accountable in your walk with God? If you struggle with a particular sin, just knowing that you'll have to give an account to someone can keep you walking straight on God's path. If you don't already have such a person in your life, begin praying today that God will give you a partner with whom you can seek His holiness and purity.

The greatest security against sin is to be shocked at its presence.

THOMAS CARLYLE

ENCOURAGERS

'But command Joshua, and encourage him and strengthen him...'

DEUTERONOMY 3:28

Have you ever had someone encourage you when you felt low or defeated? Remember how that encouragement rejuvenated you, giving you a fresh desire to persevere?

Nothing could uplift us more than the encouragement of a friend or loved one. Encouragement is the oxygen of the soul. Having run two miles, a person may need to pause to catch his or her breath before running another two. Similarly, a person facing a formidable task or even the wearying routines of life needs to pause for encouragement before tackling the work ahead. Encouragement fortifies the laboring soul.

In Deuteronomy, God instructed Moses to commission Joshua and to "encourage him and strengthen him; for he shall go over before this people, and he shall cause them to inherit the land which you will see" (Deuteronomy 3:28). Why did Joshua need such encouragement? Because God assigned him the great task of leading the Israelites into the Promised Land. God knew Joshua would need all the encouragement he could get, and He knew Moses could best give it. When Moses led the Israelites, he faced discouragement again and again: when he confronted Pharaoh, when he came to the Red Sea, and when the Israelites lamented their lack of meat in the desert. In desperation Moses cried out to the Lord, explaining that the people were too big a challenge for him. Having had these experiences, Moses readily obeyed God's command to encourage Joshua for the task that lay ahead.

Like Joshua, we all need encouragement, especially after our greatest defeats when doubt and discouragement set in. So be oxygen to the souls of those around you, strengthening them to persevere for the kingdom of God. Encourage others with God's promise to work good in all things.

Who can you encourage today?

Correction does much, but encouragement does more.

JOHANN VON GOETHE

CROWN HIM LORD OF ALL

*'But his citizens hated him, and sent a delegation after him, saying,
"We will not have this man to reign over us." '*

LUKE 19:14

Have you ever played a part in this scenario: You're having a rational discussion with someone when the subject of Christianity arises. All of a sudden, this person spouts nonsensical arguments in favor of rejecting Christ outright. Do you ever wonder why the subject of Christianity makes the most rational people irrational?

Why do so many reject Jesus Christ? Arguments against Christ seem to fly out of the human heart like bats out of a dark cave. Many people raise objections against Christ that seem absurd and ridiculous. The fallen human mind can produce an enormous amount of arguments to counter the truth of Christ despite clear evidence of His existence. This reflex rejection brings to mind Christ's trial, when no rational accusation against Him came forth.

I believe that most objections do not come from intellectual causes but from moral ones. People reject Christ not because of unconvincing arguments but because of uncontrolled appetites. Most people prefer to pass themselves off as skeptics rather than sinners, as agnostics rather than reprobates, as doubters rather than debauchers or drunks. I once read about a man who claimed to be a Christian early in life but then rejected Christ because, despite his prayers, a loved one died from a disease. Later on, however, people discovered that this man was a womanizer with a "girl in every port." His intellectual arguments didn't fuel his rejection of Christ; his sin did!

Instead of allowing sin to determine our belief in Christ, we should have an attitude like that of the aging Queen Victoria. During a performance of Handel's "Messiah," as the choir sang "King of kings and Lord of lords," she rose to her feet despite a great deal of pain. She later explained that she could not sit before the King of kings and Lord of lords. We, too, should proclaim His existence, in our arguments and our actions, striving to live right so that we might experience Him daily, leaving no room for doubt that He lives!

*All hail the power of Jesus' name! Let angels prostrate fall.
Bring forth the royal diadem, to crown Him Lord of all!*

EDWARD PERRONET

AIM HIGH

*…Shamgar…killed six hundred men of the Philistines
with an ox goad; and he also delivered Israel.*

JUDGES 3:31

How high are your ambitions to accomplish things for God's glory? Today we meet an obscure character of Scripture, a man named Shamgar, who aimed high and honored his Lord.

The Philistines had conquered Israel and were greatly oppressing the Israelites. The Philistines had taken all of the Israelites' weapons and means of defense, leaving the Israelites despondent. What could they do? They were outnumbered and defenseless. But Shamgar, a farmer, had a different attitude. He labored hard in the fields, plowing his crops with a broken yoke of oxen. Day after day he worked, despite the threat that when the harvest came, the Philistines would sweep down and carry away all his crops. And sure enough, at harvest time six hundred fully armed Philistines swept down on this one farmer armed with only a goad (a pointed instrument used to provoke oxen).

Shamgar could have made excuses: "There was only one of me. I was just a farmer. I didn't have a sword." But he didn't. Because Shamgar had faith in God and concern for his people, he decided to take a stand. As the Philistines came upon him, he took his ox goad and began to swing it! That must have been quite a battle to behold! When the dust settled, six hundred Philistines lay dead on the ground, and Shamgar went home to his harvest!

Shamgar had a goal: to free his people from bondage. Because of his faith in God, he reached that goal, despite the incredible odds against him. And we can do the same. What goals would you like to achieve? Don't sell yourself short or put limits on what you can accomplish. Through God, you can do anything! Therefore, aim high!

Not failure but low aim is the crime!

CHRISTIAN FELLOWSHIP

But if we walk in the light as He is in the light, we have fellowship with one another,
and the blood of Jesus Christ His Son cleanses us from all sin.

1 JOHN 1:7

We all need friends, and when we become Christians, we suddenly join a worldwide fellowship of friends—friends we will enjoy forever! When the Spirit of God and the love and forgiveness of God fill our hearts, all the barriers sin has erected break down. Then, by the grace of God, husbands and wives, neighbors and friends, brothers and sisters, children and parents, nations and races reunite and reconcile one to another. We become one in Christ.

Are you experiencing this wonderful friendship in your life?

Sometimes we don't experience this fellowship because we allow sin to separate us from God and each other. This division wreaks havoc in our world. As we cease to share our values, emotions, and the deepest purposes of our lives, we grow more distant, more leery of connecting with anyone. And the lack of abiding friendships in our homes, schools, families, and even churches, causes anxiety, turmoil, and insecurity in our society. The devil feeds on this division, working toward eternal separation of people from God and from one another.

But Christ stops that work. Christ unites us with God and with each other, creating a great big family, a family in the deepest, most spiritual, noblest, and holiest sense of the word. As believers, we develop a relationship so intimate that Paul describes it as one body. We unite to become the body of Christ.

The deep friendships we can have with other believers bring us great joy here on earth. They reflect the perfect unity heaven has in store for us. In fact, we can anticipate Christian communion, which will go far beyond earthly friendship, because we have brothers and sisters we have not even met but to whom we are closely linked through Christ for eternity. In an alienated and lonely world, the worldwide Church has a great privilege and opportunity to show the world true friendship.

I challenge you to build eternal friendships starting today. Can you think of a Christian brother or sister you'd like to know better? Take a step to connect today.

Is any pleasure on earth as great as a circle of Christian friends by a fire?

C. S. LEWIS

THE SLIPPERY SLOPE OF SIN

Then, when desire has conceived, it gives birth to sin;
and sin, when it is full-grown, brings forth death.

JAMES 1:15

Have you ever stood at the top of a slippery slope—perhaps a steep and icy drive-way or even a hill of dirt that crumbles beneath your feet—lost your footing, and slid down to the bottom? Sin is like that. We might justify a "tiny" sin to achieve a dearly desired goal. "After all," we say, "a little compromise won't hurt." But one little sin leads to another, and before you know it, you tumble downhill, head over heels, out of control.

We see this principle in action in a rather obscure story in 2 Kings 8, the story of Hazael. Hazael was a servant to the great king of Syria, Ben-Hadad, who had heaped upon Hazael many favors and honors. But the king fell ill, so he sent Hazael to the prophet Elisha to inquire whether he would recover from the illness. Elisha instructed Hazael, "Go, say to him, 'You shall certainly recover.' However the Lord has shown me that he will really die." Elisha stared at Hazael until Hazael felt ashamed. Hazael knew that the prophet had seen into his heart, that he could not hide his evil plans from God. But Hazael loved his own goal, his own ambition, more than he loved righteousness. So Elisha began to weep, and Hazael asked, "Why is my lord weeping?" And he said, "Because I know the evil you will do to the children of Israel." Hazael wondered aloud, "But what is your servant—a dog, that he should do this gross thing?" Hazael returned to the king and reported that the king would surely recover. But the very next day, Hazael suffocated him. And before long, Hazael invaded Israel and ravished its land and people just as Elisha had said he would.

This story shows us the inherent sin that lies within the depths of each of our souls. For Hazael, what began as ambition led down the slippery slope to murder and later to genocide.

Always be on guard. Never justify a sin, a "slight" wrong, or a white lie. If you do, you might find yourself slipping down that slippery slope.

It is much easier to repent of sins that we have committed,
than to repent of those we intend to commit.

JOSH BILLINGS

SPIRITUAL SNOBBERY

*'Take heed that you do not despise one of these little ones, for I say to you
that in heaven their angels always see the face of My Father who is in heaven.
For the Son of Man has come to save that which was lost.'*

MATTHEW 18:10–11

Do people at your church welcome strangers with open arms or spurn them with turned backs? It is tragic that many churches today display "spiritual snobbery," rejecting those of questionable reputation or faith. And this is so wrong.

This attitude prevailed even in biblical times. In fact, Jesus featured it in one of his parables. In Christ's parable of the prodigal son, the older brother displayed a smug attitude toward his wayward brother. After the joyous return of the younger brother, who had strayed from his father's house, the scene quickly changed from joy to jealousy. The brow of the older brother lowered; his face darkened; his lips curled in contempt. Inside, the house was ablaze with light and laughter. The sounds of music echoed the joy of the revelers, while outside a cold silence rested heavily on the fields, broken only by the grumbling of the older brother amid the gathering night.

In a similar way, many Christians today don't welcome prodigals into their circles. We love to have the respectable folks come into the church, the well-clothed and well-bred, but bring in the drug addict or the drunk from skid row, and some people raise their eyebrows. We invite sinners into the warm harbor of God's love, but they run smack-dab into the iceberg of the older brother.

When you really get down to it, many spiritual snobs don't really believe in conversion. Talk to them about the thief on the cross, and they become very upset, even as some of the early Christians did not believe in Saul's conversion. But "all have sinned and fall short of the glory of God" (Romans 3:23). None of us makes it to heaven except by God's grace.

Search your heart today. Do you find even a trace of spiritual snobbery there? Plan to welcome newcomers into your church, sharing God's grace with *all* who need it.

But for the grace of God there goes John Bradford.

JOHN BRADFORD (UPON SEEING CRIMINALS ABOUT TO BE EXECUTED)

THE LAST ENEMY

The last enemy that will be destroyed is death.

1 CORINTHIANS 15:26

Did you ever have an appointment you dreaded so much that you tried to get out of it any way you could? Many people seem to face death with a similar dread but never admit it to themselves. In fact, many avoid thinking of death at all costs.

The Bible says that Satan has kept the whole world in bondage throughout its history through the fear of death. Just look at the pagan cultures of the world, and you'll see a pervasive, desperate fear of the black unknown. No wonder death is called the "king of terrors."

It wasn't always this way. In the nineteenth century, people commonly discussed death. Many plays had deathbed scenes in them in which death occurred naturally. Talking about sex may have been taboo, but not discussing death. Today that is reversed. Everyone talks about sex, but nobody wants to talk about death! This attitude brings to mind a British king who charged that anyone who mentioned the word "death" in his presence would experience it shortly.

People have flouted God's laws since the beginning of time, and have always been afraid to face that great appointment with death. The Scripture says, "It is appointed for men to die once." We all have our appointment with the king of terrors. Like it or not, we can't postpone this appointment indefinitely. It's unavoidable.

But those of us who believe in Jesus Christ's saving grace needn't fear this appointment. In fact, we can look forward to it with great joy. The amazing grace of God transforms death into the very portal to paradise. Christ said, "He who believes in me has everlasting life." What a glorious promise that is!

The next time you ponder that great appointment when this life ends and eternity begins, you needn't dread it. Instead, rejoice that death has been swallowed up in victory.

Beware that moral dart [of death] for there is none but He that dwells
on high that can sustain its blow and live.

JOHN MILTON

DAVID BRAINERD

'…If anyone thirsts, let him come to Me and drink.'

JOHN 7:37

Have you ever felt intensely thirsty, so thirsty you thought you could drink a river dry? That's the same kind of thirst we should cultivate for God. We have a great example of someone who had such a thirst: David Brainerd, an eighteenth-century missionary to American Indians.

As a young lad, Brainerd's soul was parched; he thirsted for the living God. He abandoned all of his sinful ways to pursue a religious life. He prayed, went to church, and read the Bible. But despite his pure lifestyle, he still found no peace with God. One day, he reread a text he remembered from his childhood: "If anyone thirsts, let him come to Me and drink." Brainerd drank deeply from that stream of the living water, Jesus Christ, and he was quenched. As he discovered the source of the living water, he realized that multitudes of people had the same thirst he once had, and he wanted to share with them the source he had found. Brainerd thought of all the Indians in the forests of New England and knew that they must hear the good news of Christ. So he became a missionary to them.

By the end of his ministry, David Brainerd had converted only a few hundred Indians, but perhaps his greatest ministry was the intensity of his own devotion to Christ. His love for Christ burned like a brilliant flame in the night sky, attracting others to Him and animating their lives. Brainerd began early in life to keep a journal, and the revelation of his heart, soul, and mind has transformed the lives of most people who have read it. In fact, that journal inspired many people to become missionaries, to share the living waters with others!

Today and every day, seek to quench your spiritual thirst in Jesus Christ. Spend time with Him in prayer and in His Word. Then share the good news with others so that they might never thirst again.

I care not where I live, or what hardships I go through, so that I can but gain souls to Christ.

DAVID BRAINERD

ST. PATRICK

For to me, to live is Christ, and to die is gain.

PHILIPPIANS 1:21

St. Patrick, "the patron saint of Ireland," has captured the fancy of millions of people through the ages. Even those who haven't a clue what the man really stood for pay him tribute on this day by marching in parades and wearing green. Some people even get drunk to celebrate the occasion, but these people dishonor the memory of that great man who first brought Christianity to Ireland!

Patrick, who was actually born in Scotland, was kidnapped as a young lad by a band of marauding pirates. These pirates bound Patrick, took him to Ireland, and sold him as a slave to a druid chieftain. Patrick said of this experience, "It was while I ate the bitter bread of that hateful servitude in a foreign land, that the light divine broke upon my benighted soul and I called to remembrance the holy things which I had been taught in my dear old home..." Patrick's heart was transformed, and he became a new creature in Jesus Christ. By faith in the Redeemer, by a trust in the blood shed for his sins, this young man in the depths and darkness of the forests of Ireland found the Savior of the world.

After six years of slavery, Patrick escaped. But he had vowed revenge—the noble revenge of sharing the gospel with the very people who had held him captive! Patrick believed that God had called him to return to the land of his slavery. The Encyclopedia Britannica declares that Patrick himself baptized one hundred and twenty thousand persons.

St. Patrick—echoing the apostle Paul, who said, "For me, to live is Christ"—said, "For me, life is Christ." If you would know life to its fullest, then you, too, would echo what St. Patrick came to learn—that to live is Christ...that life *is* Christ!

How can *you* live your life for Christ on this St. Patrick's Day?

God's might to direct me, God's power to protect me.

ST. PATRICK

PRACTICING THE PRESENCE OF GOD

'…and lo, I am with you always, even to the end of the age.'

MATTHEW 28:20

Do you know that God is with you right now as you read these words? Do you experience His presence in everything you do?

In seventeenth-century France, a humble monk named Brother Lawrence wrote magnificent letters to a friend, letters now compiled in a little booklet entitled *Practicing the Presence of God.* Brother Lawrence had learned to practice God's presence in everything he did. He found perfect peace and tranquillity in focusing his mind upon God in every experience, whenever his mind wasn't focused on something else. He found that, during hectic times of kitchen duty and other chores, he experienced peace through focusing on the Lord through practicing God's presence.

We live in a very hectic and stressful era. But much of the stress we feel is determined by our *reactions* to the circumstances of our lives. And nothing puts life into perspective better than practicing God's presence. For this reason, I think we should strive to continually incline our hearts toward God so that after our minds turn to other things, our thoughts will automatically return to God, just as the needle of a compass points north again after moving away from something that interferes with its natural bent.

How do we continually incline our hearts toward God? Memorizing Scripture is a great start. Then, when not occupied with immediate issues, we can return our thoughts to meditating on God's Word. We can also practice God's presence by memorizing and singing hymns (even if only in our minds). The key is to constantly remind ourselves of His presence.

So today, no matter how hectic your life may be, recognize the Lord's presence within you. Practice His presence at all times…in the midst of stressful situations…between appointments…driving down the street…everywhere!

The world appears very little to a soul that contemplates the greatness of God.
My business is to remain in the presence of God.

BROTHER LAWRENCE

TRUE STRENGTH

'…"Not by might nor by power, but by My Spirit," says the Lord of hosts.'

ZECHARIAH 4:6

Some people have made the gym their second home. These people go to fanatical lengths to get their bodies in shape. I'm not devaluing caring for our bodies; in fact, I get my share of exercise. But some people make an idol of physical strength, cultivating beautiful bodies to glorify themselves.

But which one of these persons do you think is better equipped to help others: a person who works out with weights all day, developing huge muscles, or a person who is poor, weak, frail, and unmuscular? The answer isn't all that clear. A strong person may be more capable of helping people; for example, Arnold Schwarzenegger may be more physically capable of helping others than frail and tiny Mother Teresa. But it does not follow logically that he has acted to help more people than she. In fact, she has had an immeasurable impact on many people's lives.

Many of the world's greatest people haven't been strong, muscular, or even healthy. Nor have they had great wealth. But they have had to struggle with monumental problems, and through their struggles, they've learned to rely on the Holy Spirit for strength. Jesus tells us that "the meek shall inherit the earth." Nowhere do the Scriptures say that the spoils go to the strong, to the cunning, or to the wealthy. In fact, they often say the opposite. Paul makes a similar point: "When I am weak, then I am strong" and "God has chosen the weak things of this world to shame the strong." Why is that? When we rely on our own strength, then we get the credit and the glory. But when we are weak and helpless, we rely on God to work through us, and the results glorify Him.

Acknowledge your weakness today, give up your efforts to succeed on your own, and allow the Holy Spirit to use you. As you do, you'll experience true strength—God's strength working through you!

Nothing is so strong as gentleness, nothing so gentle as real strength.

ST. FRANCIS DE SALES

THE APOSTLES' CREED TODAY

'Lord, I believe…'

MARK 9:24

"No creed but Christ" is what some people claim to believe today, and that may sound good. But they forget that "creed" simply means a statement of faith and that, therefore, developing one can be valuable in helping us define what we believe. One of the oldest and finest statements of faith is the Apostles' Creed. Its roots go back to the early Church. Though not written by the apostles themselves, it carries the authority of eyewitnesses from the apostolic age. Virtually every group of Christians agrees upon this creed, so it unites us despite our doctrinal differences.

The Apostles' Creed expresses truth simply and clearly, setting forth a challenge. It is an affirmation, a declaration, a manifesto of a Messiah who has come to conquer the world! We should never mumble it or merely recite it. Because of the great truths it contains, upon which we must stake our lives, we should shout it with a fanfare of trumpets.

Here are the words of the Apostles' Creed. Today, will you recite it, pouring all your heart and soul into it?

I believe in God the Father Almighty, Maker of Heaven and Earth, and in Jesus Christ His only Son our Lord, who was born of the Virgin Mary, suffered under Pontius Pilate, was crucified, dead and buried. He descended into Hell. The third day He arose again from the dead. He ascended into heaven and sitteth on the right hand of God the Father, Almighty. From thence He shall come to judge the quick and the dead. I believe in the Holy Ghost, the holy catholic [universal] church, the forgiveness of sin, the resurrection of the body, and the life everlasting. Amen.

You don't really believe your creed until you want to say it standing at spiritual attention
with the roll of drums in your ears, the light of love dazzling in your eyes, and
all the music of the splendid world crashing out a prelude to its truth.

STUDDERT KENNEDY

SUFFERED UNDER PONTIUS PILATE

Then he released Barabbas to them; and when he had scourged Jesus,
he delivered Him to be crucified.

MATTHEW 27:26

Do you know what the key to Jesus' life was?

He suffered.

Biblical literature underscores the importance of Christ's suffering. Paul, in his epistles, virtually ignores the ministry of Christ but reminds us of what He suffered. In the Gospels, one-third of Matthew, Mark, and Luke deal with Christ's sufferings and death. One-half of John's Gospel deals with the last week of Jesus' life. The Apostles' Creed, which affirms facts about Christ's life, takes a tremendous leap from the birth of Christ to His suffering and death. It passes over His entire ministry. The creed says nothing about Jesus' great teachings, about His marvelous example, or about the incredible miracles He performed. The focus of all these works communicates the tremendous importance of Christ's suffering and pain.

Christ came as the suffering Savior because our world suffers. It has always needed a suffering head who could empathize with its pains and agonies, and Christ completely fulfilled this need. He was betrayed by Judas, deserted by the disciples, tortured and killed by the religious leaders, and abandoned by God. He has felt our pain.

Christ's death was the greatest act and event of His entire life. He was born to die. Death did not end the work of Christ—death *was* the work of Christ because through it He atoned for our sins. Three things made this atonement necessary: the abominable wickedness of our sin, God's justice and holiness, and God's love.

When you think of Christ's suffering and death, remember one thing: He came to die in your place. Oh, what love God has for you and me! Today and every day, thank Jesus for what He has done.

The heinousness of sin and the justice of God make the Cross an absolute necessity.

THE PURPOSE FOR LIVING

*'But seek first the kingdom of God and His righteousness,
and all these things shall be added to you.'*

MATTHEW 6:33

What's the purpose of life? That question was once asked in a high-school English class of some twenty students, and not one single person came up with an answer that made sense.

Do you know the purpose of your life?

One time a young man who had just graduated from Oxford University approached a friend of the family, Prime Minister Gladstone, and asked if Gladstone would listen to the plan he had mapped out for his life. Gladstone said, "Fine. Tell me." "Well, I have just graduated, and I intend to take the bar exam and practice law." "That's fine. What then?" "After some experience I hope to run for Parliament." "That's great. What then?" "I hope to make some contribution toward the betterment of our country." "Excellent. What then?" "Well, after a while, I'll retire." "Very well. What then?" "Well, I guess someday, I'll die." "That's right. And what then?" "Well, sir, I really don't know. I never really thought about it." Gladstone fixed his eyes on the young man and with a piercing gaze said to him, "Young man, you are a fool. Go home and think life through again."

Would you get the same response if you laid out your plans, your purposes, your intentions for your life before God? What is your purpose for living?

If we don't determine our purposes in life, we'll come to the end empty-handed. God has placed us on this earth to bring Him glory. Our purpose in life should be to know God and to make Him known. Everything we do should flow from that purpose.

How can you fulfill God's purpose for you today?

Here rests a man who never rested here.

EPITAPH ON A BISHOP'S TOMB

BEHOLD YOUR GOD

…Say to the cities of Judah, 'Behold your God!'

ISAIAH 40:9

In one of his sonnets, Shelley tells of a traveler from Egypt who, in a trek across a desert wasteland came upon the remains of a marble statue. All that remained on the pedestal were two feet and the lower part of two gigantic legs. Nearby, lying in the sand, was the cracked remnant of what had been the head. The face had a cruel sneer on its lips.

When the traveler rubbed the sand away from the pedestal, he found this inscription: "My name is Ozymandias, king of kings: Look on my works, ye mighty, and despair!" The traveler looked, and as far as the eye could see, there was naught but the sifting sand. Ozymandias bestowed upon himself the name "king of kings," but whatever kingdom and glory he once enjoyed had disappeared.

In contrast, the true King of kings was meek and lowly of mind when He came into Jerusalem on Palm Sunday riding a donkey's colt. Here, riding into town in great humility, was *the* King of kings and Lord of lords—the King of all creation!

Napoleon observed at St. Helena, "Can you conceive of Caesar as the eternal emperor of the Roman Senate and, from the depths of his mausoleum, governing the empire, watching over the destinies of Rome? Such is the history of the invasion and conquest of the world by Christianity; such is the power of the God of the Christians…"

Jesus is the eternal King of kings, the Lord who reigns supreme. No other has ever been or ever will be greater. Behold your God!

I know men, and I tell you, Jesus is not a man. Superficial minds see a resemblance between Christ and the founders of empires and the gods of other religions. That resemblance does not exist…There is between Christianity and whatever other religions the distance of infinity.

NAPOLEON

CHRIST BETRAYED

Now as they were eating, He said, 'Assuredly, I say to you, one of you will betray Me.'

MATTHEW 26:21

When you think of Judas Iscariot, what words come first to your mind? Perhaps "traitor"? "greedy"? "evil one"?

Judas has never been one of the more popular disciples. In the Middle Ages, people considered Judas more of a villain than we do today. We can probably attribute the medieval attitude to the way Dante portrayed Judas in his *Inferno,* a great classic that takes us on a tour of hell. In the deepest part of hell, the gigantic fiend, Satan, has a man in his jaws. Satan has already chewed off and eaten the bottom half of this man, yet as the teeth chomp and tear, the man continues to live. The man in Satan's jaws is Judas Iscariot.

On the other end of the spectrum, some modern-day authors have portrayed Judas as a hero of sorts. But to determine Judas' true character, we need look no further than the Bible. The Bible calls Judas a thief. Entrusted with the disciples' money box, which contained money to help the poor and to meet Christ's and the disciples' daily needs, Judas regularly dipped into it for his own use. Jesus warned Judas a number of times, but Judas never straightened out his heart. Jesus said, "Did I not choose you, the twelve, and one of you is a devil?" (John 6:70). Judas was a man consumed by greed, and his greed led to his destruction.

Judas was also a hypocrite. He appeared a practical man of sound reputation, which is why the apostles chose him as their treasurer. But he just played the part of a responsible man. When Judas said, "Why was this fragrant oil not sold for three hundred denarii and given to the poor?" he didn't really care about the impoverished. He just wanted more money to steal.

Judas was a greedy, hypocritical person who met the fate he was due. Christ could have used him for good, but instead Judas frustrated the cause of Christ. We all sin; remember that Peter, like Judas, denied Christ. But, just as Christ forgave Peter and used him to spread the good news, Christ will forgive us when we confess our sins. He'll use us to further His cause to the ends of the earth.

Today, check the state of your heart. Are you harboring any greed or hypocrisy? If so, avoid Judas' fate; don't betray Christ because of such hurtful attitudes. Like Peter, confess your sin before Christ, then move forward to further His kingdom in all you do.

> *It is a terrible thing, not when a man has some gold, but*
> *when some gold has a man, and Judas was had by gold.*

March 25

CHRIST IN THE HANDS OF THE POLICE

Then the detachment of troops and the captain and the officers of the Jews arrested Jesus and bound Him. And they led Him away to Annas first, for he was the father-in-law of Caiaphas who was high priest that year.

JOHN 18:12–13

Have you ever pondered all the indignities and injustices that Christ suffered on our behalf? When you do, you'll appreciate even more the sacrifice Jesus made for you and me.

In the Garden of Gethsemane, after Christ had prayed, a mob came to arrest Him. About sixty-five men, brandishing torches, swords, and spears, came to take one man, Jesus Christ, away. Judas signaled to the mob which man was Jesus by kissing Jesus' cheek. After rebuking Judas by saying, "Betrayest thou the Son of Man with a kiss?" Jesus identified Himself to the men and allowed them to bind His hands and lead Him away. Though mightier than Samson, He didn't use His power to break free.

First the mob led Him to Annas, the high priest, and then to Caiaphas, Annas' son-in-law. Both the Jews and the Romans tried Jesus, and both trials were farces. Scholars point out that, when trying Jesus, the Jews violated Jewish law thirty-five times, and the Romans violated Roman law thirteen times, making a total of forty-eight violations. Jewish law required that the people go to great lengths to find defense witnesses, but in Jesus' case the judge found false witnesses and paid them to testify against Jesus. And when the Sanhedrin asked Jesus "whether thou be the Christ, the Son of God," they forced Him to testify against Himself. The high priest declared Jesus guilty, and everyone began to spit on Him, tear His beard, and hit Him.

Josephus, the Jewish historian, tells us that the name of the high priest, Caiaphas, means rock. And Peter, Jesus' disciple, was called Cephas, which also means rock. So we have Jesus at the trial caught between two rocks—one in the courtroom accusing Him and one in the courtyard denying Him. Caiaphas' heart remained a rock, but Peter's heart broke, and Christ forgave Him.

What a Savior we have! Our Creator submitted Himself to such humiliation at the hands of His own creation so that *we* might receive His forgiveness. Thank Jesus today for all He has done for you, especially for that day when He bore such degradation in our place.

Christ was bound with the bands of your own bondage that you might be made free.

CHRIST BEFORE THE SUPREME COURT

And one of them, Caiaphas, being high priest that year, said to them, 'You know nothing at all, nor do you consider that it is expedient for us that one man should die for the people, and not that the whole nation should perish.'

JOHN 11:49–50

Have you ever considered the irony of Christ's encounter with Caiaphas, the high priest of the Jews? Christ, the true high priest of God, stood before Joseph Caiaphas, the false high priest of God. And though Caiaphas and Jesus had different motives, they agreed with each other. Caiaphas believed that, in the best interests of the people, one man should die so that the rest would live. Christ believed the same thing. Caiaphas, the false high priest, said, "Let it be Him!" And Jesus, the true high priest, said, "Let it be Me."

The great contrast between Christ and Caiaphas was that while Christ came in *obedience* to His Father's will, Caiaphas was motivated by *expedience*. Expedience comes from two Latin words meaning "to get your foot out of a trap." Caiaphas tried to set a trap for Christ, but he fell into it himself. The false witnesses that he had arranged to testify against Christ had all contradicted one another, so he had no case against Jesus. In desperation, Caiaphas screamed at Christ, "Tell us if you are the Son of God." He couldn't have expected Christ to answer this, because Christ had remained silent up to this point and because this question was illegal. (Under Jewish law no one could force someone to testify against himself or herself.) When Jesus answered, "Yes, I am the Son of God," Caiaphas shouted, "Blasphemy," tore his robe at the neck, and declared Christ guilty.

Caiaphas exemplifies many people we can describe in three words: *religious but lost.* Caiaphas, a religious liberal, denied the great truths of the Bible. He didn't believe in the Resurrection, the spirit, immortality, or angels. He supposed that his high position and his ritualistic practices would ensure his soul's eternal well-being, but alas they did not. Instead, his eternal destiny relied on the man who stood before him that day—the Christ, the Son of God.

Jesus was silent in the face of His accusers precisely because He was guilty. But the guilt He bore was not His own. It was yours, and it was mine.

THE TRIALS OF CHRIST

And those who had laid hold of Jesus led Him away to Caiaphas the high priest, where the scribes and elders were assembled...Jesus stood before the governor...

MATTHEW 26:57, 27:11

Have you ever had one of those days when it seemed as if everybody was ganging up on you? If so, then imagine what our Lord went through in the trials that lead to His crucifixion! Jesus had previously declared that He would be delivered into the hands of sinful men who would scourge and crucify Him. Now He had fallen into those cruel hands. The ordeal which would culminate in unspeakable horror for Him had now begun. The claw of the dragon was in His flesh. But Jesus mustered all His courage. He had come into the world to be the death of sin, and by that death He'd bring salvation to the world. Never before in any courtroom were the issues as momentous as when Christ stood trial. The eternal bliss or woe of countless people hung delicately in the balance!

Anyone who honestly examines Christ's trials (both the Jewish and the Roman ones) must conclude that they were, in almost every one of their details, totally illegal—that Jesus Christ received nothing but injustice when He stood before the bar of human justice. We, who are so quick to demand our rights and to demand justice, may do well to fix our eyes upon the Son of God and how He fared when He stood before the bar of human justice, keeping in mind that one day we shall stand before the bar of God's justice.

In another sense, though, Christ's trial was perfectly legal. If we try to look at it from the divine perspective, we see it in a different light. Humans attempted to convict Jesus for His own sins, but He had none; therefore, they convicted Him illegally. But God convicted Jesus of real sins—our sins—which were imputed to Him. In the deepest and highest sense, God tried and condemned Jesus for us, making Christ's punishment fit our crimes. How can we ever thank Jesus enough?

It was in our place that He was tried, and it was in our place that He was condemned.

CHRIST'S BITTER CUP

*He went a little farther and fell on His face, and prayed, saying, 'O My Father, if it is possible,
let this cup pass from Me; nevertheless, not as I will, but as You will.'*

MATTHEW 26:39

What was in the mysterious cup that appeared before Christ's face there in the darkness of Gethsemane? First of all, the cup contained *all* the sin of the world. Imagine you're visiting the Centers for Disease Control in Atlanta. You walk into a large, sealed room full of hundreds of vials containing diseases—cancer, AIDS, syphilis, gonorrhea—every dangerous and foul disease known to man. You see a technician unstopping each vial, one by one, and pouring the contents into a large beaker. How would you react if the technician asked you to touch the beaker? And if the technician asked you to drink the contents, what terror would fill your soul? But all of that is *nothing* compared to the cup of sin which Jesus drank.

The second element in Jesus' bitter cup was God's abandonment. By drinking that foul cup, Christ became the archcriminal of the universe, full of sin. God, whose holiness prevents Him from looking at any sin, turned His back on Christ, His Son, leaving Jesus abandoned and alone.

Third, since God must punish sin, He poured on Christ the great fiery cauldron of His wrath. More than that, Christ, rejected by humanity and abandoned by God, was then given over to the demons. He sank to the bottomless pit of hell, where the demons fell on Him with fang and claw.

All of this was in the bitter cup. But the most important thing about this cup is that it wasn't *Christ's* cup at all. It was *ours*. The sin was ours. The abandonment, the fiery punishment, the demons should have been ours. But Christ drank the cup for us. And because He did, today the cup of Christ is one full of blessings—love, pardon, peace, and joy. This is the cup He now offers to you and me. Take and drink of the love and freedom you can now enjoy because of the sacrifice Christ has made.

*We may not know, we cannot tell what pains He had to bear.
We only know it was for us He hung and suffered there.*

CHRIST LIFTED UP

'And I, if I am lifted up from the earth, will draw all peoples to Myself.'

JOHN 12:32

When you think of Jesus Christ lifted up on the cross, how do you want to respond?

Christ's crucifixion has a magnetic quality, drawing people to Him, and as long as we keep it centrally focused, people will continue to come to Christ. Some churches don't understand this, attempting to attract people in other ways. Unitarians, who have denied and rejected the atonement of Christ and the deity of Christ, don't have the power to attract people. One of their leaders in Birmingham, England, said that Unitarianism failed to "draw." The English public will not attend their chapels. Though Unitarians seem bewildered by this, it's no mystery. These churches don't "draw" because they've thrown away the magnet.

We don't need big signs or flashy worship services to attract people to Him. Christ's humble sacrifice has more magnetic power than anything any church could concoct.

Let's take a quick look at the immediate impact of the crucifixion to catch a glimpse of its awesome power. At the cross, the centurion—who had nailed Christ's hands and feet to the cross—saw darkness cover the sky, the sun cease to give light, the rocks quake, the earth tremble, and the tombs open. Upon witnessing all this, the centurion said, "Truly this was the Son of God" (Matthew 27:54). History tells us that this man went forth to follow Christ. A few weeks later three thousand more were drawn at Pentecost, then five thousand more, then multitudes of priests and elders and scribes were drawn, and then an exceeding great multitude were drawn, until finally the Roman Empire itself was overwhelmed by the magnetic power of Jesus Christ to draw men to Himself.

Why does the crucifixion have so much drawing power? Consider the agony Christ endured. Hanging, a firing squad, electrocution, the gas chamber—the pain of all these forms of execution could never compare to the excruciating pain of crucifixion. Jesus submitted Himself to a slow death by suffocation that could have taken several days. The crucifixion shows God's incredible love for us, the love of a Father who would give His only Son to endure the penalty for the world's sin.

Today, meditate on the Christ lifted up for your sake, and let the power of His crucifixion draw you nearer to Him in love and gratitude.

It was not the character of Christ, not His justice, nor His proclamations, nor His preaching, nor His teaching, but rather it was his death that would draw men.

BENEATH THE CROSS OF JESUS

And He, bearing His cross, went out to a place called the Place of a Skull,
which is called in Hebrew, Golgotha, where they crucified Him, and two others with Him,
one on either side, and Jesus in the center.

JOHN 19:17–18

Did you know that the Jews have built a bus stop at the foot of Golgotha? Bus after bus lines up there, waiting for passengers. When a bus leaves, it passes right by the mouth of the "skull." Once I was standing near the bus stop with a church tour group, and I pointed out the features of the skull. As I did so, four or five people not associated with our group came to see what I was pointing at. They couldn't figure it out. To them Golgotha meant absolutely nothing.

But it should mean something to all of us, because there all the ingredients came together for our salvation. The first ingredient is *humankind's sin.* If people had never sinned, Christ wouldn't have had to come to earth and die for us. The second ingredient is *God's justice.* God must punish sin because His eyes are too pure to look upon it. If He didn't punish it, He wouldn't be God. Combining humankind's sin with God's justice always and inevitably produces hell. Therefore, we need the third ingredient: the infinite, inexpressible unfathomable *love of God.* The Creator's love for His creation compelled Him to die for the creature's sin. How vast is the love God has for you and me, past our ever understanding it!

Someone once said to a minister, "There are hundreds of religions in the world, and they all have their own ideas. How do you know yours is right?" He replied. "No, there are only two religions in the world. They are either 'do' or 'done.' The other religions in the world teach that man will be saved by what he does: Do this and don't do that. But Christianity is the only religion that teaches 'It is done.' It is finished."

Which religion do you trust for everlasting life? Look toward Golgotha, where the three ingredients came together perfectly, providing for your salvation. There Christ proclaimed, "It is finished." Thank God today for granting you eternal life because of what happened at the Place of the Skull.

Beneath the cross of Jesus, I fain would take my stand,
A shadow of a mighty rock within a weary land,
A home within the wilderness, a rest along the way
From the burning of the noontide heat and the burden of the day.

FREDERICK MAKER

MAN'S GREATEST FEAR

And if Christ is not risen, then our preaching is vain and your faith is also vain…But now Christ is risen from the dead, and has become the firstfruits of those who have fallen asleep.

1 CORINTHIANS 15:14, 20

Are you afraid to die? If so, you're not alone. That fear is quite natural. But Jesus has solved this problem, the most incredible problem humankind has ever faced, generation after generation. Death has endured since humanity's fall, and people have asked, "If a person dies, will he or she rise again?" By rising from the dead Himself, Jesus gave us irrefutable evidence that the answer is "yes."

But people have doubted the truth of Christ's resurrection. Some of the most brilliant and skeptical minds of the last two thousand years have attempted to disprove it. But all those efforts have yielded nothing but the truth—that Christ rose from the dead. Let's consider some of the facts that these skeptics have had to address. First, the Christian Church has endured and grown until it has become the largest organization on the planet today. That growth began in the first century, when the apostles began to preach that Jesus had risen from the dead. Next, to disprove the resurrection, skeptics have had to explain the empty tomb; the broken Roman seal (if someone broke a Roman seal, he or she received the death penalty); and the Roman guards, who faced sure death if they left their posts or fell asleep on the job. Most important, skeptics have had to dispute Christ's appearances after His resurrection. The people saw Him, heard Him, touched Him. He fixed breakfast for his disciples. He ate fish with them. He appeared to five hundred people at one time. Furthermore, the apostles were transformed. One day they huddled in an upper room fearing for their lives, but soon after that they boldly proclaimed Christ's resurrection in public. And all except John died for what they proclaimed, sealing their testimony in their own blood.

For these reasons and many more, we have a sure foundation for our faith in Christ's resurrection. Because we know the resurrection really happened, we know Christ has conquered death, and we no longer need to fear it.

…the evidence speaks for itself. It says very clearly—
CHRIST IS RISEN INDEED.

JOSH MCDOWELL

A SURE FOUNDATION

'...He is risen! He is not here. See the place where they laid Him.'

MARK 16:6

What does it take for you to believe something that seems out of the realm of possibility? Most of us need to see some hard evidence before we lend credibility to the incredible. This is also true when people hear of Christ's resurrection. In fact, many people will develop all sorts of theories before believing that God incarnate rose from the grave.

Have you ever heard of the "Fraud Theory"? This theory asserts that Jesus didn't really rise from the dead, but rather, the disciples stole His body from the grave and then proclaimed Him risen. But the Fraud Theory doesn't mesh with the facts. For example, something happened to the disciples that changed them instantly from cowards to courageous men. The disciples credited this change with seeing the risen Christ, and despite numerous retellings, they never changed their story.

Dr. Principal Hill, a nineteenth-century theologian, put the Fraud Theory to rest when he said:

> You must suppose that twelve men of mean birth, of no education...formed the noblest scheme which ever entered into the mind of man...You must suppose, also, that men guilty of blasphemy and falsehood, united in an attempt the best contrived, and which has in fact proved the most successful for making the world virtuous; that they formed this single enterprise without seeking any advantage to themselves...with the certain expectation of scorn and persecution; that although conscious of one another's villainy, none of them ever thought of providing for his own security by disclosing the fraud, but that amidst sufferings the most grievous to flesh and blood they persevered in their conspiracy to cheat the world into piety, honesty and benevolence. Truly, they who can swallow such suppositions have no title to object to miracles.

How true that is! The Fraud Theory cannot stand against the evidence of the disciples' passion and steadfastness for the cause of Christ. You and I can rest assured that Christ's resurrection is no fraud. Christ has risen indeed!

The resurrection of Jesus Christ and Christianity stand or fall together.

JOSH MCDOWELL

SATAN'S EMPTY BOXES

Be sober, be vigilant; because your adversary the devil walks about like a roaring lion, seeking whom he may devour.

1 PETER 5:8

Have you ever done something sinful, something that seemed so exciting and promising at first, only to feel empty after actually doing it? When we pursue sin, we'll always feel that way—left high and dry.

This empty sensation reminds me of a story told by the preacher Clovis Chappel. Once there was a Christmas party in an orphanage. Beneath the tree were all sorts of beautifully wrapped packages. With all the children gathered around him, Santa Claus passed out the gifts. As he did so, everyone excitedly opened his or her present, enthusiastically examining each new toy. Everyone, that is, except for one young man, the village idiot. With no package to open, he sat, crestfallen, in the corner. Upon realizing his bad fortune, everyone became quiet, and all the children stared at him. Just at that moment, Santa Claus reached behind the tree, pulled out the biggest box of them all, and handed it to the village idiot. The young man's face lit up! Excitedly, he tore away the ribbons and wrapping paper and pulled off the lid only to find an empty box. As he stared despondently into it, all the children laughed.

Many of us have that same experience again and again in life. Life is filled with empty boxes, and we each take our turn at playing the idiot. "Give me the goods," we say, and Satan hands us an empty box. What are these empty boxes? Sin. Satan says, "Oh, just one little lie" or "one little look" or "Everybody's doing it." But when we give in, we realize he has taken us again, promising the world but delivering nothing.

The devil is the great illusionist, the great liar. He promises all manner of delights. He promises excitement, but in the end he clothes his victims in filthy rags, hunger, and misery. If these people decide to turn around and return to their Father's house, Satan sends all the bloodhounds of hell after them to overwhelm them with temptations and pull them down into the miry clay. How foolish is the man or woman who believes the promises of the father of lies. Every good gift comes down from above, not up from the pit with its hook that pulls you into the lake of fire.

Have you opened any empty boxes lately? If so, ask God to forgive you and show you how to pursue His righteousness. As you seek God, He'll help you discover the excitement and abundance of living obediently in Him.

We must not so much as taste of the devil's broth, lest at last he bring us to eat of his beef.

THOMAS HALL

AVOIDING NEGATIVITY

*...for he who doubts is like a wave of the sea driven and tossed by the wind.
...he is a double-minded man, unstable in all his ways.*

JAMES 1:6, 8

Have you ever heard the old song, "You gotta accentuate the positive, eliminate the negative, latch on to the affirmative, and don't mess with Mr. In-Between?" Today, let's talk about how we can avoid negative thinking, because if we harbor negative thoughts, sooner or later they'll destroy our lives.

One day a man tried to start his car with a jumper cable. Instead of connecting the correct part of the cable to the positive pole of the battery, he connected it to the negative pole. That mistake sparked a terrible explosion, and because of it, the man became permanently blind. In the same way, many people blind themselves by connecting to the negative pole of life.

Negativity is like a witch's wand that attaches itself to a person's forehead. The wand kills and destroys whatever it points toward. It may point toward the person who wears it, or it may point to others. You probably know people who walk around with that wand permanently pointed at their own lives. You can recognize them immediately by their negative thoughts: "I'm nobody...I really don't amount to much...I don't have many friends...I'm not too smart."

Others take that wand and point it outward. These people fail in life but blame their failures on others: their parents, their spouses, their bosses, the system, the corporation. They never accept responsibility for their own downfall. Some even point the wand at God. They say, "God could never love me. I wonder if there even is a God."

We all have negative thoughts at times, and often we don't recognize them. While we can't avoid all negativity, we can turn our attitudes into more positive perspectives. Today ask God to show you your negative thoughts and to give you the ability to look at the bright side of life.

I have begun everything with the idea that I could succeed, and I never had much patience with the multitudes of people who are always ready to explain why one cannot succeed.

BOOKER T. WASHINGTON (FORMER SLAVE)

BEING A POSITIVE PERSON

I can do all things through Christ who strengthens me.

PHILIPPIANS 4:13

Every time you open your mouth, think a thought, express an attitude, or take an action, you have a choice to do something positive or negative. Which do you most often choose?

Years ago, Art Linkletter encountered a little boy with an extremely positive attitude. On his television program, Linkletter asked the six-year-old boy, "Do you know why you were selected to be on my program?" The little boy said quite confidently, "Because I'm the smartest boy in my class." Art asked, "Oh, how do you know that? Did your teacher tell you?" "No," he replied, "I just noticed it myself." No negative thinking there!

Do you face life with a similar positive outlook? Do you respond to difficult situations by saying, "By the grace of God I can!" Or do you give up before you start, saying, "That would be too hard for me." A positive person will almost always find a way of turning a stumbling block into a steppingstone. In every situation, a positive person will ask, "Is there anything good about it?"

How do you respond to wrongdoing? Do you respond with criticism, condemnation, or gossip? Or do you respond with prayer, knowing that God can use you to bring His grace to another person's life?

If you find yourself tipping over into the negative side of the positive-negative continuum, I have good news for you: Attitudes aren't biologically determined. We don't come into this world destined to look at life one way or another. Instead, the Bible says that old things can pass away and all things can become new. That includes our attitudes. For that reason, we need to immerse ourselves in God's Word, the greatest accumulation of positive thinking the world has ever seen. As we read God's Word and seek Christ first, He makes us new, positive, and joyous people.

Do you anticipate a potentially negative situation today? If so, good! You have an opportunity to develop a positive attitude toward challenging situations! Today, allow God to work in your heart to grant you a positive outlook on life.

I have learned that success is to be measured not so much by the position that one has reached in life as by the obstacles which he has to overcome while trying to succeed.

BOOKER T. WASHINGTON (FORMER SLAVE)

FAITH, HOPE, AND LOVE

And now abide faith, hope, love, these three; but the greatest of these is love.

1 CORINTHIANS 13:13

Faith. What a magnificent thing it is to have faith in God! Faith lifts us to new heights. Do you believe that God is with you, that He will never leave you, that He will help you, that He will turn everything for your good? What a tremendous difference to know that you're a child of the King, a member of the House Royal; that you will live forever; and that God will do great things through you.

Hope. How marvelous to have hope! Do you have the confidence that God will accomplish His perfect plan in your life and that He'll bring you to Paradise to live with Him forever? That hope destroys the dark gray cloud that obscures your pathway, and it opens the view to your destination: the glorious, radiant, setting sun that will give way to that new and eternal morning of Paradise.

Love. Who is your best friend in this world? You probably cherish most the person who brings out your best. As the sonnet says:

> I love you not for what you are but for what you are helping me to become
> Overlooking my faults and reaching down into my heaped-up heart
> And making of the lumber of my life, not a tavern, but a cathedral.

When others help us reach our potential, we know they love us, and in return we love them.

Faith, hope, and love produce a joyful life. As we cultivate faith, hope, and love in our Lord, He gives us joy. I encourage you to memorize Scriptures on faith, hope, and love and to speak those verses back to the Lord in prayer. Sing His praises in your daily worship. As you do these things, He'll bring His joy into your life.

Joy is prayer—joy is strength—joy is love—joy is a net of love by which you can catch souls.

MOTHER TERESA

ONE MEDIATOR

For there is one God and one Mediator between God and men, the Man Christ Jesus.

1 TIMOTHY 2:5

Have you ever stood on one side of a canyon and marveled at the canyon's depth and breadth? Can you imagine what it would take to bridge such a chasm?

Our sinfulness has created an unfathomable chasm between us and God, but Christ has bridged it. He is our Mediator, the one who connects us to God the Father. How do we know this? First of all, Jesus said so. He said, "I am the way, the truth, and the life. No one comes to the Father, but by me." Jesus said this because He is God, the creator of the world, the one who existed before anything else existed. He promised that one day He would come in the flesh to save us, and He did. He conquered the power of sin and death.

Second, no one else has the qualifications for the job. Sin separates us from God, and only a sinless mediator can remove it. Buddha, Mohammed, and Confucius all taught that certain behaviors would enable humans to reach God, but they themselves never promised to save anybody. And even if they had made such a promise, they could never have come through. Like us, they were sinful human beings. They had no power to save, and we can never save ourselves regardless of the number of good deeds we do. The Bible teaches that we are saved by grace, by believing in Christ. Christ promises to save all who believe in Him, and He *can* follow through on His promise because He is sinless and because He is God.

As our mediator, Christ exercises a three-fold office. He is prophet, priest, and king. As prophet, He saves us from our ignorance of sin. The greatest prophet the world has ever known, Christ seasoned His words with grace, and the common people heard Him gladly. As priest, He saves us from the guilt of sin. He was a perfect priest because, being sinless, He could offer Himself as a perfect and holy sacrifice, paying for our sin once and for all. As king, He saves us from the dominion of sin over our lives. He is the King of kings before whom *every* knee shall bow.

Today give thanks that Christ has become your mediator, building a bridge between you and God the Father.

The devil would have us set ourselves forth as our own savior.

WHEN THE FLAME BURNS LOW

…'Sir, we wish to see Jesus.'

JOHN 12:21

Do you feel a little low, as if your spiritual gas tank is on empty? Has the fire of Christ's joy within you dwindled to an ember? If so, you're not alone. In fact, you're in very good company. Many people in the Bible experienced the same weariness and loss of zeal. David cried, "Restore to me the joy of Your salvation" (Psalm 51:12). Solomon said, "Hope deferred makes the heart sick" (Proverbs 13:12). Job lamented, "May the day perish on which I was born, and the night in which it was said, 'A male child is conceived'"(Job 3:3). Moses entreated, "I am not able to bear all these people alone, because the burden is too heavy for me. If You treat me like this, please kill me here and now" (Numbers 11:14–15). Paul explained, "For we do not want you to be ignorant, brethren, of our trouble which came to us in Asia: that we were burdened beyond measure, above strength, so that we despaired even of life" (2 Corinthians 1:8).

What causes spiritual weariness? Often we find ourselves spiritually drained because we have unconfessed and unrepented sin in our lives. I once left my car parked at the beach on a windy, humid day. When I returned several hours later, the windshield was coated with a thick, salty encrustation. I could hardly remove the salty layer with the windshield wipers. Unconfessed sin does the same thing to the soul. It clouds it and takes away its sparkle. Do you have unconfessed sin weighing you down and tiring you out?

We also grow spiritually weary when we lead hurried lives. As we do more and more for Christ, we have less and less time to spend in private devotions, our time of spiritual rejuvenation. Our lives become like the bottom of a soda sucked dry through a straw. The Bible tells us, "Be still, and know that I am God" (Psalm 46:10). Can you set aside some extra time today to rest in your Father's arms?

Sometimes we lose our spiritual edge because we've taken our eyes off our Savior and Lord. As we walk across the sea of life, we can stay on top of the tumultuous waves as long as we focus on Jesus. But when we look away, the breakers come crashing in and knock us down. Do you need to refocus your spiritual sights on your Savior today?

God, I pray Thee, light these idle sticks of my life, that I may burn for Thee.
Consume my life, my God, for it is Thine.

JIM ELLIOT (MARTYRED MISSIONARY)

GLORIFY THE LORD

Oh, magnify the Lord with me, and let us exalt His name together.

PSALM 34:3

The doxology we sing in church summarizes well our true purpose in life: "Praise God from whom all blessings flow. Praise Him all creatures here below. Praise Him above ye heavenly host. Praise Father, Son, and Holy Ghost. Amen." The Westminster Catechism says that our chief end in life is to "glorify God and enjoy Him forever."

Do you ever wonder how you can glorify God? First, we honor God by giving Him the praise and worship He deserves. When we acknowledge His greatness and His provision, we bring glory to His name. But we can magnify the Lord in everything else we do as well. I believe that if we determine to use our God-given talents, time, strength, and wisdom to glorify Him, we find ourselves involved in something exciting, something bigger than ourselves. As we do our jobs well, we glorify our Father. As we strive to cultivate loving and happy families, we glorify our Father. When we share the good news of Christ and introduce men and women to His kingdom, we glorify our Father.

By doing all for God's glory, we fulfill God's purpose for us. Johann Sebastian Bach certainly glorified God in his life. Many musicians consider Bach the greatest musician who ever lived. On his music scores are phrases such as "Soli Deo Gloria," which means "To God alone be the glory." William Wilberforce, the great evangelical statesman, brought glory to the Lord as he strove to end slavery in the entire British Empire. While God hasn't necessarily called you to be a Bach or a Wilberforce, you can bring glory to His name whoever you are and with whatever unique talents and gifts you have. Today, seek to glorify God in all you do. This focus will give your life a grand and magnificent purpose!

In commanding us to glorify Him, God is inviting us to enjoy Him.

C. S. LEWIS

RENEWING OUR STRENGTH

So He Himself often withdrew into the wilderness and prayed.

LUKE 5:16

When was the last time you sat still and stared into space? I'm not talking about the short daydreams that float through your mind during the day. I mean true, relaxed, uninterrupted, peaceful nothingness. Have you had any of that lately?

We lead busy lives, and because of our many commitments, we tend to keep going and going. We look for results in everything we do, and if we do something that produces nothing, we view the time spent as wasted.

But we need that time of space, of nothingness. We need to pull ourselves away from the hustle and bustle to regroup, reflect, rejuvenate. Jesus, our great example in life, *often* withdrew. He had thousands of people to minister to and heal. He had disciples to teach and only three short years to get the job done. Yet despite His great mission of saving the world, He took time away, spending time alone with His Father.

Life is a pilgrimage, and as we travel, we need strength along the way. This journey is a struggle, a battle, warfare. And as good soldiers of Christ, we need strength to win that battle. We don't gain that strength by continuing to strive. We gain it by waiting on the Lord. The prophet Isaiah declared the great truth that He who gives life can continually renew it. The Scripture reads, "Even the youths shall faint and be weary, and the young men shall utterly fall, but those who wait on the Lord shall renew their strength; they shall mount up with wings like eagles, they shall run and not be weary, they shall walk and not faint" (Isaiah 40:30–31). What a marvelous promise that is!

When we get physically or spiritually tired, we need quiet time with the Lord. A tree does not bear fruit always. It has seasons for blooming and seasons for growth and seasons for rest. So it is with us. We have times of service, then we need times to come away with God and allow Him to renew our strength.

Do you feel a little worn out today? Do you need strength to face the challenges before you? Then come away today. Spend some time alone with the Lord. Allow your Father to give you what you need—rest.

Christians who don't come apart for a while will just come apart.

ANONYMOUS

THE TOWER OF BABEL

Therefore its name is called Babel, because there the Lord confused the language of all the earth; and from there the Lord scattered them abroad over the face of all the earth.

GENESIS 11:9

Have you ever visited a foreign land and tried to get directions from a native? Perhaps you've felt the relief of finding someone who speaks a tongue you both know. Or perhaps you've experienced the uncertainty and confusion of getting nonverbal directions from someone who doesn't speak your language.

All that confusion began with the Tower of Babel. Until the time of the Tower of Babel, all people spoke the same language. Because they could understand each other, they could collaborate to build a spectacular tower that would reach the heavens, a tower intended to be the center of civilization.

People of all civilizations have built magnificent towers, but the builders of the Tower of Babel caught God's attention. Why? Because of their motive for building this tower: making a name for themselves. The builders of the Tower of Babel didn't want to build the City of God; they wanted to build the City of Humankind. All was for the glory of humanity, for dominion over others, and for the glory of *self*.

God recognized that because these people had one language and were united, they would accomplish not only this project but also anything else they decided to do. So God intervened. The problem, God said, was that the people were unified. That has a strange ring to our ears. Why? Because we're always told to seek unity, not division. And yet God divided these people. He saw their unity and decided it could mean only harm. God knows that the heart of humankind is sinful and that the unity people create among themselves always inclines toward evil. So God confused them. He diversified their speech and scattered them.

But in Christ, all curses are reversed, including this one. On the day of Pentecost, what do we see? People speaking in tongues previously unknown to them. Through the Spirit of Christ we discover a unity that is holy and good. We see people from all nations, tribes, and languages uniting in Him, the head of the Church.

Are you experiencing confusion and division between yourself and someone else? Perhaps you're not speaking the "same language." You're experiencing the impact of our fallen nature. But you also know where the remedy comes from— Jesus Christ. Invite His Spirit to bring unity between you and others today.

They that have despised the word of God, from them shall the word of man also be taken.

C. S. LEWIS, "THE CURSE OF BABEL" FROM THAT HIDEOUS STRENGTH

FEELING THE FAITH

For we walk by faith, not by sight.

2 CORINTHIANS 5:7

Have you ever said to yourself or to someone close to you, "I just don't feel that I have faith"? Have you ever doubted the steadfastness of your belief in God because you didn't feel happy or excited about your relationship with Jesus Christ?

Many Christians confuse faith with feelings. They think that if they really have faith, they'll feel certain emotions. But faith isn't based on feelings. Feelings are like the waves of the sea, in constant motion and continual change. Our feelings change from day to day and from hour to hour. But faith underlies all of that like the rock beneath the waves. Faith is about trusting in Jesus Christ, who never changes.

One day Martin Luther, that great man of faith, experienced one of his frequent periods of depression. While in this depression, Luther's arch-enemy, Satan, came to him and asked if he felt his sins had been forgiven. Luther responded that he knew that his sins were forgiven because God had declared that truth in His Word. The Scripture does not say, "Believe on the Lord Jesus Christ, then thou shalt *feel* saved," but "Believe on the Lord Jesus Christ and thou *shalt* be saved." And so, even as he *felt* depressed, Luther had *faith* based on scriptural truth.

Charles Spurgeon tells us that a good illustration of faith is the limpet. The limpet is a small creature that dwells by the sea and clings to rocks. If you manage to sneak up on one and strike it with a stick, it falls from the rock. But if you hit a neighboring limpet, the first limpet becomes aware of potential danger. At that point, you can hit that limpet until you break your stick, and it will never fall off because it clings to the rock for its life. "That," said Spurgeon, "is an illustration of faith."

Faith is clinging to Jesus Christ, not some fleeting feeling. So no matter how you feel today, tenaciously hold onto Jesus Christ. When in doubt, don't gauge your faith by your feelings. Go to God's Word, and read His promises. Stake your faith on God's promises, clinging to them for your very life, because when the waves of your emotions roll over you, God's promises will remain steady beneath you.

Often our feelings have more to do with our digestion than with our religion!

LOVE RESTORED

...God is love.

1 JOHN 4:8

In the beginning, God said, "Let us make man in our image, after our likeness." As He did so, He made us able to give and receive love in relationships with each other and with Him. He created us in His perfect love.

But now we bear few signs of that love. In our sinfulness, we have distorted His kingly nature and have all but destroyed the image of God in us. And with that, we have distorted and destroyed our experience of love.

How can we love again as God created us to love? On our own, we can do nothing to restore God's image or His perfect love within us. No effort or striving can perform the task. A little child can take an egg in his hand and crush it, but all the skill in the world could never restore it. All the knowledge, power, and technology that can split atoms and place man on the moon cannot restore that egg to its original form. How much less can we, by our own wisdom or strength, restore God's image—His perfect love—to our souls.

But in Christ, love is restored. Christ pours His love on humankind as He poured out His life in atonement for our sins. Though we're unworthy, Christ's sacrifice lights the fragile flame of love in our hearts, making it burn strong and clear. As the flame of Christ's love ignites each of us, those around us will catch the fire, and Christ will restore His love to the whole world.

Today let God fill your heart with His love, and as He does, let His love flow through you to those around you. One by one, as He restores His love to each of us, He'll restore His love to the whole world.

From heaven [love] came, to heaven returneth.

ROBERT SOUTHEY

THE BIBLE AND ECONOMICS

For even when we were with you, we commanded you this:
If anyone will not work, neither shall he eat.

2 THESSALONIANS 3:10

Do you dread going to work or tending house, viewing labor as a curse on your life because of the Fall? Well, it isn't. Before sin ever touched this earth, God commanded Adam to tend the garden. God created us to have meaningful employment and to earn our keep. And He created a context in which we could live and prosper.

God reveals that context in His Word. While the Bible isn't an economics textbook, it does say a great deal about how we can thrive. The Bible says that if a person does not work, that person shall not eat. (Of course, this principle doesn't refer to a person unable to work.) The Eighth Commandment, "Thou shalt not steal," makes it clear that we can own property, ruling out certain economic systems such as communism. In fact, I believe free enterprise is a biblical principle. Most people didn't understand this until 1776, when Adam Smith wrote his famous book on economics, *The Wealth of Nations*. This book sparked the worldwide spread of capitalism. Before that time, most people lived a hand-to-mouth existence, spending about ninety percent of their income on food. But between 1800 and 1850, wages quadrupled as people pursued scriptural economic principles, and from 1850 to 1900, wages quadrupled again. This was especially true in America, where free enterprise had its freest reign.

But in this century, we've turned from some of those biblical principles. A misapplication of the concepts of *justice* and *charity* have created in our nation "social justice" (in other words, welfare). Public welfare is neither just nor charitable, because it forcibly takes money from one person and gives it to another. Public welfare also tempts people to take advantage of public money and to fight for as much of it as they can get. It destroys private charity and creates vice and laziness.

I challenge you to apply biblical principles of economics in your life and to cultivate a responsible work ethic. Resolve today that whatever task comes your way, you'll work for God's honor and glory. As you do, He will bless you for your obedience.

America will last until the populace discovers it can vote for itself largess
[gifts or handouts] out of the public treasury.

ALEXIS DE TOCQUEVILLE

FULLY PERSUADED

[Abraham] did not waver at the promise of God through unbelief; but was strengthened in faith…and being fully convinced that what He had promised He was also able to perform.

ROMANS 4:20–21

Are you fully convinced that what God has promised He is able to perform?

If you'd like a surefire way to test the strength of your faith, then stretch your wings in the area of stewardship. Tithe as God has commanded, and watch Him perform as He has promised in Scripture. Paul tells us, "My God shall supply all your need according to His riches in glory by Christ Jesus." We need to trust God's promise, go about our daily work, and know that He will supply all we need. God gives a second promise that goes beyond the first one. God has said, "Bring all the tithes into the storehouse…and prove Me now in this…if I will not open for you the windows of heaven and pour out for you such blessing that there will not be room enough to receive it" (Malachi 3:10). And God makes yet another promise which goes beyond the first two. We find this promise in Mark 10:29–30, where Jesus says to us, "There is no one who has left house or brothers or sisters or father or mother or wife or children or lands, for my sake, and the gospel's, who shall not receive a hundredfold now in this time…and in the age to come, eternal life."

You might consider today's standard of living and balk at giving away some of your hard-earned money. But we all need to keep in mind that our God is not limited by inflation or other problems with the economy. The only thing that limits God is our unbelief. Stewardship and God's fulfillment of His promises aren't matters of money; they're matters of faith.

Do you believe that God can and will do all He has promised? Then put your money where your mouth is. Exercise your faith by being a good steward of all He has given you. If you refuse to waver in the face of God's promises, being fully convinced that He can fulfill them, you'll find that He will abundantly bless you.

We cannot serve God and mammon, but we can serve God with mammon.

ROBERT SPEER

GODLINESS WITH CONTENTMENT

But godliness with contentment is great gain. For we brought nothing into this world, and it is certain we can carry nothing out.

1 TIMOTHY 6:6–7

Do you ever feel caught up in "keeping up with the Joneses"? Do you often feel a twinge of jealousy when a neighbor or friend shows off a new purchase, or are you content with what you own?

Many people are in love with this world's goods whether they have them or not. I think of a man who started out well. He succeeded in business. He lived his life as John Wesley encouraged: "Make all you can, save all you can, give all you can." This man tithed regularly, and God blessed him as he did so.

But as this man became more and more prosperous, he found tithing more and more difficult. One day he came to Peter Marshall, the famous Senate chaplain of decades ago, and said, "Dr. Marshall, I have a problem. I've tithed now for some time. It wasn't too bad when I made $20,000 a year. I could afford to give the $2,000. But, you see, doctor, I now make $500,000 a year, and there's just no way I can afford to give away $50,000 a year."

Dr. Marshall said, "Yes, sir. I see that you do have a problem. I think we ought to pray about it. Dear Lord, this man has a problem, and I pray that you will help him. Lord, reduce his salary back to the place where he can afford to tithe."

This man started out having mastery over things, but ultimately things had mastery over him. Maybe you know someone like this man…maybe it's you.

Money makes a wonderful servant but a terrible lord. Yet many people are completely enslaved by it. They give all their thoughts to money. If they're not thinking about how to get more of it, they're thinking of how to hold on to what they have. That is a form of slavery!

Many people have lived in small cottages and managed to gain very little of this world's goods. Yet their hearts were fixed upon God. Some Christians are poor; some are wealthy. The important thing is *"godliness with contentment."* These two combined are "great gain."

Are you the master of your money and possessions, or are they your master? If you find that the latter is true, pray that God will reverse that trend, and then watch as He answers your prayers!

Own your possessions. Don't let your possessions own you.

ANONYMOUS

WHY DO WE PRAY?

…you were called into the fellowship of His Son, Jesus Christ our Lord.

1 CORINTHIANS 1:9

"Why do we have to say our prayers?" asks a little boy as his mother prepares him for bed. This child's simple question echoes the sentiment in the hearts of many people much older and supposedly much wiser than he. Do you ever ask that question? And if so, have you found any answers?

One of the key reasons we pray is to commune with God. Prayer fosters a two-way relationship between us and the God who loves and cares for us. Consider a child growing up in a home where his parents have given him every-thing: life, love, food, clothes. In everything, the parents have provided the very best they could afford. But as the child gets older, he decides that he doesn't have time for his parents, so he hardly ever comes home except when he has to. When he does, he stays busy in his room, rarely responding to his parents. Finally, the child grows into a man, goes out on his own, finds a job, and gets married. He never visits his parents; he never writes; he never calls.

What would you call such a child?

What would you call a person who receives life and love from his Father in heaven, the Father who watches over him and provides everything he needs in this life, including the food he eats and the clothes he wears? He receives innu-merable blessings, and yet he grows up, never talking to his Father, never visit-ing His house. Unconcerned with his relationship with his Father, he never prays. What do you call such a person? The Scripture calls such a person a "pagan," a person without God, a godless human being.

But we who know the Lord delight in spending time with Him. Why do we pray? Not so that He will do more than we ask or think, although He does. We pray so we can walk with God.

Today, spend some time with your Father. Tell Him what's on your mind and in your heart. And listen for Him to tell you about Himself, too. He wants a daily, two-way relationship with you more than you could ever imagine.

Prayer does not change God, but changes him who prays.

SOREN KIERKEGAARD

WHO HOLDS THE FUTURE?

*…I know whom I have believed and am persuaded that He is
able to keep what I have committed to Him until that Day.*

2 TIMOTHY 1:12

The year was 1943. Halfway around the world, a young pilot was flying his Corsair above the scattered islands of the Pacific, scanning his radar for the enemy. Suddenly, out of nowhere, he saw enemy planes. Before the young pilot knew it, one of them was on his tail. He rolled his plane over and dove down, back up again, turning, twisting, diving, doing everything he could to escape. But he had an expert fighter pilot on his tail. In the end, a burst of machine-gun fire pierced not only his plane but his body as well.

Mortally wounded, the young pilot somehow managed to land his disabled plane on one of the jungle islands of the South Pacific. He struggled to crawl clear of the plane in case it exploded. Five days later his body was found. He had, clutched in his hand, a scrap of paper on which he had written his last words: "When peace like a river…" That was all. His final words were the beginning of that wonderful hymn that goes like this: "When peace like a river attendeth my way, when sorrows like sea billows roll; whatever my lot, Thou hast taught me to say, it is well, it is well with my soul."

Here was a young man who had learned somewhere—whether in his home or at church—Who held his future. When we recognize and acknowledge that God holds the future, we can be assured that whatever comes our way, even if it's the worst scenario we can imagine, God can transform it into a blessing. Only when we place our entire trust in Him will we have the kind of assurance in our future that this young man had.

Are you walking through a peaceful river or through rolling sea billows today? Whatever your lot, place your full trust in the Lord. Only when we trust the One who holds the future will it be well with our souls!

I have no fear…Christ is the Captain of my soul.

DOROTHEA DAY

IF GOD BE FOR US

What then shall we say to these things? If God is for us, who can be against us?

ROMANS 8:31

We cannot possibly fail with Christ's love in our corner. Paul says, in what I call the "Golden Shield" of faith, "If God is for us, who can be against us?" Who can fight against us and succeed? No one! God's love shields us from all attacks of the evil one and his followers. Despite such attacks, we are safe and secure for eternity. Who can be against us? The world, the flesh, and the devil may try to defeat us, but *all* will fail.

To grasp the truth of Paul's statement, think of the persecution the early Church endured. In the first few centuries of Christianity, Christ's followers went through the most difficult persecution ever seen on this planet. For nearly three hundred years, in ten great waves of persecution, the Christian Church was under attack. The Roman pagan state used all of the hatred it possessed to try to destroy the Church. Everything the depraved and demonic mind could conceive of, the Romans did. They crucified Christians right side up and upside down; they burned Christians alive; they put Christians in sacks with vipers; they gave Christians to bulls to gore; they fed Christians to the lions. Yet *nothing* could break the Christian will. The Roman Empire eventually perished, but the Church remains to this day. The greatest persecution the world has ever seen (rivaled, perhaps, only by that of the Communists in our century) was unable to break the Herculean might of Christians armed with nothing but faith, prayer, and the Word of God.

This applies to us today as well. With such a Golden Shield, we may deflect all of the attacks against us (from without and from within) because of what Christ has done for us. Come what may, *nothing* can separate us from the love of Christ. If God is for us, who can *possibly* be against us?

Caesar and Christ had met in the arena [Colosseum], and Christ had won.

WILL DURANT

HAPPY IN THE HOLY SPIRIT

Rejoice in the Lord always. Again I will say, rejoice!

PHILIPPIANS 4:4

Have you ever noticed that people who are constantly morose and miserable just don't seem to get along with others? Everywhere the gloomy person goes, he or she runs into interpersonal problems such as rejection and poor treatment. On the other hand, have you ever noticed that happy people don't seem to have many enemies? A joyful person finds very few relational problems. This type of person doesn't quickly take offense and doesn't offend people very often; rather, this person brings gladness into any situation.

How does a person maintain such a consistently joyful attitude? Does God want us pretending to be happy when we're not? Not at all! God wants us to have *true* joy. So how do we cultivate this attitude? The Scripture says, "In your presence is fullness of joy; at your right hand are pleasures forevermore." This is the wonderful secret God would have us know: We find fullness of joy in God's presence. By spending time with the Lord we will have joy infused into our souls. We'll discover the truth that Christ is indeed no killjoy but is in fact the great King and source of *all* joy.

Often, we don't feel joyful because we haven't spent enough time with God. But if we wait in the Lord's presence, He'll fill us with His joy. If we seek the fullness of His Holy Spirit, we'll receive the fruit of joy. If we confess any sin that hinders us from rejoicing in the Lord, we'll experience the joy of our salvation.

If you're running a bit low on joy today, spend some quality time with God. Allow Him to saturate your soul with His joy. Then, as you go through the day, rejoice at every opportunity you have! Again I will say, rejoice!

Life is a duty…Life is divine when duty is a Joy.

HENRY VAN DYKE

APOSTASY

They went out from us, but they were not of us; for if they had been of us, they would have continued with us...

1 JOHN 2:19

Do you know someone who once seemed on fire for the Lord but then backslid into spiritual oblivion? If so, then you know the grief of watching someone slip from God's grasp, especially when that person is someone you love. You might wonder what this person's eternal future will be, hoping God's grace continues to cover him or her. But you also might wonder whether this person was truly a Christian in the first place.

People who fall away from the Lord are called apostates. "Apostasy" means spiritual defection. The great apostate of all time was Judas Iscariot. Unfortunately, many people have followed his pattern.

Charles Spurgeon tells about a great hulk of a man in the village where Spurgeon first preached. This man was a fine-looking giant of a man but a drunkard as well. He often brawled in the local bar with those who dared to cross his path. And he would have nothing to do with religion, until one day when, to the amazement of all, this man asked Jesus to be his Savior. He joined a church, attended every service, and volunteered for any work that needed to be done.

But this man's former companions made fun of him for turning to religion. After enduring about ten months of their laughter, he succumbed to their mocking. First he dropped away from the works. Soon he didn't attend prayer meetings. For a while, he continued attending Sunday morning church, but his attendance became more and more irregular until he stopped attending altogether. He never completely returned to his former self, but often people saw him staggering drunkenly about the town. And when his unbelieving friends saw him like that, they said to each other, "Ha, there is your Christian! Hypocrites! That's all they are."

Was this man really a Christian? The Bible plainly teaches that God will preserve until the end the ones who are truly His. Whenever the genuine work of salvation happens in the heart of a man or woman, boy or girl, God will see that it perseveres until the day of Christ. But those with sham faith will eventually fall away.

If you know someone who once seemed to follow Christ but has since turned away, pray for that person today. Ask God to do a work of true salvation in that person's heart so that he or she may know the fullness of life in Christ.

Those who have denied Christ have manifested the spirit of the Antichrist.

LITTLE THINGS

Catch us the foxes, the little foxes that spoil the vines, for our vines have tender grapes.

SONG OF SOLOMON 2:15

In the Song of Solomon, we read of *little* foxes that ruin the vineyards. What are "little foxes"? I see them as the small things that don't seem important but can spoil "tender grapes" such as a relationship, a career, or a life dedicated to Christ. How many marriages have failed because spouses paid no attention to the little things? How many athletes have lost competitions because of tiny bobbles or missteps? Many of us can see the big pictures of our lives and of our relationships with God but we neglect the details necessary for bringing the larger picture into focus. God neglects neither the great nor the small, and neither should we.

Have you attended to the "little foxes" in your life, the "minor" behaviors that can either draw you to or push you from the Lord?

Michelangelo, that marvelous genius and magnificent sculptor, was sculpting a figure from a block of marble while a friend looked on. After an absence of several months, the friend returned and said, "I see that you have not been working on your statue." Michelangelo answered, "Oh yes, I have been working on it each day." The friend asked, "Oh, how can that be?" The great artist replied, "I have softened this line here—the hem of this garment. I have straightened the lip and brought out this muscle more clearly…polished this…sharpened that." "Well," said his friend, "those are just trifles." To that Michelangelo responded, "Trifles they may be, but you will remember that trifles make perfection; that perfection is no trifle."

We must attend to the "trifles" if we ever hope to succeed. Attention to detail will determine the ultimate outcome and success of our lives. And as we act faithfully in the little things, God will bless us with greater opportunities for service. We will develop the faithfulness and obedience needed to conquer the great issues in the battle of life.

What "little foxes" do you need to attend to today? Commit yourself to addressing these "minor" issues, and watch how your conscientiousness affects the grander scheme of your life.

Little things ultimately make a big difference in life.

April 22

HE DIDN'T LIFT US UP TO LET US DOWN

'For to everyone who has, more will be given, and he will have abundance;
but from him who does not have, even what he has will be taken away.'

MATTHEW 25:29

Does this text seem fair to you? After all, why would someone who has an abundance get more? And shouldn't the person with nothing receive something?

Jesus described the principle of this passage on five separate occasions in different forms. This verse is the basis for the principle of use: "Use it or lose it." We see this principle at work in a variety of contexts. For example, in the physical realm, the arm of the blacksmith or the body of the football player becomes more and more muscular through exercise. In the work world, the person who has the ability and desire for a job usually finds more opportunities to work and improve his or her skills. As for moral conscience, our character develops in proportion to the Bible-based choices we make day after day.

And, of course, this principle applies to the spiritual realm. Charles Spurgeon spoke of two great principles of grace. The first one is that God gives grace to the empty, needy, poor, and humble. The second one is that to those to whom God has granted His grace, He continues to grant more. The more grace we need, the more grace He makes available to us.

To receive more grace from God, we must use the grace He has already given us. Some people are like the little boy riding the rocking horse—they exhibit a lot of motion but little progress. These people keep bustling with activity in hopes of earning salvation, but they haven't taken advantage of the grace God has already freely given. Others may resemble a grapevine that doesn't grow because, instead of being planted in deep soil, its roots dangle into an empty well. Instead of growing in grace, some people wither spiritually because they haven't planted themselves in God's grace from the start. And others are like a sailboat with sails full of wind yet unable to move because it is still anchored to the ocean floor. Instead of moving forward in God's grace, people like this let sin weigh them down.

Have you received the grace God makes available to us all? Determine today that you will use to the fullest all the grace God has given you. Then watch as he gives you more!

When God pours out his initial grace upon us, it is a harbinger of grace to come.

April 23

ENTERING THE PROMISED LAND

...'So I swore in My wrath, "They shall not enter My rest" '...

HEBREWS 4:3

Have you ever had a relationship with someone who didn't have faith in you? If so, how did you feel, knowing you would never fail that person yet that person failed to trust you?

God feels the same way when we don't believe in His power or desire to bless us. God feels pleased when we have faith in Him, and He feels angry when we don't. In fact, our unbelief often short-circuits the blessings He has in store for us.

Consider, if you will, this tremendous lesson from the Old Testament. God promised to deliver the Israelites into the Promised Land. To get them there, He gave them straightforward directions: Go directly to the mount, receive the Ten Commandments, proceed to Kadesh Barnea, enter the Promised Land, and occupy it. Moses sent twelve spies to scope out the land in advance, to determine the obstacles that would have to be overcome before taking possession of the land. When the twelve spies returned, ten of them reported that the giants and walled cities were greater than the Israelites could conquer. Because of the Israelites' reliance upon themselves and unbelief in God, God condemned them to wander for forty years in the wilderness! God said, "So I swore in my wrath, 'They shall not enter My rest.'" The Israelites did not place their trust in God; instead, they trusted in their own plans. And because they did, they delayed their entrance into the Promised Land. Their unbelief kept them from experiencing God's perfect will for their lives.

God's plan is perfect, and we need to submit to it. Otherwise we may find our hearts and souls in the midst of a vast wilderness, wandering because of our inability to trust Him. I encourage you to pray that God would give you the will to trust Him and His perfect plan. As you believe in His ability and desire to care for you, He will surely lead you to the Promised Land. He'll lead you there even if you make the tiniest step of faith toward him by praying as the doubting man in Mark 9 did—"Lord, I do believe; help thou my unbelief!"

If you've missed God's perfect will for you in the past because you've lacked faith, don't be discouraged. You can still experience His will for you as you believe in Him. Trust in Him today, for He is faithful.

When unhappy, one doubts everything. When happy, one doubts nothing.

JOSEPH ROWE

April 24

TOTAL SURRENDER

*I beseech you therefore…that you present your bodies a living sacrifice,
holy, acceptable to God, which is your reasonable service.*

ROMANS 12:1

Many Christians live their whole lives without ever fully grasping some of the great spiritual truths of God. Foremost among these truths is that God wants to *bless* our lives. Anything other than that is alien to Him, for God acts out His true nature when He blesses His children. He is a God of all grace who wants nothing more than to make His love known to us. He delights in opening the windows of Heaven and pouring blessings upon us, blessings far more wonderful than most of us have ever dreamed.

Isn't that an incredible truth to hang onto?

But God has a basic condition for His blessings. The apostle James says, "You ask and do not receive, because you ask amiss." Many times when we seek God's blessings, we ask amiss because we do not meet God's condition for the full outpouring of those blessings: total surrender to Him! That is what God demands. In numerous places, God says the same thing over and over: Yield yourselves to God; offer your bodies as living sacrifices; present yourselves to God as those who are alive from the dead; yield not your members as instruments of unrighteousness, but as instruments of righteousness unto God.

Is there anything in your life that holds you back from fully enjoying God's blessings? anything you need to surrender to Him? God wants to bless our lives, but first He wants us to surrender. If we can do that, we'll discover the blessings of heaven in a way that is far beyond our dreams.

…throughout the whole universe there is nothing good but that which He works.

ANDREW MURRAY

CHRIST IN THE HEART

…that Christ may dwell in your hearts through faith…

EPHESIANS 3:17

A five-year-old Christian boy was very ill, so ill that he required open-heart surgery. After a successful operation, the doctor checked on the little boy in his hospital room. With bright and eager eyes, the little boy asked, "Doctor, was He there?" The doctor asked, "Was who where?" The young lad replied, "Was He there? Did you see Jesus in my heart?" At that, the doctor suppressed a smile and replied, "Yes, son, He is there."

What does the Great Physician say about your heart today? Is Jesus there? For us to grow in grace, Christ must first dwell in our hearts. The apostle Paul prayed that Christ would dwell in our hearts through faith and that as we become rooted and grounded, we would know Christ's love and be filled with God's fullness. We must grasp the significance of that tremendous metaphor. Theologians say that Christ comes into our hearts, and by the continual supply of His grace and love, we grow spiritually. When Christ comes to dwell in a person's heart, He digs the tree of that person's life out of the bitter soil of the old nature, and He transplants it into the new, rich soil of His love. As we allow Jesus to do this, we flourish and bring forth the fruit of the Holy Spirit.

Have you invited Christ to take up residence in your heart? If not, allow Him to transplant your life from your old nature into His immeasurable love. As you do, He will cause you to grow in grace and in the knowledge of Jesus Christ.

God has two dwellings: one in heaven, and the other in a meek and thankful heart.

IZAAK WALTON

THE WEAKER BROTHER

But beware lest somehow this liberty of yours become a stumbling block to those who are weak.

1 CORINTHIANS 8:9

God has given us tremendous liberty. He has freed us from all sin. Yet our liberty doesn't come without limits. According to Scripture we have three classes of actions: those commanded by God, those forbidden by God, and those which God neither commands nor forbids—"things indifferent." To these "things indifferent," we must apply our liberty carefully. If we, in our liberty, choose an action that causes a weak brother or sister to stumble in the faith, then we become responsible for his or her downfall.

In Corinthians, Paul addresses a "thing indifferent," an issue that the Corinthians had hotly debated: whether or not to eat meat offered to idols. We can't relate to this issue since we don't sacrifice meat to idols these days, but we can consider it in the same light as the issue of whether or not to drink alcohol. In the Corinthian's situation, it appears that the stronger brethren wrote to Paul, and since Paul championed liberty, the brethren expected him to say they could eat the meat. But instead, Paul told them that while nothing forbade them from eating it, they shouldn't do anything that would cause their weaker brethren to stumble. This principle has become known as the "Royal Law of Love." We must freely forsake our liberties for the sake of our more vulnerable brothers and sisters.

In one sense, the weak always control our lives. Often the baby decides whether you go out or stay home. The sick child decides what you do in the evening. The sprained ankle decides the rest of your physical activity. In the same way, we must place the spiritual needs of our weaker brothers and sisters ahead of our desire to indulge our liberty.

As our ultimate example of this, we can look to Jesus. Because of our liberty, we may feel we have rights to certain "things indifferent." We may resent having to give up those rights for the sake of our weaker brethren. But for us, weak as we are, Jesus gave up His rights—the right to sit at the right hand of the father, the right to be adored, the right to be worshiped and ministered to by the angels.

Today, thank the Lord for your liberty. And if you have a choice about doing something that would make a weaker brother or sister stumble, choose Christ's Royal Law of Love and sacrifice your rights for that person' spiritual well-being.

Love sacrifices all things to bless the thing it loves.

EDWARD GEORGE BULWER-LYTTON

RING THE BELLS

Bless the Lord, O my soul; and all that is within me, bless His holy name.

PSALM 103:1

Think for just a moment of two things. First, when was the last time you asked God to give you something? Got it in mind? Now, when was the last time you praised God just because of Who He is?

So often we get on our knees and pray, "O Lord, bless my soul." We constantly ask God to touch our lives. In contrast, the psalmist who wrote Psalm 103 got on his knees and said, "O my soul, bless the Lord." A complete antithesis! Why? Because the psalmist was in the "graduate school" of prayer. He had risen to that elevated atmosphere of praise and adoration. As we read the rest of the Psalms we find everywhere the same note of praise: "Praise the Lord!" "Give thanks unto the Lord for He is good."

Do your prayers begin in a similar fashion?

Such an element of praise and adoration, I believe, can change our lives completely. How? First, it will make a difference because we will become much more pleasing to our Father…and that will be the beginning of some wonderful things. Second, we should ring the bells of praise not only for God's sake but also for the sake of others. Praise draws people to God, even as ringing church bells filter over the community and draw people to hear the gospel. We need to become a steeple set with bells. We need to ring out the happy bells of thanksgiving, the golden bells of praise, until the whole world abounds with the echoes of that sound.

What praise can you "ring" to God today? Unbelievers yearn for real joy and praise, and when we express gratitude and praise to God, those unbelievers will be drawn to Christ. So today ring the bells of praise!

If Christians praised God more, the world would doubt Him less.

CHARLES JEFFERSON

ALL THINGS FOR OUR GOOD

And we know that all things work together for good to those who love God,
to those who are the called according to His purpose.

ROMANS 8:28

Have you ever looked back on a difficult time in your life and been amazed at how, in an entirely unforeseen way, it turned out positively? As we go through life, God operates behind the scenes, working everything for good on behalf of those who love Him. We may not recognize it in this lifetime, but when we get to heaven and God replays the pictures of our lives, we'll discover the positive end to each trial we've endured.

I hope you'll claim this truth today. I hope you know God has *everything* under His control, even the chaotic times in your life. He has a plan for everything you undergo. You may face an avalanche of trial, trouble, and tribulation. Maybe you face it even today. Anyone in that situation would feel discouraged. I have often found myself in the deep, dark pit of despair and discouragement, wondering how I'd ever get out. But in those times God encourages me by reminding me of His promise: He works everything for good. We must view everything that comes our way, even the most difficult situations, through the filter of God's love.

I invite you to do that today, whatever trial you face. Remember that God has a perspective on your problems that you can't see as a limited human being here on earth. Be encouraged that God *can* see the big picture and that He'll put the pieces of your life together to an end far beyond your wildest dreams.

God moves in a mysterious way, His wonders to perform.

WILLIAM COWPER

SACRIFICE

'Whoever desires to come after Me, let him deny himself, and take up his cross, and follow Me.'

MARK 8:34

Have you ever noticed how virtually all of the people we call heroes have made great sacrifices in one way or another? To achieve the ends they deemed worthwhile, these people sacrificed their time, their finances, their health, even their lives. And because they willingly relinquished any claims to these things (which we take for granted), we view these people as heroes, worthy of honor and emulation.

Throughout the centuries, God has used sacrifice as the marble from which He carves greatness. Here are some people we call heroes for the sacrifices they made:

•the apostles who gave their lives at stakes, on crosses, and in other torturous ways;

•the early Christians in the Colosseum of Rome, who watched iron grates rise and famished lions charge;

•Christians who were tied to stakes and watched as torches ignited kindling beneath them;

•the Pilgrims who, in the dead of winter, sailed across tumultuous seas to the inhospitable coasts of New England;

•George Washington and his brave soldiers at Valley Forge, who left bloody footprints in the snow as they departed; and

•Jesus Christ, who made the ultimate sacrifice, His life, at Calvary.

What sacrifice can you offer to God this day? What material will you give Him so that He can carve greatness from your life?

There has never yet been a man in our history who led a life of ease
whose name is worth remembering.

THEODORE ROOSEVELT

TO SEE GOD

'Blessed are the pure in heart: for they shall see God.'

MATTHEW 5:8

Some have called the concept of seeing God "the brightest star in the Beatitudes' constellation." For ages, Christians have longed to see God. The mystics of the Middle Ages rejoiced in the concept of seeing God, calling it the "Beatific Vision." This vision was the great quest of theology and even the quest of science as originally constructed—through the examination of the cosmos, humans hoped to more clearly see the Creator.

But Scripture explicitly states that no human can see God directly and live. Yet many still seek to do so. Philip the Apostle said to Jesus, "Lord, show us the Father, and it is sufficient for us." Even pagan princes have sought to see God. In the ancient Roman Empire, Trajan said to a believer in the true God, "I understand that you believe your God is everywhere…I should very much like to see Him." The believer responded, "I am afraid, sire, that no mortal eye can look upon His glory." Nonetheless, the king commanded the believer to show him God. The believer suggested to the king that he first look at God's ambassadors before he look God in the face. With that, the believer led the king outside on a bright, dazzling day and told the king to look at the sun. The king responded, "I cannot, for the light dazzles my eyes!" The believer then explained that if the king could not look at a mere ambassador that carries a message of God's creation, how could he possibly look into the face of God Himself?

We cannot see God with our limited human eyes. But we *can* see Him with our souls, experiencing His joy, His peace, and His serenity. I hope that you have the blessing of seeing God this way as you foster a pure heart.

Jesus, the very thought of Thee, with sweetness fills my breast, but even more
Thy face to see and in Thy presence rest.

ST. BERNARD OF CLAIRVEAUX

May 1

A NATIONAL DAY OF PRAYER

'If My people who are called by My name will humble themselves, and pray and seek My face, and turn from their wicked ways…'

2 CHRONICLES 7:14

A multitude of presidents through the years have declared this date our National Day of Prayer. And our country needs prayer! In fact, I think this country needs our prayers now more than ever before, except perhaps during the War for Independence and the Civil War. We desperately need a national revival. Unless we have one, I believe that America, as we know it, won't exist much longer. And if America falls, virtually the entire missionary enterprise of the Church could come to a screeching halt. But if America turns back to God, He could prevent this country's demise.

If we need to be convinced of the importance of national revival, we need look no further than the Israelites. In ancient Israel prophets arose and proclaimed the destruction of Israel unless that nation turned back to God. But the people mocked the prophets and ignored them, telling them to go tell their doleful tales elsewhere. Yet true to the prophets' words, the Assyrians came down like wolves in a pack, fiercely and cruelly defeating Israel, and ancient Israel (not to be confused with ancient Judah) never recovered. Had the Israelites turned back to God when He spoke His intentions through the prophets, they wouldn't have met with such a devastating fate.

If our nation, like Israel, needs national revival, then what is it and how can we bring it about? William Sprague defines national revival like this: "Wherever you see religion rising up from a state of comparative depression to a tone of increased vigor and strength, wherever you see professing Christians becoming more faithful to their obligations and behold the strength of the Church increased by fresh accessions of piety from the world, there is a state of things which you need not hesitate to denominate a revival of religion."

How can we bring this about? By doing what our government has set this day aside for us to do—pray. Today will you join me and millions of others in praying for the spiritual revival of this great nation?

Give me one hundred men who fear nothing but sin, and desire nothing but God, and I will shake the world.

JOHN WESLEY

NATIONAL REVIVAL

'...then I will hear from heaven, and will forgive their sin and heal their land.'

2 CHRONICLES 7:14

Yesterday we discussed our need for national revival. Today and tomorrow I want to continue with this theme.

Revival is a rebirth, a restoration of God's power, and I believe that it can happen in America! God can yet change this land. He can stay the hand of chastisement acted out in our mean city streets and spreading into the countryside.

But to have revival, we must pay a price. God says, "If My people who are called by My name will humble themselves, and pray." Revival begins with God's people praying prayers of brokenness, of humility, of acknowledgment of our own sins. How often do we pray for the sins of others and neglect repenting of our own sins that prevent us from being effective witnesses for God? We need to fall on our knees and get our own lives straight with God.

God doesn't do His work in unbelievers until His people renew their devotion to Him. But when that happens, watch out! He has promised that when we humble ourselves and pray and seek His face, He will hear, forgive our sin, and heal our land. The spiritual renewal of God's children inevitably issues forth a tremendous outbreak of evangelism that has fresh power and works in ways never seen before. God can release His power to bring the entire nation to Him.

The Great Awakening in America began when a few people prayed, seeking God's face, week after week, time after time, until finally God began to pour out His Spirit. Christians met to pray. They began to expect great things of God. And people became Christians! For years this revival went on. At its peak, fifty thousand people a week were born into God's kingdom.

Will you join me in praying for national revival? Will you humble yourself before God and seek His face so that He might bring revival to this land through you? Let's all do this so that we might not hinder God from drawing this nation to Himself.

Take a piece of chalk, and draw a circle on the floor.
Then step inside the circle and pray, 'Lord, send a revival inside this circle.'

GYPSY SMITH (ON BEING ASKED HOW TO START A REVIVAL)

SEND A GREAT REVIVAL!

…O Lord, revive Your work in the midst of the years!…

HABAKKUK 3:2

Today we'll take our last look at revival. Particularly, we'll look at some great revivals of the past.

Perhaps the most notable revival of the twentieth century happened in 1904 and 1905 in the tiny land of Wales. This revival started with a few people fervently praying. The prayers of these people had powerful results. Churches that had been one-fourth full of apathetic Christians began to come alive. The Spirit of God fell on various towns, moving everywhere. Within five months, over a hundred thousand people in that small land converted to Christianity! The bars in many towns had to shut down completely, and the jails were emptied and closed!

Another powerful revival happened years ago on the battleship *North Carolina*. While this battleship anchored in New York harbor, four young men out of a thousand got together. They could find no other Christians, but they asked for a room where they could meet and pray. They were assigned a little room way below the waterline, and day after day they faithfully met together to pray. They prayed that God would pour His blessing upon that ship. Finally one day the Spirit of God descended, the sailors' hearts burned within them, and they knew that God was present. They began to sing praises to God, and their hymns of praise wafted up through the ship. Hearing the singing, rough sailors came down to mock the four men, but when these rough men entered the room, the power of God's Spirit gripped them. These men fell to their knees. Eventually, hundreds converted to Christianity, and a great revival swept the entire ship. In fact, the revival carried from that ship to others.

The same God who changed these men, the same God who changed Saul of Tarsus into Paul the Apostle, can change anyone. Today pray that God will bring revival to our nation, especially to the people whom you'd least expect would give their lives to Christ. He can work through you as you faithfully pray.

It [revival] is a sovereign act of God, whereby He intervenes to lift the situation completely out of human hands and works in extraordinary power.

JEFFREY KING

THE CLAIMS OF CHRIST

'I and My Father are one.'

JOHN 10:30

Have you ever really thought about some of the things Jesus Christ said about Himself? Have you ever pondered the fact that Jesus Christ made claims that today would put someone in a lockup?

Jesus said He was the "light of the world." Talk about delusions of grandeur! (But only if the claim weren't true.) Jesus also claimed an eternal origin—He said, "Before Abraham was, I AM." His hearers, the Jewish leaders of His day, knew that those words were a claim to deity. (Recall that, in Exodus 3:14, God identified Himself to Moses as "I AM.") Jesus also claimed the power to forgive sins, something only God can do. As well, Jesus presented Himself as equal to God when He said, "I and My Father are one."

The Jewish leaders knew the meaning behind Jesus' words, and they didn't like what they heard. They recognized Jesus' claim to deity and almost stoned Him for blasphemy.

If you really think about it, either Jesus was crazy, he was a deceiver, or He was telling the truth. C. S. Lewis, the great Christian writer, put it so well:

A man who was merely a man and said the sort of things Jesus said would not be a great moral teacher. He would either be a lunatic—on a level with the man who says he is a poached egg—or else he would be the Devil of Hell. You must make your choice. Either this man was, and is, the Son of God: or else a madman or something worse. You can shut Him up for a fool, you can spit at Him and kill Him as a demon; or you can fall at His feet and call Him Lord and God. But let us not come up with any patronising nonsense about His being a great human teacher. He has not left that open to us. He did not intend to.

—*Mere Christianity* (Macmillan, 1952)

Whenever you find yourself thinking about Jesus, take a moment to stop and consider Who He really is. He revealed His identity in His words, and He'll back up His words by showing His power in your life.

We believe in one Lord, Jesus Christ, the only Son of God, eternally begotten from the Father, God from God, Light from Light, true God from true God, begotten, not made, one in Being with the Father. Through Him all things were made...

NICENE CREED

JESUS CHRIST OUR LORD

'…learn from Me, for I am gentle and lowly in heart…'

MATTHEW 11:29

The four Gospels present four rather different pictures of Christ from different perspectives, from different backgrounds, and through different events. As we read those Gospels, a character rises up from the pages, a character unique and altogether lovely. We begin to see a face and hear a voice, a voice that speaks with a music and a poetry never heard before. His message? "Come to Me, all you who labor and are heavy laden, and I will give you rest…learn from Me, for I am gentle and lowly in heart."

Have you heard and responded to that message?

That voice has reverberated through the centuries. Ah, the skeptics have come with their scissors and their paste, cutting up the Gospels and pasting them back together anyway they've wanted. Still that character stands and speaks an everlasting message. The invitation still comes, the music still sounds. "Learn from Me, for I am gentle and lowly in heart."

Antagonists have attempted to refute Jesus' claims. Nietzsche condemned Christ, mocking His humility and dubbing Him a slave. Nietzsche died in a madhouse, but the voice of Christ still resounds. Hitler, following in Nietzsche's footsteps, declared that he, as a pure pagan, would uproot Christianity from the earth. Hitler became a charred cinder, his name a byword for one who does evil. But the voice of Christ continues to resound throughout the world. The Communists tried to kill just about every Christian they could get their hands on. But today in those lands more people follow Jesus than follow Karl Marx.

So it goes that Christ, whose message has outlasted all his detractors, criticizes His critics and becomes the final Judge of all His judges, and all the while His voice still exhorts, even today, "Learn from Me, for I am gentle and lowly in heart, and you will find rest for your souls."

Today let that lasting message reverberate through your heart, encouraging you in all you do.

Jesus shall reign where'er the sun does his successive journeys run.

ISAAC WATTS

WHAT IS HE TO YOU?

…'Behold, this Child is destined for the fall and rising of many in Israel…'

LUKE 2:34

Whoever you are, you cannot avoid Jesus Christ, either in this life or the next. He is the Lord of lords and the King of kings. He is the One "with whom we have to do." I once heard about a secular talk-show host who flippantly remarked, "Jesus means absolutely nothing to my life." How wrong she is, for one day, like all of us, she will stand before Him in judgment.

The Bible teaches us that we can experience Jesus Christ as either a steppingstone that raises us to new heights or a stumbling block over which we trip and fall. Christ is as salt—permeating, penetrating, and seasoning all with which He comes in contact. You cannot avoid His influence. You cannot avoid the working of Christ any more than you can avoid the working of fire—stand before the fire, and it shall warm and comfort you; thrust your hand into it, and it will burn you.

An Eastern fable tells of a magic mirror that remained clear when the purehearted looked into it. But when the glance of a vile, unholy person fell upon it, the mirror clouded over instantly. Thus, the owner of that mirror could immediately tell the character of his visitors as they glanced into it. In the same way, Christ reveals our true natures to others, to God, and—if we pay attention—even to ourselves. Notice the reactions to Christ when He first came into this world: Mary and Joseph loved Him; the innkeeper was too busy for Him; the shepherds worshiped Him; Herod hated Him; both Anna and Simeon in the Temple praised God for Him. And so, Jesus Christ reveals our true character when we come into contact with Him.

What do you discover about yourself as you look into His face?

Whoever you are, the Gospel must be to you a savour of life or of death.

CHARLES SPURGEON

May 7
GROWING IN GRACE

*'I am the vine, you are the branches. He who abides in Me, and I in him,
bears much fruit; for without Me you can do nothing.'*

JOHN 15:5

When you were a child, did you look forward to growing up? Perhaps your mother or father marked your physical growth on a wall, charting your progress toward adulthood.

Just as we anticipated physical growth when we were children, we need to pursue spiritual growth daily. Repeatedly the Scriptures speak of spiritual growth. A psalmist declares that when we meditate on God's Word, we become "like a tree planted by the rivers of water, that brings forth its fruit in its season" (Psalm 1:3). Jesus explains how we must be like branches grafted into the vine, growing to produce fruit. We are told to grow into the fullness of the stature of Jesus Christ. God has most definitely designed us to grow spiritually.

How can we tell if we're growing according to God's plan? One of the signs will be the fruit of graciousness, becoming like the all-gracious God, having an unselfish love and concern for others' needs. Another sign is joy. As we grow in grace, we'll rejoice in everything life hands us, good or bad. Conversely, if we grumble and complain about everything, continually sad and dejected and depressed, we're clearly not growing in grace. Those negative attitudes reflect our spiritual immaturity. Consider the great admonition of the Bible: "Rejoice in all things." We can fulfill that command only when we've grown in grace.

How can we pursue spiritual growth? Think of Olympic weight lifters, who need just the right food and exercise to build strength. In a similar way, we as Christians grow by taking in the spiritual food of God's Word, prayer, and our consistent devotional lives, then by exercising ourselves in the faithful performance of Christian duties such as works of mercy and evangelism. As we engage in these spiritual disciplines, we grow in grace and in the knowledge of our Lord Jesus Christ.

Where are you along the "wall" of spiritual growth? I encourage you to chart your progress today. Then set your sights on a higher mark, and commit to at least one spiritual discipline that can get you there.

All growth that is not towards God is growing to decay.

GEORGE MACDONALD

May 8

FORWARD!

And the Lord said to Moses, 'Why do you cry to Me? Tell the children of Israel to go forward.'

EXODUS 14:15

Have you ever encountered an obstacle so huge, you just didn't know if you could get around it? Perhaps you are facing one today…

If you need a testimony of victory against tremendous obstacles, read the book of Exodus. The tenth plague had come upon Egypt, striking the firstborn of all the houses of Egypt. Meanwhile, the Israelites sat terrified in their homes amid the shrieks, wails, moans, and cries of the mourning Egyptians around them. The angel of God had passed through the land, slaying the firstborn of every house that did not have blood upon the doorpost and lintel. The next day, Pharaoh gave the Israelites permission to leave Egypt, and so they headed out of the land. But while Moses led the Israelites to the edge of the Red Sea, Pharaoh hardened his heart and sent his men to pursue the Israelites. As the Israelites looked back from the Red Sea, hundreds of Egyptian chariots bore down on them! They had no place left to go. With the Red Sea in front of them and the Egyptians behind them, "The Lord said to Moses, 'Why do you cry to Me? Tell the children of Israel to go forward.'" At once the Red Sea parted, and God provided them safe passage.

Forty years later, the Israelites (now under Joshua's leadership) faced the Jordan River, and it appeared impossible to cross. But God had told them that when they stepped into the water, it would disappear. The river flowed menacingly along, but because of God's instruction and promise, they went forward. At the moment the Israelites' feet touched that water, it parted, and the people walked across on dry ground to the Promised Land!

When we face obstacles, God always provides a way. He has promised in His Word that He will make our paths straight. God calls us to go through our obstacles, whatever they may be, because He calls us *forward* to a glorious destiny, the Promised Land. So if you face a tremendous obstacle today, wait for God to provide you a way through it, and when He calls you forward, go in the faith that He will fulfill His promise to you.

When the good Lord closes a door, somewhere He opens a window.

THE SOUND OF MUSIC

PERSEVERANCE

'But he who endures to the end shall be saved.'

MATTHEW 24:13

Do you have stick-to-itiveness? When you up come against an obstacle, do you push through to the end? Persistent effort pays off. Paul tells us in Galatians 6:9, "And let us not grow weary while doing good, for in due season we shall reap if we do not lose heart."

What makes people decide to quit? Sometimes people quit because they feel their efforts have brought little or no success. Once a man, determined to find gold, spent time and money digging a mine shaft. But after digging down one mile, he gave up and sold the mine. The person who bought the mine dug down only three more feet and struck gold! People also quit because of setbacks in their health, finances, or other arenas of their lives. Criticism by others, especially the criticism of a spouse, parent, or friend has caused many people to give up. The ingratitude of those they have tried to help has discouraged others.

But we can't let lack of success, devastating setbacks, criticism, or ingratitude hinder us from pursuing worthwhile goals. The first time Benjamin Disraeli spoke before the English House of Commons, the members laughed at him. But instead of throwing in the towel, Disraeli vowed that one day those people would listen to him. He went on to become a great orator and the first Jewish prime minister of England. William Carey, a missionary to India, faced devastation, but he never gave up even though a fire burned his house and, with it, many years of Bible translation work. Instead of quitting, he reworked his translations, and when finished he believed his second translations were better than the first.

We *can* persevere, even when times get tough. But we can't do it alone. Isaiah 40:31 says, "But those who wait on the Lord shall renew their strength; they shall mount up with wings like eagles, they shall run and not be weary, they shall walk and not faint." As we wait on God, He gives us the strength to endure.

Are you about to lose heart? If you want to quit a work the Lord has given you to do, ask God to strengthen you so that you may continue. As He gives you strength, take hold of your goal and never let go.

A lot of impulsive mistakes are made by people
who simply aren't willing to stay bored a little longer.

FRANK CLARK

HEART CARE

Keep your heart with all diligence, for out of it spring the issues of life.

PROVERBS 4:23

Have you had a heart exam recently? I don't mean the kind in which a doctor listens to the physical health of your heart through a stethoscope. I mean an examination in which the Holy Spirit determines the *spiritual* state of your heart.

The Bible always addresses sources of things, and as shown in Proverbs 4:23, Scripture recognizes that people are more frequently moved by their emotions than by their intellect. Our emotions influence our intellect more than our intellect affects our emotions. We do base our faith on rational thought, but faith is not without emotion or passion. Indeed, the very heart of our faith is the Passion of Jesus Christ.

Why do we need to understand the relationship between the heart and the head? Because Jesus said that out of the heart proceeds all manner of evil: adultery, murder, theft, and so on. Out of the heart "springs the issues of life." Therefore, we need to watch our hearts very carefully.

What kinds of "heart disease" do we need to watch for? The heart can become inflamed by passion and lust, so we need to watch its "temperature" and not allow such things to start. Unfortunately, the temperature of the heart often reaches high degrees quickly, and if left unchecked, all sorts of immorality can break forth. The Bible clearly communicates that Christians must check evil at the very first impulse. No one can imprison us for our thoughts, but our unchecked thoughts may very well land us in hell because evil thoughts testify to an evil heart.

The Scripture says that we need to bring every thought into captivity to Christ. To do that we need to set a guard, a watchman, over our hearts in the same way the Bible tells us that we should place a guard at the door of our lips to watch what we say.

Do you have a guard over your heart? If you don't, invite the Holy Spirit to take that post today, examining your heart regularly to keep you in tiptop spiritual condition.

Private victories precede public victories.

STEPHEN COVEY

THE CROWN OF A GODLY MOTHER

*…when I call to remembrance the genuine faith that is in you, which dwelt
first in your grandmother Lois and your mother Eunice…*

2 TIMOTHY 1:5

What influence has your mother had on your life? If someone wanted to quote you on the impact your mother has had on you, what would you say?

Many outstanding people in this world have attributed their accomplishments to their mothers. Thomas Edison, that famous inventor, wrote, "I did not have my mother long, but she cast over me an influence that has lasted all my life. The good effects of her early training I can never lose…My mother was the making of me." Charles Spurgeon, perhaps the greatest preacher who ever lived, said, "I cannot tell how much I owe to the solemn words and prayers of my mother." Dwight L. Moody, the great evangelist of a century ago, said, "All that I have ever accomplished in life, I owe to my mother." We even have a statue to a mother in this country. We know it in another context—as the Statue of Liberty. Auguste Bartholdi, its sculptor, used his own mother as his model!

G. Campbell Morgan, one of the great preachers of this century, and his wife reared four sons, all of whom became ministers. At a family reunion, a friend asked one of the sons, "Which Morgan is the greatest preacher?" The son looked at his father for help in answering. His father replied, "Mother!" Her "preaching" had a great impact on their character!

Today, thank God for your mother and for the impact she has had on your life. Make sure to thank her, too, through a phone call, a letter, or a thoughtful gift. Let her know how much you cherish her and her influence.

*At the end of your life, you will never regret not having passed one more test,
not winning one more verdict or not closing one more deal.
You will regret time not spent with a husband, a friend, a child or a parent.*

BARBARA BUSH

"I WILL ANSWER YOU"

*'Call to Me, and I will answer you, and show you great and mighty things,
which you do not know.'*

JEREMIAH 33:3

"Call to Me…" God says in Scripture, yet so many of us are slow to respond to that invitation. Why do we pray so meagerly? I believe it's because unbelief whispers in our ears, "Your prayers won't work. God won't hear them. Others may come and receive all sorts of bounty from God, but not the likes of you, not the one who has so often broken His commandments. God doesn't even want to hear from your lips." Do thoughts of unworthiness creep into your mind, building a wall between you and God? Yet against these whispers of Satan, God's Word speaks to us, "Call to Me…" God reaches out to us, inviting us to reach out to Him.

Yet doubts still discourage us from praying. Inside our heads we hear, "Prayer will do no good because God will not answer. I've tried before, and I haven't received answers." Have you ever felt that way? Then read the second part of Jeremiah 33:3, an assurance that stills such doubts: "I will answer you." God has promised to respond to our prayers.

When we call on God, we can feel confident that He has made us worthy of approaching Him and that He has promised to answer us. We should also keep in mind all the other principles that the Bible teaches concerning prayer. For example, to maintain an open prayer line to God we must confess our sins and ask for forgiveness, while forgiving those who have sinned against us. Another principle is that we must call upon God in faith, believing He will do that which we ask of Him. The Scripture says that whatsoever you shall ask, believe that God will give it, and you shall have it. We should also call upon God with great perseverance and ask according to His will. Finally, we should pray with gratitude, thanking God for all He has already done.

How's your prayer life these days? Are any of the concerns I mentioned earlier stopping you from fully enjoying your connection to God? I invite you to call to God and remember His promise to answer you. Do these things, and wait for God to show you "great and mighty things"!

More things are wrought by prayer than this world dreams of.

ALFRED LORD TENNYSON

HEROES WANTED!

*'Now therefore, give me this mountain...It may be that the Lord will be with me, and
I shall be able to drive them out as the Lord said.'*

JOSHUA 14:12

Suppose, as you looked for a job, you came across this ad in the classifieds: "Heroes wanted. No cowards need apply." Would you apply for that job? Are you a hero?

Most of us have never even considered this matter, but we should, because we desperately need heroes in the army of God. Over and over in Scripture, we read of valiant, mighty men and women, and we're encouraged to follow their examples. The Bible exhorts us to endure hardship as good soldiers of Christ. It admonishes, "Fear not," "Be not afraid," "Be of good courage," "Fear not the face of men." Such courage is the mark of a hero.

Why do we need so much courage? Because Jesus has commissioned us as His soldiers to witness for Him. We have the privilege of serving as Christ's ambassadors to this dying world, sharing the good news of what Jesus can do for people.

Yet tragically, many people who profess to be Christians have gone AWOL (Absent WithOut Leave) in this regard. The battle for lost souls rages on, but many of us hide in our own secure corners of the world, leaving the lost vulnerable to the enemy.

This should not be true of the soldiers in Christ's army. After all, our leader, Christ, is the greatest hero Who ever lived. Not only did He single-handedly take on all the hosts of mankind, an apostate Jewry, a hostile heathenism, and His own friends who forsook Him, but He also took on the forces of death, hell, Satan, and the demons, overcoming them one and all! And as God's soldiers, we have Christ's death-defeating power on our side! We need not fear as we share the gospel of Jesus Christ. As we face the fray, Jesus Christ heats the heart and fuses the shifting sands into rock, making heroes out of cowards. Christ stands ready to do that for each of us.

Will you allow Christ to grant you his courage today? If you do, be a faithful soldier, using that courage to share Christ's good news with somone who desperately needs to hear it.

...Brethren, we are treading where our Captain trod...

"ONWARD CHRISTIAN SOLDIERS" (HYMN)

May 14
TRUST IN THE LORD

Trust in the Lord with all your heart, and lean not on your own understanding;
in all your ways acknowledge Him, and He shall direct your paths.

PROVERBS 3:5–6

We can go through this world in one of two ways: remembering God, focused on eternity, and trusting Him with all our hearts or forgetting God and leaning on our own understanding to make it through this life.

Which camp are you in?

"Trust in the Lord with all your heart...and He shall direct your paths." God makes this great promise to us, a covenant that offers great blessings to those who will heed it daily. "Trust in the Lord with all your heart." It's a primary lesson of Christianity, a seemingly simple essential of our faith. Yet we seem to find it so difficult to learn. We learn to trust in God just a little bit and think we've made great progress in the spiritual realm. But then we face situations that reveal vast areas of our hearts that we've never entrusted to God.

In these times, we may believe we've given our trust to God and wonder why He hasn't responded. But really, we lean on our own understanding and strength to work it out. We attempt to achieve our will through praying certain ways and doing good deeds. But it isn't until we've exhausted our resources and truly trusted God, laying our burdens at His feet, that He provides a way. "Acknowledge Him, and He shall direct your paths."

Who are you trusting to carve out your life pat—you or the Lord? God says, "Trust me." How can you do that today?

...They who trust Him wholly find Him wholly true...

"LIKE A RIVER GLORIOUS" (HYMN)

SELF-CONFIDENCE OR CHRIST-CONFIDENCE

*Some trust in chariots, and some in horses; but
we will remember the name of the LORD our God.*

PSALM 20:7

Let's say you've come up against the toughest trial of your life, an obstacle many others have failed to overcome. (Maybe you're facing it today!) What's your first response? Do you forge ahead, or do you fall to your knees?

Israel faced an obstacle too big for its own might to overcome; his name was Goliath. All of the armies of Israel had self-confidence until they faced this giant. Then where did their self-confidence go? It failed them. But one young man, David, completely lacked self-confidence. He had another kind of confidence— confidence in the living God. David said to Goliath, "I come to thee in the name of the Lord of hosts…whom thou hast defiled." When everyone else cowered in fear, David, the boy whose confidence was in God, went forth to victory.

We all need confidence. But the question at hand is: "Confidence in whom?" If we rely on our own power, we lean upon a weak reed indeed. When we have confidence in ourselves, two things invariably follow: (1) If we succeed, we become prideful, and (2) if we fail, we are cast into despair and depression.

We live in a day when hundreds of books and seminars preach self-confidence. But these messages fly in the face of the God's Word, which declares, "Cursed is the man who trusts in man and makes flesh his strength" (Jeremiah 17:5). Self-confidence is a snare and an illusion.

How much better to trust the One who made you than to trust in yourself. Confidence in God delivers us from pride by giving us gratitude to God for victory in our lives. It delivers us from despair because we know that whatever comes to pass, God will work it together for our good. Those who trust in God go through life with a certain tranquillity that allows them to pass over the rough spots of life virtually undisturbed. We need to trust in God not only for our eternal salvation but also for the everyday affairs of our lives. When we would fail ourselves, God will never disappoint us!

Are you facing a Goliath in your life today? Like David, place your confidence in God, and wait for your victory through Him.

Jesus never fails.

CHRISTIAN SONG

THE LEGACY OF CHRIST

'Peace I leave with you, My peace I give to you; not as the world gives do I give to you.
Let not your heart be troubled, neither let it be afraid.'

JOHN 14:27

Do you ever feel that life moves too fast? Perhaps you can relate to the old saying "Stop the world—I want to get off!" Sometimes the world spins too fast; one day melds into the next; and, despite our frenzied and harried pace, we fall further and further behind on our obligations.

But God doesn't want us to live this way. He wants us to *"be still* and know that I am God." Jesus says to us, "Come unto me all you who are weary, and I will give you rest." In fact, God instituted the Sabbath, an important time of rest. When was the last time you sat still in God's presence, enjoying His rest?

We desperately need "downtime." Dr. Richard Swenson, author of *Margin,* a book about reducing stress, says that we need to restore what he calls our "margins," our reserves. He points out that we live overloaded lives today. But, Swenson says, we can't deplete our spiritual, emotional, physical, financial, and time reserves for too long without paying for it in one way or another.

Jesus left a legacy to His disciples, a legacy we share in, a legacy that keeps us from depleting all our resources. What is this legacy? His peace. Christ declares to us, "Peace I leave with you, My peace I give to you." Oh, how we need it in these troubled times when people's hearts literally fail them for fear! Threats of terrorists and crime rob millions of people of peace. Job insecurity steals people's serenity. Nervous breakdowns abound. Pharmacies sell tranquilizers by the millions of pounds each year. We desperately need Christ's peace, and to gain it, all we need to do is surrender ourselves to God. We find the secret of peace in trusting in His perfect will for our lives, yielding ourselves to rest in His trustworthy arms.

Do you need a dose of peace today? Just look to Christ, the sovereign Lord of all history. He will bring His perfect will to fruition as you trust in Him. Whatever your problems, fix your eyes upon Jesus, and peace will flood your soul.

Don't wrestle, just nestle.

CORRIE TEN BOOM

THE COLD PHARISEE

*'I tell you, this man went down to his house justified rather than the other; for everyone who
exalts himself will be abased, and he who humbles himself will be exalted.'*

LUKE 18:14

Do you have confidence that God finds you acceptable? If so, upon what do you
base your confidence?

The Pharisees believed that God found them acceptable based on their
goodness. The Pharisees trusted in their works. Jesus tells us that they even
prayed to themselves: "The Pharisee stood and prayed thus with himself." As
time went on, they became increasingly holy in their own eyes.

But Christ found them greatly lacking. He didn't base their acceptability on
their deeds; he based it on the state of their hearts.

We can classify sin in many ways. Let's consider the notion of "hot" and
"cold" sins. Hot sins are those of passion. These would include such things as
adultery, stealing, anger, murder, fornication, and rape. Most of us consider
these the most heinous of all sins, and to be sure, the Pharisees avoided such
actions. But to the cold sins God turns His hottest words. He scorns sins of self-
righteousness, harboring a condemning spirit, pride, and despising others.
Against this sort of sin Christ leveled His greatest attacks, and the people most
guilty of them were the Pharisees.

So often we trust in ourselves, building our hope of heaven on nothing
more than our own self-righteousness, our own piety, and our own benevolence. We believe we can achieve our own salvation by keeping the commandments and fulfilling ceremonial duties. But if we base our salvation on such
things, we'll find ourselves sadly mistaken. We could *never* do enough to earn
our own passage to heaven. Only Jesus Christ can save us through His blood.

Today thank Jesus for His sacrifice, which has made your sanctification
possible. Ask God to give you a humble and thankful heart every day that you
may remember the true Source of your salvation.

People who are wrapped in themselves make small packages.

BENJAMIN FRANKLIN

HE RESTORES MY SOUL

He restores my soul…

PSALM 23:3

Have you felt run-down lately? Do you need a little refreshment or maybe even a full-blown vacation? We all feel that way at times. Because of the Fall, everything in this world runs down, including us. We experience this in the spiritual realm as well as in the physical.

But Jesus Christ is the great restorer. When we feel drained, we can rely on Him to rejuvenate us. He says, "Behold, I make all things new," and nothing exists that he can't rebuild or renew. Jesus restores:

speech to the dumb;	sight to the blind;
food to the hungry;	hearing to the deaf;
sanity to the demoniac;	tranquillity to the sea;
strength to the weak;	life to the dead;
joy to the bereaved;	health to the sick;
purity to the prostitute;	dignity to the despised;
hope to the believer;	grace to humankind.

He is indeed the great restorer of all things! And He can make our souls new, even if we've backslid. I spoke recently with a man who at one time walked with Christ but then fell away significantly. But, he told me, God had restored his soul and given him a joy he hadn't known in decades. Many times when we fall, we think God is angry. Satan accuses us, "You've blown it! It's all over. He wants nothing to do with you anymore." But that's not true. Just as a shepherd searches for a lost sheep, so Christ the good shepherd will come seeking us if we've gone astray. He'll restore our souls as we return to Him.

For whatever reason you may feel run-down, ask Jesus to restore you. Allow His love and power to rejuvenate you as you rest in Him.

When Satan reminds you of your past, remind him of his future.

BUMPER STICKER

THE PARABLE OF THE WEDDING FEAST

*'…when the king came in to see the guests, he saw a man there who did not have on
a wedding garment. So he said to him, "Friend, how did you come in here without
a wedding garment? And he was speechless.'*

MATTHEW 22:11–12

Can you imagine being invited to a royal wedding? For most of us, our first response would be "But I have nothing to wear!" Then we'd go to great lengths to prepare for the event, scouring all the best stores for the most suitable gown or tuxedo, not to mention all the appropriate accessories!

Well, the invitations have gone out, not for the wedding of the century, but for the wedding feast of the ages. And *you* are invited!

In the parable of the wedding feast, Jesus says that the King of kings has invited many to come celebrate with Him, but some of them won't come. So the King invites more to attend. Those who accept the invitation must carefully choose what to wear. Would any store sell a dress fine enough? Would any tailor sew an outfit appropriate for the great wedding feast of the Lamb? No, nothing we could find would be good enough, so God Himself has provided a shining white robe for each of us to wear. That robe is the righteousness of Jesus Christ. It is the only proper outfit, and woe to the person who tries to get into the banquet—heaven—without it.

God will immediately spot those at the banquet who do not wear the wedding garment. In the parable, the man without a wedding garment represents all those who have joined the Church for reasons other than love for Christ. He represents all who profess what they do not possess. Many people claim to be Christians, but they haven't truly given their hearts to Jesus Christ. As the king in the parable cast out the man without the wedding garment, so, too, will God cast from heaven those who do not wear the robe of Christ's righteousness.

Don't miss out on the wedding banquet. Dress for true success by taking Christ's righteousness upon you. Allow His grace to usher you in to the celebration of all time!

Morality may keep you out of jail, but it takes the blood of Jesus Christ to keep you out of hell.

CHARLES SPURGEON

WHO ARE YOUR FRIENDS?

Be not misled: 'Bad company corrupts good character.'

1 CORINTHIANS 15:33, NIV

We are all influenced by each other, and our ideas, thoughts and even mannerisms are shaped by the people around us. Who we choose as friends is critical in terms of who we ultimately become. Choosing godly friends will build us up in the faith and help us to become godly. Conversely, choosing ungodly friends will pull us down.

From the beginning of time, peer pressure has been a major factor in leading people astray. The book of Proverbs contains many practical warnings for us. For example, Proverbs 1:10 instructs: "My son, if sinners entice you, do not consent." Solomon goes on to describe how ungodly acquaintances will try to persuade you to join in their activities.

How can we become close friends with such people and not be influenced by them? We can be friends with the ungodly inasmuch as we attempt to be gracious witnesses to them, but certainly we cannot, as children of God, take our cues from them or engage in their wicked activities.

The destructive effect of friendships with the wrong people can be seen in the results of a recent survey of inmates in an Illinois prison. Do you know the main reason for their criminal behavior? Not broken homes, poverty, or lack of positive opportunities in life. The main reason the prisoners cited for their wayward lives was their friends: peer pressure.

Don't be misled: Bad company corrupts good character. Let's commit to choosing our friends and associates carefully—even prayerfully.

Associate yourself with men of good quality…'tis better to be alone than in bad company.

GEORGE WASHINGTON

THE PRODIGAL SON

Then He said, 'A certain man had two sons.'

LUKE 15:11

Author Charles Dickens, who knew a great tale when he heard it, remarked that the greatest story in all literature was the parable of the prodigal son. For the next few days, we'll examine this story that earned such distinction.

To begin our examination, let's briefly review the story. You will recall that the parable is about a father and his two sons. The younger son came to his father, asking for his share of his inheritance. The father gave it, and the young man left for a far country and squandered the money he received on wild living ("prodigal" means wasteful). The younger son ended up broke and in dire straits, so he returned to his father in repentance. The father embraced him, rejoiced at his return, and celebrated with a feast. The older brother, who had never left home, was jealous of his father's attention toward the younger brother. But the father told the older son that they had good cause to celebrate—the prodigal son had been dead and now was alive. (For the complete parable, read Luke 15:11–32.)

One theologian has pointed out that Christ is always crucified between two thieves: license and legalism. So it is with these two sons, the younger representing license and the older legalism. These two sons paint a picture of the entire human race, the depiction of two apparently opposite and yet related types of sinners. Both rebel in their own ways, alienating themselves from their father. Yet the father loves them both with a love beyond comprehension.

This rich parable teaches many deep truths, but the greatest of these is the love of the Father, who welcomes home those who have fallen into all kinds of sin. Whether we live wildly or we self-righteously judge those who do, the Father loves us and welcomes us home as His children.

Love is God's essence; power but his attribute; therefore is his love greater than his power.

RICHARD GARNETT

THE FAR COUNTRY

'…the younger son gathered all together, journeyed to a far country, and there wasted his possessions with prodigal living.'

LUKE 15:13

Someone once said that people can be divided into two types: givers and takers. The prodigal son in Christ's parable was most definitely a taker. We can paraphrase his first words in the parable as "Gimme. Gimme the goods that fall to me." "Gimme" is his attitude and the attitude of millions of people in our world today.

So the father divided the wealth and gave the son his living. With his newly acquired access to wealth, the prodigal set out for the "far country." Where was that far country? Well, the original hearers of Jesus' parable might have thought it was Babylon or Rome or Corinth. Today a prodigal might set out for New York, Los Angeles, or San Francisco. Harvey Cox described the "far country" as the secular city, the place where most people live today, a world bounded by time with no thought of eternity or of God. People who adopt the secular philosophy don't deny God outright; they merely ignore Him, considering Him irrelevant.

The prodigal son did just that to his father as he set off for the far country. But the far country wasn't all he had dreamed it would be. The prodigal son soon found that out. The more he did what he liked, the less he liked what he did. He looked for liberty; he found tyranny. He looked for friends; he found pigs. He looked for sensuality; he found starvation. Those were the realities of the far country. When the prodigal had spent all he had in riotous living, a mighty famine came over that land, and he found himself in great need. To survive, he ended up feeding pigs, a most debasing task for a Jew. Further, he felt so hungry that he longed to fill his stomach with the slop he fed them! Such are the ravages of sin. It may look so glamorous at first, but it ends up so debasing.

The good news is that though we may venture to that far country, the Father anxiously awaits our return. If we repent and return to the Father, no matter how far we've strayed, He will welcome us in. Have you wandered off? Turn around and come back today. The Father is waiting with open arms.

That which we call sin in others is experiment for us.

RALPH WALDO EMERSON

THE LOVE OF THE FATHER

*'And he arose, and came to his father. But when he was still a great way off, his father
saw him and had compassion, and ran and fell on his neck and kissed him.'*

LUKE 15:20

Do you remember the last time you waited to see someone dear to you? Perhaps
your best friend from childhood visited you from a faraway place. Maybe a
child came home from college. Whoever it was, how did you feel when that
person finally arrived?

The joy we feel at a reunion with a cherished family member or friend is just
the tiniest reflection of our heavenly Father's joy when one of His lost children
returns to Him. We get a wonderful picture of this in the parable of the prodigal
son. When the son returns home, the father runs to greet him and welcomes him
with open arms; so great was the father's love for his child.

The prodigal had finally realized the frivolity of leaving his father's house.
He recognized the error of his ways. As he arose and made his way home, his
father waited and watched. The father's hair had now turned gray, and his heart
had long been broken. Nevertheless, he sat on his rooftop, looking and yearn-
ing and waiting for his beloved son to return.

After waiting for so long, one day the father saw a head rise up over the hill,
then a torso, then a body; and even though the person was clothed in rags, he
recognized the gait. It was his son! The father rushed down the stairs; made his
way out of the house; and, to the amazement of all the servants, took off running.

Some sinners say they'll repent someday…one of these days or when they
lie on their deathbeds. But every day they wait, they put off the tremendous
reunion that awaits them. God waits to take them in at the slightest indication
that they want to come home. To say, "I am going to turn to Christ next week"
or "next month" or "tomorrow" means only that the sinner will spend that
much more time in spiritual squalor while the Father's love and the homecom-
ing celebration wait.

Ah, dear prodigal, you who suppose you have sunk so deeply into the mire
of the far country that God would never want to set His eyes on you again, Jesus
has delineated for you a perfect picture of God's unfathomable love, if you just
turn to God once again, in true confession and repentance. He'll be there, running toward you to embrace you and welcome you home.

[He] who sins and mends commends himself to God.

CERVANTES

May 24

THE OLDER BROTHER

'But he was angry, and would not go in…'

LUKE 15:28

After the prodigal son had returned to his father, there was great rejoicing. Everyone celebrated the prodigal's return…everyone, that is, except the older brother. Instead, he moped, and he lashed out at his father for celebrating his brother's return.

We can put sin into two categories: sins of the flesh, which the prodigal son embodied, and sins of the disposition, which are typified by the older brother. Pride was the older brother's main sin. C. S. Lewis, the great Christian author, has said, "It is pride which has been the chief cause of misery in every nation and every family since the world began. Other vices may sometimes bring people together: you may find good fellowship and jokes and friendliness among drunken people or unchaste people. But pride always means enmity—it is enmity. And not only between man and man, but enmity to God." Since pride produces nothing but misery and division, it is not surprising that the older brother felt miserable and separated himself from his family.

Some people have tried to excuse the older brother's tantrum by saying that it was only a fit of temper and nothing to concern ourselves with. But Jesus had enough concern about it to include it in this parable. We can't dismiss the older brother's outburst, for his tantrum reveals the rottenness of pride at the core of his being, pride which rose to the surface when his brother returned and would rise again the next time someone threatened his self-righteousness.

For as bad as the prodigal's sins were, the older son's sin was worse. While the prodigal came to the father and confessed his sins, the older brother never did. He never entered the house. Night fell and left him outside. And the story ends there. Why? The story ends with the older brother outside in the dark because a person with such a spirit can never enter heaven. That kind of person must become grateful anew for salvation given in grace, never earned. The love of Christ must come into that person's heart to remove the pride from his or her soul.

Does this hit a little close to home? Have you ever found yourself a tad indignant that someone who has sinned so greatly receives the same salvation God gives you? Then confess that pride today. Ask God to remove it from your heart. And thank God that His mercy extends to prideful sinners, too!

Pride and grace dwelt never in one place.

JAMES KELLY

LET US REMEMBER

'…My people have forgotten Me days without number.'

JEREMIAH 2:32

Do you know anyone—a relative, a friend, a hometown hero—who has given his or her life for our country? Memorial Day is a day when we remember those who have made that ultimate sacrifice, who have given their lives that we might enjoy the freedom we have in America today. How easily we forget the terror that filled the hearts of young men when they landed on the beaches of strange islands they had never heard of. How easily we forget the spilled blood of those who lay wounded in foxholes. We forget all those sacrifices in the midst of our modern pleasures and preoccupations.

But today we remember, and well we should. Let us remember Lexington, Concord, Valley Forge, Yorktown, the Battle of New Orleans, Gettysburg, Pearl Harbor, Bataan, Normandy, the Battle of the Bulge, North Africa, Iwo Jima, Guadalcanal, Pork Chop Hill, Korea, Vietnam, and the Persian Gulf, where hundreds of thousands of Americans laid down their lives that we might enjoy this day of peace and freedom.

As we remember those brave men and women, we also need to remember what they fought for. Did they sacrifice their lives for what we see happening in our nation these days, for our plummeting moral standards? Never in the history of the world, one writer has said, has any nation so quickly thrown off its belief system. For scores of years founders, presidents, and Supreme Court justices have said, "This is a Christian nation." But we have forgotten or rejected our heritage by the choices so many of us have made.

Is there anything you can do today to remember not only the men and women who have given their lives for this country but also *why* they gave up their lives? Is there something you can do today—within yourself or with those around you—to help our nation get back on course? May God grant that we return to our roots and remember our rich Christian heritage and those who shed their own blood to preserve it.

…the Almighty Being…has kept us in His hands from the
infancy of our Republic to the present day…

ANDREW JACKSON

LOVING CHRIST

'…love the Lord your God with all your heart, with all your soul,
with all your mind, and with all your strength.…'

MARK 12:30

Have you had the wonderful experience of falling in love with someone? If you have, then you know how it changes your whole outlook on life. The grass looks greener. Music sounds more beautiful. Everything becomes more positive.

If this is true for human love, how much more for divine love? Christ loves us intimately, and He is more than worthy of our affections in return. Since the Son of God came to earth, we have the great privilege of knowing Him personally, walking humbly with Him each day, and loving Him intimately.

How can we tell if we love Jesus? Of course, we know we love Him when we obey His Word. But we can also tell whether we love Jesus in the same way we know whether we love a fellow human being. When we truly love someone, we love to talk with that person. We desire to pour out our hearts and souls to them. We feel confident that our beloved understands us and likes to listen to us. But we also love nothing more than to hear from our beloved. If he or she is away, we eagerly anticipate phone calls and letters from that person. And each time we interact with our beloved, we want to discover more and more of that person's character, thoughts, likes, and dislikes. We're not satisfied until we know that person well, knowing what he or she thinks about everything. And when we really love someone, we want to become the type of person he or she wants us to be.

Such things are second nature when true love is present. And they are the same thoughts and desires we should have for our relationship with God. Do you desire to love God with all of your heart, mind, and soul? If you feel that your relationship with Him could use some improvement, then look to the Cross. Look to that great source of love, and ask Christ to bring a coal from the altar of His love and set a flame in your heart—one that will never be extinguished so you may love Him with *all* your being.

Pray that this day you will fall in love with Jesus afresh.

May 27

THE UNIQUENESS OF CHRIST

'Nor is there salvation in any other, for there is no other name under heaven given among men by which we must be saved.'

ACTS 4:12

Have you ever had an unbeliever tell you that all religions are the same and that one is just as good—or bad—as the other? Many non-Christians seem to believe this. But the truth is that while many religions exist, only one gospel prevails. While many teachers have gained followings, only one Teacher—Jesus Christ—has saved us.

Christ is the solitary and unique Savior of the world. He is unique, first of all, because, unlike prophets of other religions, Jesus Christ founded His religion on Himself, not on His teachings (although His teachings are extremely important). For example, Laotzu, founder of Taoism, said, "Here is the way; walk in it." He taught his followers *a* way. But Jesus said, "*I* am the way, the truth and the life." Christ is the cornerstone of Christianity. You could be a Muslim without knowing much about Mohammed. You could be a Buddhist and know very little about Buddha's life. But you cannot be a Christian without knowing Christ.

Jesus is also unique because, unlike the founders of all other religions, Christ rose from the dead. Go down into the caverns of the dead, and cry out, "Mohammed?" "Here!" "Buddha?" "Here!" "Confucius?" "Here!" "Jesus of Nazareth? Jesus of Nazareth?" You'll hear nothing, because as the angel said, "He is not here, for He is risen, as He said."

Make no mistake: All religions are not the same. Only Christ brings life and immortality to light. Only in Him do we have certain confidence of life everlasting.

If I might comprehend Jesus Christ, I could not believe on Him.
He would be no greater than myself. Such is my consciousness of sin and inability
that I must have a superhuman Saviour.

DANIEL WEBSTER

May 28
SORROW AND SYMPATHY

...the God of all comfort, who comforts us in all our troubles, so that we can comfort those in any trouble with the comfort we ourselves have received from God.

2 CORINTHIANS 1:3–4, NIV

The problem of suffering, or as C. S. Lewis called it, "the problem of pain" has troubled believers for centuries. In fact, an entire book of the Bible—Job— addresses the issue of enduring pain and sorrow. Why does God allow us to go through heartbreaking times of tribulation? Have you ever asked that question? Have you ever cried in despair to God, desperately asking, "Why?" Maybe you're experiencing suffering even now. And if you're like the rest of us, you want nothing more than to purge yourself of all pain, trouble, hurt, and sorrow.

Despite our desperate cries, God often doesn't remove troubles and sorrows from our lives. Why? Because God uses suffering to prepare us for helping others. Through our troubles and sorrows, God molds us into sympathetic and compassionate people. The Bible speaks of comforting those in trouble through the comfort that we ourselves have received from God. Only those who have endured the shadow, who have known suffering and trouble, can adequately comfort others.

In the Old Testament, when a man was ordained to the priesthood, he had water sprinkled on his head, his hands, and his feet. We who are the priests of God, in the universal priesthood of all believers in the new covenant, experience a baptism of tears that prepares us for the office of sympathy.

Where did Paul get the wisdom to write his comforting epistles? Where did David get the inspiration to write those solacing psalms that play such an important role in every believer's life? Where did John get the foresight to write that tremendously hopeful conclusion to the book of Revelation? Each one of them gained the ability to comfort others by experiencing his own tears.

If you know someone experiencing hard times right now, comfort that person. Pray for him or her. Show sympathy and compassion. And if *you* are enduring a difficult time, don't view it as a hopeless, needless tragedy. Perhaps God is using your trial to prepare you for an important work. Ask God today to transform your sorrows into sympathy and empathy.

Sweet are the uses of adversity.

WILLIAM SHAKESPEARE

THE PARABLE OF THE SOWER

...'Behold, a sower went out to sow. And as he sowed, some seed fell by the wayside; and the birds came and devoured them. Some fell on stony places, where they did not have much earth; and they immediately sprang up because they had no depth of earth. But when the sun was up they were scorched, and because they had no root they withered away.'

MATTHEW 13:3–6

Why do some people fall away from the faith and others continue to the end? A person's spiritual staying power depends on his or her inclination upon hearing God's Word. Jesus explained this in detail by telling the parable of the sower. In this parable a farmer sows seeds on four kinds of soil; three were bad, and one was good. Each type of soil represents a way that people might hear God's Word. Today let's consider the first two types of soil and what they represent.

Seed first fell along the wayside path. In Palestine, small farms were divided by paths trampled hard by many feet, both human and animal. As the farmer sowed the seed, some of it fell on this hard-packed dirt. Because the seed was vulnerable on the path, the birds gobbled it up. This hard-packed soil represents the hearts of wayside hearers. Trampled hard by the hoofs of Satan and his herd of lies, lusts, and vanities, God's Word has no place to sink in and take root.

Second, seed fell on rocky soil. This kind of soil was actually slabs of rock protruding from the hills or mountains with only an inch or two of soil on top. That soil was easily warmed by the sun, encouraging the seed to sprout quickly. But when the sun rose high, it scorched the seed. Having no root, the seed died. In the same way, rock-soil hearers feel enthusiastic about God's Word when they first hear it. But while their hearts seem tender to the Word on the outside, inwardly they have no intentions of allowing the Word to change their hearts and lives. The instant that tribulation comes because of God's Word, these people stumble spiritually, unable to withstand the heat.

Do you know people who fall into these two categories? Ask God to soften the soil of their hearts, preparing them to hear His Word and bear its fruit in their lives.

Tomorrow we'll address the third type of soil.

Almighty God of truth and love, To me Thy pow'r import;
The burden from my soul remove. The hardness of my heart.

CHARLES WESLEY

THE CARES OF THE WORLD AND THE DECEITFULNESS OF WEALTH

'…the ones that fell among thorns are those who, when they have heard, go out and are choked with cares, riches, and pleasures of life…'

LUKE 8:14

Yesterday we considered two kinds of "hearers" of God's Word: the wayside hearers and the rocky-soil hearers. Both had hardened their hearts, refusing to allow the Word to penetrate and change their lives. Today we're going to discuss the third kind of hearer that Jesus spoke of in the parable of the sower: the thorny-soil hearer. The farmer cast the seed everywhere, and some of the seed fell on thorny soil. Although the soil richly nourished the seed, the thorns choked the plant so that it couldn't bring fruit to maturity. In the same way, thorny-soil hearers can hear and absorb God's Word, but the cares of the world and the deceitfulness of riches choke them, preventing them from bearing any fruit.

I have known so many people like this. I think of a dear man I know who once told me, "Oh, I haven't got time for spiritual things. I have to make a living. It is so hard these days." Thorny-soil hearers pay too much attention to the cares of this world, forgetting that they will one day die and face God and their cares will disintegrate in His presence. And yet people continue to allow bills, jobs, worries, and anxieties to crowd out the Word. These cares choke out time to serve Christ and to bear fruit. I know of too many people who have gone this way, spiritually strangled to death, never bringing forth fruit to maturity.

What about the deceitfulness of riches? I have seen many people who have prospered, so blessed by God that they no longer concern themselves with the cares of this world, but they have now let riches deceive them. Everything has come their way, and they want more. Instead of God's goodness leading them to trust Him more, their wealth simply brings forth more thorns in their lives. They buy every sort of new gadget and toy and invest in every new luxury to make life exciting. They have no time for God, no time for church. Instead, they say, "I must look after my portfolio." Money in itself is not bad, but the love of money is; it has shipwrecked the faith of many.

Instead of being wayside, rocky, or thorny soil for the seeds of God's Word, we need to be good soil, hearing God's Word, understanding it, and bearing fruit for His kingdom. Today, read God's Word, and let it really sink in. Then let it do its work in your heart so that you might bear its fruit in your life.

The poorest man I know is the man who has nothing but money.

JOHN D. ROCKEFELLER

THE NAME ABOVE EVERY NAME

'And she will bring forth a Son, and you shall call His name Jesus,
for He will save His people from their sins.'

MATTHEW 1:21

Many people are given exalted names but never live up to them. Charles Spurgeon tells about wandering in a cemetery and seeing a headstone inscribed with these words: "Sacred to the memory of Methuselah Coney. Age, six months." (Recall that the biblical Methuselah lived more than nine hundred years!)

The most important name the world has ever heard is the name of Jesus, and Jesus lived up to everything that name foretold. To make sure Mary and Joseph named Jesus properly, God sent angelic messengers to proclaim what His name should be and why. "Jesus" means "Jehovah saves," and Jesus saved all of us from sin. The Bible has many other names for Jesus, but "Jesus" was His personal name, the name we call Him as our friend, the name that celebrates Him as our Savior.

Of course, we've Anglicized Jesus' name. In His Hebrew home, people would have called Jesus "Joshua." That name, common in that time and in ours, celebrates the memory of Joshua, one of the great heroes of Israel. Joshua led God's people into the Promised Land of Canaan and fought to drive out all the Israelites' enemies. During his lifetime, Joshua kept God's people in line so that they walked with the Lord.

Joshua lived up to his name. He saved God's people from earthly enemies and led them to the Promised Land. Jesus lived up to His name by doing something even greater—saving His people from eternal foes and delivering them into an eternal promised land.

As you go about your business today, honor the name of Jesus. Each time His name comes to mind, dwell on the fact that He has lived up to the promise of His name by saving you from sin and death for eternity.

Jesus Christ [is] the condescension of divinity and the exaltation of humanity.

PHILLIPS BROOKS

THE TEN COMMANDMENTS TODAY

Now by this we know that we know Him, if we keep His commandments.

1 JOHN 2:3

In numerous classes, to hundreds of people, I have posed this question: "Can anyone tell me any one single thing any person can do that would please God other than obey His law?"

What would you say?

It's a tough question, and so far, no one in my classes has come up with an answer. Some have said, "Well, we could love God," and to do so would be to obey what Jesus said was the first and greatest commandment: to love the Lord our God with all of our heart, strength, and mind. But many others hold the erroneous belief that because Christians are saved by faith—without having done anything to earn our salvation except receive Jesus' free gift of grace—that we do not have to keep God's laws after we're saved.

That's not what the apostle Paul teaches. In Romans 3:31, he asks and answers the question about keeping the law: "Do we then make void the law through faith? Certainly not! On the contrary, we establish the law." When God gave His law in the Old Testament, He also promised to purify us and write His law on the walls of our hearts. Then we would no longer be like the wild horse that does not want to submit to a bridle and does everything in his power to fight against it. Instead, we'd be like the tame horse that willingly and gladly submits to the guidance of his master and wears the bridle.

God promised to take away our wildly rebellious hearts and give us new hearts of glad submission. Because of our new hearts, we can say with David, who was called a man after God's own heart, "Oh, how I love thy law. It is my meditation day and night." This should be the attitude of our heart. We should believe, as the apostle Paul did, that God's law is good and just and holy. We should remember Jesus' teaching, "If you love me, keep my commandments."

Will you covenant with me today to obey God's commandments, showing your gratitude to and love for Him by doing so?

If we do not have a law of God, how shall we know His will?

HORATIO BONAR

HOW TO INTERPRET THE TEN COMMANDMENTS

'I am the Lord your God, who brought you out of the land of Egypt...'
EXODUS 20:2

In the next few days, we'll take a close look at each of the Ten Commandments. But before delving into each one, let me make a few general observations that should help you better understand all of them. First, each commandment contains both a negative action and a positive action for us to obey. For example, when a commandment forbids murder, it inherently commands us to sustain life. When it forbids adultery, it commands purity. When it forbids theft, it commands honesty. As we dwell on each commandment in the next few days, think of both sides to each one, and brainstorm ways to incorporate the positive action in your life.

Second, when a commandment condemns one offense, this offense represents and includes all similar offenses. For example, when a commandment forbids adultery, it also forbids all other forms of unlawful sex—fornication (sexual intercourse between unmarried people), incest, sodomy or homosexual offenses, and beastiality. When reading about each commandment, spend a moment or two thinking of how each commandment extends to other actions. Commit yourself to being obedient in these implicit areas as well as in the explicitly commanded one.

Third, whatever a commandment forbids is forbidden in actions, *words,* and *thoughts.* The commandments reach into the secret places of our hearts. They don't allow us to call ourselves righteous when we cover up evil motives with charming behavior. For example, Jesus said, "Whoever is angry with his brother without cause shall be in danger of the judgment." So consider ways you can obey each commandment not only in deed but in word and thought, then commit yourself to maintaining high standards in all three areas.

As you meditate on the Ten Commandments in the coming days, keep all these things in mind. As you do, you'll discover how to better express your love to God. And the more you obey Him, the more He will show Himself and His will to you.

God gave us the Ten Commandments, not the Ten Suggestions.

TED KOPPEL (PARAPHRASED)

NO OTHER GODS

'You shall have no other gods before Me.'

EXODUS 20:3

A class of college students had the assignment of ranking the Ten Commandments in order of importance as they saw them. The students ended up reversing the order. At the bottom of the list, they placed the command "You shall have no other gods before Me."

Where would you have ranked this commandment?

Many people today utterly forget their Creator. They offer Him no praise or thanks. They don't even give Him a second thought.

When God says we must have no other gods before Him, He doesn't give us free license to have other gods as long as we place Him in front of the line. God didn't want the Israelites—or us—to have any other gods at all. The Hebrew people lived in the midst of a society that worshiped the gods Moloch, Baal, and Mammon. Moloch was the god of cruelty who demanded child sacrifices. Baal was the god of lust. Mammon was the god of money. Many today still worship these three gods, although not by the same names.

The First Commandment covers a multitude of actions we should avoid. Some of the sins forbidden by the First Commandment are: atheism (denying or not having a God); idolatry (worshiping any other god instead of the one true God); not standing up for God; neglect of anything due or required by Him; hatred of God; self-love and self-seeking (putting self above God); anything that takes our mind off God completely or in part, such as unbelief, heresy, distrust, despair, hardness of heart, and pride; tempting God; lukewarmness; consulting with the devil; slighting and despising God; resisting and grieving His Spirit; and accusing God falsely.

After reviewing such a list, who can possibly claim not to have violated this commandment? But, thankfully, if we confess our sins, God is faithful and just to forgive our sins and to cleanse us from all unrighteousness.

Do you need to put away any behaviors that hinder you from honoring God first and completely?

Eternal Father of my soul, let my first thought today be of Thee, let my first impulse be to worship Thee…let my first action be to kneel before Thee in prayer.

JOHN BAILLIE

BESIDE ME THERE IS NO OTHER GOD

For I do not desire, brethren, that you should be ignorant…

ROMANS 11:25

Do you know God? Not just know *about* Him, but really *know* Him? Do you know that we *can* know God, for He has come into this world and revealed Himself to us through Jesus Christ?

Agnostics believe that God is essentially unknowable. Thomas Huxley coined the term "agnostic" in the nineteenth century. The term comes from two Greek words: *nosis* (to know) and *a* (to take away). Although "agnostic" is a relatively new English word, its Greek equivalent occurs frequently in the Scriptures. Paul says, "I do not desire, brethren, that you should be ignorant." The word "ignorant" is a Latin word derived from the Greek word *agnostis*. "Agnostic" and "ignorant" mean exactly the same thing: "not to know God."

While agnostics claim that any attempt to know God is futile, Scripture tells us differently. The Bible says that we can know God because He has revealed Himself to us. In Isaiah, Jehovah says, "I am Jehovah. I am God, and beside Me there is no other God." He also says, "I am Jehovah, I am the Savior and beside me there is no Savior." In the New Testament, we read of the One set forth as God: "In the beginning was the Word, and the Word was with God, and the Word was God." "And the Word became flesh and dwelt among us." And Thomas knelt at the feet of Jesus and said, "My Lord and my God!" Luke tells us that "there is born to you this day in the city of David a Savior, who is Christ the Lord."

Jesus Christ is the "down-to-earth" revelation of God as expressed in the New Testament. He is none other than the great *"I Am,"* the great Jehovah, the Creator of the universe. God in the form of Jesus Christ has come to bring us out of the bondage of our sin through His sacrificial death.

You and I have the privilege of knowing God—the all-powerful, all-knowing creator of the universe—on a personal level! Allow God to reveal Himself to you through Scripture, through Jesus Christ, and through the ways He touches your life today.

I am convinced of God by the order out in space.

EUGENE A. CERNAN (ASTRONAUT)

GRAVEN IMAGES

'You shall not make for yourself any carved image, or any likeness of anything that is in heaven above, or that is in the earth beneath, or that is in the water under the earth.'

EXODUS 20:4

Read that verse again. Think about it. What does it mean to you?

Over the years, people have held varying interpretations of that verse. Some people believe that the Second Commandment forbids *any* kind of visual art including television, motion pictures, books, paintings, and pictures. But this interpretation doesn't fit with God's instruction to Moses to build a tabernacle that included visual representations such as embroidery and pictures of flowers and trees. Others believe the Second Commandment forbids three-dimensional art such as statues. But this interpretation doesn't fit either. If this interpretation were correct, then why would God command Moses to adorn the tabernacle with three-dimensional figures of oxen and cherubim?

These interpretations rely on extremely literal readings of the verse. Let's take a step back to grasp the bigger picture behind the words. The Second Commandment doesn't forbid any art form in and of itself. In fact, God loves beauty and has given it to us in abundance. We can use Christian art to glorify God and to produce additional beauty in the world. We can also use it to communicate God's truth. Pictures bring to mind great scenes of Jesus finding the lost sheep, healing the blind man, or inviting all to come to Him.

Instead of forbidding artwork, the Second Commandment actually forbids *idolatry*—worshiping a work of art in place of worshiping the living God. That's why the Israelites shouldn't have made the golden calf, not because it was a three-dimensional statue, but because they worshiped it instead of God. The Second Commandment commands intolerance of other gods and other religions. While intolerance sounds harsh, God means it for mercy. God is like a parent who won't tolerate His child eating junk food because it deprives the body of nutrients—He knows that when we worship a false god we deprive ourselves of His greatest blessings and highest good.

Today take a few minutes to evaluate what you worship. If you find it isn't God, then reorder your priorities so that He is first in your life, before anything humankind has created.

God forbids us to have other gods instead of Him…That is when we fear, love, or trust any person, thing, or creature as we should fear, love, and trust in God alone.

MARTIN LUTHER

IDOLS OF THE MIND

'…He who has seen Me has seen the Father…'

JOHN 14:9

There are many idolaters among us today. We may not carve gods from wood or stone, but we often shape an idol in our mind—a cheapened image of God. We carve God up until we've whittled Him down to our own liking. Then we bow down and worship the image we've made. We deceive ourselves into thinking we're worshiping the true God when we're doing nothing of the kind.

We need to throw away our limited understanding of God and seek out His true nature. How can we do this? By looking to Jesus Christ. The New Testament declares that Jesus Christ is the exact image of the invisible God. In all of His attributes—His mercy, purity, sinlessness, grace, love, holiness, and righteousness—Jesus Christ reflects God's image because Jesus Christ *is* God in the flesh. Only by examining Jesus Christ can we ever discover what God is like.

Michelangelo once found a great slab of marble so large that no one else would use it. He had a specific purpose for this marble. Before he began his work, Michelangelo built a shed around the marble so that no one could see it. For months he worked, allowing no one to view his progress. Finally, it was completed, and Michelangelo unveiled his great statue of David. Why didn't he allow anyone to see it before completion? Because he didn't want people forming wrong ideas about it until it had reached perfection.

In the same way, God in Old Testament times forbade humans to make any image of Himself because their view of Him was incomplete. Finally, in the fullness of time, God revealed the exact and perfect image of His own nature in the person of Jesus Christ.

Superficial minds see a resemblance between Christ and the founders of empires and the gods of other religions. That resemblance does not exist.

NAPOLEON

HONORING GOD'S NAME

'You shall not misuse the name of the Lord your God,
for the Lord will not hold anyone guiltless who misuses His name.'

EXODUS 20:7

Can you remember the last time you heard someone using God's name in vain? People do this so regularly that it often doesn't register in our minds anymore. In fact, blasphemy and profanity are so common these days that Hollywood film producers feel they must include them in their pictures to draw crowds.

This wasn't always so. In Old Testament times, no one could even speak God's name (Yahweh) except the high priest, who could say it only once a year (when he entered the Holy of Holies). Whenever the scribes who copied the Old Testament Scriptures came to God's name, they had to bathe, change their clothes, change their pens, confess their sins, and pray before they could write it. Then with great reverence they'd dip their pens into the ink only once. They wouldn't dip their pens again in the middle of writing God's name. That's the kind of reverence God's name deserves.

Some people say, "Taking God's name in vain is just a habit. I don't mean anything by it. I don't even realize I'm doing it." How sad that we sin so repeatedly that our consciences have become seared and hardened, making us unaware of our ungodliness and wickedness. Such people often find their lives crumbling around them, and they don't know why. They don't realize that God punishes those who take His name in vain.

Despite God's clear command to treat His name reverently, many continue to swear. Jesus tells us the reason for this. He says that the mouth speaks from the abundance of the heart. If your heart is a sewer, your mouth will be a gutter. But when God cleanses your heart, your lips become clean.

Do you struggle with taking God's name in vain? If so, ask God to purify your heart. As you submit to His cleansing, He will replace your foul speech with a purity only He can give.

Surely a good actor can communicate his intentions without resorting to profanity.
In the golden age of Hollywood, they did all the time.

June 8

KEEPING THE SABBATH HOLY

'Remember the Sabbath day, to keep it holy.'

EXODUS 20:8

When Sunday rolls around, do you take the day off to play, rest, dwell on God, and interact with family and friends? Or do you see Sunday as another day to clean the house, catch up on work, weed the garden, and wash the car?

While under attack by many today, the Sabbath is a blessing, not a curse. When God created the earth, He created the Sabbath as part of the weekly cycle of life. It is a day of *rest*—something sorely needed these days. In commanding us to observe the Sabbath, God has given us a greater life—time to rejoice and laugh and praise Him. We need to set aside this time to be with our families, to study the Bible in depth, to serve, to rest.

In 1618, Great Britain's King James I wrote a book on sports in which he encouraged all Englishmen to play sports on the Sabbath afternoon. This idea upset many Christians and pastors, becoming one of the reasons the Puritans left England within the next couple of decades. In fact, the Pilgrims and Puritans sacrificially dedicated themselves to obedience of this command. The Pilgrims' voyage to America on the *Mayflower* took many months. A storm finally blew them into Plymouth on a Sunday morning and landed them on Clark's Island across from the rock where they finally came ashore. Despite their long containment on the boat, they didn't rush off it on that Sunday morning. Instead, they honored the Sabbath, attending worship services and praising God. The next morning they landed on Plymouth Rock.

Eric Liddell, the hero of *Chariots of Fire,* also observed the Sabbath and received tremendous blessing for it. Though the Olympic committee had planned his race for a Sunday, he refused to run. He gave up his spot that day, and for all he knew, he had given up his chance for an Olympic medal. But the committee allowed him to run the 400-meter race (which he had never before run), and despite his inexperience, Liddell won the gold medal.

If you don't already observe the Sabbath, I encourage you to give it a try this week. Set aside Sunday to worship, rest, and rejuvenate. As you do, I'm certain you'll discover the Sabbath is a *blessing* of renewal and rest, for God's glory and your good.

As the Sabbath goes, so goes the nation.

THEOLOGICAL MAXIM

HONOR TO PARENTS

*'Honor your father and your mother, that your days may be long
upon the land which the LORD your God is giving you.'*

EXODUS 20:12

Do you remember the old slogan from the sixties "Never trust anyone over thirty"? For many in our culture, "authority" has become a dirty word. While all authority figures have been the target of this attitude, it seems particularly directed toward parental authority. But God, who is outside our ever-fluctuating social trends, tells us something quite different. In fact, He *commands* the opposite. In the Fifth Commandment, He tells us to *honor* our parents.

Some people suppose that this commandment deals only with children obeying their parents. It is true that when we are children, we must obey our parents, but later we can honor them, show them respect, and care for them. As we grow into adulthood, our relationships with our parents and our responses to their authority will determine our responses to other authority figures. In our egalitarian society, we tend to lose sight of the fact that the world consists of relationships between superiors and subordinates—teacher to student, employer to employee, and God to creature, for example. So the Fifth Commandment addresses an aspect of human nature that extends to every phase of a person's life.

What do we gain by obeying this commandment? God tells us that if we honor our parents we will have long lives. Although this promise is a general principle and not an unconditional promise, we often see that people who honor their parents live to a ripe old age.

How is your relationship with your parents? Do you honor them? Whether they are living or dead, you can show respect to them. How can you honor your parents today?

The thing that impresses me most about America is the way parents obey their children.

DUKE OF WELLINGTON

June 10

GODLY DADS

*And you, fathers, do not provoke your children to wrath, but bring them up
in the training and admonition of the Lord.*

EPHESIANS 6:4

Are you a father? If so, how is your relationship with your children? Are you enjoying a close, nurturing relationship or tolerating a distant, divided one?

Karl Marx once said that in order to take over any nation, one must create a breach between one generation and the next, preventing the transfer of strong values, morals, and beliefs. We saw this in our own nation as the famed "generation gap" between the youth of the sixties and the generation before them came closer to dividing fathers from sons and daughters than anything else in the history of this country. Since that time, we've seen the unraveling of the moral fabric of our nation, making our country vulnerable to influences of all kinds.

But we can have hope. The last verses of the Old Testament describe the greatly anticipated day of the Lord, saying that just before Christ returns, God "will turn the hearts of the fathers to the children, and the hearts of the children to their fathers" (Malachi 4:6). At that time, children and their fathers will bond together once again. Even now we've begun to see a uniting, in heart and mind, of fathers with their sons and daughters.

Are you a father? If so, what part do you play in this promised bonding? Before you know it, your children will be gone. What spiritual and emotional legacy will your children carry with them into adulthood?

I hope that on Father's Day this year all of us who are dads will commit to being godly fathers, bringing up our children in the nurture and admonition of the Lord. We need to teach our children the doctrines of our holy religion. We need to pray with them and for them, especially in these days of moral decline. Today, pray that God will give you the strength and courage necessary to devote your life to Him and to be a godly father.

I believe...that husbands hold the keys to the preservation of the family.

JAMES DOBSON

DO NO MURDER

'You shall not murder.'

EXODUS 20:13

This commandment, though stating a value we all hold, has tipped off some of the most heated debates in our society.

For example, people often debate how this commandment applies to abortion. Some contend that abortion can't be murder because they believe that life doesn't begin at conception. However, the Bible clearly states that a baby has life the moment he or she is conceived. In fact, unlike our culture, the Bible uses the same word for the baby inside the womb as for the baby after birth. Because babies are clearly human beings in God's eyes, even from the first moment of conception, abortion is murder and forbidden by the Sixth Commandment.

Another hot topic tipped off by this commandment is capital punishment. If taking another human life is wrong, how can we turn around and take a murderer's life? Let's go back to the Hebrew to get the answer. In writing the Sixth Commandment, Moses intentionally passed over *nine* different Hebrew words for "kill" and chose the one that means "murder" (*ratsach*). In Exodus 21 God commands that people who commit certain sins should receive the death penalty. The word *ratsach* is not used in these cases, so capital punishment does not equal murder. (Note that killing in self-defense is not murder. In Exodus 22:2 we read that if a thief breaks into a house and the owner kills the thief, the owner won't receive the death penalty because he or she defended home and family.)

Not only does the Sixth Commandment address hot topics, it goes deeper, penetrating to the secret motives of our hearts. Jesus said, "Whosoever is angry with his brother without cause shall be in danger of the judgment." Thus, unrighteous anger is a violation of this commandment. And to fully observe the Sixth Commandment, we must not only avoid murder and unrighteous anger, but we must proactively save lives. Jesus commanded us to feed the hungry, clothe the naked, comfort the sick, visit those in prison, and share the gospel with others.

While most of us don't murder people outright, we may harbor unrighteous anger, or we may neglect helping those in need. What do you need to do to ensure that you obey the Sixth Commandment completely?

Anger is never without a reason, but seldom with a good one.

BENJAMIN FRANKLIN

June 12

ON TAKING YOUR OWN LIFE

…[Judas] went and hanged himself.

MATTHEW 27:5

Yesterday we looked at murder; today we look at suicide, the leading cause of death among young people in America today.

Suicide is the murder of ourselves, and since murder is wrong according to the Sixth Commandment, suicide is wrong. The Bible makes it plain that we have no more right to take our own lives than to take the life of another. Scripture mentions the sin of suicide just five times. In over four thousand years of biblical history, only *five* people took their lives. All five were wicked men such as Judas, who sold the Savior for thirty pieces of silver.

Those who commit suicide take the precious gift of life that God has given them and fling it back in His face. They demonstrate their lack of faith in God's existence and in the fact that God will work all things together for good.

William Cowper, a young Englishman who lived in eighteenth-century London, was so filled with hopelessness that he decided to take his own life. He bought some poison and ate it, but it only made him sick. Then he bought a gun, but it was defective and did not fire. Cowper subsequently tried to hang himself, but the rope broke. Finally he decided he would take a cab to the River Thames and drown himself, but it was so foggy that his cabdriver could not find the river. After two hours, the cabby drove Cowper home. In his room, Cowper opened his Bible and read about how much God loved him. Then and there, he asked Jesus into his heart and wrote the great hymn, "God moves in a mysterious way His wonders to perform; He plants His footsteps in the sea and rides upon the storm."

Jesus can turn even the bleakest circumstances into something beautiful. He not only gives new hope, He is the way, the truth, and the *life!*

Life is worth the living, just because He lives.

"BECAUSE HE LIVES" BY BILL GAITHER

AVOIDING SEXUAL SINS

'You shall not commit adultery.'

EXODUS 20:14

As you well know, we live in a society that laughs at "outdated" ideas about sexual purity and marital faithfulness. Those who live by God's standards are anomalies, called "old-fashioned" and "narrow-minded."

Pardon me for getting a little personal, but how have our society's attitudes affected *your* attitudes?

Let's quickly refresh ourselves on God's commands regarding marital fidelity. God created marriage vows and the marriage union in which a woman and a man become one flesh. A person commits adultery when he or she engages in a sexual union with a person other than his or her spouse. Such unfaithfulness often breaks up marriages, and it's one of the two biblical grounds for divorce. (The other is desertion by an unbelieving spouse.)

What many people don't understand is that splitting up a marriage for any reason other than biblical ones puts both spouses in positions to commit adultery (Matthew 5:32). By marrying, divorcing, remarrying, divorcing, and so on, many people today practice "serial polygamy": having adulterous relations with one person after another, all supposedly blessed by marriage.

Jesus also taught that we could commit adultery in our minds. He said that "whoever looks at a woman to lust for her has already committed adultery with her in his heart" (Matthew 5:28). Considering how pervasive pornography is today, many people violate this command.

God has warned us that no adulterer, no fornicator, no homosexual will go to heaven (1 Corinthians 6:9–10). No matter what we call it, God calls adultery *sin*. God created the Seventh Commandment because He wants the best for us. Sexual immorality destroys the mind, the body, happiness and satisfaction in marriage, and ultimately, the soul. Our heavenly Father doesn't want us to experience any of those consequences.

If you're married, do whatever it takes to guard your precious sexual union. When we follow God's ways, we find what's best for us. But if you've already gone astray in this area, remember that in Christ you can find forgiveness for and freedom from all these things. Confess, repent, and resolve through the Holy Spirit to remain obedient to God's command.

I know Christ can give the power to say no, because He gave it to me.

STEALING

'You shall not steal.'

EXODUS 20:15

Some years ago, the state of Delaware opened a new turnpike. Motorists without exact change could pick up an envelope at the automatic toll booth, take it home, and mail the toll to the state at their convenience. During this experiment, which lasted twenty days, motorists took 26,000 envelopes but returned only 582. Some of the returned envelopes had paper and junk in them, but virtually *none* contained any money.

What would you have done if given the same opportunity?

As our nation moves further away from God, stealing is becoming epidemic. People learn to steal in part because of their upbringing. Once some parents spanked their little girl for stealing. Afterward that little girl dried her tears on a towel her parents had "taken" from a hotel. Schools have also played a part because they no longer post the Ten Commandments on their walls and because they teach that there are no absolute rights or wrongs in life.

But as Christians, God's Word is our standard, and Scripture clearly forbids us to steal. It also commands the opposite positive action—that we be honest and generous. Christ taught that a person must repay what he or she has stolen. In Luke 19, Zacchaeus paid back four times the amount he had stolen as a tax collector. God wants us to have the same repentant attitude when we take what isn't ours.

"But," you say, "I'm not a thief! I've never stolen anything!" While most of us have never held up a bank, a large majority of us have helped ourselves to others' belongings through seemingly harmless actions. Here are some "innocent" ways in which we break the Eighth Commandment (see if you can read this list without wincing): shoplifting, cheating for grades in school, cheating on taxes, ripping pages from library books, marrying or divorcing for money, taking kickbacks on contracts, faking insurance claims, stuffing ballot boxes, borrowing things and not returning them. We also rob God by not paying our tithes.

Do you have a habit or two you need to break to fulfill God's Eighth Commandment? Thankfully, if we've broken the commandment, God grants us mercy and forgiveness through Christ. May God help you be completely honest in all your dealings with others.

A kleptomaniac is a person who helps himself because he can't help himself.

HENRY MORGAN

TO TELL THE TRUTH

'You shall not bear false witness against your neighbor.'

EXODUS 20:16

The Hare Krishna cult (a form of Hinduism) believes there are five circumstances in which one may lie and remain sinless: in marriage, to gratify lust, to save one's life, to protect one's property, and on behalf of Brahma (the highest caste of Hindus). But God is Truth, and He abhors and abominates *all* lying.

The Ninth Commandment forbids lying on several levels. The worst level is perjury—lying about someone in a court of law. Our courts of law recognize this as a gross crime, but in Old Testament times, the people took it even more seriously. A witness who committed perjury would receive the same penalty as the criminal, such as death by stoning. Another level of lying includes the sins of talebearing, faultfinding, and criticizing. We must do nothing that will harm a person's reputation. The third level is speaking falsely to someone.

Just as the Ninth Commandment forbids these three levels of lying, it also requires the opposite positive actions of speaking truthfully and witnessing for God's truth. We must faithfully witness for the Lord and His gospel, even if it costs us our lives. (The word "witness" in Greek is *marturia*, from which we get the word "martyr." This developed because many people in the New Testament lost their lives for bearing witness to the gospel.) Jesus was the ultimate true witness. At the same time that Peter lied in the courtyard, saying, "I do not know this man," Jesus was inside before the Sanhedrin bearing faithful witness to the truth.

Have you lived in line with the Ninth Commandment? If not, choose today to avoid lying on all levels, to speak truthfully, and to witness to God's truth.

The trouble with stretching the truth is that it's apt to snap back.

SATURDAY EVENING POST

BEWARE OF COVETOUSNESS!

*'You shall not covet your neighbor's house…your neighbor's wife…
nor anything that is your neighbor's.'*

EXODUS 20:17

We've all done it, and yet it has been called the sin no one commits. One priest declared that in fifty years of hearing confessions, not one person had ever confessed to committing this sin. Another minister declared that in decades of leading prayer meetings, no one ever mentioned it.

What is this sin? It's covetousness: desiring another's possessions, eagerly wishing for what we don't have. Covetousness is a root sin, a sin committed in the heart that can lead to sins committed outwardly, such as stealing. Covetousness is linked to greed, and the apostle Paul said greed was idolatry.

You can see covetousness everywhere in our culture, including messages that pour out of Madison Avenue. Advertisers prey on our lack for their financial gain. Even bumper stickers often appeal to covetousness, such as the ones that say "Born to shop" or "Whoever dies with the most toys wins." (I prefer the bumper sticker that says, "He that dies with the most toys wins—nothing.")

One day Abraham Lincoln was walking down the street in Springfield, Illinois, holding the hands of his two little boys, who were wailing and crying. A neighbor stepped out of his doorway and said, "Mr. Lincoln, what's the matter with the boys?" Answered Lincoln, "Just the same things that's the matter with the whole world: I have three walnuts and each boy wants two!"

So what's the cure for covetousness? The Bible has the answer. Covetousness, essentially, is fixing our hearts and desires upon the things of this world. But the Bible says, "Set your mind on things above, not on things on the earth" (Colossians 3:2). We need to replace covetousness with contentment, our greed with gratitude.

Today ask God to show you whether covetousness is an unconfessed sin in your heart. Then ask for His grace to give you contentment with and gratitude for the gifts He has given you.

Greed has poisoned men's souls.

CHARLIE CHAPLIN (ON THE EVE OF WORLD WAR II)

THE GREAT COMMANDMENT

' "You shall love the Lord your God with all your heart, with all your soul, and
with all your mind." This is the first and great commandment.'

MATTHEW 22:37–38

Can you imagine someone *commanding love?* We can understand how God can command certain actions or even tell us how to speak or think. But to go into that innermost closet, into the depths of our hearts, and to command us to love, seems a breach of our free will. Yet God *commands* us to love Him.

Why is this the case? There are several reasons. God knows that we're built to love something supremely. If we don't love God, we'll adore something less honorable, less exalted than He. And whatever we love most, we'll inevitably resemble, just as we become like that which we worship. This is why God says that He's a jealous God and that we should have no gods before Him—not for His sake but for ours. God doesn't need our love, nor does He need our worship. In fact, He doesn't need anything from us! But we most definitely need Him. We need to worship and love Him so that our lives might be purified by that love.

If anything can ever lift us from the mire of our sin, it's the power of love. As we love God and others, we'll resist breaching our relationships with sinful thoughts and actions.

Today fix your gaze on Jesus Christ, the Bridegroom, and His love for you, His bride. Let God's love for you kindle in your heart and spirit a greater love for Him.

Oh, how I love Jesus…Because He first loved me!

FREDERICK WHITFIELD

THE MORAL LAW OF GOD

Oh, how I love Your law! It is my meditation all the day.

PSALM 119:97

What is your relationship to God's law? Are you passing acquaintances who wave "hello" from across a great distance but never interact? Or are you in such intimate communion that you hide the Law in your heart, thinking of it constantly?

If you feel a bit distant from God's law, perhaps understanding its origin and purpose will give you the desire to know it better. In the Old Testament, God gave humankind three types of laws: civil laws, ceremonial laws, and moral laws. The *civil* laws helped people interact as a country. God laid down the civil laws because He Himself was King of Israel; no one else had authority to create such laws. If someone broke a civil law, that person would receive a punishment such as bodily harm or even death. These laws disappeared in A.D. 70 when Israel was no longer a theocracy.

The *ceremonial* laws dictated which days to commemorate as a nation—the Passover and the Day of Atonement, for example. These laws also carefully delineated how to celebrate each holy day. The ceremonial laws foreshadowed Christ's coming; since He has come, we no longer observe them.

The third type, *moral* laws, reflect the eternal, holy, and unchangeable nature of God. All the moral laws are summed up in the Ten Commandments. God's moral laws have never passed away and will never pass away. We must obey them always. We need the moral laws because they draw people to Christ. They restrain wicked people. They smash our pride and drive us to our knees. They guide us in the way we should live.

In considering the moral laws, people make two basic errors. Some people believe they can save themselves by keeping the laws. Others believe just the opposite—that if they are saved, they don't have to keep the moral laws. But God wants to create a perfect kingdom of righteousness where, in joyful and willing obedience, men and women yield themselves gladly to God's eternal law because of their love for and gratitude to their Savior and Lord.

Today ask God to show you how to delight in His law. Invite Him to make His law a constant companion for your soul.

It is impossible for us to break the Law. We can only break ourselves against the Law.

CECIL B. DEMILLE (DIRECTOR OF THE TEN COMMANDMENTS)

LAW AND GOSPEL

Do we then make void the law through faith?
Certainly not! On the contrary, we establish the law.

ROMANS 3:31

Now that we've spent the past few days looking at the Ten Commandments, we need to clarify the relationship between the Law and the gospel. Many people don't understand this relationship, but unless we do, we'll live our faith on false pretenses.

The Law reveals to us our need for the gospel. It shows us our sinfulness, for no one, except the Savior, has kept the Law fully. The Law doesn't save us; it condemns us. It shows us our need for salvation. We can gain that salvation only by believing the gospel, the good news that God sent His only Son to die in our place.

This relationship between the Law and the gospel distinguishes Christianity from all other religions. We could boil all those belief systems into a single two-letter word: "do." This is the essence of every pagan religion's message: "Do this; don't do that." Even distortions of Christianity base salvation on that one word.

But the basic message of Christianity is not "do," but "done." "It is finished" were the last words Christ spoke before He died. It is done! Finished! Christ paid the full penalty for our sins. And now, all who trust in Him may have eternal life freely.

We're not saved *by* good works. We're saved *to* them. When God's grace touches our lives, we naturally desire to do good works. As you continue to meditate on the Ten Commandments, remember their rightful place; in obeying them you thank God for that which He has done through the gospel.

The world has many religions; it has but one Gospel.

GEORGE OWEN

June 20

ASSURANCE OF SALVATION

*These things I have written to you who believe in the name of the Son of God,
that you may know that you have eternal life, and that you
may continue to believe in the name of the Son of God.*

1 JOHN 5:13

Do you know for sure that when you die, you'll go to heaven? If you've given your life to Christ, you can *know* that you'll have eternal life because the Bible promises that to you. His Word is true, and it has greatly comforted those at death's door, the great and wise as well as the poor and humble.

When Sir Michael Faraday, the brilliant scientist who discovered magnetism, was on his deathbed, someone asked him, "Sir Michael, what speculations do you have about life after death?" And he replied in astonishment, "Speculations! Why, I have no speculations! I'm resting on certainties! 'I know whom I have believed and am persuaded that He is able to keep that which I have committed unto Him against that day.'"

An elderly Scottish lady lay at death's door. Her pastor asked her, "Sadie, suppose that after all God has done for you, when you die He should still allow you to perish; what then?" She said, "Well, that's up to Him. He will do what He will. But if He does allow me to perish, then He will lose more than I. For though I lose my soul, He will lose His honor. He has promised me in His Word, 'He that trusteth in Me shall never perish.'"

An old fisherman who lived by the sea also came to the end of his days. A friend asked him, "John, do you believe you're going to heaven?" John replied, "Look out the window. Are the seven great stones still there?" The friend said, "Yes." "Is the old mountain crag there?" He said, "Yes." "Are the Three Maidens [a set of mountains] still there?" He said, "Yes." John leaned back and said, "'The mountains shall disappear and the hills shall be cast down, but My Word shall last forever.'"

Today praise the Lord that His Word is true, and thank Him for the assurance you have as you rely upon His Word—that you will live in heaven for eternity.

Blessed assurance, Jesus is mine. Oh, what a foretaste of glory divine.

FANNY CROSBY

MARY SLESSOR OF CALABAR

'...learn from Me...'

MATTHEW 11:29

Would you like to know a great spiritual secret? You can find it in three of Jesus' words: "Learn from Me." When we learn from Him, He will change us from the inside out. Let's consider the example of a great heroine of the faith who submitted to and learned from her Savior.

Mary Slessor, originally from Scotland, is considered one of the first female missionaries. According to her own testimony, she had lived as a "wild lassie" until, by God's grace, she entered the kingdom and eventually traveled to faraway lands to spread the gospel. Barely over five feet tall, Mary was nevertheless a giant among people, a woman of tremendous courage and faith.

In her passion to share the good news with those who desperately needed to hear it, Mary set off to Calabar, the ghetto of Africa. Calabar comprised the worst of nature, both environmental and human. The people who dwelt there were bloody, savage, and cruel. They were fetish worshipers, headhunters, and cannibals. Nonetheless, Mary proclaimed to them the gospel, and, astoundingly, God opened up their hearts. They became willing to hear. One after another they yielded their lives to Christ. And as they did so, they abolished the horrible customs that had plagued them for years.

Mary Slessor gave of herself to Africa for forty years. When she died, thousands of former fetish worshipers, headhunters, and cannibals mourned, saying, "The mother of us all is dead." What was the secret of Mary's life? She had learned from Christ. She had learned of His compassion and His concern for souls. She had learned of His courage. Mary Slessor prayed to and trusted God, saying that prayer was the greatest power God has given into our hands for service. She believed that by God's power she could do all things.

I hope you, too, take this great secret to heart. As you learn from Christ, rely on Him, and seek to do His will, He'll make His power available to you for whatever challenges you face.

Jesus Christ is the center of all, and the goal to which all tends.

BLAISE PASCAL

TO LIVE IS CHRIST

For to me, to live is Christ, and to die is gain.

PHILIPPIANS 1:21

If someone asked you what you live for, how would you respond? Some people seem to live for their next vacation. Others live for their retirement. Still others live for the weekend! But Paul expresses the best way to live. He declares that to live is Christ, and to die is gain.

Too often, people want to rewrite the verse, replacing "Christ" with "pleasure." "For to me, to live is pleasure," cry a whole host of voices today. But pleasures fade quickly, and this lifestyle leads to ceaseless striving for one more thrill, one more good feeling.

Others would replace "Christ" with "money." "For to me, to live is money." These people spend most of their waking hours, energy, and thoughts trying to make money. Some of them desire to be truly wealthy, while others want just a little bit more than they presently have. A reporter once interviewed a fantastically wealthy man and asked him, "How much do you want?" The wealthy man replied, "Just a little bit more." Do you live to gain wealth? If so, may I say that at the end of your life, your wealth will turn to ashes in your mouth, and you'll find that the great deceiver has deceived you.

Others would say, "For to me, to live is fame." They give their whole lives to accomplishment. Perhaps they rise to the top of the ladder. But then where are they? Many people who "make it" find themselves saying, "Is this all there is?" Like many who have risen to the pinnacle of success, they find nothing but the same emptiness that hounded them from the very beginning.

"For to me, to live is Christ." This is the secret of life! Furthermore, it is the secret of consecration, the secret of commitment. I do not believe that you could take the meaning of consecration and commitment and express them more succinctly than Paul has in those seven words. Today ask God to show you how to live so that you can say, "For to me, to live is Christ." Then follow the way He shows you so that you may live a life consecrated and committed to Him.

Our business is to do the will of God. He will take care of the business.

ANONYMOUS

THE SHADOW OF THE ALMIGHTY

He who dwells in the secret place of the Most High
Shall abide under the shadow of the Almighty.

PSALM 91:1

What is your greatest fear, the one thing above all others that makes your eyes widen and your heart race? Some fear death the most. Others fear public speaking even more than death. And still others fear dental exams. Newspaper counselor Ann Landers reports receiving about ten thousand letters each month from people with all kinds of issues that can be reduced to one common problem: fear.

When our faith in Christ disappears, fear takes its place. The Bible says that in the Last Days people's hearts shall fail them for fear. Shakespeare puts it this way: "Cowards die many times before their death; the valiant never taste of death but once." The Bible exhorts us to courage, saying, "Fear not," "Be not afraid," "Be of good cheer," "Be courageous and very strong." This is not advice; it is a commandment.

If you find yourself feeling fearful, Psalm 91 can help you ward off your fear. This psalm was the invocation of the early Church during a time when the disciples suffered great trouble and persecution. Many a young person has gone off to war leaning heavily on its promises. Psalm 91 promises to protect those who "dwell" in God's presence. Someone once said that there are two kinds of people: those who dwell in God and occasionally visit the world, and those who dwell in the world and occasionally visit God. When we dwell too long in the world, fear can overcome us. To experience God's strength and peace, we must abide in Him.

The secret dwelling place of God is His Word. In His Word, God reveals the wonders of His grace and love. Dwelling with God means hiding His Word in our hearts by memorizing it and meditating on it. We also dwell with God when we commune with Him in prayer and seek His purpose in our lives.

Do you often live in fear? If so, begin now the practice of abiding in God's presence. Read His Word, and spend time with Him in prayer. Draw near to Him, and He will grant you His courage.

The emotion of fear is, in itself, no sin. It is the act of cowardice that matters.

C. S. LEWIS

WHERE THERE IS NO VISION

Where there is no vision, the people perish…

PROVERBS 29:18, KJV

Do you have a great vision for your life? Do you have a purpose in mind, a purpose in heart that comes from a vision that inflames your heart with a blue-white flame? Or do you simply live your life because every morning you wake up again and there you are, having to endure just one more miserable day?

I believe we need to have vision for our lives, dreams to reach for, goals to accomplish. As we develop vision, we discover purpose for our lives. If we lack vision, says the Bible, we perish. Though we may not die physically, we become part of the walking dead who view life as having no meaning.

Vision gives significance, value, and meaning to our very existence. If we want our lives to have significance, then each of us needs to take hold of a vision and pursue it. And as Christians, we need to seek God's vision for our lives. We are not free to choose our own; we have been bought with a price. We have a Master and Lord to serve. And our Lord has clearly described His vision for us: reaching the world for Christ. How does God envision fulfilling that goal through you?

If you lack vision for your life, pray that God would reveal to you His vision for you. Ask Him to show you how you fit into His overall purpose: to spread the gospel to those who need to hear it. Then adopt His vision for you as your own.

The poorest man is not he who is without a cent, but he who is without a dream.

PENNSYLVANIA SCHOOL JOURNAL

"WHAT IS YOUR NAME?"

'Be strong and of good courage...'

DEUTERONOMY 31:6

I admire people who display great courage. One man in history known for his courage was Alexander the Great. One day, Alexander held court in Nebuchadnezzar's great palace in Babylon. He sat upon the great golden throne, pronouncing sentences for the crimes charged to his soldiers. The sergeant-at-arms brought in one soldier after another and read their crimes. No one could deliver them from Alexander's severe judgments.

Finally, the sergeant-at-arms brought in a young Macedonian soldier and read aloud his crime: fleeing in the face of the enemy. This cowardice Alexander could not tolerate. But as he looked on this young soldier, Alexander's countenance changed from stern to soft. Smiling, he said to the lad, "Son, what is your name?" The boy said softly, "Alexander." The smile left the king's face. He said, "What did you say?" The young man snapped to attention. "Alexander, sir." The king turned crimson and shouted, "WHAT IS YOUR NAME?" The boy began to stammer and said, "Al...Alex...Alexander, sir." The king burst out of his chair, grabbed the young man by the tunic, stared him in the face, then threw him on the ground and said, "Soldier, change your conduct or change your name!"

All of us have a name from our royal lineage. What is that name? Christian! And we need to live our lives in a manner worthy of that name. Dear friend, I encourage you to be strong. Be courageous. Obey the Lord. Allow God to give you courage in Him—courage to do what God has told us to do, courage to avoid the things God has told us not to do, courage to stand up for Christ. Let us not cower under fire but stand firm in the Lord's name, living up to our calling as Christians.

Courage is the virtue that makes other virtues possible.

WINSTON CHURCHILL

GEORGE WHITEFIELD

'…unless one is born again, he cannot see the kingdom of God.'

JOHN 3:3

Do you ever think about our nation and wonder whether God will renew a land that has sunk to the moral depths that ours has? Is there any hope for the society in which we live? Perhaps we can take a cue from another time, another society.

The period in which we live is not unlike that of the opening half of the eighteenth century, especially in England. At that time, adultery, fornication, gambling, drunkenness, and the breaking of the Sabbath were commonplace. Crime was rampant, and sin was the norm. Sounds rather contemporary, doesn't it?

But then John Wesley and George Whitefield came on the scene, and revival began. It came as an electric shock and galvanized the people of England. As revolution took place in England, the morality and religion of the country changed completely. (In fact, historians say that the Victorian period was in many ways a byproduct of the Wesley-Whitefield revivals.)

God used George Whitefield not only in England but also in America. Whitefield preached in various colonies and helped found the University of Pennsylvania. So great was the change Whitefield sparked that it became known as the Great Awakening.

Whitefield had made England and America his parish. Tens of thousands would come from miles around to hear him preach. What was his life-changing, culture-changing message? The same text that had pulled him into the kingdom of God: "Unless one is born again, he cannot see the kingdom of God." Near the end of Whitefield's life, one of his friends asked him, "Why is it that you preach so often from that text, 'Ye must be born again'?" Whitefield answered, "Because ye must be born again." With this simple message, Whitefield helped transform the core of two countries.

To save our great nation, we, too, must declare throughout the land, "You must be born again!" Perhaps today you can share this message with someone you know.

Take care of your life, and God will take care of your death.

GEORGE WHITEFIELD

WILLIAM CAREY

'For God so loved the world that He gave His only begotten Son...'

JOHN 3:16

How big is your God? Is He bound by the limitations of what you can see, hear, and think? Or do you have a God who can do anything at any time? Today, let's consider a great man who believed in a *great* God—William Carey, the father of modern missions. Carey lived by the motto "Attempt great things for God. Expect great things from God."

For centuries, worldwide missions had come to a virtual standstill. But William Carey, a cobbler who lived in England in the eighteenth century, explored God's Word and became increasingly convinced that God was concerned about the *whole* world—"For God so loved the *world.*" This conviction began a burning in Carey's heart. He envisioned millions of people perishing throughout the earth, people who needed to hear about Jesus Christ. Being a man of action, Carey convinced a group of ministers in 1792 to form the first foreign missionary society. But that was not enough. Carey himself felt led to the mission field, so he traveled to India. He mastered more than a dozen Indian languages then translated the entire Bible or portions thereof into those languages. Every day, he preached to the natives. The result? Not one single convert among the Indians for seven years. But Carey persevered, believing that God could and would do great things. Finally, in 1800, Kirshna Pal was the fist convert of the modern missionary movement. Soon hundreds, thousands, and millions followed!

In the thirty-five years after Carey went to India, missionary societies sprang up all over Britain, Europe, and America. The result was an outpouring of missionary activity, labor, and zeal, the likes of which had not happened since the first century! All of this came about through the hard work of a humble cobbler who believed in God's greatness and obeyed God's call. When ordinary people with ordinary talents yield fully to God, He uses them to accomplish extraordinary things.

What can *you* do for God today?

When I am gone, speak less of Dr. Carey and more of Dr. Carey's Saviour.

WILLIAM CAREY

THE KEY TO A HAPPY HOME

*Let no corrupt communication proceed out of your mouth, but what is good
for necessary edification, that it may impart grace to the hearers.*

EPHESIANS 4:29

Of all the contributing factors that make our homes happy, good communication must be high on the list.

As we relate to people, we communicate on many levels—everything from "Hi, how are you?" to divulging facts, expressing emotions, and ultimately sharing our true selves. To make a home run smoothly, we need communication on all levels, but especially on that most intimate level of revealing ourselves to our housemates and families.

But that kind of communication can feel threatening. Sharing at the deepest, most intimate level makes us vulnerable, and many people don't want to risk rejection. But as these people stay on "safer" levels of communication, they never discover the real glory of intimacy.

People avoid intimate conversation not only because they fear rejection but also because they have built up resentment against people who have hurt them in the past. As they refuse to forgive and as they continue to keep records of wrongs, these people maintain barriers between themselves and others. While they may feel safer that way, these people miss the joy of reconciliation and better understanding. We must express tenderheartedness and forgiveness toward one another as God, for Christ's sake, has forgiven us. If we don't let go of our anger, we will clam up or blow up. "In your anger, do not sin," and "Let not the sun go down upon your wrath." These admonitions from Ephesians can help us forgive others and let go of pent-up resentment.

We also need to avoid faultfinding and blame. If we negatively evaluate someone, that person will not risk any deep communication, and we'll experience isolation. Instead of focusing on the negative things, focus on the good in the people you care about. When we start focusing on the positive, the positive will increase, and we will "administer grace" to each other.

What are some ways you can foster deeper communication in your home today? Do you need to share yourself on a deeper level, to forgive someone, to refrain from harshly judging others? Take a risk today, and see how those you live with respond as you pursue intimate communication and relationships.

Until I truly loved, I was alone.

CAROLINE NORTON

June 29

HENRY DRUMMOND

…but the greatest of these is love.

1 CORINTHIANS 13:13

How is your love life? Or put differently, is yours a life of love?

Today I'd like to focus on a man who exemplified Christian love. Henry Drummond, a nineteenth-century Scottish evangelist and writer, influenced lives wherever he went. He's perhaps best known for his book entitled *The Greatest Thing in the World,* an exposition on the love chapter of 1 Corinthians.

Drummond discovered that the most important thing he could do in life was to learn to love. He set his heart and mind and soul on this goal. In learning to love, he became one of the most influential men of his time. He always kept company with a myriad of people, from well-known citizens to unconventional, vagrant bohemians. Everyone was his type of person. Dwight L. Moody said that most Christians make an occasional sojourn into the thirteenth chapter of 1 Corinthians, but Henry Drummond seemed to live in that chapter all his life, and it poured out from his pores. His love for others radiated from his face.

Have you made the joyful discovery that the greatest thing in the world is to give love (not get it)? When we look back on our lives, we will see that in our moments of selfless giving, our lives took on their truest significance. Compared with all other things, love stands out as the greatest. But we cannot share this love on our own; we must receive it from Him who is love. Ask God to fill you with His love so that you might share it with others. Pray that His love would flow from you in all that you do.

Love is life, and lovelessness is death.

FRANCES PAGET

FAITHFUL AND TRUE

And Moses indeed was faithful in all His house as a servant,
for a testimony of those things which would be spoken…

HEBREWS 3:5

Have you ever struggled to remain faithful to God in certain areas of your life? To be faithful literally means to be "full of faith." The practical outworking of faithfulness is remaining true to God and His Word regardless of the cost or adverse circumstances.

Consider one man of faith, General William Booth, who founded the Salvation Army. In his later years, he lost his eyesight. He visited the doctor for help, but the doctor could not do much for him. His son, Bramwell Booth, had to give his father the final report: "I am afraid that there is little that they can do for you." General Booth said, "You mean that I will never again see your face?" His son replied, "I am afraid the likelihood is that you will never again see my face in this world." To this, General Booth declared, "Well, I have served God and the people with my eyes, and now I will serve God and the people without my eyes." What an incredible example of faith in the midst of a tremendously adverse circumstance!

If we want to faithfully seek and serve God, we must remain true to God even in the face of possible loss, as Abraham remained true to God even when he faced losing his son, as Daniel remained true to God even as he faced the horrors of the lions' den. To be faithful to Christ means to forsake this world with all its trappings and temptations. But even when we lapse in our faithfulness to God, He remains steady in His faithfulness to us. If you have trouble being faithful to God's call, then ask the Lord for His strength and help. Bolster your faithfulness by studying His Word and obeying its commands.

I do not want merely to possess a faith, I want a faith that possesses me.

CHARLES KINGSLEY

DISCOURAGEMENT

...It is enough! Now, Lord, take my life, for I am no better than my fathers!

1 KINGS 19:4

Has discouragement dogged your path recently? You're probably all too familiar with that sick feeling: A friend has let you down or the promotion has fallen through or your car just clutched its chest and died.

Life often seems riddled with letdowns, and if you haven't experienced such discouragement yet, you're in for a rude awakening because, sooner or later, discouragement elbows its way into all of our lives. Even spiritual giants such as Elijah experienced discouragement. After the greatest triumph of Elijah's career—his defeat of the prophets of Baal—he fled for his life. When Jezebel, the Queen of Israel, threatened Elijah's life for what he had done to the prophets, Elijah cried, "It is enough! Now, Lord, take my life, for I am no better than my fathers!" Elijah was in the pit of despair even though he had just experienced great victory through God's power.

Whatever discouragement we face, God's Word tells us that we can have hope. Scripture tells us that whatever comes our way, God will use it for good in our lives. He promises us that He will deliver us from our despair, although we may have to suffer for a while. Why does God allow us to suffer? Because through the fires of our affliction, God consumes our impurities and refines our gold. After all, what is a precious jewel but a piece of earth that has gone through some rather traumatic experiences? God is in the process of creating beautiful gems out of us so that we may adorn His crown.

Life can either wear us down or polish us up. If you feel discouraged today, trust Christ to use your discouraging times to mold you into a precious jewel, a person of great strength and character. Allow those thoughts to comfort you in tough times.

If you believe God is living, act like it!

KATHERINE LUTHER

HOW I KNOW THE BIBLE IS GOD'S WORD

All Scripture is given by inspiration of God, and is profitable for doctrine,
for reproof, for correction, for instruction in righteousness.

2 TIMOTHY 3:16

The more I read the Bible, the more I realize what an incredible book it is. Charles Wesley, the great hymn writer, said the Bible was written either by angels and good men, by demons and bad men, or by God. I am convinced that God wrote the Bible, and I have a lot of evidence to back up my conviction.

I believe that God wrote the Bible, because in the Old Testament alone God says twenty-six hundred times that He did so.

We can trust the Bible as God's Word because two thousand of its predictions have already come true. Over one hundred prophecies address the city of Babylon, including its destruction and the fact that it would never be rebuilt. Three hundred and thirty-three prophecies concern Jesus Christ, accurately predicting His place of birth, His character, and His crucifixion.

The Bible is from God because it is unified in thought. It contains sixty-six different books by approximately forty different authors writing in three different languages—Hebrew, Aramaic, and Greek. Yet the same golden thread of redemption runs through it—God by his grace saves us when we believe in Jesus Christ, His Son.

We know God gave us the Bible because He has preserved it from destruction. It has survived twenty-six hundred years of attack. It has survived philosophical debates, wars, persecutions, and burnings.

We know the Bible is God's Word because archaeology has confirmed it. For example, the Old Testament mentions the Hittites some forty times, but secular literature makes no mention of them at all. Because of this, some people have said that the Bible is inaccurate. Then archaeologists dug up the great Hittite empire and proved the Bible right.

We know the Bible is from God because it has the power to transform. It transforms individual lives, societies, countries. It has produced literacy, liberty, and a republican form of government.

We have so much proof that indicates the Bible is God's Word. Since He has taken great care to communicate and preserve His Word for you, treasure it, and take the time to know it well. Let it speak to your heart today.

Not one single archaeological discovery has ever controverted the Bible.

NELSON GLUECK

BLESSED IS THE NATION

Blessed is the nation whose God is the Lord…

PSALM 33:12

This time of year is always a perfect time to dwell on the founding of our nation. Did you know that God's providence played an enormous part in the settling and founding of this country? George Washington alluded to God's providence many times as he recounted our nation's development. Let's look at just one stunning example, forgotten by many today.

In the first year of the Revolutionary War, America almost lost the entire conflict. British General Howe had cornered Washington's army in Brooklyn Heights. The British forces surrounded the American forces in a great semicircle, and behind them British ships could close them off at any time. In fact, the British intended to do just that the next day and thus end the war.

The Americans had no way to escape. Nevertheless, that night, Washington endeavored to escape, realizing the helplessness of his position. He collected every vessel he could find, from rowboats to sloops, and set about to evacuate his troops by night. Counselors advised against such an escape because the British would see them in the moonlight and hear the splashing of their oars. But Washington was determined to go ahead anyway. Just as the American troops began to launch their vessels, a strange and unusual fog rose up and completely covered all of them! The next morning, when General Howe gave the orders to close the trap, he was astonished to find that Washington and his entire army had disappeared!

Precisely because of many incidents like these, Washington wrote after the war: "I am sure that never was a people, who had more reason to acknowledge a divine interposition in their affairs, than those of the United States." Today, thank God for His providence during the formation this great nation. And please join me in reminding people of God's hand in founding it. Let's give credit to Whom it is due.

The hand of Providence has been so conspicuous in all this, that he must be worse than an infidel that lacks faith, and more than wicked, that has not gratitude enough to acknowledge his obligations.

GEORGE WASHINGTON

AMERICA: A CHRISTIAN NATION

If the foundations are destroyed, what can the righteous do?

PSALM 11:3

Do you ever wonder about the direction in which the United States is heading, worried that the fabric of our society is fraying around the edges? If you're like me, you may read the newspaper headlines and shake your head in dismay at the choices our fellow citizens make.

Our country wasn't always this way. Take an honest inventory of our history, and you can have no doubts that America began as a Christian nation. The early settlers of America clearly intended to advance the Christian faith when they came ashore in New England. Before stepping foot off the *Mayflower*, the Pilgrims drew up what became America's first contract of government—the Mayflower Compact. This compact clearly states the Pilgrims' purpose in making their historic voyage: "…undertaken for the glory of God and the advancement of the Christian faith…"

Jumping ahead to the founding fathers of this country who framed the Declaration of Independence and the Constitution, we find that the book they quoted most often in their *political* writings was the Bible. And in 1892, after a thorough review of all of America's foundational history, the Supreme Court declared this country a Christian nation.

America was founded upon Christ and His Word. But this foundation is under siege by those who would have our history otherwise. These people have rewritten our history books, erasing God from the pages. They've removed the Bible and prayer from the classrooms, only to replace any hint of Christianity with policemen and metal detectors!

Ah, my friends, Uncle Sam needs your prayers. I urge you to pray for the leaders of this nation—not only on the Fourth of July, but every day. Pray with me that we as a nation might return to Him. Pray and work as if our very future as a country depends on revival. After all, it does!

The highest glory of the American Revolution was this: that it connected
in one indissoluble bond the principles of civil government with the principles of Christianity.

JOHN QUINCY ADAMS

GOVERNMENT: A FEARFUL MASTER

*Let every soul be subject to the governing authorities. For there is no authority except from God,
and the authorities that exist are appointed by God. Therefore whoever resists the authority
resists the ordinance of God, and those who resist will bring judgment on themselves.
For rulers are not a terror to good works, but to evil. Do you want to be unafraid of the authority?
Do what is good, and you will have praise from the same. For he is God's minister to you for good.
But if you do evil, be afraid; for he does not bear the sword in vain; for he is God's minister,
an avenger to execute wrath on him who practices evil.*

ROMANS 13:1–5

Do you ever listen to the news and find it hard to believe that God has ordained all governments? Whatever our opinions about governments around the world, the Bible tells us that God has appointed all governing authorities and we must submit to them.

The Bible teaches three truths about government that our founding fathers clearly understood, but which today have been blurred and obscured. If we understand these truths, we will place government in its appropriate place as God has ordained. The first truth is this: Government is under God and separate from the Church. The early founders knew nothing about a secular state (except for one caused by the ghastly French Revolution). They knew only about a nation under God. They knew that God Himself is above government, and that God, not the government, grants us our rights. The second truth is this: The purpose of government is justice. God has commissioned governments to legislate and administer laws for fairness among the people. Today the government has departed from this concept and attempts to practice benevolence. Governmental benevolence is incredibly wasteful, ineffectual, and harmful. The third truth is this: Government is a terror to evil works and not to good. God has ordained governments to punish evil deeds. Unfortunately, today we often see that, because humankind is basically sinful, government is becoming a terror to good works as well. We see the government beginning to direct oppressive tendencies toward the Church and its schools.

The government is a fearful master, but God is a faithful master. Today pray for those who run your local, state, and national governments; pray that God will use them for His glory and His will.

Government is a dangerous servant and a fearful master.

GEORGE WASHINGTON

THE CHRISTIAN VIEW OF POLITICS

And He put all things under His feet, and gave Him to be head over all things to the church.

EPHESIANS 1:22

Have you ever wondered if you should *always* obey the laws of our government? This is an important question because the government influences almost every aspect of our lives. To help us answer this question, the Bible delineates a few principles.

Principle number one: *The Triune God is sovereign over the whole universe.* He is sovereign over *every* area of life, not just the Church. This includes the government.

Principle number two: *The ultimate source of authority is not in the government or in the people; it's in God.* God has set government in place to enact and execute the laws He has given us in His Word—the moral laws of God, which He has written on our hearts. The authority of the government comes from God, and the government must answer to God.

Principle number three: *The government has limited authority and power*. The government does not encompass all things. We have other spheres that influence our lives: family, church, education, art, and science. Each of these spheres has its own authority and responsibility, and we must work out our lives freely in the various spheres in which we live. This means that if anyone in any sphere of activity oversteps his or her authority, the Christian has the obligation to disobey. If the government commands the Christian to do something contrary to the clear teaching of God's Word, then the Christian must obey God and not humans. For example, some governments have forbidden Christians to pray, worship God, and witness. Clearly, these governments have created laws contrary to God's commandments.

Are you willing to stand up for God's laws when they conflict with those of your government? Ask God to give you wisdom as a citizen and the courage to obey His Word despite any governmental opposition.

It is no more possible for man to build a political state without the help of God than it was for the builders of Babel.

BENJAMIN FRANKLIN

LEGISLATING MORALITY

'The God of Israel said…"He who rules over men must be just, ruling in the fear of God." '

2 SAMUEL 23:3

Have you ever heard the statement "Christians shouldn't impose their morality on the rest of us"? Many seem to feel this way, opposing any kind of law or ordinance that might support Christianity. I was in the Senate many years ago when someone introduced legislation designed to protect the integrity of the family. The author of the bill had based each of the various articles on some moral view of what the family should be. Some people viciously attacked this bill because it was contrary to their own legislation that in the end would cause further disintegration of the family. From this example, we see that some morality concerning the family, as in everything else, will be legislated. So the question comes down to this: Whose morality will we write into law: God's or humanity's? Will we legislate a Christian nation—a nation under God—or a humanist nation—a nation under people?

The frightening thing about a humanist state is that in creating legislation, people have nothing to appeal to beyond humans themselves. The founders of this country said that people have been created equal and have been endowed by their *Creator* with certain unalienable rights. Therefore, the state doesn't give us our rights, extending or withholding them as it pleases, but rather *God* has given them to us. We have an appeal beyond people, beyond the state, to God Himself. Many people have lost sight of the fact that our absolute God said, "By *Me* kings reign," and that Jesus Christ is the King of kings and Lord of lords. The whole world is His kingdom, and He is sovereign over all.

Do you long for our nation to once again submit to God's morality? If so, will you join me in prayer and in action to restore this great land as one nation under God?

The issue is not whether or not someone will impose his morality on legislation.
The question is whose morality will he impose?

July 8

THE GOD OF ALL COMFORT

Blessed be the God and Father of our Lord Jesus Christ, the Father of mercies and God of all comfort, who comforts us in all our tribulation, that we may be able to comfort those who are in any trouble, with the comfort with which we ourselves are comforted by God.

2 CORINTHIANS 1:3–4

Have you ever gone through a terrible trial, yet through it all felt completely surrounded by God's love? God is the God of all comfort, and when we struggle, He comforts us by His presence, His power, and His Word. Here are some of God's words that might comfort your heart in times of great difficulty:

•When people persecute you: "Rejoice and be exceedingly glad, for great is your reward in heaven" (Matthew 5:12).

•When you're sick: "Be of good cheer, daughter; your faith has made you well" (Matthew 9:22).

•When you're weary: "Come to Me, all you who labor and are heavy laden, and I will give you rest" (Matthew 11:28).

•When you're afraid: "Be of good cheer! It is I; do not be afraid" (Mark 6:50).

•When you need help: "If you ask anything in My name, I will do it" (John 14:14).

•When you're worried: "Let not your heart be troubled, neither let it be afraid" (John 14:27).

God's comfort is wonderful in difficult times. But God doesn't comfort us just for our own sakes; He comforts us so that we may comfort others. I remember when a woman in our church lost her son in a swimming pool accident. Many people tried to comfort her, and she appreciated their concern, but she didn't experience true comfort until someone who had also lost a child came and talked to her.

When we experience tragedy, we can thank God for the comfort He gives us in our time of need. And later, we may look for opportunities to comfort others who are going through similar trials. Allow God to work through you, maybe even today, to bring His comfort to others with the comfort He has given you.

Christianity is a religion of comfort. Our God is not only 'the God of all grace,' He is also 'the God of all comfort.'

BILL ELLIOT

BEER INTO CARPETS

'…One thing I know: that though I was blind, now I see.'

JOHN 9:25

In nineteenth-century England, a nonbeliever once taunted a Christian who was a converted drunkard. The nonbeliever sneered, "Surely you don't believe those Bible miracles, such as Christ turning water into wine." The ex-drunkard replied, "If you think that's a miracle, come to my home, and I'll show you how Christ changed beer into carpets, chairs, and even a piano!" Christ had come to dwell in the heart of that converted drunkard and had transformed his inward life as well as his outward circumstances. As the Bible says, "Therefore, if anyone is in Christ, he is a new creation; old things have passed away; behold, all things have become new" (2 Corinthians 5:17).

Have you allowed Jesus Christ to transform *your* life?

Jesus Christ is in the business of changing lives. He has done it throughout the centuries and continues to do it in our own day. And all of those changed by Him can echo what the blind man said when Christ gave him eyesight for the first time in his life: "One thing I know: that though I was blind, now I see."

I often express this transforming power in economic terms: Jesus Christ changes many societal liabilities into societal assets. Many who, earlier in their lives, seemed to have nothing to offer have become great spiritual leaders. The Church couldn't exist without people whose hearts Jesus Christ has transformed.

Have you been changed by receiving Christ's lovingly offered gift of eternal life? If not, I urge you to give your life to Him today and watch Him change you for the good from the inside out.

I wish that there were some wonderful place called the Land of Beginning Again,
Where all our mistakes and all our heartaches and all of our poor selfish grief
could be dropped like a shabby old coat at the door, and never be put on again.

POEM

THE CONQUESTS OF THE CONQUERED

Therefore He says: 'When He ascended on high, He led captivity captive, And gave gifts to men.'

EPHESIANS 4:8

What does the phrase "He led captivity captive" mean? It may seem like a puzzle, but it's not as confusing as it seems. Let me explain.

Before Christ came, all who died went to a place called, in the Hebrew, "Sheol." Some people believe there were two compartments in Sheol, one for the wicked, and one for the righteous, but the Bible simply says that everybody went there. In this shadowy land controlled by Satan and his demons, believers waited for the Messiah to come set them free. After His crucifixion, before He ascended into heaven, Jesus went to Sheol and rescued from the bonds of eternal death and torment all the saints of the Old Testament (those who had trusted in the promised Anointed One). Jesus led His beloved saints triumphantly to heaven. This triumphant procession was the greatest victory march of all times, greater than any this world will ever see.

Because Jesus "led captivity captive," we as Christians are all winners. We can partake in His victory and in the spoils of the spiritual war that rages all around us. However, in order to partake, we must first totally surrender our lives to Christ. We can't hang onto control of our own lives. When British General Cornwallis surrendered to George Washington, he came dressed in his finest uniform and began to praise the American's skill as a commander and military tactician. He continued in this way until Washington interrupted him and said, "Your sword, sir!" You see, Cornwallis hadn't fully surrendered until he handed over his weapon. In the same way, we will not experience spiritual victory until first we have been conquered by Christ and have surrendered our lives to Him. Then by faith we can enter into that triumph as we identify ourselves with Him. By faith we can know that He has already won the victory. Since He turns our defeats into triumphs and works all things together for our good, we know we can face today with confidence in Him, come what may. Jesus is the ultimate "Commander in Chief."

Is there anything that stands in the way of your complete devotion to Christ? If there is, I encourage you to surrender it to God right now. Don't waste one minute before you start enjoying the spoils of your victory in Christ!

If you are a Christian, God guarantees that you are to be a winner.

DEATH SWALLOWED UP

O Death, where is thy sting? O grave, where is thy victory?

1 CORINTHIANS 15:55, KJV

Someone once asked, "Who has not at some time in his life trembled at the thought of death? Who has been able to resist him?" All of our might and wisdom, all of our cunning and power have been to no avail before death's invincible might.

But do you know that the great specter of death that has always clouded the horizon has been vanquished? Do you know that you no longer need fear the grave?

Against the heartless monster of death, God commissioned His Son, who sat at His right hand. Jesus willingly responded, "Lo, I have come to do Thy will." Christ took upon Himself the task of confronting and overcoming our temptations, and He bore our sorrows. Finally, Jesus Christ gave Himself to mortal combat with death, laying down His life for us. He passed through that greatest of all ordeals so we wouldn't have to; He allowed Himself to be bound in the grave that He might once and for all "break the bands of death."

By His substitutionary death, Christ undermined the power and foundation of the grave. Christ's light has overtaken the darkness of the grave, and His victory has disempowered the king of terrors—death. Because we share in this victory, we Christians should rejoice! The world over, people lack hope when anticipating death. But we who trust in the great Prince of Life need no longer fear death. We can look forward to heaven, where the shadow of that specter shall never fall upon the threshold. Those dark, hollow eyes of the king of terrors, that have so inspired horror in millions, will then have become a joke. No longer will that bony finger of death beckon to anyone to come and follow him.

In light of Christ's resurrection, Paul wrote, "O death, where is thy sting? O grave, where is thy victory?" In the same way, you and I can rejoice today, knowing that death has been swallowed up in victory—all thanks to Jesus Christ!

When the stars have burnt out, we who trust in Christ will have just begun to live.

AS THE TWIG IS BENT

*'...these words which I command you today shall be in your heart; you
shall teach them diligently to your children, and shall talk of them when you sit in your house,
when you walk by the way, when you lie down, and when you rise up.'*

DEUTERONOMY 6:6–7

Are you ever discouraged with your children? Let me encourage those of you who have children or hope to have children someday—whatever challenges you face in parenting, don't ever give up. "As the twig is bent, so grows the tree." This familiar saying contains a biblical truth: "Train up a child in the way he should go, and when he is old he will not depart from it." Knowing how much parents love their children in all their moods and phases, God has given parents the responsibility for "bending the twig," for training children in all aspects of life.

Surprising as it may seem, the American habit of sending children to public schools with the expectation that the schools will teach them everything is a relatively recent development. From the time the Pilgrims landed in the early 1600s to the middle of the nineteenth century, parents maintained responsibility for their children's education. When public education first began, parents didn't need to worry about what the schools would teach their children because, for the first hundred years, the curriculum included Bible reading and prayers. Today, I am sad to say, our society has allowed the eradication of both of these.

Because we can no longer rely upon the school system to support our Christian views, we must work even harder to ensure that our children grow in Christ. How do we bend the twig? Our children need a God-centered education, one that teaches sound moral principles, emphasizes their creation in God's image, and presents the salvation message. They need to have high academic standards set for them and to have direction toward attaining these standards through discipline that includes guidelines, boundaries, and rewards. And we need to teach our children patriotism. Though our country has many flaws, it is still the most blessed nation on earth.

So don't give up. Keep bending the twig. If you do, you will one day have a tree that stands tall and bears much fruit for God's glory.

*Have thine own way, Lord! Have thine own way! Thou art the potter; I am the clay.
Mold me and make me after thy will, while I am waiting, yielded and still.*

ADELAIDE POLLARD

THE BRIDGE OF FAITH

For by grace you have been saved through faith, and that not of yourselves; it is the gift of God, not of works, lest anyone should boast.

EPHESIANS 2:8–9

Have you ever tried to explain to someone what the word "faith" means? If you have, then you know that it's a difficult concept to explain. Here's a story that might help others understand the meaning of faith.

It was a dark night on the main road from Jackson to Vicksburg, Mississippi. It had rained heavily, but the storm had finally broken, and the pavement was not so slippery. A truck driver traveled down that stretch of highway, and since conditions had improved, he began to relax a bit. Suddenly he saw the twin taillights of the car in front of him melt into the road and disappear. The truck driver sat bolt upright with his startled eyes wide open. Such a thing could not happen! In the next fraction of a second, he saw the gaping black hole where once a bridge had spanned the river. The truck driver slammed on his brakes, and the wheels stopped instantly, but there was no longer a road beneath them. His truck sailed silently and eerily into the black void before him. As the truck sank into the water, the driver broke out the window, got out of the truck, and managed to swim to shore. Like a dripping scarecrow, he scrambled up the embankment to the road. As he climbed, he heard one car after another zoom smoothly into the gap and disappear. The only trace was a booming splash preceded by startled shrieks or cries. Finally, the truck driver made his way to the road and frantically waved his hands at the oncoming cars in the dark. But they did not stop. Sixteen people died that night because they had faith in a bridge that was no longer there.

In life, we maintain faith in many bridges—the bridge of successful achievements, the bridge of good deeds, the bridge of "I tried as hard as I could"—but all of these bridges are out. Faith in Christ is the only bridge we can rely on. It's the only bridge that will get us across the river of temptation, the river of trial and affliction, the river of sin and guilt, the river of death. Without the bridge of faith in Jesus Christ, the dark waters would swallow up every one of us. As a survivor, will you warn others about the bridges that are out? You may be the only signal of the danger ahead.

To believe on Christ is initial faith…to assimilate Him is active faith.

CORNELIUS WOELFKIN

LIBERTY VERSUS LICENSE

Now the Lord is the Spirit; and where the Spirit of the Lord is, there is liberty.

2 CORINTHIANS 3:17

Are you ever confused about what's right and wrong in our world today? You're not alone. Part of the problem is a confusion between liberty (which we could define as the freedom to do right) and license (which we could define as the freedom to do wrong).

Our salvation is not a license to sin. It is a deliverance from sin. When Jesus first began His public ministry, what did He say? Repent! Though we have saving faith in Christ, we must still turn from sin and to God. The apostle John writes, "Do not love the world or the things in the world" (1 John 2:15), for loving the world is antithetical to loving the Father.

Neither God nor the founders of this country intended for anyone to abuse liberty as license. However, today many openly confuse liberty with license to do whatever their desires lead them to do! Sin has become flagrant in our society. Many people today look upon Christianity as an impediment to their "freedom," that is, their freedom to sin. But these people have transformed liberty into license, and in the worst form of licentiousness, they don't want anybody speaking against their actions or in any way restraining them. Ironically, claiming freedom to do whatever they want, these people are actually in bondage to their sinful natures, for whoever sins is a slave to sin. But Christ came to free us from sin and from the penalty of sin. Let's walk, then, in that liberty today by yielding ourselves to Him afresh.

He is the best friend of American liberty who is most sincere and active
in promoting pure and undefiled religion.

JOHN WITHERSPOON

THE CHRISTIAN AT THE JUDGMENT

*…each one's work will become manifest; for the Day will declare it, because it will be revealed
by fire; and the fire will test each one's work, of what sort it is.
If anyone's work which he has built on it endures, he will receive a reward.*

1 CORINTHIANS 3:13–14

Let us get it clear once and for all: Heaven is a "free gift," not an "earned reward."
I once saw a pamphlet with this question on the cover: "What must you do to
go to heaven?" I opened it up, and the inside was blank! This pamphlet clearly
communicated the message that we can do *nothing* to earn our salvation. Jesus
has already paid the price in full for you and for me. Isn't that an incredible
truth?

We can't save ourselves through good deeds, but we can do good works as
a way of thanking God for our salvation. The Bible says that God will reward us
in heaven for these works of thanksgiving. Scripture doesn't tell us what rewards
we'll receive, but it does tell us how to earn them. God sets aside rewards for
those who experience persecution for Christ's sake (Matthew 5:12). He also
rewards those who are good stewards of the things God has given to them
(Matthew 25:21). God has also planned special rewards for those who love their
enemies (Luke 6:35) and especially for those who faithfully witness to others
(John 4:35–36).

Keep in mind that at the Final Judgment the fire will try our works to see
which will last as heavenly rewards. According to the Bible, some of us build
with gold, silver, and precious stones, while others of us build with wood, hay,
and stubble. Through the fire, the gold, silver, and precious stones will remain,
but the wood, hay, and stubble will go up in smoke. The worst disaster that
could befall a human being is to lose his or her soul, but those of us who believe
in Jesus' gift needn't fear that fate. However, we may face the second-worst disaster—watching all the work of our lifetimes burned up in the fire at the Final
Judgment (1 Corinthians 3:15).

Are you investing your time this day to make an eternal impact? Are you
building with gold, silver, and precious stone or with wood, hay, and stubble? I
encourage you to do good deeds with eternity in mind, so that at the Final
Judgment you may receive the best reward of all—hearing God say to you,
"Well done, good and faithful servant!"

*The only test that really matters in life is that ultimate one,
which will test the quality of our life's work.*

TO TEMPER OUR TEMPER

'Be angry, and do not sin': do not let the sun go down on your wrath…

EPHESIANS 4:26

How is your temper? Do you keep your anger in check, or have you let anger sink its roots into your life? Unfortunately, an untold number of people go through their entire lives angry. Virtually any psychiatrist or psychologist would say that as many as ninety percent of their patients have problems somehow related to anger. Sadly, our anger seeps its way into our happiness, homes, and friendships, eroding the foundations of these blessings. Clearly, God desires better for us.

So how do we temper our temper? The Bible has a few pointers for us. First of all, we need to realize that any unjustified anger is a serious sin. Jesus said, "But I say to you, that whosoever is angry with his brother without a cause shall be in danger of the judgment." Knowing that unjustified anger is a sin, we need to repent of it, and by God's grace, do all we can to rid ourselves of it. Second, we need to forgive those who have slighted us. Remember that when the Jews and Romans wounded Jesus, He did not wound in return. Rather He said, "Father, forgive them." We need to forgive from our hearts those who have injured us. Third, we need to redirect our anger. If possible, we need to turn our anger away from those who hurt us and use it constructively to resolve the problem at hand. We need also to live by the important Biblical advice given to us: "A soft answer turneth away wrath."

No emotion in and of itself is evil, including anger. It becomes evil when we allow it outside the limits and structure that God has established. When our anger gets to that point, we need to confess it and repent of it. If you feel angry today, don't let the sun go down on your wrath. Bring it to God, and allow Him to begin a healing work in your heart. Do what you can to reconcile with the person you feel angry with. Determine, by the power of the Spirit, to forgive and to work constructively toward a solution.

It is he who is in the wrong who first gets angry.

WILLIAM PENN

July 17

HEAVEN

And I saw a new heaven and a new earth, for the first heaven and the first earth had passed away…Then I, John, saw the holy city, New Jerusalem, coming down out of heaven from God, prepared as a bride adorned for her husband.

REVELATION 21:1–2

Do you ever wonder what heaven will be like? I know none of us can possibly imagine its splendor! In the last two chapters of Revelation, we do get a glimpse of the glory to come as John pulls the curtain aside for a few moments. What marvelous pictures he paints as he dips his hand into all earthly beauty and heavenly light. He has taken the most magnificent things known to humankind and used them to paint the picture of the holy city, the new Jerusalem. What a marvelous place it must be—a city with foundations and walls made of precious stones, with streets and buildings and towers made of pure gold. The tree of life will stand by the crystal river, and all the treasures of the nations will be brought in. Should we take John's picture literally, or is it merely a symbol? If John's representation is just a pale picture of some greater reality, then heaven's glory is beyond the ability of the human tongue to declare.

When earth seems intolerable to you, think of heaven, our true home. It seems our longing for heaven diminishes with the increase of our material goods. But when we have great need, when our troubles increase, then we long for heaven. Perhaps God even allows a certain amount of our needs to go unmet or certain troubles to come our way so that our longing for our true home will not grow too dim. "For where your treasure is, there will your heart be also."

We are pilgrims and strangers here, so let's not get too attached to our earthly existence. Our true citizenship is in heaven. Today, whether you endure great trial or experience tremendous joy, set your sights on heaven. Remember and long for your true home.

When all my labors and trials are over, and I am safe on the beautiful shore,
just to be near the Lord I adore, that will be glory for me.

CHARLES H. GABRIEL

LOYALTY

And Ittai answered the king and said, 'As the Lord lives, and as my lord the king lives,
surely in whatever place my lord the king shall be, whether in death or life,
even there also your servant will be.'

2 SAMUEL 15:21

Have you ever been betrayed by a friend? Have you experienced the heartache of disloyalty? In our mobile society where divorce, the breakdown of families, corporate mergers, and hostile takeovers are commonplace, loyalty is sometimes a rare quality. Often it seems that everybody's out for "number one." Yet loyalty is one of the most fragrant and lovely of all the flowers that grow in the garden of the soul. Does it grow in your soul?

We can learn about loyalty from an obscure Bible character, Ittai the Gittite. When David's rebellious son, Absalom, tried to steal the throne from his father, forcing David into temporary exile, many within the kingdom went over to Absalom's side. Others remained loyal to David and fled with him. When David saw Ittai the Gittite among those who had followed him, David warned Ittai to turn back lest he be killed. But Ittai said that he would follow David to help him, even if it meant death.

Ittai was a tremendously loyal person. He was willing to sacrifice his life to be in the presence of the one who held his affections. Something about David captured Ittai's heart. Despite David's one great fall, he had a great, generous, and noble spirit that attracted so many. Ittai was drawn to him and attached his heart to him, pledging his loyalty even to the point of death.

We, too, have Someone to whom we must remain loyal, Someone of great, generous, and noble spirit—our Lord and Savior, Jesus Christ. He is worthy of our attaching our hearts to Him. As we pledge our loyalty to Christ, we could change the world.

It will cost me to be loyal to Christ—but it will also pay.

ELEANOR DOAN

NEWER AND NEWER

Therefore, if anyone is in Christ, he is a new creation; old things have passed away; behold, all things have become new.

2 CORINTHIANS 5:17

Have you ever felt discouraged because you've noticed a wrinkle where you once had smooth skin or a little extra "padding" where you once had muscle? Maybe recently you've spied just one gray hair too many.

In this world, the Second Law of Thermodynamics (which asserts that all things tend toward disorder) constantly works upon everything, including us. All things eventually run down, wear out, and grow old. You've seen it at work. As soon as you buy or make something new, immediately it starts to age, decay, wither, and disintegrate.

We can never overcome the Second Law of Thermodynamics—we can't even break even! But in the kingdom of Christ, we do not wear down, disintegrate, or age as the things of this world do. God makes us new creations, and He'll continue to do so until that day when He will make all things new. We can never mend or repair our old, broken-down, corrupt, evil nature. Instead, we allow Christ to remove them. The old must diminish while the new grows. The diminishing of the old nature is called mortification. The growing of the new nature is called vivification. Put the two together and the result is sanctification—one of the great doctrines of the Christian faith.

If we walk with Christ each day, He renews us. As we come to know Christ better, our spirits change more and more. He molds us day by day into His image, chipping away at our old nature and replacing it with the new. Only Christ can do this work, and He does it by the continual supply of His grace.

Do you feel the need for renewal today? Then invite God to do His work of grace in you. Submit to His rejuvenating power, and watch as He continues to make you a new creation for His glory.

Since we are born into God's family we should bear a family resemblance!

PAUL LEE TAN

July 20

THE CAUSE AND CURE OF SADNESS

Restore to me the joy of Your salvation, and uphold me with Your generous Spirit.

PSALM 51:12

The greatest lie that Satan has ever told the human race is this: We shall find joy through sin; we'll achieve true happiness by disregarding the commandments of God and letting ourselves follow our passions. Have you ever believed and trusted this lie, only to find yourself miserable and defeated?

Sin is a great deceiver. Before it binds, it blinds. Think of Samson, who was blinded and made to grind grain like an ox. Sin is subtle, a slippery slope that pulls us into things we never expected we'd do. When the prophet predicted that Hazael would become king of Syria and massacre thousands—not only men, but women and children as well—Hazael replied in horror, "But what is your servant—a dog, that he should do this gross thing?" (2 Kings 8:13). Yet, Hazael did the very things he abhorred. Robespierre, who in his younger days resigned his position as judge because he didn't want to give criminals the death penalty, sent thousands of people to the guillotine during the reign of terror in Paris!

Sin not only brings death; it brings sadness. David wept because he knew his own sin had caused his beloved son Absalom to rise against him in rebellion. What had originally seemed so good brought grief into David's life.

Although sin brings death and sadness into our lives, we can have joy again. As we submit to Christ's will, we find true joy and fulfillment. The King of Joy has washed away our sins forever and put new spirits within us. Today, thank God that, despite this sad, dying, sinful world, we can have fullness of joy in Him today and for eternity.

There is happiness in holiness.

TAKING THE STRAIN OUT OF LIFE

Thou wilt keep him in perfect peace, whose mind is stayed on thee...

ISAIAH 26:3, KJV

Many people run themselves into the ground because of stress, strain, worry, and anxiety. I suppose a proper epitaph for most people in America today would be "Hurried, worried, buried."

Did I just write your biography?

Many times we wish we could wash our hands of all our responsibilities and worries. The executive of one small company decided he would. Even though his company was headed for bankruptcy, he decided to quit worrying about it. So this executive called in his first vice-president and said, "I have had it with worrying about this company. If you'll take over and handle all my worrying for me, I will add $50,000 to your salary." Startled and perplexed by this generous offer (knowing the financial condition of the company), the vice-president asked, "But where are you going to get an extra $50,000?" The boss replied, "That's your first worry."

William Gladstone, perhaps the greatest prime minister England ever had, was a fine Christian man who served the Lord. On the wall of his bedroom hung a large plaque embroidered with this text: "Thou wilt keep him in perfect peace, whose mind is stayed on thee." It was the first thing Gladstone saw when he awoke in the morning and the last thing he saw before retiring at night.

"Thou wilt keep him in perfect peace, whose mind is stayed on thee." *There* is the secret of peace. We can have this peace because we know that the One upon whom we've stayed our minds is the One who works all things together for our good.

Is the frantic pace of modern life robbing you of your peace today? If so, slow down and refocus on the Lord. Realize that He's with you, and He's in control no matter what comes your way. Stay your mind on Him, and let Him grant you His peace.

Give me, O God, this day a strong and vivid sense that Thou art by my side.

JOHN BAILLIE

THE ALCHEMY OF GOD

*And we know that all things work together for good to those who love God, to
those who are the called according to his purpose.*

ROMANS 8:28

Have you ever had a rock and wished you could change it into a diamond?
Years ago, before the advent of chemistry, a science called alchemy existed, and
alchemists had a similar passion: finding a way to transform worthless metals
into gold. Of course, they never succeeded.

But God is the master alchemist. He has a passion for taking *all* things and
working them for good. Charles Spurgeon tells about one man who had complete faith that God would work everything for his good. During the reign of
Queen Mary I of England, this man was captured for preaching the gospel. He
received the sentence of being burned alive at the stake in London. When he
heard the sentence, he said, "Well, never mind. God will work all things together
for my good. I don't know how, but He will." On his way to London, the guards
treated the man roughly. In fact, they even threw him down to the ground, and
in doing so, they broke his leg. Then they mocked the man, saying, "Well, tell
us how this will work together for your good." He said, "I don't know, but it
will." Before they could continue their trip, the guards had to take time to put
the man's leg into a splint. Because of this delay, the group arrived in London a
day later than the guards had planned. But the night before they arrived, Queen
Mary died, and Elizabeth had taken the throne. Instead of burning the man at
the stake, Elizabeth pardoned him. So, although his broken leg was a bad thing,
God used it for his good, saving his life through the delay it caused.

Do circumstances often seem to work in opposition to your expectations?
Do you sometimes despair of any good coming from your situation? Remember
that God is in charge. He sees the big picture; He knows the future. He controls
all things, and He loves you more than you can imagine. Through your experiences, He'll shape you, transforming you into the best person you can be. Trust
Him and even thank Him for situations that seem bad, because He works all
things together for your good.

God, the mighty alchemist, transforms the lead of our lives into gold.

DEATH SWALLOWED UP

O death, where is thy sting? O grave, where is thy victory?

1 CORINTHIANS 15:55, KJV

Someone once asked: "Who has not at some time in his or her life trembled at the thought of death? Who has been able to resist it?" All our human might and wisdom have no power against its invincible might.

But as Christians, we needn't fear. The great specter of death that has always clouded the horizon does not reign supreme. Against this heartless monster, God commissioned His Son, Jesus, who sat at His right hand. Jesus declared, "Lo, I have come to do Thy will," and He took upon Himself the task of confronting and overcoming death. He laid down His life for us, passing through that greatest of all ordeals so we wouldn't have to. He allowed Himself bound in the grave that He might forever "break the bands of death." Jesus Christ, sinless human and almighty God, undermined the power of the grave and rose triumphant over it.

What a glorious truth! We who trust in the Prince of Life need no longer fear death. It holds no power over us now. In that celestial city of heaven, the shadow of death shall never fall upon the threshold. No longer will that bony finger beckon through the door to come and follow him. Instead, we will live in Christ's light for eternity. Paul wrote, "O death, where is thy sting? O grave, where is thy victory?" Death has been swallowed up in victory—all thanks to Jesus Christ!

When the stars have burnt out, we who trust in Christ will have just begun to live.

July 24

VICTORY BY FAITH

…this is the victory that has overcome the world—our faith.

1 JOHN 5:4

Do you ever feel overcome by the cares of the world? We may often feel on the brink of defeat, but God has destined that *we* overcome *the world*. What does "world" mean in this context? It stands for the worldly system under Satan's rule with all its lust, greed, animosity, and self-centeredness. This world system is antithetical to Christ and must be overcome.

But how do we overcome it? Through faith. As a well-known hymn declares: "Faith is the victory…that overcomes the world." We can only overcome the world when we entrust our lives to Christ, the first to overcome the world. I'm sure that as John wrote the words of our text (1 John 5:4), he hearkened back to that solemn night—the night Jesus went into Gethsemane before He was arrested, stripped, and nailed to a cross. After Jesus and the disciples had finished their supper that night, Jesus said, "In the world you will have tribulation; but be of good cheer, I have overcome the world" (John 16:33). What an astonishing statement! Jesus had none of this world's goods; He didn't even have a place to lay His head. The Jewish leaders hated Him and would soon arrest and crucify Him. And yet Jesus said, "I have overcome the world."

Jesus Christ was an overcomer. Refusing to be deceived or defeated by this world, He fixed His eyes on the eternal kingdom of God. We should do the same. When you feel that the world is getting the best of you, remember that Christ has overcome the world on your behalf. Have faith in Christ, and claim your victory.

Beside us to guide us, our God with us joining,
Ordaining, maintaining His kingdom divine.
So from the beginning the fight we were winning;
Thou, Lord, wast at our side, all glory be Thine!

"WE GATHER TOGETHER" (THANKSGIVING HYMN)

C. T. STUDD

'For with God nothing will be impossible.'

LUKE 1:37

Do you face a difficulty today that seems impossible to resolve? For a bit of encouragement, consider one of God's choice servants who believed that God would accomplish the impossible for him.

C. T. Studd was born in England into great wealth and was educated at Cambridge. While at university, Studd became the premier cricket player in all of Great Britain. He then devoted his life to Christ and the mission field, becoming one of the greatest missionaries ever.

Studd set sail for China in 1885. Upon his arrival, this English aristocrat resolved to become Chinese. He donned a Chinese robe, shaved his head (all but a pigtail), and lived like the poorest of the Chinese. Through this experience he learned a great lesson: He could trust God to provide for all of his needs. God used Studd mightily in China, bringing many to Christ.

After years of loyal service in China, Studd felt the Lord calling him to India. This was remarkable, for seldom does a missionary go from one great field to another. Studd's father had made a fortune seeking gold in India; now the son wanted to seek souls for Christ. So Studd labored hard for Christ in India. After six years his health began to wane, so he returned home to England. But even his failing health couldn't impede the vision God had given him. Against the wishes of family, friends, and his doctor, Studd set sail for Africa, not once but twice. There, just as he had done in other lands, he brought many to the living Savior.

C. T. Studd was a man of great faith. He wasn't interested in pursuing things that seemed possible; He believed that God would do impossible things through him. What a difference each one of us could make if we, too, remembered that nothing is impossible for God. As you face challenges beyond your strength and abilities, keep this old saying in mind: "God and I can do anything God can do alone!"

Christ wants not nibblers of the possible, but grabbers of the impossible.

C. T. STUDD

STUDYING JESUS

Be diligent to present yourself approved to God, a worker who does not need to be ashamed, rightly dividing the word of truth.

2 TIMOTHY 2:15

Someone once wrote out the Constitution of the United States, using longhand to achieve an amazing effect. As you read the document, you see just the words. But if you move back from it, you get another picture—a beautiful portrait of George Washington made by the variation of light and dark pen strokes. It is a magnificent work of art.

So it is with the Bible. When we first read it, we may see only stories about seemingly unrelated things. But after a while we discover that all of Scripture points to Jesus Christ, the Lord of glory. The Old Testament foretells His coming; the Gospels describe His coming; the Epistles explain the reasons for His coming. As we look at the big picture of the Bible, we should see Jesus Christ.

Every Christian wanting an intimate relationship with Jesus needs to read and study God's Word daily. And yet, so often we don't study His Word at all. Imagine claiming to love someone who fights a battle in a far-off land. If that person wrote you letters, would you leave them sitting unopened on the coffee table? Of course not! You'd rip them open right away, read them, and read them again. Well, somewhere in our houses sit sixty-six love letters from God, from Genesis to Revelation. If we love God, let's make sure we read those letters.

Set aside time regularly to delve into God's Word, meditating upon it and hiding it in your heart. Get the Bible handbooks and dictionaries that supplement serious study of His Word. As you get to know the Bible better, you'll discover more about and draw closer to the central figure of that book, Jesus Christ.

The New Testament is the very best book that ever was or ever will be known in the world.

CHARLES DICKENS

YOU CAN!

I can do all things through Christ who strengthens me.

PHILIPPIANS 4:13

Do you dream big dreams for your life? If you were given absolute assurance of success, would you act on those dreams? Well, God has promised us such victory. Read Paul's claim from Philippians again: "I can do all things through Christ who strengthens me." What an incredible promise! But all too often we talk ourselves out of our dreams with two simple words: "I can't." These words of unbelief crush our dreams. Instead of trusting God's promise to strengthen us for all things, we rely on our own volition, our education, our physical prowess, or perhaps even our social standing. And when we perceive a lack of resources to accomplish our dreams, we fail to even try.

Jesus said, "Without me ye can do nothing." If we ever want to fulfill our dreams, we must keep our eyes on Jesus Christ. And as we do, the possibilities are limitless. But first, we must align our aspirations with God's Word and with His will for us. Second, we must steadfastly work toward our goal, never losing sight of it. Paul serves as a great example of this two-step strategy. He had a dream that every nation, tongue, and tribe would know the gospel. Paul's goal was completely in line with God's truth. And despite his suffering as he strove toward his goal, Paul never lost sight of it. Because of his perseverance and his reliance on God's strength, Paul's dream lives on as the good news continues to spread to the ends of the earth.

God intended His children to soar like eagles. He wants us to live in His world of infinite possibilities, relying on His strength to make our dreams realities. Do you have a dream, something you think you could never achieve? Then ask God for strength to achieve it. As you set your faith in God and seek His will, He will make your dreams come true!

For they conquer who believe they can.

VIRGIL

THE GUILT IS GONE

In whom we have redemption..., the forgiveness of sins.

COLOSSIANS 1:14

Have you ever felt so guilty you couldn't look someone in the eye? Guilt is tremendously motivating. While the possibility of feeling guilty may not stop us from doing something wrong, once we feel guilty, we'll do almost anything to avoid being found out. Sir Arthur Conan Doyle, the creator of the famed fictitious detective Sherlock Holmes, once played a terrible practical joke. He wrote an unsigned letter and mailed it to twelve prominent men. It said, "All is discovered. Flee at once!" Within forty-eight hours all of them had left the country. Guilty!

Though people in our society rarely use the word "sin" in conversation anymore, we can't get rid of guilt, and it has a powerful effect on us. Guilt weakens and destroys. It can create a sense of anxiety—a nameless, unknown fear. It can produce a depression that hangs over our heads like a black rain cloud. It can make us feel unclean, soiled, worthless. It can give us such a poor self-image that we become our own worst enemies. Guilt can even create physical illness; after David sinned with Bathsheba, he said, "My bones grew old through my groaning all day long" (Psalm 32:3).

There is a difference between *guilt* and *guilt feelings*. You may have bad feelings even though you're not guilty. Psychiatrists may help you get rid of guilt feelings, but they don't know how to handle guilt. Many of them don't even like the word. They use "confused" or "mixed up priorities" instead. But the Bible says, "For all have sinned and fall short of the glory of God" (Romans 3:23) and "There is none righteous, no, not one" (Romans 3:10). Our guilt is so permanent, it seems engraved in granite. We cannot blame it away. We cannot push it down or trade it for another emotion.

We can get rid of our guilt in only one way—by asking Christ for forgiveness. Do you need to ask His forgiveness for something today? Confess to Him, and unburden your heart. Allow Him to wash you perfectly clean.

What can wash away my sins? Nothing but the blood of Jesus.
What can make me pure within? Nothing but the blood of Jesus.

MARY RUNYON LOWRY

WHEN YOUR LOVE GROWS COLD

Greater love has no one than this, than to lay down one's life for his friends.

JOHN 15:13

As human beings we go through an enormous variety of emotions. Feelings are part of life's color; when we don't feel anything, life can seem flat and drab.

As tough as it is to admit, loving our Lord falls in this category. While His love for us is constant and eternal, some days, because we are human and sinful beings, we don't naturally feel a sense of love overflowing toward Him.

When we find loving our Lord difficult, how can we renew our love for Him? We do this by remembering His suffering for us. I am amazed at how glibly we repeat those words, "Christ died for my sins," without considering the incredible truth contained therein. When we remember Christ's anguish in the Garden of Gethsemane, the agony He suffered at the hands of the high priest and Pontius Pilate, the excruciating death He endured on the cross, then love for our Lord and Savior should flood our hearts. This is why the Lord's Supper is so important. It reminds us of His sufferings on our behalf. When we fix our minds on that thought—that our *Creator* died for us—our love for Him will be renewed.

Whenever you feel that your love for the Lord has grown cold, climb the mountain of Calvary and breathe in the fresh air from Heaven. This will renew your soul and increase your spiritual vitality.

I love Thee, because Thou has first loved me, And purchased my pardon on Calvary's tree.
I love Thee for wearing the thorns on Thy brow; if ever I loved Thee, My Jesus 'tis now.

WILLIAM R. FEATHERSTONE

HE SHALL RETURN

For the Lord Himself will descend from heaven with a shout, with the voice of an archangel, and with the trumpet of God. And the dead in Christ will rise first. Then we who are alive and remain shall be caught up together with them in the clouds to meet the Lord in the air. And thus we shall always be with the Lord.

1 THESSALONIANS 4:16–17

As Christians we have an incredible event to anticipate—Christ's second coming. Why do we know this will happen? Because more than three hundred times in the New Testament, the Scriptures very boldly state that Jesus Christ will return; even more prophecies are found in the Old Testament concerning His second advent. And Jesus Himself declared it unequivocally, "I will come again, and receive you unto myself." History marches on to that very moment; His return will be the great climax of all time!

Are you ready for it?

Every Sunday for centuries, the Christian Church around the world has confirmed Christ's second coming. In the Apostles' Creed, we declare, "From thence He (Jesus) shall come to judge the quick and the dead." This is confirmed by the Nicene Creed, the Constantinople Creed, the Westminster Confession, the Thirty-Nine Articles of the Church of England, the Augsburg Confession, and all of the other great confessions of the Church. Jesus Christ is coming back to this world!

Are you prepared?

Although we know for certain that this event will happen, we don't know when. Numerous people have claimed to figure out the exact day and time. (Imagine that—the angels don't even know, but people rush in where angels fear to tread, and they proclaim both year and date.) But the Scripture says that Jesus will come at an hour when we won't expect Him. He'll come suddenly, like a thief in the night. He might come today or a thousand years from now.

Either way we must be ready. Would you want the Lord to come today? Are you ready to be in His presence? From now on, live each day as if it's the day He'll return.

His [Jesus'] teaching on the subject quite clearly consisted of three propositions:
1. That he will certainly return.
2. That we cannot possibly find out when.
3. And that therefore we must always be ready.

C. S. LEWIS

THE RETURN OF THE SPIES

Then Caleb quieted the people before Moses, and said, 'Let us go up at once and take possession, for we are well able to overcome it.'

NUMBERS 13:30

Have you ever faced a daunting task, one that looked not even remotely feasible? At times like this, God, who can do the impossible, wants us to have faith in His presence and in His ability to see us through.

The ancient Israelites serve as an excellent example of what *not* to do under pressure. Faced with an overwhelming task, they failed to respond in faith. Moses had just sent twelve spies (one representative from each tribe) into the land to spy it out and bring back intelligence reports concerning the nature and strength of their adversaries. After some days, the spies returned from their trip throughout Canaan. They gave two reports: the majority report given by ten and the minority report given by two, Joshua and Caleb.

The majority report said: "It [the land] truly flows with milk and honey…Nevertheless the people who dwell there are strong; the cities are forti- fied." Upon hearing that, Caleb could not restrain himself. He had heard enough negative nonsense. He leaped to his feet and said, "Let us go up at once and take possession, for we are well able to overcome it." But the ten other spies shot back: "The land through which we have gone as spies is a land that devours its inhabitants, and all the people whom we saw in it are men of great stature." Then the people's hearts melted within them; all night they "raised their voices and wept aloud." Joshua and Caleb submitted the minority report, reminding the Israelites that with God's help, they could take the land. But the people wouldn't listen. These two men were the only ones with faith in God. And they became the only ones from that generation who eventually entered the Promised Land!

These two men based their faith on God's promises. That's how they over- came their fears and fought to enter the Promised Land. We need to do the same thing. When circumstances overwhelm you and the task at hand is daunting, place your full faith in God and trust that He will deliver you into your promised land.

With God, go over the sea—without Him, not over the threshold.

RUSSIAN PROVERB

TO FORGIVE

'And forgive us our debts, as we forgive our debtors.'

MATTHEW 6:12

When was the last time someone hurt you? What has been your response to that person since that event? Are you holding onto a grudge, or have you forgiven that person for the pain he or she caused you?

God clearly directs us to forgive people who have wronged us. But forgiving people is so difficult, especially when we still feel hurt by their choices. Nevertheless, we must obey God's command. So how do we obtain a forgiving spirit, willing to release even the worst offender from any debt owed us? Here are some steps that can help:

1. Avoid seeking revenge. Remember God has said, "Vengeance is mine; I will repay." Leave retribution in His hands.

2. Release people from human judgment. It's so easy to judge others when they have hurt us. But God is the ultimate judge. Shall we usurp the judgment of the Creator of the universe?

3. Reconcile with the offender. The Bible says, "Be reconciled to thy brother." As this is not always possible, the Bible also says, "inasmuch as it is up to *you*, be at peace with all men."

4. Pray for your enemies' good. Jesus said, "Pray for them which despitefully use you." Do you pray for the good of those who hurt you?

5. Love your enemies. Difficult as it sounds, we must treat our enemies with Christ's love. Fortunately, God doesn't leave us to our own devices on this one; He enables us to do it.

6. Overcome evil with good. The Scripture says, "Be not overcome of evil, but overcome evil with good." What a tremendously powerful concept that is! Resolve to do good to others, even if they've breached your trust.

Is there someone whom you cannot forgive? Then, my friend, you need to ask Jesus Christ for His power to forgive that person. Let Christ's love work through you. Then, if you still find forgiving that person difficult, look into the face of Him who hung on the cross and said, "Father, forgive them, for they know not what they do."

Everyone says forgiveness is a lovely idea, until they have something to forgive.

C. S. LEWIS

August 2

CHANGE YOUR ATTITUDE AND CHANGE YOUR WORLD

For as he thinks in his heart, so is he. 'Eat and drink!' he says to you,
but his heart is not with you.

PROVERBS 23:7

A student of flying was taking his first solo flight. All went well until he had to land his plane. Suddenly, he heard a voice over the radio saying, "Correct your attitude!" He thought to himself, "My attitude? My attitude is just fine." Because the student didn't heed his flight instructor's warning, he crashed his plane.

After the crash, his instructor showed him this definition for "attitude" in the flight manual: "the plane's inclination toward the earth."

Our inclination toward life can destroy us or make us successful. Why? Because our attitudes affect our relationships with others, with ourselves, and with God. Chuck Swindoll, a popular radio preacher, once said, "I am convinced that life is ten percent what happens to me, and ninety percent how I react to it."

A young lady once came to her pastor with a problem. She said, "I have the meanest, orneriest, most foul-mouthed father-in-law you've ever seen, and he lives with us. Whenever he gets mad, he curses me. I have not been a Christian very long, and I've got a temper of my own. I'm about ready to let him have it. What can I do?"

The pastor asked, "What does he like to eat?"

She replied, "Fudge. He likes fudge."

The pastor said, "The next time he curses you, fix him some fudge."

About a week later, the father-in-law was sitting in the kitchen when the young lady accidentally splashed some hot food on him. He began cursing her. However, she remained calm, prepared some fudge, and handed it to him. At first, he just looked at it. But after a while, a big tear dripped off his cheek and splashed onto the plate of fudge. Then he put his arms around his daughter-in-law and said, "Daughter, I want you to forgive a mean, ugly, old man." This woman had the joy of leading her angry, ornery father-in-law to the Lord right there in her kitchen! Why? Because she exhibited a loving attitude.

Do you need to correct your attitude today? Change your attitude, and you can change your world!

A man's life is what his thoughts make it.

MARCUS AURELIUS

CRUCIAL CHOICES

*'And if it seems evil to you to serve the LORD, choose for yourselves this day whom you will
serve, whether the gods which your fathers served that were on the other side
of the River or the gods of the Amorites, in whose land you dwell.
But as for me and my house, we will serve the LORD.'*

JOSHUA 24:15

People of little resolve never accomplish anything. General Julius became Julius
Caesar because he made a tough decision: He dared to cross the Rubicon, a
river all Roman generals were forbidden to cross even with the smallest band of
soldiers. He said, "If I cross not this river this instant then my life shall be overcome with calamities." And laying the reins upon the neck of his horse, he
plunged into the river with this cry: "The die is cast!" He crossed to the other
side, ready for battle and ready for destiny.

Our "Rubicon" is the choice to serve God's kingdom. We all serve something. Even if we decide to ignore God's service and live for pleasure, Jesus tells
us, "Whosoever committeth sin, is the servant of sin." We need to actively
choose who we'll serve, not wavering somewhere in neutral ground. Charles
Spurgeon talks about a group of people he calls "betweenites." Spurgeon says
when the forces of Christ and the forces of Satan gather on opposing hills for
that final battle, the "betweenites" will be milling around in the valley below and
will be trampled by both sides.

The choice to serve God is urgent; we shouldn't put it off. You have to
decide for yourself—will you serve God, or won't you? No one can make that
choice for you. We all shall die alone and stand alone before God's presence to
account for our choices. In that day we shall be without excuse.

Cross the Rubicon today—choose to serve the Lord with all your heart. Say
with Joshua, that tremendous leader of the Israelites, "As for me and my house,
we will serve the LORD."

*Rise up, O men of God! Have done with lesser things;
give heart and soul and mind and strength, To serve the King of kings.*

WILLIAM MERRILL

LET US REMEMBER AND GIVE THANKS

Bless the Lord, O my soul; and forget not all His benefits.

PSALM 103:2

"Thank you!" Two simple words that let us know we're appreciated for what we do and who we are.

When was the last time those words crossed your lips as you prayed to God?

I believe the Scriptures place a great deal more emphasis upon gratitude than we realize. In fact, the Scriptures consider thankfulness and its antithesis, thanklessness, as extremely important issues. Throughout the Bible, we're called again and again to praise and thank God.

Most people have Christianity absolutely backward. They suppose that the motive of the Christian life is to perform good deeds in the hope of gaining eternal life. And if that were the case, we wouldn't need to express thanks to God; we would have earned our own passage to heaven with no one to thank but ourselves. But we can't achieve eternal life on our own; we can gain salvation only through God's grace by faith in Jesus Christ. And this truth engenders a heart of thankfulness and praise. God's amazing grace inspires us to express our deepest gratitude to our Lord and Savior.

When we freely offer God our thanks and praise, our lives change. As we count our many blessings, one by one, we may become overwhelmed by what God has done in our lives. We may also learn to trust Him for future needs as we review God's perfect track record of taking care of us.

I encourage you to keep a spiritual journal, where you record your prayer requests and the Lord's answers. The ancient Israelites often ran into problems because they didn't remember all God had done for them in their past, such as parting the Red Sea to save them from Pharaoh and the Egyptians. But if you keep a prayer journal, you won't suffer from the same "amnesia." As you regularly write down God's answers to your prayers, you'll remember His wonderful care for you, and you'll automatically be filled with gratefulness and adoration toward God.

A thankful heart is…the parent of all other virtues.

CICERO

August 5

DRIFTING!

Therefore we must give the more earnest heed to the things we have heard, lest we drift away.

HEBREWS 2:1

Have you ever rowed a raft on a river? If you have, then you probably know that when you row upstream, away from the falls, you have to keep going. If you stop rowing, you'll inevitably drift backward, silently, imperceptibly toward the falls, toward danger. But as this happens, you may not realize that you're drifting away.

The Christian life is like paddling against a rapidly flowing river. It takes a definite decision of our wills to live for Christ, but it takes no such definite decision to drift away. All you have to do is neglect your faith, even for a brief time, and before you know it, you're headed straight for spiritual destruction.

You've probably heard the classic story about the wife who complained that her husband never sat next to her in the car anymore. He, the driver, turned to her and said, "But, dear, *I* never moved." We're the same way with God. Though sometimes we may feel far from Him, He never forsakes us. Instead, we allow ourselves to drift away from Him.

Such drifting in the Christian life seldom happens instantly. When we neglect our relationship with Jesus Christ, even for a short while, the drifting begins. Continued neglect leads to disaster. Someone has put this truth into an easy-to-understand word picture. To maintain a flow toward Christ, we must apply ourselves to the "oars"—the oars of Scripture reading and prayer which together provide for our devotional life. As we "row" toward Christ, we grow closer to Him and further from the crashing falls. But if we just let the oars sit in the water, we go wherever the river runs, in a direction toward crashing defeat.

If you've been drifting away from the Lord, then I urge you to draw near to Him today. Make a conscious decision to apply yourself to the oars of faith, interacting with God daily through His Word and through prayer.

> *...Prone to wander, Lord, I feel it, Prone to leave the God I love,*
> *Here's my heart, O take and seal it. Seal it for Thy courts above.*

ROBERT ROBINSON

GREATNESS

'But he who is greatest among you shall be your servant.'

MATTHEW 23:11

Do you want to be great?

The pursuit of greatness has been an almost universal quest on the part of humankind. For five thousand years, people have toiled up the path toward greatness as they see it—to the way that leads to fame and fortune, to power and privilege and ease.

But Jesus stands beside that path with outstretched arms saying, "You seek greatness, but you're not even on the right path. The pinnacles of greatness which you see are illusory. The path to greatness lies not in being served, but in serving." Does that truth surprise you? It's exactly the opposite of what we think, the opposite of what the world tells us.

The world's view of greatness bombards us constantly. Every time we open the newspaper or read a magazine or turn on the television, the world sets before us its view of greatness—its perversion of God's view of greatness, the devil's view of greatness—with so-called great people gaining more possessions and notoriety and expecting others to take care of their every need. Millions of people within the Church have allowed this incorrect view to unconsciously seep into their minds and hearts with all its deadly tendencies.

We need another view—Jesus Christ's view. Just as Jesus said that we descend to rise and that we die to live, He said that the one who seeks greatness must first seek servanthood. He said that even the Son of Man came not to be served, but to serve and give His life as a ransom for many. He demonstrated his view of greatness on the night before He went to the cross. At the Last Supper, Jesus washed the feet of His disciples, stunning them by His humble act of servanthood.

So I ask you again, do you want to be great? If so, then imitate Jesus, who came to minister rather than to be ministered to. Start today by finding, or even making, an opportunity to serve someone else.

What we have done for ourselves alone dies with us.
What we have done for others and the world remains and is immortal.

ALBERT PINE

HUMILITY

By pride comes only contention, but with the well-advised is wisdom.

PROVERBS 13:10

When you think of humble people, what images come to your mind? What characteristics and attitudes contribute to humility?

We often hold misconceptions about humility. Some people believe they can gain humility only when they deny the talents they possess. But that's not humility; it's foolishness. When we deny our abilities, we deny the goodness and grace of God, the giver of every good and perfect gift.

Rather, humility comes from a proper perspective about our God-given gifts and talents. We can admit that we have talents, abilities, and intelligence and still remain humble as long as we acknowledge we've received them all from God. Therefore, we don't take the glory but instead give thanks to God who is the source of our talents and abilities. We also thank Him for our accomplishments. We shouldn't say, "I can't brag about the talents I've received, but just look at what I've done with them!" Again, we acknowledge that God works through us and that without Him we can do nothing.

Foster humility in your life today. Thank God for giving you abilities and for accomplishing His work in and through you. May you give glory to God as you use your gifts and talents for Him today.

By the grace of God I am what I am: Not I, but the grace of God in me.

JOHN KNOX

SEEKING SUCCESS

'But seek first the kingdom of God and His righteousness…'

MATTHEW 6:33

Would you call yourself a successful person? What measure do you use to determine your answer to that question?

Many people define success as being happy. But if that's our definition, few who seek success find it. Happiness is a byproduct of seeking something outside ourselves, something we cannot control. So if we bank our success on it, we'll often experience frustration. But ultimately, it's a lie that happiness is the evidence and result of a successful life.

If we're ever to experience success, we first need to understand the true definition of it. Jesus Christ described success for us in Matthew 6:33: "But seek first the kingdom of God and His righteousness." Those who seek God's kingdom and His will for their lives are usually those who experience God's richest blessings. These people find that which others spend their whole lives pursuing: gifts God gives to those who seek Him.

Consider the words of David Livingstone who, after great suffering and personal loss, wrote, "My Jesus, my Christ, my God, my King, my all, I again consecrate my life entirely unto Thee. I will place no value upon any thing or any relationship except as it relates to Thy Kingdom and Thy cause." A great hero of the faith, Livingstone opened up Africa to the gospel, sharing God's good news with millions who had never heard it before. Livingstone's words and actions exemplified true success: seeking first the kingdom of God.

If the whole world applauds but Christ says, "Nay," then one's life is a tragic failure. Today set your heart first and foremost toward God's kingdom, forsaking anything that might stand in your way. Do this, and you shall no doubt succeed, at least by the standards that really count in life!

The Bible never tells us to seek the Kingdom of God; it tells us to seek it first.

CHARLES SPURGEON

HUMANISM

'Cursed is the man who trusts in man and makes flesh his strength…'

JEREMIAH 17:5

Humanism—faith in humankind—seems to creep further and further into our society. How does this perspective affect our culture?

To understand the impact humanism has on our society, we must first understand humanistic theory. Let's look at the four principles upon which it is based. First, humanism touts the doctrine of *atheism*. Whereas our catechism says that humankind's chief end is to glorify God and enjoy Him forever, the humanist says that humankind's chief end is to glorify humankind. The originator of humanism, the ancient Greek philosopher Protagoras, put it this way, "Man is the measure of all things." Humanism also asserts the doctrine of *evolution*. Humanists believe the universe is self-existing and not created. Humans simply evolved from lesser forms and are therefore nothing more than animals. The third doctrine of humanism is *amorality*. Humanists don't believe in absolutes but instead view truth as relative. Finally, humanists believe that we must have a *collectivist society*, sacrificing individual well-being for the common good, and that we must establish this society immediately. Some have said that humanism is nothing other than communism in philosophical garb.

Since humanism seems to have a system of doctrinal beliefs, is it a religion? The *Humanist Manifesto* of 1933 calls it such nine times. Not only is humanism a religion, it's an insidious one. It uses our public schools as church buildings; some school teachers serve as its ministers; its high priesthood is the National Education Association; its property is valued in the hundreds of billions of dollars. Every year our nation spends tens of billions of dollars in the propagation of humanism's doctrines and tenets. Humanism is particularly dangerous because, unlike any other religion in America, it is endorsed in the public schools and established in every department of the government of the Unites States.

We know Who wins in the end, but tragically, many souls will be lost as humanism's influence increases. Today pray that Jesus will save those who promote the false religion of humanism and for all who believe in it.

If God is dead, then all things are permissible.

FEODOR DOSTOEVSKY

CHRIST IN YOU

*To them God willed to make known what are the riches of the glory of this mystery
among the Gentiles: which is Christ in you, the hope of glory.*

COLOSSIANS 1:27

Do you ever get involved in a good mystery story, intrigued by the twists and turns, trying to figure it out until, in the final scene, you discover whodunit?

God's Word contains many mysteries, and God's mysteries are greater than any other mysteries in the world. No one, not even the most clever detective, can solve them. We can only discover the truth when God, the great revealer, chooses to make it known.

God has revealed one great mystery to us, a mystery which had previously lain hidden for centuries: Christ in us, our hope of glory. This is the great secret of Christianity. Christ doesn't just go *before* us as a leader; *beside* us as an encourager; *behind* us as a teacher, pointing the way we should go; or *above* us as a counselor to whom we turn in times of need. He is all of that, but—far, far more—He is Christ *within* us as the regenerator, the transformer, the sanctifier, and the strengthener who provides all we ever need. When the ever-living Christ with His supernatural, wonder-working power comes into the heart of the most hardened sinner, He transforms that sinner into a new person. We must all have Christ *in us*. Only those who allow Christ to reign in their hearts will enter Paradise.

Some have called inviting Christ into our hearts "being born again." With that truth, we have these options: "Born once, die twice; born twice, die once." If you have been born twice—once physically and then spiritually—you will die only once. You will be spared the second death, and instead you will pass from this life directly into the presence of God's glory. And eternity with Christ is another great mystery—one that only Christians will know.

*Every character has an inward spring; let Christ be that spring.
Every action has a keynote; let Christ be that note to which your whole life is attuned.*

HENRY DRUMMOND

ON RECEIVING AN INHERITANCE

In whom also we have obtained an inheritance, being predestined according to the purpose of Him who works all things according to the counsel of His will.

EPHESIANS 1:11

Has someone ever included you in his or her will? If so, you might have a small inkling of what it means to be included in the will and testament of God. When God's will and testament are read, we shall receive glorious things beyond even our wildest imagination! No one in the world could possibly have the slightest conception of the full wonders that God has provided for those who love Him. As Christ's heirs we receive deliverance from death and the promise of eternal life. He vows to meet all our needs from His abundance, and He works all things together for our good. And one day He will take us to live with Him in Paradise.

Don't you wonder what Paradise will be like? We've seen countless wonders God has created on this earth—how much more splendid will heaven be? What will it be like when there is no more pain, sorrow, or separation? In this life, many people endure great pain. Many suffer sorrow and heartache over loved ones. Others feel depressed. Yet others are separated from those whom they love. But in heaven we'll have no more separation, sickness, heartache, loss, pain, or death. The things of this earth will have passed away. Our release from these things is part of the inheritance God has prepared for His children.

How can you and I receive this inheritance? Paul tells us: "In him we were also chosen…that we, who were the first to hope in Christ, might be for the praise of his glory. And you also were included in Christ when you heard the word of truth, the gospel of your salvation" (Ephesians 1:11–13, NIV). Put your faith in Jesus, and He will reserve this inheritance for you!

The key to heaven is shaped like a cross and those that would enter therein do so by trusting in the cross of Christ.

INTEGRITY

'But let your "Yes" be "Yes," and your "No," "No."
For whatever is more than these is from the evil one.'

MATTHEW 5:37

A little boy was once asked in Sunday school to define the noun "lie." In response, the boy said, "A lie is an abomination to the Lord and a very present help in time of trouble." We may laugh at this child's perspective, and yet doesn't it hit a little close to home? Have you found yourself justifying a lie here and there? Many of us do. But we need to avoid compromising the truth.

We need to cultivate truthfulness in our lives for several reasons. First, as Charles Hodges says, truthfulness is the very substratum of deity. By that definition, a being who would lie couldn't be God but merely a false god or lying idols of the heathen. Truthfulness is the very essence of God's character. If God lied, we could have no confidence in Him whatsoever.

Second, truthfulness is essential to God's purpose for humankind. We can never reach God's full potential for us if we lie. The Scripture tells us that our goal is to become like God and Jesus Christ. Therefore, we must become like Him who cannot lie under any circumstances.

Third, lying destroys the fabric of society. Social harmony depends on a certain amount of trust based on truthfulness. How can there be any trust among us when we justify telling lies?

Can you truthfully say that honesty and integrity are qualities in your life? We need to remember that we will stand before God and be held accountable for every idle word. Therefore, in the words of the psalmist, "Keep your tongue from evil." Let's pray that our truthfulness as Christians will shine like a beacon in a world steeped in darkness and lies.

White lies are but the ushers to black ones.

ELEANOR DOAN

ONCE AND FOR ALL

So Christ was offered once to bear the sins of many…

HEBREWS 9:28

Have you ever experienced the joy of giving someone a gift with no strings attached, no expectation of thanks, no anticipation of reciprocation? Then you have a small taste of Christ's joy in providing salvation for us. And yet we find it so hard to accept this gift at face value. We seem to want to add to it just for good measure. But we have nothing to add. Jesus' sacrifice was perfect, atoning for all sins forever. He has paid our debt in full.

I recall once reading of a master wood craftsman who spent months constructing a beautiful coffee table for his friend. He carved all manner of intricate designs around the side of the table and applied seventeen coats to the surface, a Parisian finish, until it glistened. You could see your face in it as if it were a mirror. The craftsman brought the table wrapped in a soft cloth to his friend, unveiled it, and said, "Voilà! There it is—the long-anticipated gift."

Though the table was indeed a thing of consummate beauty, the craftsman's friend said, "Oh, I…I think it is just magnificent, but I couldn't simply accept it as a gift. You have done all the work. Surely I must do my part." With that the friend picked up a piece of sandpaper and started to sand the top of the table. The master craftsman grabbed his friend's wrist and said, "Stop that! You'll ruin it all. It is finished."

So it is with the great redemption wrought by Christ. Just before He gave up His spirit, Christ said, "It is finished!" Done! Complete! We can add nothing; indeed, we in our sinfulness have nothing to offer. But nothing is needed. Christ's sacrifice is perfect. Christ suffered infinitely upon the cross and paid an infinite price—in full.

The only "sacrifice" we can now give to the Lord is a sacrifice of praise for what He has done! So, if you haven't already, accept the gift. Stop trying to earn it; just take it from Christ with a heart full of gratitude.

Jesus paid it all, all to Him I owe.
Sin had left a crimson stain; He washed it white as snow.

ELVINA M. HALL

KEEP YOUR EYES ON JESUS

But when he saw the wind, he was afraid and, beginning to sink, cried out, 'Lord, save me!'

MATTHEW 14:30, NIV

Have you ever faced a storm in your life, one so big that you thought you'd never see the light of day again? Maybe you face one even now, and you feel threatened and dismayed by the waves crashing around you.

Peter knew exactly how you feel. After a long, hard day of ministry, Christ had sent his disciples to sail across the Sea of Galilee while He climbed a mountain alone to commune with His Father. The disciples' crossing was anything but smooth. The winds had whipped the sea into a frenzy, and the disciples struggled to control their boat. Unable to make headway, the disciples feared for their lives.

Then, in the last watch of the night, Jesus came to them—walking on the water! When the disciples saw Jesus coming toward them, they were terrified. They thought they had seen a ghost, and they cried aloud. But Jesus said, "Take courage! It is I. Don't be afraid."

Peter responded, "Lord, if it's you, tell me to come to you on the water." Jesus replied, "Come." As Peter began to walk on the surface of the water, he focused his sights on Jesus. Step after step, he walked on top of the water! But, as the sea continued to churn around him, Peter looked at the water and began to sink. He cried out in terror, "Lord, save me!" So Jesus reached out His hand and rescued him, saying, "You of little faith." As long as Peter kept his eyes trained on his Lord, he had safe passage in the midst of a raging storm. But when he focused on the churning waters, he lost sight of Jesus and lost his footing, too.

As you face storms in your life, don't look at the waves crashing around you. Instead, keep your eyes focused on Jesus. He can steady and sustain you through any storm. Look at Him and walk toward Him—He'll give you safe passage through the raging seas.

Turn your eyes upon Jesus. Look full in His wonderful face.
And the things of the earth will grow strangely dim in the light of His glory and grace.

HELEN LEMMEL

EDUCATION

'And these words which I command you today shall be in your heart; you shall teach them diligently to your children, and shall talk of them when you sit in your house, when you walk by the way, when you lie down, and when you rise up.'

DEUTERONOMY 6:6–7

Who has the primary responsibility for the education of our young? The state? Local schools? Principals and administrators? Teachers? The Bible tells us that *parents* have the primary responsibility for teaching their children how to survive and succeed in life. Unfortunately, in today's anti-family milieu, a growing number of the social elite think that the state should regulate what children learn.

It wasn't always this way. When the Pilgrims and Puritans came to America, they placed a high priority on education. In 1647, not long after their arrival, the Puritans passed the "Old Deluder Satan Act," the first law in the English colonies to require education. The law's title refers to the devil, who gets his foothold into people's lives by distracting them from learning Scripture.

But in the early nineteenth century, Horace Mann, who did not believe in Christ's deity, established the modern public education system in order to take control from the Church, where virtually all the education had taken place, and put it into the hands of the state. Eventually, the schools became almost entirely secularized, and real learning has plummeted as revealed again and again in countless standardized tests.

Often what public schools teach contradicts what parents want their children to learn. This is tragic because in the long run, God holds *parents* responsible for their children's education. We as a Church need to support the young families in our midst to provide and support educational alternatives for them such as Christian schools or home schools. We need to lobby and vote for ballot measures that support parents' rights to determine what their children will learn in school. We must do all we can to help parents rear their children in the knowledge of God.

Christianity is par excellence a teaching religion.

J. D. DOUGLAS

THE TEST OF A TRUE FRIEND

A man who has friends must himself be friendly…

PROVERBS 18:24

Think for a moment of the best friend you've ever had. What made that person such a great friend? What was it about that person that made you want to reciprocate friendship?

Good friends are hard to come by in our mobile, "rootless" society. With so much to do and so little time, many of us don't invest what it takes to develop true friendships, instead settling for temporary "acquaintanceships." But in doing so, we miss out on the richness that deep, abiding, and significant friendships bring to our lives.

Do you wish for more from your present relationships? To foster devotion, we must give of ourselves. This isn't easy for most of us, but if we do it, we experience tremendous rewards. Every person who has ever engaged in a truly selfless friendship has found that in giving, personal horizons expand. These people discover that true happiness is found, not in comfort, but in sacrifice.

We in America balk at any type of sacrifice, avoiding anything that might result in the slightest discomfort. But the Bible says of Jesus that "for the joy that was set before Him He endured the cross despising the shame." Because of Christ's love for us, He endured the ultimate sacrifice. And when someone acts as a true friend in that way, we want to respond in kind, and we don't experience it as a burden but as a joy.

A little girl walked down the street carrying a boy much too big for her to bear. An old man stopped and asked the little girl if the boy was too heavy for her, and she replied, "He's not heavy; he's my brother!" Is there a friend or a potentially new friend whom you can carry today? How can you give of yourself to someone who really needs you, someone you can care for with great joy in your heart? For as you give of yourself out of love—without complaint or irritation—you'll discover genuine friendship.

Life begins when you begin to serve.

ANONYMOUS

MASTER OR GENIE

…Jesus Christ is Lord…

PHILIPPIANS 2:11

Is Jesus the Lord and master of your life, or is He but a genie in a bottle, there to answer your every beck and call? In some quarters of today's Church we find a sort of theology that says one may accept Jesus as Savior and reject Him as Lord. This is heresy. People who believe this come into "faith" still hanging onto *their* plans, *their* goals, *their* agenda. They receive Christ as a genie in a "theological bottle" that they call forth through prayer.

People like this miss the full meaning of Christianity. To believe in Christ means to accept Him as Lord and master of our lives. Napoleon in his latter days at St. Helena said, "Across a chasm of eighteen hundred years, Christ makes a demand which is above all others difficult to satisfy. He asks for that which a philosopher may often seek at the hands of his friends, or a father of his children, or a bride of her spouse. He asks for the human heart, for his very own, exclusively his. Wonderful! In defiance of time and space, the soul of man with all its powers becomes an annexation to the Empire of Christ."

George Matheson describes the human personality as a palace of many chambers. In this palace is the room of memory where Calvary may have the central place. There's a sunny chamber of affections where we may love Christ fondly. There's a lofty chamber of imagination where we plan the great things we'll someday do for God. But above all, there's the throne room of the human will. When we invite Christ into our hearts, we must allow Him to reign on the throne of our will. And as we do, suddenly a corridor opens and connects all the other chambers, for when Christ controls our will, He controls all else.

Have you surrendered the throne of your will to the King? If you haven't, do so today. Allow Christ to reign in your heart, guiding every decision you make. Then watch as He opens to you a life beyond your wildest dreams.

Gimme this. Gimme that. Bless me, Lord, I pray.
Grant me what I think I need to make it through the day.

CHRISTIAN SONG

A NOBLE ORIGIN AND DESTINY

But one testified in a certain place, saying: 'What is man that You are mindful of him, or the son of man that You take care of him? You have made him a little lower than the angels; You crowned him with glory and honor, and set him over the works of Your hands.'

HEBREWS 2:6−7

How you view humanity has a great impact on how you treat people. So what do we make of the fact that humans have killed more of their own in the twentieth century than in any of the previous centuries? What does this tell us about the way we view ourselves?

I believe we can attribute the rise in the rate at which humankind kills its own to the rise in the number of people who believe in evolution. People no longer believe that humans are just a little lower than the angels; instead, we're just a little more advanced than the apes. Bertrand Russell, an evolutionist and author of the book *Why I Am Not a Christian,* said, "We started somewhere, we don't know where; we are here, we don't know why; we are going to some great oblivion, we know not whither." The evolutionary view of humans, taught in so many of our schools today, has led many young people into hopelessness.

By contrast, we Christians have a high view of humankind because the Bible has definite answers to life's basic questions, answers that give us hope. Where did I come from? I came from the heart and mind of the omnipotent and omniscient God, who made me in His image. Who am I? I am a child of the King, a prince/princess of the royal realm. Why am I here? I am here to serve and glorify the Almighty and to enjoy Him forever. How should I live? I should live according to the commandments which He has given me in His Word, commandments designed for my good and advancement. Where am I going? I am going to a Paradise far beyond my comprehension: "Eye has not seen, nor ear heard, nor have entered into the heart of man the things which God has prepared for those who love Him" (1 Corinthians 2:9).

Today thank God for your divine origin and for the hope it gives. Treat those around you as the divinely created beings they are. Remember, each one (including you) is a little lower than angels!

For the Christian, for the creationist, man has a noble origin and a noble destiny. And in between, his life is crammed full of meaning, value, significance, and purpose.

THE GLORY OF HIS MAJESTY

Declare His glory among the nations, His wonders among all peoples.

PSALM 96:3

In your opinion, who is the most awe-inspiring person ever to have lived? What makes that person so incredible? Now think of God. Isn't it amazing that no matter how awe-inspiring some people are, none can compare to the majesty of our great God?

Today let's dwell on God's awesomeness. First of all, God is a Spirit. While He is a personal Spirit who touches each individual life, He is also an infinite Spirit, inhabiting every place, filling heaven and earth and reaching beyond the farthest star. Psalm 139:7–8 says, "Where can I go from Your Spirit?...If I ascend into heaven, You are there; if I make my bed in hell, behold, You are there." His Spirit is everywhere.

God is also eternal. He has existed forever. He is the great I Am, not the great I Was. Psalm 90:2 says, "Before the mountains were brought forth...You had formed the earth and the world, even from everlasting to everlasting, You are God." He was here before time began and shall remain after time ends.

As well, God never changes. Malachi 3:6 says, "For I am the Lord, I do not change." He doesn't continually evolve or learn; He is complete and perfect already. Nor do His counsels change. Psalm 33:11 says, "The counsel of the Lord stands forever, the plans of His heart to all generations."

God is infinite, eternal, and unchangeable not only in His being, but also in His power. Jeremiah 32:17 says, "There is nothing too hard for You." To grasp even the smallest inkling of God's immenseness, think of our entire universe as a tiny grain of sugar on God's finger. While this picture doesn't accurately depict God because it implies that He is finite, it does give us an idea of His magnitude.

When we catch even a glimpse of God's Majesty, we can do nothing but respond in continual praise. Today, take some time to dwell on the awesomeness of our God, and offer Him praise for His majesty.

Atheism is so senseless. When I look at the solar system, I see the earth at the right distance from the sun to receive the proper amounts of heat and light. This did not happen by chance.

ISAAC NEWTON

"PREACH THE GOSPEL"

…'Go into all the world and preach the gospel to every creature.'

MARK 16:15

When we first come to the Savior, we come with empty hands, empty of anything that could commend us to His kingdom. With empty hands we embrace His Cross and trust in His redeeming work to save us. But when we meet Christ in heaven, we hope our hands will be full to overflowing with the souls we've led into His everlasting kingdom.

If you were to meet Christ in heaven today, what would you hold in your hands to offer Him?

Christ has commanded us to give witness of Him to the world. He said, "Go into all the world and preach the gospel to every creature." Our world is lost and dying, and we Christians have within our hands the only cure: the good news that Jesus Christ has saved us. We need to share that good news freely to bring hope and healing into the world.

As we share Christ with others, we'll gain a real sense of significance and purpose for our lives. And as we walk in faith, giving away the abundant resource of God's grace, we gain even more spiritual growth in return.

Not only is witnessing to people a command from Jesus Christ, it's a tremendous privilege. Do you know someone who needs to hear the good news today?

Must I go, and empty handed, thus my dear Redeemer meet?
…Not one soul with which to greet Him: Must I empty handed go?

CHARLES C. LUTHER

TRAGEDY OR TRIUMPH?

For to me, to live is Christ, and to die is gain.

PHILIPPIANS 1:21

If you knew that you were going to die today, how would you feel until the moment arrived? Death can be either the most frightening or the most delightful prospect to an individual. How a person feels about death depends totally on his or her relationship with the Lord. Consider how one man changed his perspective on facing "the king of terrors" as his relationship with Jesus Christ changed.

John Wesley was an unbeliever and a clergyman all at the same time, at least in the early part of his ministry. He knew all the facts about Christianity, but he hadn't developed an intimate relationship with Jesus Christ. During this time of unrecognized spiritual confusion, Wesley was sailing on a ship bound for England when a great storm overwhelmed the vessel, ripping its sails to shreds and threatening to destroy the masts. Wesley was terrified! As the wind howled in the darkness of that night, Wesley felt certain he'd soon face his Maker. He knew that he was getting ready to leap into the darkness of death, and he didn't know where he would land.

Suddenly, over the howling of the winds, Wesley heard the sound of singing. He looked to see where it came from, and he saw three men holding onto the other side of the ship, singing praises to God. Wesley staggered over to these men and shouted against the wind, "How can you sing? You are going to die this very hour!" To his astonishment they replied, "If the ship goes down, then we go up to meet the Lord!"

"How can they know that?" thought Wesley. Only later, in London, would he discover their secret—the secret of eternal life through faith in Jesus Christ.

Dying means totally different things to the saved and the unsaved. At death, the unbeliever is ripped from the arms of the world and cast into the fires of hell. But the Christian leaves this world to rest eternally in the everlasting arms of Jesus, who has made our entrance into heaven possible by His death!

What's your attitude toward death? If you feel fear, you needn't. You can trust your life to Jesus Christ, accepting His free gift of grace, your passage to heaven when this life ends. And as you receive that gift, you can experience the joyful anticipation of an even greater life to come when this life ceases.

The best of all is, God is with us. Farewell! Farewell!

JOHN WESLEY'S DYING WORDS

ON GIVING AND RECEIVING

But this I say: He who sows sparingly will also reap sparingly, and
he who sows bountifully will also reap bountifully.

2 CORINTHIANS 9:6

When you have an opportunity to give away money, what's your attitude? Do you give generously, with a happy heart?

The Bible tells us that God loves a cheerful giver. It also says that we shouldn't give grudgingly or from compulsion. But many people do just that. They look on their giving not as sowing but as throwing, such as the man who put a dollar in the offering plate and afterward sang with all his might, "When we asunder part, it gives us inward pain." Do you have a similar attitude toward giving away your money?

God honors those who give generously. A man named William decided to give ten percent of his income to the Lord. As he grew more wealthy, he increased his giving to twenty percent of his income, then to fifty percent. Eventually he gave away one hundred percent of his income. Who was this man? William Colgate. Of the millions of people today who brush their teeth with Colgate toothpaste, very few know that this man succeeded because he obeyed the law of sowing. Other successful men followed this principle, too, such as Mr. Heinz of Heinz Ketchup and Mr. Kraft of Kraft Foods.

Although we might not have as much wealth as those gentlemen, we still need to obediently and faithfully give tithes to the church and offerings to those in need. Often we have good intentions but fail to come through when we have opportunities to give. But we can trust that when we give, God will give back to us abundantly. He has promised that He will do that very thing.

Years ago I tested God's promise by increasing my giving as I had the opportunity. I now give back one hundred percent of my salary to the church. In every one of those years as I increased my giving, God increased my income and opened the windows of heaven. I ended up with more money than I would have had if I had held on tightly to every penny.

Let me make it clear: God doesn't need our money. He doesn't command us to give because He needs it. He commands us to give because we need to trust God's provision. Money is nothing to God except an index to our souls. Our giving shows how much we trust God to provide for us.

Do you believe that God will take care of all your needs? If so, then give what you can expectantly and gladly, believing in God's generosity and faithfulness. Remember, no one could ever outgive God.

There was a man, some called him 'mad.' The more he gave, the more he had.

ANONYMOUS

GOOD FOR EVIL

*'...bless those who curse you, do good to those who hate you, and
pray for those who spitefully use you and persecute you.'*

MATTHEW 5:44

Remember the last time someone wronged you? Maybe a friend betrayed a confidence. Or perhaps someone attacked your character or lied to you or...well, any one of thousands of scenarios. Whatever the offense, how did you respond?

In matters of good and evil, our responses can take one of four directions. First of all, some people return *evil for good*. This is the devil's way of doing things. We see this attitude demonstrated by criminals and by cruel and tyrannical governments. You offer these people your best, and they hurt you in return. Then some people return *evil for evil*. These people aren't devil-like; they're beast-like. Animals, especially wild animals, generally react this way. If you step on a snake's tail, you can soon expect to find its fangs in your ankle. Others return *good for good*. This isn't devilish or beastly; it is a natural human response, the response of an unregenerate person. We don't find this hard to accept. In fact, when we do good to others, we expect good in return. But the fourth response, returning *good for evil,* makes us halt in our tracks. Jesus says, "But I tell you not to resist an evil person." He then gives some illustrations of this: If someone takes away your coat, let that person have your cloak also; if someone borrows from you, do not turn away; and if anyone compels you to go a mile, go two. If we were to put such a response into practice, we'd see God do tremendous things through us.

Jesus, in His great love and compassion, has told us how to respond to others, especially those who hurt us! But we can't respond this way on our own; it's not part of our human nature. Instead, we must turn to Christ Himself, who returned ultimate evil with ultimate good. Christ went into the very depths of ruin and hell for our evilness, and in His goodness He suffered for us and conquered evil for all time. Only through Christ can we gain the ability and the desire to go the second mile, to turn the other cheek.

Has someone done you wrong recently? How can you return good for evil today?

*Never does the human soul appear so strong and noble as when it forgives
revenge and dares to forgive an injury.*

EDWIN HUBBELL CHAPIN

LESSONS FROM A CATERPILLAR

'...I say to you, unless one is born again, he cannot see the kingdom of God.'

JOHN 3:3

Have you ever considered the amazing lessons that nature, one of God's greatest preachers, offers us? We learn friendliness from the dog. We learn diligence from the ant. And we learn about new birth from the caterpillar.

Caterpillars do not lead very exciting lives. In fact, you might even pity them. They never travel very far, and when they do travel, they must exert a tremendous amount of effort to get anywhere. And since they grovel in the dirt, they don't see much of the world.

Although this existence doesn't sound appealing to us, it's the only existence to which caterpillars are accustomed. Have you ever heard the story of the two caterpillars who laboriously made their way across the muddy earth, when one of them looked up and spied a butterfly fluttering by? As this caterpillar watched the butterfly dipping and flitting about, picked up by the breeze and carried off into the ethereal blue, he turned to his companion in the mud and said, "You'd never get me up in one of those things!"

While we may think it crazy that a mud-groveling caterpillar would never want to become a beautiful, soaring butterfly, the unbelieving world seems to have the same view when it comes to that mysterious doctrine of the "new birth." Why believe in a faith based on such a preposterous notion? But the only kind of Christian that exists is a born-again Christian, whether Lutheran, Presbyterian, Methodist, Roman Catholic, Greek Orthodox, or any other denomination. The doctrine of regeneration—the necessity of the new birth—has existed since the beginning of Christianity, and if we want to spend eternity in heaven with Jesus, we must fulfill it.

Spiritually speaking, are you a caterpillar or a butterfly? Have you been born again? If not, I urge you to be so today, by repenting of your sins and asking Jesus Christ into your life as your Lord and Savior.

Born once, die twice; born twice, die once.

ANONYMOUS

EFFECTUAL CALLING

...whom He predestined, these He also called; whom He called, these He also justified; and whom He justified, these He also glorified.

ROMANS 8:30

Have you ever called to someone—maybe your child playing in the yard or a friend you see across a room—and that person didn't respond to your call? While people may not respond to us for a variety of reasons, God never has this problem. He is sovereign. The ones He calls always come to Him. In theological circles, this truth is known as the doctrine of "effectual calling." ("Effectual" means "producing results.") From the beginning of the world, God chose the ones who would be His, and He presently goes about calling His chosen to Him.

God calls His chosen people in two ways: outwardly and inwardly. The outward call comes from God's Word, the inward call comes from the Holy Spirit, and the two interact to draw us to God. When we hear the Word of God preached, the Holy Spirit works in our hearts so that we'll respond to it. (The doctrine of effectual calling is also "irresistible grace" because the Holy Spirit calls us so lovingly and powerfully we can't possibly resist Him.) A person whom God has not chosen gets only the outward call. Such a person hears the Word but cannot respond to it because the Holy Spirit hasn't worked in his or her heart.

Some people believe that God gives only an outward call, that they hear God's Word and have the power to accept or reject it. But this cannot be true because it would mean God doesn't have enough power to choose whom He wants. His call would not be effectual. It would also mean that people wouldn't need God to choose them because they would be all-powerful. But we know this is not true. Until God chooses us, we're dead in sin with our minds darkened and unable to understand or choose spiritual things.

None of us deserves God's choosing. In His infinite mercy, He chose us according to His good pleasure. The fact that the Lord wanted to choose any of us and that He sent Jesus to seek us is an awesome mystery. He revealed it so that none of us would boast of our salvation.

Do you hear God's call? Be sure to respond today!

I sought the Lord, and afterward I knew He moved my heart to seek Him seeking me.

THE THINGS OF THE WORLD

Do not love the world or the things in the world. If anyone loves the world, the love of the Father is not in him. For all that is in the world—the lust of the flesh, the lust of the eyes, and the pride of life—is not of the Father but is of the world. And the world is passing away, and the lust of it; but he who does the will of God abides forever.

1 JOHN 2:15–17

"Eat, drink, and be merry," says the world, "for tomorrow we die." Well, the world is half right: Tomorrow we die. Suppose *you* were to die tomorrow. How would your obituary read? Consider it for a moment...

Having considered your potential obituary, answer this question: How much of that obituary pertains to God's kingdom?

Only one life and soon 'tis past;

Only what's done for Christ will last.

How many obituaries are written in sand about the things of sand! Sadly, worldliness—the love of the things of this world—has rendered many professing Christians ineffective. The Bible speaks plainly about the dangers of a worldly heart. "Adulterers and adulteresses!" says James, "do you not know that friendship with the world is enmity with God?" (James 4:4). The world hates God, and those who befriend the world become God's enemies. Worldliness makes people focus on outward, rather than inward things. By having this focus, people ignore God's kingdom within them, and Satan gains prime opportunities to drag their souls into the pit for eternity.

The Bible gives us the key to overcoming worldliness. It boils down to what we set our hearts on. "Set your mind [or affections] on things above, not on things on the earth" (Colossians 3:2). If we allow Christ to reign in our hearts, then we will dwell on the spiritual world and not on the world around us.

Today ask God to search your heart for any worldly ways that separate you from Him. Confess those areas to God, and ask Him to forgive you. Then ask Him to show you how you can set your mind and heart on "things above."

What is this world? A net to snare the soul.

GEORGE WHETSTONE

GENESIS

In the beginning God created the heavens and the earth.

GENESIS 1:1

When you look at our world and see both the bad and the good, do you ever wonder how our society has gotten to this point? Do you ever ask yourself, "How did it all begin?"

God has answered that question for us, and to find it, we need look no further than the book of Genesis. Genesis explains the beginning of all things: the universe, humankind, marriage, evil, language, government, culture, nations, religions, chosen people. Genesis puts the rest of the Bible in context; without it, we couldn't possibly understand the entirety of God's Word.

For this very reason, many have attacked Genesis. Ken Ham, a cartoonist and a defender of Genesis, has created a vivid, descriptive picture of these attacks. One of Ham's cartoons shows two castles, each built upon a foundation. The castles have walls, turrets, towers, and flags. One castle is named "Christianity"; the other, "Humanism." On the wall of each castle stands a man with a cannon. The Christian fires his bombs at the flags flying over the humanism castle, flags labeled "gambling," "homosexuality," "divorce," and "abortion." But the humanist has his cannon aimed downward and blasts at the foundation of the Christian castle. This foundation is labeled "Genesis." As depicted in this cartoon, the world wages its war against the Genesis accounts of our beginnings, hoping that as it pokes holes in Genesis, all of Christianity will crumble.

To carry this illustration a little further, the Christian, who shoots only at the flags, would do better if he aimed his cannon at the foundation of the humanism castle. This foundation is labeled "evolution." To join in the fight, to uphold our own foundation, we need to understand that evolution and the Bible are totally incompatible. Evolutionists are atheists. They have stated in their own words that if the God of Genesis existed, He would not allow them to sin. With that premise, evolutionists can only believe that everything came into being by chance.

But we know differently because God has revealed to us how everything began. By doing so, He has given us the ability to understand the rest of His Word and the world we live in. Today as you observe what happens around you, thank God for showing you how it all began.

[If Genesis were somehow removed from the Bible] the rest of the Bible would be incomprehensible. It would be like a building without a ground floor, or a bridge with no support.

HENRY MORRIS

FAITH'S ULTIMATE TEST

And Abraham stretched out his hand and took the knife to slay his son.

GENESIS 22:10

Do you face a test of faith today? Is God calling you to leap into the unknown, into uncertain, perhaps even treacherous waters? If so, maybe Abraham's story will inspire you.

God's familiar voice rang out, "Abraham." And Abraham responded, "Here I am, [Lord]." The Lord gave Abraham instructions: "Take now your son…and go to the land of Moriah, and offer him there as a burnt offering…" Perhaps no more painful words have ever been heard. All of Abraham's joy disappeared in a flash. However, Abraham did not question; he simply obeyed. First thing the next morning, he prepared for the journey to the mountains. No questions, just obedience. For three long days he walked with Isaac at his side, Isaac who knew nothing of his father's mission. Only God and Abraham knew what lay at the end of this journey. Silently, Abraham and Isaac climbed to the top of Mount Moriah.

Once there, father and son erected an altar together. Then Abraham bound his son and, summoning all of his strength, laid Isaac upon the altar. With his heart about to break, Abraham lifted the knife above Isaac's chest. As Abraham began to plunge the knife downward, he again heard that familiar voice, "Abraham, Abraham…Do not lay your hand on the lad." God intervened and provided a ram in Isaac's place.

God didn't want Abraham to sacrifice his son. God wanted obedience. Through this incident, God tested Abraham's faith. He wanted to know which would win out: a father's love for his child or his obedience to his God. When we truly have faith in God, we will trust Him and do whatever He asks of us. Abraham was a man of tremendous faith—he trusted God with his son's life, believing that God could raise the dead (Hebrews 11:17–19). Faith trusts that whatever God commands must be done, and what God has promised He will perform in His own time.

So, back to you and your test of faith. Ask God to show you clearly what He wants you to do. And when He does, follow Him without question or dispute. He can (and did!) raise the dead; He can surely work good through your obedience.

Doubt sees the obstacles—faith sees the way.

IRA LEE ESHLEMAN

HOPE

Blessed be the God and Father of our Lord Jesus Christ,
who according to His abundant mercy has begotten us again to a living hope…

1 PETER 1:3

What's your outlook on the future? Do you view the future with hope for great things or with despair?

Two thousand years ago, Cicero said, "Where there is life, there is hope." These words ring true to a certain extent. When we struggle against all sorts of odds, even if we face imminent death, as long as we have life, we have hope. However, for many people, the following statement seems more relevant: Where there is not hope, there is not life—nothing but darkness, despair, and death.

When we lose hope, we lose all of our joy. Just imagine facing any one of many difficult trials—betrayal, loss of a job, death of a loved one—without having any hope. Without hope, we have no foundation to stand on when the going gets rough. We also lose the meaning of life when hope slips away. When we have no hope, nothing has purpose. Under these conditions, the everyday struggles of life become burdens too heavy to bear and too difficult to endure.

But we need not lose hope! Because of Christ's resurrection, we have great hope for our future! We don't just hope for something that is to come; we find our hope in something that has already taken place. The Resurrection, a documented fact in history, is a solid, unmovable rock, and everyone who hopes in it has great joy. Christ has vanquished death and hell. We have the hope of going to heaven to spend eternity with Him. And even in this life, Christ has promised never to forsake us.

Christ gives us hope. If you're feeling a little low on hope today, ask Jesus to give you some. Remember that He has secured your future, and in that truth you can have great hope for today and every day.

Everything that is done in the world is done by hope.

MARTIN LUTHER

TO REAR A CHILD

*'Whom will he teach knowledge? And whom will he make to understand the message?
Those just weaned from milk? Those just drawn from the breasts? For precept must be upon
precept, precept upon precept. Line upon line, line upon line, here a little, there a little.'*

ISAIAH 28:9–10

If you're a parent or hope to be one someday, then you've probably already considered how you'll raise your children. Allow me, if you would, to put my oar in the water and give you a few thoughts about godly parenting.

When we first look at our newborn children, we are full of hopes and dreams for them and their future. To guide our children toward reaching their potential, we can rely on promises and principles from God's Word. Biblical parenting boils down to two main things: We must train our children in God's Word and discipline them according to God's principles.

"Training our children" means teaching them line by line, precept by precept, a little bit here, a little bit there about the things of God. A father must fulfill his role as spiritual head of his household, teaching his family the things of God: "And you, fathers, do not provoke your children to wrath, but bring them up in the training and admonition of the Lord" (Ephesians 6:4). This includes teaching the Ten Commandments, the gospel of Christ, the importance of memorizing Scripture, and how to pray. And because our lives speak louder than our words, we must teach by both precept and example.

Disciplining our children must be done in love, not anger. We shouldn't raise our voices. We should listen to our children and refrain from disciplining them until we hear all the facts. We should set explicit and reasonable boundaries, enforce them consistently, and make it clear that Mom and Dad will always have the final say. We should encourage good behavior by offering positive rewards. A father once paid his son to read certain books and write book reports on them. When in college, the son often expressed gratitude to his father, because his knowledge of those books put him far ahead of his classmates. This father's initiative helped the son reach his potential.

Parenting is tough but worth every effort we make. As we train our children in God's ways, we can feel confident that our children will reach their full, God-given potential. Today, pray for your children. Ask God to help them grow in Him. And ask Him to give you the wisdom you need to train them in the way they should go.

You cannot change your ancestors, but you can do something about your descendants.

ANONYMOUS

LIVING THANKFULLY

As you have therefore received Christ Jesus the Lord, so walk in Him, rooted and built up in Him and established in the faith, as you have been taught, abounding in it with thanksgiving.

COLOSSIANS 2:6–7

A secular author was researching the subject of gratitude. As he did, he examined two large dictionaries of modern psychology and could find no mention of the terms "gratitude," "thankfulness," or "giving of thanks." He then scanned the card catalog of a large university library containing hundreds of thousands of volumes. Through his search, he found not one single card giving any reference to the terms "gratitude" or "thankfulness." Indeed, as one humorist put it, "If you're looking for gratitude, you'd better look in the dictionary. That's the only place you're going to find it."

If someone looked into your heart today, would that person find thankfulness and gratitude?

Someone once said that thankfulness is the least of the virtues and ingratitude the worst of the vices. We consider gratitude an easy virtue to attain, yet so few people distinguish themselves by their thankfulness. Meanwhile, in the first chapter of Romans, Paul, in cataloging the descent of humankind into the mire of depravity, begins by saying that "although they knew God, they did not glorify Him as God, *nor were thankful*" (Romans 1:21, emphasis mine). He then describes humanity's fall into all sorts of base immorality. The slide from godliness into wickedness begins with ingratitude.

Shakespeare once said, "How sharper than a serpent's tooth it is to have a thankless child!" But the Bible repeatedly calls upon us to remember our blessings and express gratitude. It says, "Bless the Lord, O my soul, and forget not all His benefits" (Psalm 103:2).

What blessings can you thank God for today? Beginning now, cultivate a grateful heart. Make it a regular practice to thank the Lord for who He is and for all He has done for you.

As a rule, a man's a fool. When it's hot, he wants it cool.
When it's cool, he wants it hot. Always wanting what is not!

ANONYMOUS

THE WISDOM OF THE WORLD

Where is the wise? Where is the scribe? Where is the disputer of this age?
Has not God made foolish the wisdom of this world?

1 CORINTHIANS 1:20

Our world prides itself on nothing more than its vaunted wisdom. Having confused sophistication for wisdom and knowledge with understanding, our world looks down on those who believe in God and trust in His Word. Yet the Bible says that God has made the wisdom of this world *foolishness*. Most, however, do not really believe that. Sadder still, even Christians are impressed and intimidated by the world's apparent wisdom.

But let's take a quick look at what the world's wisdom has accomplished through the years. Wisdom supposedly reached a pinnacle in the Golden Age of Greek philosophy. Socrates, Plato, and Aristotle brought to light vast stores of knowledge that the world had not hitherto known. Yet their writings have done little to regenerate humankind and alleviate humanity's problems. More recently (several hundred years ago), we ushered in the Age of Reason, supposedly a golden age of wisdom. But in truth, these were some of the bloodiest years France has ever seen. The guillotine, like some huge monster, consumed its victims until the streets of Paris ran with blood, and that Age of Reason became a very unreasonable, frightening, and terrible time. Even in this modern age, we haven't learned our lessons. We've accumulated great stores of knowledge, so much that we cannot even measure it. Yet have we really arrived at wisdom? The twentieth century has been history's bloodiest era!

Do we really want to rely on the world's "wisdom" if it has resulted in all this bloodshed? Let's bank our lives on the wisdom of God, wisdom that resulted in a different type of bloodshed—the blood shed by Jesus as He hung on the cross to die for you and me. God's wisdom can do more to ennoble human life and alleviate the pain of human existence than anything conceived by the wisdom of this world.

Wisdom is the something that enables us to use knowledge rightly.

PAUL LEE TAN

THE AGE OF ANXIETY

'But the very hairs of your head are all numbered.
Do not fear therefore; you are of more value than many sparrows.'

LUKE 12:7

A couple of years after the end of World War II, the British author W. H. Auden wrote a poem about the age in which he lived. Auden entitled this poem "The Age of Anxiety." Amazingly, the label still describes our time though Auden coined it half a century ago!

Do you ever lie awake at night, worrying about this and anxious about that? If so, you know how distressing that experience can be, tossing and turning, trying to sleep while your concerns hound you. But if you're a Christian, you needn't allow worry to plague you. Instead, you can turn over your anxieties to your heavenly Father, casting them on the One who cares for you. I heard about one Christian man who envisioned lifting each of his big burdens, like a large stone, and handing it to Jesus. When Christ took hold of it, suddenly the rock shrank to a pebble! Our worries do indeed shrink when we leave them in God's care.

A missionary was teaching a Hindu woman, who had just accepted Christ, how to pray the Lord's Prayer. The woman prayed, "Our Father, which art in heaven." Then she said, "Stop! Do you mean that God is our Father?" The missionary said, "Yes." She said, "That's enough! If God is our Father, then there's nothing to worry about!"

Do you remember being a child, trusting your parent or guardian to take care of all your concerns? Remember how, no matter how frightened you might have been, all your fears dissipated when you put your hand into the hand of a loving parent? In the same way, we have a divine and heavenly Parent on whom we can still cast our burdens, no matter how big or how small they are.

Do you have a burden causing you to worry today? Hand it to God, your Father who cares for you. Allow Him to give you the peace that comes from trusting Him with everything that concerns you.

When you have nothing left but God, then for the first time you
become aware that God is enough.

MAUDE ROYDEN

POWER

*That He would grant you, according to the riches of His glory, to be strengthened
with might through His Spirit in the inner man,*

EPHESIANS 3:16

Leap tall buildings in a single bound! Run faster than a locomotive! Defeat villains with superior wit and strength! You know who I'm talking about, right? We've all seen characters such as Superman and Batman bending steel beams and knocking out criminals, and we cheer as good wins over evil.

Perhaps we cheer because we see a kind of power that can affect our world. We know we don't have that kind of power within ourselves, so we live vicariously through the superheroes our culture has created. Through them, we attempt to compensate for what we so obviously lack.

We all need the power to triumph over evil. However, our real need lies not in the external world but in the internal combat zone where we fight our moral battles. None of us will ever need to leap a tall building or bend steel beams with our bare hands. But we do need to conquer sin, overcome temptations, and bend our iron wills in obedience to God. And we can't do those tasks without strength and power.

As Christians we have only one source for such might: the explosive power of Jesus Christ in our hearts. Not only does Christ's power expel the evil within us, it conquers the attacks from without. Christ calls us to triumph, but He never leaves us to fight on our own. Jesus always leads us forth in triumph, exhorting us to "go and conquer in my name." With Christ's power inhabiting our souls, we can conquer evil and draw people to Jesus. God can use us to transform people and thus the society around us.

Christ is the only true superhero, and He lives within us and works through us. Allow Him to empower you for the challenges and temptations you face this day. By Christ's power, you can conquer all evil that comes your way.

Satan trembles when he sees the weakest saint upon his knees.

OLD ENGLISH HYMN

NEVER QUIT

'…Be faithful until death, and I will give you the crown of life.'

REVELATION 2:10

What is one goal you've reached that you feel particularly proud of? Is it graduating from school? running a marathon? teaching your children good morals? bringing a friend or family member to Christ?

Now, what did it take for you to reach that goal?

Columbus set the goal of sailing around the world. Every day of his voyage, he penned these words in his diary: "And this day we sailed on." Columbus achieved incredible results because he continued the pursuit of his goal day after day. In the same way, if we want to reach any goal, we need perseverance and faithfulness. How well we *start* doesn't really matter. In any goal we set out to achieve, we need to persevere until the end.

Would you like to know a couple of secrets about living successfully? Then read with me a verse from Genesis which contains two great secrets of success in any sphere of life: "And Abram took Sarai his wife, and Lot his brother's son, and all their substance that they had gathered, and the souls that they had gotten in Haran; and they went forth to go into the land of Canaan; and into the land of Canaan they came." Do you see in these words the two great principles of success in life? "And they went forth to go into the land of Canaan." The first secret to succeeding in life is this: We must set out to achieve noble goals, goals worthy of our effort as people who will dwell eternally in Jesus Christ's presence. Second, we must keep going. Abram and his family made it to Canaan because they persevered. They traveled toward Canaan day in and day out until they arrived. If we expect to lead successful lives, we can't give up after we've set out to achieve a goal. Instead, we must everlastingly keep on keeping on.

If you haven't already determined some goals for yourself, choose a goal today, a goal worthy of your time and effort. Then set out to meet that goal, persevering today and in the days to come.

There aren't any hard and fast rules for getting ahead, just hard ones.

ANONYMOUS

September 5

EXCELLENCE IN ALL THINGS

Do you see a man who excels in his work? He will stand before kings;
he will not stand before unknown men.

PROVERBS 22:29

A gentleman was walking down the street, and he passed a large construction site where a group of men were laying brick. He asked one of the workers, "What are you doing?"

The man answered, "I'm laying bricks, stupid. What does it look like I'm doing?"

The gentleman asked another man, "What are you doing?"

The second man replied, "I am making a wall."

The passerby asked a third man, "What are *you* doing?"

He said, "I am building a magnificent cathedral to the glory of God!"

What's the difference between the narrow vision of the first two men and the great vision of the third man? The third man saw the ultimate purpose of his work: to glorify God.

We need to have the same focus in whatever work we do, whether we work directly for the Church or in a secular profession. As the Shorter Catechism of the Westminster Confession states, the chief end of humankind is to glorify God and to enjoy Him forever. So as we live and work, our ultimate purpose should be to glorify God.

How can you and I glorify God in our work? By pursuing excellence in all we do. Too often, work done in the Church by professing Christians is sloppy or below par. But when we do things well, God is glorified. For this reason, Christian books should be of a higher caliber than secular books, and Christian videos should be of a higher quality than secular ones.

Whatever God has called you to do, pursue excellence both professionally and personally. Make it your end to glorify God in all you do, and God will help you achieve the highest quality of which you are capable. Remember that even the smallest, most mundane task will ultimately result in a magnificent cathedral of glory to our God.

Excellence in all things and all things to God's glory.

MOTTO OF CORAL RIDGE PRESBYTERIAN CHURCH

MODERN MYTHS: THERE ARE NO ABSOLUTES

'And you shall know the truth, and the truth shall make you free.'

JOHN 8:32

Over the next few days we'll look at some modern myths—assertions by our society that contradict biblical truth.

The first and perhaps most prevalent is "There are no absolutes; all truth is relative." Have you perceived this attitude recently? You can hear it in statements such as "Things change, and what we believed ten years ago no longer fits"; "That may be true for you, but it's not true for me"; "That concept works in America, but it would never work in China."

The statement "There are no absolutes; all truth is relative" contradicts itself because it's an absolute statement. When people assert that no absolutes exist, they really claim that God doesn't exist because God is the ultimate absolute. "No absolutes" means no inspired Word of God. It means no Jesus Christ.

But absolutes *do* exist. The Bible constantly deals with absolutes: life and death, obedience and disobedience, righteousness and sin, saved and lost, light and darkness, good and evil, faith and unbelief, heaven and hell, God and Satan. Not only do absolutes exist, but we can know and understand them. The Bible says, "These things I have written to you…that you may know that you have eternal life, and that you may continue to believe in the name of the Son of God" (1 John 5:13). We can know that we must receive Christ as our Lord and Savior; that no one can mock God; that all have sinned; that one day we shall all give an account of ourselves; that Christ is the way, the truth, and the life; and that Christ prepares a place for us in heaven.

When we know the absolute truth, it sets us free to realize God's will in our lives. Don't let cultural relativism fool you into thinking that each person can determine his or her own "truth." We all may perceive minor aspects of truth differently, but that doesn't support the idea of relative truth. Truth is eternal and unchangeable.

Do you want to know the absolute truth? Then look into God's Word today. Search the Scriptures for God's truth, and let it set you free.

Those who deny moral absolutes find themselves in even greater bondage to sin.

MODERN MYTHS:
PEOPLE ARE BASICALLY GOOD

As it is written: 'There is none righteous, no, not one.'

ROMANS 3:10

Most people in America today believe that people are basically good. This belief astonishes me because it flies in the face of biblical teaching and contradicts much of human history.

Today we hesitate to mention the word "sin." We don't talk about "right and wrong"; we talk about "right and stupid." A person doesn't admit to sinning but instead says, "I did something dumb. I acted stupid. I should have been more careful." We no longer label violent criminals as "evil." Instead, we say they are "victims of illness."

But the Bible expounds on humankind's basically evil nature. "The heart is deceitful above all things, and desperately wicked; who can know it?" (Jeremiah 17:9). "But we are all like an unclean thing, and all our righteousnesses are like filthy rags" (Isaiah 64:6). "If we say that we have no sin, we deceive ourselves, and the truth is not in us" (1 John 1:8). Jesus also believed in humanity's evilness. He said that we are all sinners; children of Satan; hypocrites; filled with evil thoughts—murder, adultery, fornication, and theft; vipers; fools; and blind. History confirms humanity's evil nature. Historians tell us that one-third of all human beings who have lived on this planet have died at the hands of their fellow human beings.

We're *all* sinners. God knows our base, evil nature. He knows that none of us could ever be good enough to have a relationship with Him. So He made a way for us to spend eternity in heaven by placing all our sinfulness on Christ and having Him die in our place. Praise God that He hasn't left us to our own devices but instead has forgiven us and imputed to us Christ's righteousness. By God's good grace, we have Christ's basic goodness resident within us.

The greatest saints, down through the centuries, have all
acknowledged themselves to be the greatest of sinners.

MODERN MYTHS: WE CAN HAVE MORALITY WITHOUT RELIGION

And so it was, when Jesus had ended these sayings, that the people were astonished at His teaching, for he taught them as one having authority, and not as the scribes.

MATTHEW 7:28–29

What part does your relationship with God play in your life? Your answer to that question will affect your reaction to the myth we look at today.

Many people believe that they can have morality without religion. What do you think about that statement? It's a myth so ingrained in the modern American mind that people take it for granted. In fact, we continue to build our current educational and legal systems upon it, despite the warnings of great people in history. For example, George Washington, in his farewell address, warned us to avoid this myth: "And let us with caution indulge the supposition that morality can be maintained without religion." Dostoevski, an author of the last century, reminded us, "If there is no God, then everything is permissible." John Paul Sartre echoed Washington and Dostoevski: "[Without God] all activities are equivalent…Thus it amounts to the same thing whether one gets drunk alone, or is a leader of nations."

And I say: We cannot have morality without religion. Why? Because people don't follow a code of ethics when a fellow human being has drawn it up. While the humanists have drawn up a Humanist Manifesto that many have chosen to follow, this manifesto includes many things originally forbidden by God—divorce, suicide, free love, fornication, adultery, and euthanasia. No one can impose his or her morality on others. The atheists and humanists have only accomplished this because they've legislated whatever behaviors they've wanted to sanction. We also can't have morality without religion because if we get rid of God, we have nothing left to guide us except what we see other people doing. And what someone *is* doing is not necessarily what he or she *should* be doing. You cannot get an "ought" from an "is."

No one but God is just enough, powerful enough, or wise enough to create a moral code by which humankind must live. God not only created this code, but He sent His Son to pay the penalty for all our violations of it. Today, thank God not only for the creation of His code but also His fulfillment of it through Jesus Christ. Then submit your will to Him, allowing His moral code to guide you in everything you say and do.

And let us with caution indulge the supposition that morality can be maintained without religion.

GEORGE WASHINGTON

MODERN MYTHS: GOD HELPS THOSE WHO HELP THEMSELVES

For by grace you have been saved through faith, and that not of yourselves;
it is the gift of God, not of works, lest anyone should boast.

EPHESIANS 2:8–9

No doubt you've heard the statement "God helps those who help themselves." What is your reaction when I tell you that this, too, is a myth of our culture? Do you feel shocked? indignant? relieved?

We've heard this statement again and again, sometimes from deeply spiritual people whom we trust. In fact, we've heard it in church so many times that many people think it comes from the Bible. But it doesn't. We buy into this myth because it has that can-do, pioneer spirit that built our nation, but it often leads us astray.

God does expect us to help ourselves in some things, such as working diligently. But when it comes to salvation, we must rely entirely on God's provision and mercy. From the beginning, we've tried to help God provide us with salvation, but He has put up a sign that clearly states, "No help wanted or needed." As the late Anglican bishop, Taylor Smith, received a shave from his barber, the bishop brought up the topic of salvation. The barber snapped, "I do my best, and that is good enough for me." Through the rest of the shave, the bishop remained silent, and when the barber finished, Smith paid his bill. In the meantime, another man had come in for a shave. The bishop picked up a razor and said, "I'll give this man a shave." The barber exclaimed, "I don't think that's a good idea, bishop." The bishop said, "Ah, but I assure you, I'll do the best I can." The barber said, "But I'm afraid your best will not be good enough for this gentleman." The bishop replied, "And neither, sir, is your best good enough for God."

Our best falls far short of what God accepts for our atonement, and for that reason, we can't help ourselves. And fortunately, we don't need to. Christ has already fully paid our debts. As far as salvation is concerned, God helps the helpless who trust in Him. Today, thank God for that truth, and rest yourself in Him and in His provision for your atonement.

Not the labors of my hands can fulfill Thy law's demands
All for sin could not atone; Thou must save and Thou alone.

"ROCK OF AGES" (HYMN) BY AUGUSTUS TOPLADY

MODERN MYTHS:
SUICIDE IS A VIABLE OPTION

But he who sins against me wrongs his own soul; all those who hate me love death.

PROVERBS 8:36

Explore with me one final modern myth: "Suicide is a viable option."

Dr. Arthur Caplan, the director of the University of Minnesota's Center for Biomedical Ethics, says that the most significant bioethical event in our country's history "is not artificial hearts; it's not grandmothers who give birth to their grandchildren. It is the matter of doctor-assisted suicide because it is a break from a two-thousand-year-old tradition that says [in the words of the Hippocratic oath] doctors cannot harm." We can't tell what harmful actions will follow in the wake of doctor-assisted suicides. We can trace the atrocities of the Holocaust to a small beginning: the blurring of the line between physicians healing people and killing them. As serious as this subject is, it has generated its own class of humor. Picture this: A cartoon shows a doctor's waiting room full of elderly patients with their crutches, canes, and wheelchairs. The nurse steps cheerily to the door and announces, "The doctor will kill you now."

Advocates for doctor-assisted suicide call it "death with dignity." But that watered-down term masks the reality that this practice is self-murder. Charles Hodge of Princeton Seminary put it this way, "Suicide is…self-murder in the sight of God…We have no more right to take our own life than the life of another…It is a crime which admits of no repentance and consequently involves the loss of the soul."

If you have lost a friend or loved one to suicide, let me hasten to make something clear. I believe that a Christian may fall prey to intense, overwhelming despair and could, in such a mental state, commit suicide without forfeiting his or her soul. But for the most part, as Hodge says, "Suicide is most common among those who have lost all faith in Christianity." Remember that God has given you your life as a precious gift. Cherish and preserve it whatever difficulties come your way.

Let us not be cowards, deserting our posts,
flinging back thanklessly in the face of God the gift of life.

THE ULTIMATE CHOICE

'…choose for yourselves this day whom you will serve…'

JOSHUA 24:15

Decisions, decisions! Many people nowadays drown in a sea of options. Perhaps you feel that way today! But fortunately, despite the myriad of decisions you must make every day, most decisions are not particularly life changing. On the other hand, we can examine decisions in history that changed the course of nations. Someone once asked Alexander the Great, "How did you manage to conquer the whole world?" Alexander replied, "By not wavering." Is decision-making really that simple? Well, it may be more profound than we think. But often we find that as we hesitate, ponder, and consider things, we don't conquer much of anything—not even our own indecision!

We do have one decision we must make as soon as possible, and it *is* life changing. Joshua laid this same decision on the line for the Israelite people. He had gathered the Israelites together at Shechem, which, before the conquest of Jerusalem, was the most holy place in all of Israel. At Shechem, Abraham had built an altar when he came from Ur of the Chaldees. At Shechem, Jacob had purchased a parcel of land. At Shechem, Joseph's bones had found their final resting place after the Israelites brought them from Egypt. At Shechem, tribes had gathered to hear the curses and the blessings from Mount Ebal and Mount Gerizim. At this most historic place, Joshua once more gathered the tribes of Israel and delivered his equivalent of Washington's farewell address. Joshua rehearsed God's goodness and His mercies to the people over the years and called upon the Israelites to make a decision. He said, "Choose for yourselves this day whom you will serve."

Sooner or later we all must decide whether or not we'll live for God and serve Him. Joshua ended his farewell address with the words that many a godly family has made its own: "But as for me and my house, we will serve the LORD." Do those words describe your life, your home? Today, if you haven't already, make the decision to serve the Lord with all you have and all you are. This is one decision you'll never regret.

The rich young ruler, in his famous interview with Christ, asked the right question,
asked the right person, received the right answer, but made the wrong choice.

BILLY GRAHAM

ATHEISM: THE RELIGION OF FOOLS

The fool has said in his heart, 'There is no God.' They are corrupt, and
have done abominable iniquity; there is none who does good.

PSALM 53:1

The statement "Atheism is the religion of fools" may make some people angry, but let's examine its veracity. First of all, we know atheists are fools because God says so in His Word (see today's text). Second, reason confirms the irrationality of atheism. For an atheist to prove that God does not exist, he or she would have to explore every corner of the universe. Logic calls this the "fallacy of the universal negative." You cannot prove a "universal no" because you cannot "know" everything. You cannot know for sure that no little green men inhabit the universe because you cannot visit every planet and every star. In the same way, you cannot prove that God doesn't exist. Third, experience demonstrates that atheism is foolishly destructive. The twentieth-century atheistic philosophies of Nazism and Communism have butchered some 170 million people. This total tops the sum of all those who died in all the preceding wars in history. As well, atheism has in some cases led to hopelessness and insanity. Nietzsche, founder of the "God is dead" movement, went stark, raving mad during the last eleven years of his life.

Only a small number of Americans label themselves as atheists. In fact, many consider themselves Christians. Some attend church on Sunday, but the rest of the week they ignore God, so in reality these people are "practical atheists." Others who might, in past years, have called themselves atheists now hide their true identities under the names of humanism or secularism. The atheist says, "Down with God." The humanist says, "Up with man." These are seemingly opposite statements, but they communicate the same thing.

The good news is that atheism is not accomplishing its goals. Today more people believe in God than at any other time in history. So even when Christians appear as fools in the world's eyes, we know that God has chosen the "foolish" to shame the "wise."

Today pray for your atheist friends. Pray that they would join you as followers of Christ. Pray that they may experience God in such a powerful way that they can never again doubt His existence.

The greatest question of our time is not communism versus individuality; nor Europe versus
America; not even the East versus West. It is whether men can live without God.

WILL DURANT

THE UNSEDUCIBLE

…that she caught him by his garment, saying, 'Lie with me.'
But he left his garment in her hand, and fled and ran outside.

GENESIS 39:12

Have you ever thought about what makes someone a hero? A hero is brave against all odds! A hero will fight for what's right, even it if costs his or her reputation, health, wealth, power, social position, or even life.

Joseph was a hero. Even though he lived centuries before God gave the Israelites the Ten Commandments, Joseph knew what God's law required, and he lived by it. The evil practices of Egypt had not corrupted him. When Potiphar's wife tried to seduce him, Joseph said, "How then can I do this great wickedness, and sin against God?" He called a spade a spade. And in the face of temptation, he fled. But Joseph was punished for his honesty, thrown into prison for a crime he did not commit. At this point in time, Joseph could have reasoned that if God had not abandoned him when He allowed Joseph to be sold as a slave, He had certainly abandoned him now. But Joseph heroically kept believing and trusting in God.

Have you ever thought of what the results might have been if Joseph had yielded to temptation? He wouldn't have been cast into prison where he met the baker and cupbearer and interpreted their dreams. Pharaoh wouldn't have summoned Joseph to interpret his dreams of cows and haystacks. Pharaoh wouldn't have made Joseph the second-highest official in Egypt, commissioned to gather food in preparation for the famine. God would have had to fulfill His purposes in some other way.

Our obedience to God can have far-reaching consequences; in the same way, our disobedience to Him can have devastating effects. In Joseph's case, we see that a young man's fidelity, refusing to compromise his honor with a lustful woman, resulted in enormous good.

Do you face strong temptations today? Don't yield to them. Instead, flee from them. God will bless you for remaining true to his Word.

[When faced with temptation] it is better to lose a good coat than a good conscience.

MATTHEW HENRY

NO MORE TEARS

'And God will wipe away every tear from their eyes…'

REVELATION 21:4

Amid all the trouble we experience on an ongoing basis, with "Murphy's Law" seeming to work overtime and deep sorrows occasionally gripping our lives, can you imagine the day when God will take us to heaven and wipe every tear from our eyes? How we long for that day!

In heaven, we'll experience so many new things, things more wonderful than we could ever imagine! Yet we'll no longer see many things we know quite well. We'll have no need of sun or moon, for the glory and brightness of God and the Lamb will light everything. There will be no darkness, no night. And we'll no longer have limited bodies. God will make us perfect—we won't even need to sleep!

Churches and temples will no longer exist because we'll always and forever be in God's presence. We'll no longer pray or meditate because we'll talk to our Father face to face. And no false religion will exist to obfuscate the truth and deceive people.

No longer will we endure death or sorrow or sadness or pain. We'll no longer experience separation—we'll reunite with our loved ones who have gone before us, and we'll never have to bid anyone a painful farewell again.

In heaven, we'll no longer sin. We won't even think a sinful thought. We will finally be fully sanctified, perfect in our white robes, washed in the blood of the Lamb.

But the most glorious thing about heaven is that Jesus is there. It is He who makes it perfect. Soon you will cast yourself in the Savior's arms and thank Him for getting you home safely. All the pain of this world will fade away forever. How we long for that day!

Then I shall bow in humble adoration. And there proclaim,
'My God, how great Thou art.'

CARL BOBERG

September 15

JOHN KNOX

'And this is eternal life…Jesus Christ, whom You have sent.'

JOHN 17:3

How fervently do you wish for our nation to know God? Do you desire it so much that you're willing to pray, "Oh, God, give me America, or I die!" What tremendous things God could do in this country if we all prayed that prayer!

Five hundred years ago, Scotsman John Knox, one of the great reformers, prayed, "Great God, give me Scotland, or I die." Knox lived at a time of tremendous religious turmoil. People confused about Christianity persecuted those who tried to spread the truth. In fact, the great turning point in Knox's life came when he watched his spiritual mentor, George Wishart, suffer a horrible death by being burned at the stake for preaching the gospel. From this point in his life, Knox knew that God had called him to the ministry of Jesus Christ.

And he, too, suffered persecution. Not soon after delivering his first sermon, the French, who had come ashore as part of a religious war, took Knox captive. Knox suffered the fate of a galley slave, chained to the rowing bench of a French war vessel. After managing to secure a pardon, he fled from Scotland and went to Geneva where he translated the Scriptures from Hebrew to English. From Knox's work (along with the help of others), we received the blessing of the Geneva Bible.

At this time, Mary, Queen of Scots had persecuted as heretics people all over Scotland. And yet John Knox had the desire to bring even her to Christ. People were astonished when Knox entered the queen's castle and challenged her with the gospel's truth. Those who stood nearby could not believe that Knox had no fear of a woman who had the power and desire to send him to the stake. Yet even Mary, Queen of Scots came to fear Knox and his great intellect.

Knox's anchor, God's Word, had held strong through his long and stormy life. What a great example to each of us is John Knox's faith and courage in Jesus Christ! Today pray that God would give us our country, and that more and more people would give their hearts and souls to Jesus Christ. Ask the Lord for courage to do your part in bringing salvation to this nation.

Here lies a man that never feared the face of men.

KING OF SCOTLAND (WHEN KNOX DIED)

THE CHURCH IN THY HOUSE

'Therefore you shall lay up these words of mine in your heart and in your soul, and bind them as a sign on your hand…You shall teach them to your children, speaking of them when you sit in your house, when you walk by the way, when you lie down, and when you rise up.'

DEUTERONOMY 11:18–19

A woman once told me, "When I was a child, we didn't have family devotions in our home, but I had a friend in the neighborhood who did. I often visited her and sat and watched as this family lifted their hearts together to God. My soul was touched. I vowed I would never marry a man who couldn't pray and lead in family worship. God answered that prayer, and I have such a man." What a blessing!

Do you worship with your family on a regular basis? Some families make such family time a part of their weekly schedules. Others don't, not because they lack the desire, but because they don't know what to do. So let me suggest ways you can incorporate worship time into the life of your family.

First of all, set aside a worship time when every family member, including your young children, can participate; some families choose to do this after a meal. I believe that the spiritual head of the family should lead the devotion. As you enter into this time, encourage attitudes of joy, love, and peace—including peace with each another. If any family members have unresolved conflicts with each other, encourage them to come to peaceful terms before this time of unified devotion before God.

Worship times can have a variety of formats, and I recommend that you vary your own format over time to keep things interesting. Each time you have a family devotion, you might want to choose a specific topic to address such as integrity, purity, or honesty. Whatever topic you choose, focus on meditating upon the Word of God. You can do this in a variety of ways such as reading from a Bible, a children's Bible, or a hymnal. If possible, pray, sing, and memorize Bible verses, as well. I know of one family that keeps track of prayer requests and God's answers to those requests. They feel blessed as they see God at work in their lives.

If you haven't already, I encourage you to institute a regular family worship time. Family worship can bring blessed peace into your home, binding all family members together in love and understanding. Ask your family today how you can bring worship into your home regularly.

Family worship is a matter of conviction, not convenience.

THE LEGEND THEORY

*For we did not follow cunningly devised fables when we made known to you the power
and coming of our Lord Jesus Christ, but were eyewitnesses of His majesty.*

2 PETER 1:16

If you've been a Christian long enough, you've more than likely had, at one time or another, a conversation with a skeptic claiming that Christianity is based on myths. Unfortunately, a lot of anti-Christian voices have arisen in our culture, even among seminary professors and "Bible scholars." Many of these people believe the "legend theory," the idea that the "myths" surrounding Christ, His miracles, and His resurrection just gradually evolved over the decades and centuries.

This view, popular in the nineteenth century, largely collapsed in the twentieth century with the rise of modern archaeology. Even secular historians point out that the Church of Jesus Christ began in A.D. 30 in Jerusalem because the apostles preached a crucified and resurrected Christ. The apostles focused their teaching on this fact. And they had no time for myth making or legend spinning. As Peter said, "We were eyewitnesses." John said, speaking of Jesus, "That which was from the beginning, which we have heard, which we have seen with our eyes, which we have looked upon, and our hands have handled...we declare to you" (1 John 1:1, 3). The apostles spoke of that which they had experienced.

What's more, most of the apostles died deaths that testified to their absolute belief in what they proclaimed. They were crucified; they were stoned. And they endured all this for believing a legend which hadn't even developed, which wouldn't develop for another 100 or 150 years? That's absurd!

As well, according to Josh McDowell, eighteen different first-century pagan writers present more than a hundred facts about Christ—His birth, teachings, miracles, crucifixion, resurrection, and ascension. These secular authors corroborate the disciples' claims, the claims that have endured for centuries, the claims you and I make as Christians. Christianity is no legend that built up over the centuries. It's the truth.

If people challenge you for believing in a so-called myth, you can rest assured that the Bible contains the reliable account of Christ's life. No legend could ever come close to emulating such incredible truth!

*The first fact in the history of Christendom is a number of people
who say they have seen the Resurrection.*

C. S. LEWIS

REJOICE

…sorrowful, yet always rejoicing…

2 CORINTHIANS 6:10

In the midst of a recent illness, at a time when I felt such pain that tears coursed down my cheeks and fell to the floor, I could honestly say to my wife, "I believe that God is good and will yet lift me up out of this." And in my heart, in the midst of the pain and tears, I rejoiced in God's goodness. I rejoice because my faith rests upon those things that God has told me; therefore, no matter what my circumstances are, I always have something to rejoice about.

How can God command us to rejoice when we feel miserable? One reason is very clear: A joyful Christian serves as the best possible testimony for Jesus Christ. When we rejoice, the world sees that Christ has fulfilled His promise to give us His joy abundantly. That joy goes beyond what we can summon up within ourselves and cannot be diluted by the challenges life hands us. Paul wrote his famous words, "Rejoice in the Lord always" while in the depths of a Roman prison. He was in chains, awaiting a capital trial. His prospects were dreary, his hope almost nonexistent, and his comforts nil. Yet despite all this, he said, "Rejoice in the Lord always."

The secret, of course, is found in the words "in the Lord." So many people seek happiness and do not find it. Happiness is determined by happenings, and happenings fluctuate constantly; they are ever-changing and ever-shifting about us. But if we seek Jesus, we will find joy. He is the wellspring and the source of all joy. Rejoice in your circumstances? No! Rejoice in the Lord…in His good-ness…in His grace…in His mercy…in His patience…in His faithfulness. We rejoice in what He has done for us on the cross and through His resurrection. That is the secret of rejoicing, of singing and making a melody in your heart to the Lord in all circumstances.

Do you have that joy today? Whatever your circumstances, seek the Lord and allow Him to give you His joy.

In Thee is gladness, amid all sadness, Jesus sunshine of my heart.

JOHANN LINDEMANN

HIS SECOND ADVENT

*Behold, He is coming with clouds, and every eye will see him, and they also who pierced Him.
And all the tribes of the earth will mourn because of Him…*

REVELATION 1:7

Have you ever noticed how different people perceive the same event as either good news or bad news depending on their perspectives? Well, when Christ comes again, that's exactly what will happen.

When Jesus came the first time, He brought good news for all the world. He came to prepare a way for us to spend eternity with Him in heaven. Freely He offered Himself to us, even unto death on the cruel cross. And through these twenty centuries, He has continued to reach down from heaven with His pierced hands to lift up human souls.

But when Christ comes again, the time of grace will have ended. All who have given their lives to Christ will rejoice, for they shall finally go to their true home, heaven. But all who do not belong to Christ will experience the most awful disaster possible. They will lose everything in that hour. Nonbelievers even now realize they will have no hope when faced with the end of the world as we know it. "The best we can hope for," said the unbelieving British philosopher Bertrand Russell, "is unyielding despair." The French existentialist Jean-Paul Sartre echoed, "Unyielding despair, and upon this foundation, we must build our lives." Nobel Prize-winning scientist and evolutionist Harold Clayton Urey said, "I am a frightened man myself. All the scientists I know are frightened—frightened for their lives—and frightened for your life."

In that day when the stars begin to fall, the unbeliever's fear will be justified; for destruction and everlasting fire will descend upon those who did not believe in Christ. But today the sun of His grace still shines in the sky, and the offer of salvation still stands: "Come unto me," He says, "and I will give you rest." I encourage you to share this offer of salvation with friends and family who have yet to believe. Strive that, in that moment that Christ returns, all around you may experience His coming as good news.

What death is to each man, the Second Coming is to the whole human race.

C. S. LEWIS

FELLOWSHIP WITH THE FATHER

That which we have seen and heard we declare to you, that you also may have fellowship with us; and truly our fellowship is with the Father and with His Son Jesus Christ.

1 JOHN 1:3

Do you realize how much God wants to have fellowship with you? It's difficult to imagine, but it's true. He loves you and wants to be with you far more than you could ever dream.

What can we do to meet Him halfway, to play our part in developing fellowship with God? A story by the English evangelist Charles Spurgeon may hold the answer.

Suppose a great plague comes to London. People are dying everywhere. Those who are still alive feel such terror that they've boarded themselves up in their homes. Suppose an English nobleman has a son who is a great physician. Together they determine to help as many people as they can. The son searches for the sick and brings them to the house he and his father share. The father smiles approvingly at the son's compassion. The son goes out again and again, searching for victims.

Suppose one day the son finds you lying hopelessly on a street corner. He picks you up tenderly in his arms and takes you to his home. As you recover, you begin to realize that nothing in the world compares to the work happening in that house. So you enter into a sympathetic understanding of the father and son's mission. Yet if you want to actually enter into fellowship with that great man and his son, you must go further. You must come to the place where you ask them how you can help. When you do, they give you the task of carrying basins and bringing towels. You now have some part in their fellowship, yet you cannot understand it fully until the day you say, "Sir, I see that what you are doing is the only thing in life that really matters. I want to give my whole self over to it. I want to go out and join your son in bringing in the sick." At that point, my friend, you begin to enter into and understand the deep mystery of fellowship with the father and his son.

If you'd like to enter into a deeper fellowship with the Father and His Son, ask God to show you the first step you should take. Ask Him to send someone into your life whom you can bring to Him.

With heart toward God and hand toward man.

SLOGAN OF THE SALVATION ARMY

TALK TO THE BOSS

Casting all your care upon Him, for He cares for you.

1 PETER 5:7

Do you have a concern today? Does something burden your heart? Well, whatever it is, cast your care upon God, for He cares about you and can do something about your concern.

Some years ago, I read an interesting book by an unbeliever who attempted to "do in" the Christian faith. Despite his lack of belief, I found insightful something he said regarding prayer. This author called prayer the most incredible conceit in the history of humankind. He argued that if you worked for General Motors as a lowly employee and wanted to see the boss, you'd not have even the remotest chance of ever entering the boss' office. Think about it. What would happen if a citizen tried to speak to the President of the United States? I've thought about putting in a person-to-person call just to see what would happen. I'd probably speak to an undersecretary of an assistant to somebody, but not likely to the president. "And so," says my skeptical friend in his book, "what an incredible conceit it is to suppose that at any moment we can talk to the boss of the whole shebang."

Well, the concept of prayer *would* be an incredible conceit...if it weren't true. But it *is* true, and it's the most incredible condescension on the part of a gracious God! Have you ever thought about it? You could probably never speak to the highly placed people in this world, yet the most highly placed Person in all the universe—"the Boss of the whole shebang"—waits patiently to hear what you have to say to Him. Don't you find that amazing?

So remember, this day and every day, you have the great privilege of prayer. *You* can "talk to the Boss"! Tell the Boss your worries and cares. Share with Him your triumphs and joys. He *always* has time to listen to you!

Daily prayers lessen daily cares.

ANONYMOUS

J. S. BACH

…'Behold! The Lamb of God…'

JOHN 1:29

Johann Sebastian Bach is considered the father of classical music and, in the opinion of many, the greatest musician ever to have lived. But he not only wrote and played music excellently, he also sought to glorify God in all he did. For three centuries now, Bach's music has taken people beyond themselves and toward God.

In addition to composing music, Bach also fulfilled countless other obligations. He raised a large family. He taught music on a regular basis. He served as a church musician as well as conductor for the church choir and orchestra. He also fulfilled an obligation to compose new music for every Sunday. He regarded himself as a conscientious craftsman doing a job to the best of his ability for his supervisor's satisfaction, for others' pleasure and edification, and above all, for God's glory.

Many historians have noted that all over his manuscripts Bach wrote notations such as "S.D.G." *(Soli Deo Gloria)*, meaning "Solely to the glory of God" or "I.N.J." *(In Nomine Jesu)*, meaning "In the name of Jesus." Throughout his great masterpieces appear these words from Scripture: "Behold! The Lamb of God" (John 1:29). In his music, Bach honored the Lamb of God who had taken away his sin and had given him the peace and joy that pervaded his life…the Lamb of God to whom he ascribed all glory and to whom he appealed every day. According to Bach, music was worship, and he told his music pupils that unless they committed their talents to the Lord Jesus Christ they'd never become great musicians.

J. S. Bach did not live for fame or fortune. He lived for God's glory. That focus pervaded his life. We, too, should have this goal as our singular focus.

Where there is devotional music, God is always at hand with His gracious presence.

J. S. BACH

WILLIAM WILBERFORCE

…those who live should live no longer for themselves, but for Him who died for them…

2 CORINTHIANS 5:15

Do you have a high and holy cause you're working toward, one you'd like to see resolved before the end of your life? William Wilberforce, the model Christian statesman of all time, had a cause for which he fought most of his adult life. His dedicated service is an example to all who would reach for a seemingly unattainable goal, one worthy of a lifetime of effort.

Wilberforce was born into great wealth and comfort in England in 1759. After attending Cambridge University, he was, at the age of twenty-one, elected into the House of Commons. Wilberforce found life in Christ, and after his conversion, he dedicated himself wholeheartedly to freeing the slaves.

What drove a man of such wealth and comfort to give of himself so completely? To live for Christ, and thus to live for others, became his consuming passion. His friend William Pitt, the prime minister of England, declared his belief that Wilberforce was the man to lead the way toward the abolition of slavery. Wilberforce believed, after much prayer, that God had spoken to him through his friend, calling him to a lifetime crusade. After intense study, Wilberforce took the floor of Parliament and introduced a bill to abolish slavery. Parliament overwhelmingly defeated Wilberforce's bill that year, but he didn't give up. Year after year, Wilberforce fought relentlessly for the emancipation of the slaves, beginning with the abolition of the slave trade. Wilberforce's bill didn't pass until at least twenty years after he had begun his crusade. A few years after that bill passed, Parliament passed legislation freeing all the slaves held in all British territories. On that day, seven hundred thousand British slaves were freed. Wilberforce was greatly moved to know that his lifetime of effort had finally resulted in the end he had sought. He thanked God that he had lived long enough to see the final results of his efforts.

If you work toward a heartfelt cause, toward fulfilling God's call on your life, allow Wilberforce's life to encourage you. Don't ever give up. What God has called you to, He will most certainly fulfill.

O Heavenly Father, give me a heart like the heart of Jesus Christ,
a heart more ready to minister than to be ministered unto,
a heart moved by compassion towards the weak and the oppressed.

JOHN BAILLIE

PROSPERITY

*Honor the Lord with your possessions, and with the firstfruits of all your increase;
so your barns will be filled with plenty, and your vats will overflow with new wine.*

PROVERBS 3:9–10

God offers us blessings in many different forms. He blesses us with peace, joy, love of family and friends, emotional stability, and a host of other things. But God also promises to provide for all our material needs "out of His riches in glory." We don't provide for ourselves from *our* paychecks, *our* abilities to make money, or *our* bank accounts; rather, God takes care of our needs from *His* riches in glory.

Have you (excuse the pun) banked on this promise? So many people worry about paying their bills, but God has promised to make ends meet for us. Yet because they lack faith, many people hold on tightly to what God gives them, and as a result, they rob God of their tithes and offerings. They don't honor the Lord with their substance by giving as God has instructed. Instead, they withhold from Him the "firstfruits" of their income. Therefore, God withholds His blessing from them. Hear what God says through His prophet Haggai to the ancient Israelites who neglected to tithe: "You have planted much, but have harvested little. You eat, but never have enough. You drink, but never have your fill. You put on clothes, but are not warm. You earn wages, only to put them in a purse with holes in it" (Haggai 1:6, NIV).

God doesn't want us to tithe so He can have our money. He has all He needs. But He wants us to *honor* Him in this area of our lives. When we give tithes and offerings to God, we exhibit recognition that the Lord has given us *everything* we have. We give to Him because we're grateful for all His blessings. Most of all, we give because He has commanded us to do so. We submit ourselves to His will by giving to Him first.

God promises to bless those who give faithfully (see Malachi 3:10) and invites us to test Him in this. If you haven't already, give a tithe of your income, even if you believe you can't afford it. As you obey Him by tithing, God will pour out His blessings upon you.

Religion begat prosperity…

REV. COTTON MATHER

THE ART OF BIBLE READING

Be diligent to present yourself approved to God,
a worker who does not need to be ashamed, rightly dividing the word of truth.

2 TIMOTHY 2:15

When you receive a letter from someone you love, you open it right away and read it again and again, right? Well, in your Bible you have sixty-six love letters from God's heart to yours. What a tremendous profession of His undying love! Don't you want to read them again and again to get every last nuance of His dedication to you?

We need to read our Bibles daily. When God gave manna from heaven, He told His children not to store it up, but to go out and collect it each day. In the same way, we need to feed ourselves daily on our spiritual food—God's Word. But despite our good intentions, we often find it difficult to remain dedicated to daily Bible reading. Let me make a few suggestions that may help you delve into God's love letter to you.

First of all, develop a plan for your Bible reading. For example, read from both the Old Testament and the New Testament on the same day, perhaps from the New Testament in the morning and from the Old Testament in the evening. Then take time to meditate on what you just read. Ask yourself, "What did this passage say? Does it communicate a theological doctrine? Is it a command I should obey? a promise I can claim? a warning I should heed? an example I should follow or avoid? How is God trying to speak to my heart?" Then resolve to live by the truth the passage shows you. If you need help understanding what you read, get a good commentary, such as *Matthew Henry*, which has stood the test of time and blessed thousands of lives. When you interact with other Christians, make a habit of sharing what you've learned from your personal Bible reading, and invite your friends to share, too. You can also benefit greatly by studying the Bible with other believers. Sometimes group interaction helps you see a truth you would have missed if you had studied alone.

The Bible is an amazing, unique, life-giving Book. If you have neglected to read God's love letters to you, ask Him to forgive you and to help you become a student of His Word.

The Bible is our only safe guide.

DANIEL WEBSTER

FILLED WITH THE SPIRIT

And do not be drunk with wine, in which is dissipation; but be filled with the Spirit.

EPHESIANS 5:18

God gives every Christian the Holy Spirit when he or she accepts Christ as Savior, but not every Christian is *filled* with the Holy Spirit. Do you know whether you're filled with the Spirit? Perhaps you wonder how you can know. Paul gives us some answers. In his Epistle to the Ephesians, Paul lists three results of being filled with the Holy Spirit. First of all, we will sing and make melody to the Lord in our hearts as God fills us with His joy. Second, we will give thanks for all things. We will know that the omnipotent, sovereign God holds us gently in His hands. Nothing can come to us that does not first pass through the filter of His love. Nothing happens to us that He can't make good. Therefore, by faith, we can give Him thanks for all things. A third result of being filled with the Spirit is that we will submit ourselves one to another in the fear of the Lord. Why does that indicate being filled with the Holy Spirit? Because when we draw close to Jesus Christ, we see our sins clearly; we see how unworthy we are of the least of His favors. Our pride diminishes, and we become filled with humility. We therefore willingly submit ourselves to one another.

Do you see those results in your life? Whether or not you do, invite the Holy Spirit to fill you today. Some suppose they can be filled with the Holy Spirit once for all time, but such filling needs to occur daily, moment by moment. Ask God right now and each day to fill you with His Holy Spirit, that the Spirit may empower you to serve Him with joy.

By 'riches of grace' the apostle means all the spiritual resources that are at the disposal of Christians through the redeeming work of Christ and the gracious presence of his Holy Spirit.

HENRY W. DUBOSE

September 27

COMMANDED TO SING

*Speaking to one another in psalms and hymns and spiritual songs,
singing and making melody in your heart to the Lord.*

EPHESIANS 5:19

Do you ever find yourself, without even realizing it, humming a praise song? Did you know that as the Holy Spirit fills you, the joy you experience will express itself in song? The Bible makes it clear that God is bound up with singing. When God created the world, the morning stars sang together for joy. The seraphim and the cherubim praise God around His throne forever, not because God has commanded them to do so, but because in Paradise their song inevitably rises like a wellspring from their hearts to their lips. Even the birds continually sing their praises to God.

Do you have a song of joyfulness in your heart today?

The great saints of the faith expressed their God-given joy in song. Moses wrote songs. The Bible contains a whole collection of prayers and praises written by that sweet psalm-singer of Israel, David. Jesus and the apostles sang. When they partook of the Passover, they sang a hymn. Before his conversion, St. Augustine heard Christians singing songs of praise to God, and because those praises filled his heart to overflowing, he wept for joy.

Christianity is a singing religion more than any other. We have the great hymns of the Reformation, such as Luther's "A Mighty Fortress Is Our God." Wesley wrote hundreds of hymns, and many other Christians have given us hymnals filled with songs of praise. Other religions may have their sad and mournful chants, but only in Christ do people find joy that rises in song. Christians, therefore, should be a singing people. A gentleman of the Church recently told me, "The most exciting day of my life was one day when I was home fixing my dinner. I was just thanking God for everything! I was thanking God for the food, for the pan to cook it in, for the stove, for the hands I had to hold the pan. And I just broke forth in song!" God wants us to have that kind of overflowing joy.

Do you have a favorite song that expresses your joy in Christ? Then sing it today! Sing it as you go about your business, letting your joyfulness overflow in musical praise to God!

*I sing because I'm happy! I sing because I'm free!
For His eye is on the sparrow, and I know He watches me.*

HYMN

JOHN MILTON

...to Him be glory and dominion forever and ever...

REVELATION 1:6

How blessed we'd be if we could give ourselves over, body and soul, to the glorification of our Savior Jesus Christ. John Milton, England's most profound poet, did precisely this. He was a man molded by the Scriptures, and many consider Milton one of the highest examples of Puritanism. Though he lived much of his life in blindness, God granted him the vision to see things in the vast universe that lie beyond what the rest of humanity can see.

John Milton saw the power of sin that, left unchecked, brings death. He saw the reality of Jesus Christ, the second Adam. His masterpieces, *Paradise Lost* and *Paradise Regained,* involve two principal characters: the first Adam, by whose disobedience all of humankind plunged into sin; and the second Adam, Jesus Christ, the beginning of the new creation. Milton's epic poems describe the tremendous power and deception of sin that had come into this world, wreaking havoc and misery upon the earth. They also contain another reality—Jesus Christ, who gave thirty-three years of perfect obedience to God's commands, who regained the kingdom for those of us who trust in Him.

Milton was a poet of the invisible. He splashed on a vast canvas the history of the world from eternity to eternity, painting with his pen the greatest panorama of all time. He saw things that no one had ever seen before. And he has shared that vision with others, opening the eyes of millions. Milton believed that humankind has a high calling—to glorify the living Christ—and he fulfilled this calling in all he wrote. May we all have that same vision to be a blessing to God, to open the eyes of others by glorifying Jesus Christ in all we do.

Beyond compare the Son of God was seen,
Most glorious; in him all his Father shone,
Substantially expressed, and in his face,
Divine compassion visibly appeared,
Love without end, and without measure grace.

JOHN MILTON

POSSIBILITIES UNLIMITED

I can do all things through Christ who strengthens me.

PHILIPPIANS 4:13

What would you try if you knew you could not fail? Would you climb a mountain? learn to fly an airplane? share the gospel with your family? The Scripture promises us that we can do "all things." Have you claimed that promise? A person who professes to believe he or she "can do all things through Christ" and does not exercise that belief is like a miser who has a hundred million dollars in the bank but goes hungry day after day.

For many of us, our belief is more like this: "I can do a few things through Christ, who gives me a little help." Why do we sometimes believe that we can do only "a few things"? We believe this because we listen to the lies Satan speaks through his voice of discouragement. We believe this because we allow persecution to stop the Lord's work.

But if we want God to use us, we have to bank on that verse. Those who have turned the world upside down—Hudson Taylor, Adoniram Judson, and William Carey—believed God could do mighty things through them. They made this verse their life verse, and it transformed them. And even though the apostle Paul was beaten, stoned, shipwrecked, and left for dead, he attempted great things for God because he expected great things from God. He lived by the verse he had penned—"I can do all things through Christ who strengthens me."

If you let the truth of this verse permeate your thinking, it can transform your life! We achieve only a fraction of what we could because we don't take God at His Word. Are your expectations too low? Do you dream big dreams but never act on them? Then ask God to plant this promise deep in your soul and help you live in His power!

Man, with God's help and personal dedication, is capable of anything he can dream.

CONRAD HILTON

THE QUEST FOR LIFE

*'For whoever desires to save his life will lose it, but whoever
loses his life for My sake and the gospel's will save it.'*

MARK 8:35

When, at the end of your life on earth, you look back over your life, what do you hope to have accomplished or experienced? I think we would all like to "go for the gusto," pursuing life with a capital L. But many pursue this goal in the wrong way. Sadly, even many Christians seek life with a capital L in a way that will prevent them from ever attaining it.

People miss out on abundant life because it is a paradox. The way we truly gain life runs 180 degrees counter to the way we *think* we gain life. Jesus tells us, "For whoever desires to save his life will lose it, but whoever loses his life for My sake and the gospel's will save it." Yet most people frantically do all within their power to save their lives by heaping upon themselves all manner of comforts, pleasures, delights, and securities, not realizing that everything they do destroys the very thing they want to save. As they attempt to gain life, they lose it.

Jesus' words are difficult. Many people read them, shrug them off, and go on their way, hoping that somehow those words don't apply to them. For many, those words seem beyond understanding. But let me make it clear: If we focus all our attention and energies upon our material well-being, upon our lives in this world, then we shall lose that higher, greater, and more abundant life that we can have in Christ. Only when we release our lives to Christ, allowing Him to do whatever He wishes through us, do we gain life and gain it abundantly. Live for Jesus every day, including today, and you'll experience life with a capital L!

Aim at Heaven and you will get earth 'thrown in;' aim at earth and you will get neither.

C. S. LEWIS

GEORGE WISHART

If I must boast, I will boast of the things that show my weakness.

2 CORINTHIANS 11:30, NIV

How well do you do when an occasion calls for going above and beyond the call of duty? If you need some encouragement in this area, then consider George Wishart, a sixteenth-century Scotsman. You may have never heard of Wishart, but he is one of the great heroes of our Christian faith. Even before the Reformation came to Scotland, he preached the gospel of Jesus Christ.

Wishart lived in a time when a plague decimated great numbers of people on the continent of Europe. As that plague drew near to one of Scotland's cities, the people panicked and raced to call for the most godly and saintly man they knew. The man they chose was Wishart. Wishart answered the call and went outside the gates of the city. There he knelt on his knees and prayed to God to cease the plague's onslaught. History reports that the plague spread no further!

After this tremendous victory, Wishart went immediately to one of the cities that had already been hit by the plague. Those who had contracted the plague huddled outside the city gates, locked out of the city, while those untouched remained inside, cringing in fear. Wishart climbed on top of the city wall and began fearlessly preaching the gospel to those who were dying without and those who were cringing within. Yet, in spite of his courage, his willingness to venture all for Christ, the people declared him a heretic in those dark days and condemned him to burn at the stake.

Outside the gates of the castle, the people erected the stake and piled up the wood. As Wishart approached the stake, he knelt down, lifted his face to heaven, and prayed, reciting parts of the psalms. Then Wishart stood, took the executioner by the shoulders, and kissed him on the cheek, explaining to him that the kiss was a token of forgiveness. Once they had bound Wishart to the stake, they lit the timber, and the flames carried George Wishart's soul into Paradise.

Wishart remains an example to us of prayer and courage. If you face a situation that requires you to go above and beyond the call of duty, let Wishart's story encourage you. Trust in God to give you what you need to make it through, and go forth willingly to fulfill His call for your life.

Christianity has made martyrdom sublime, and sorrow triumphant.

EDWIN H. CHAPIN

GOD'S TRANQUILIZER

The Lord is my shepherd; I shall not want.

PSALM 23:1

On a scale from one to ten (ten being the highest), what is your daily level of stress? Do you cruise through life at level two? Or do you constantly run on all cylinders at level nine?

Seventy-five years ago, the only people who used the term "stress" were engineers talking about the physical pressure placed on objects. But now we use the term to express the pressure we feel mentally and emotionally as we live through each day. Many physicians and researchers spend all of their time dealing with stress-related disorders, as hospital beds fill up with businessmen, bricklayers, housewives, and children. There's no question about it—this is the Age of Anxiety.

But God never intended us to live stress-filled lives. The Bible states that worry is a sin, commanding us to "be anxious for nothing" (Philippians 4:6). Yet we don't live in line with this command. Instead, we worry and fret about our jobs, our families, our financial status, and everything else under the sun. Many of us don't know how to cope because we don't have the internal strength to withstand the pressures from without. Many seek solutions in drugs and alcohol. But God has given us a far more effective tranquilizer: Psalm 23.

This jewel of Scripture can so effectively take away our fears and worries that I commend it as a prescription from the great physician Himself, Jesus Christ. Psalm 23 is God's tranquilizer. Take it regularly, and you'll find what the world is desperately looking for and finding: the peace that passes all understanding! Grasping even the first sentence, "The Lord is my shepherd; I shall not want," can do wonders for the human heart.

Author Thomas Carlyle made this astute point, which can reduce our stress: "Our main business is not to see what lies dimly at a distance, but to do what lies clearly at hand." Thus, with God's help, we should live one day at a time, trusting God to take care of our daily needs!

Do you feel stressed today? Then remember that the Lord is your shepherd who will take care of every concern you have. Turn your worries over to Him today, and allow His peace to guard your heart.

Peace is such a precious jewel that I would give anything for it but truth.

MATTHEW HENRY

LIVING SERENELY

Do not be anxious about anything, but in everything, by prayer and petition, with thanksgiving, present your requests to God. And the peace of God, which transcends all understanding, will guard your hearts and your minds in Christ Jesus.

PHILIPPIANS 4:6–7, NIV

One of the best definitions of worry that I've ever heard is "interest you pay on debts you may never owe." Have you paid interest like that recently?

Worry and anxiety take a great toll on our minds and bodies. For example, research has shown that anxiety causes high blood pressure. Researchers placed a mouse in a cage. At another location within the mouse's sight, they placed a cat in a cage. The cat had no contact with the mouse: their cages weren't close together, the cat never escaped from its cage, and the cat never had an opportunity to threaten the mouse. But the cat was in the same room, and the mouse knew it! The mouse kept its eyes on the cat all the time. Six to twelve months of testing revealed the mouse had developed very high blood pressure. Nothing had happened to it. Its life had never been in jeopardy. But worry almost killed it!

So many of us are like that mouse, seeing potential danger and borrowing trouble that may never come. Worry is the sand the devil wants to throw into the machinery of your life. If you let it, worry will tear up your body and rip apart your mind.

Instead of worrying, we should pray about our concerns, giving them to our Lord. As one person said, "When I worry, I go to the mirror and say to myself, 'This tremendous thing which is worrying me is beyond a solution. It is especially too hard for Jesus Christ to handle.' After I have said that, I smile and then I am ashamed." If we would only learn the secret of faith, we could live serene lives. Paul said, "Be anxious for nothing." Paul's word for anxiety (*merimnao*) means "to rip in half." Don't let potential problems rip you in half. Stop paying interest into that bank. Instead, hand your concerns to Jesus today. Let Him take care of them and, in their place, give you peace that surpasses understanding.

Worry is the advance interest you pay on troubles that seldom come.

ANONYMOUS

CHRIST CAN MEET OUR EVERY NEED

And my God shall supply all your needs according to His riches in glory by Christ Jesus.

PHILIPPIANS 4:19

Do you often find yourself at month's end with more bills than you have money to pay? Do you have any needs that are going unmet? Well, Jesus Christ is our all in all; He meets all our needs, whatever they may be.

Too often, though, we miss out on His blessings because we foolishly cling to the tattered rags of our own ability; we constantly look to ourselves for our provision. But we don't have to. Scriptures make it clear that God will take care of all our needs (and even some of our wants). Take, for example, the specific promise Paul recounts: "And my God shall supply all your needs according to His riches in glory by Christ Jesus" (Philippians 4:19). Russ Johnston observes that this verse doesn't say, "And my God shall supply all your needs according to *your ability to make money*"; rather, it says, "according to *His riches in glory by Christ Jesus.*"

I believe the "Jehovah texts" in the Old Testament can help us remember that Jesus will meet all our needs. The first of these, Jehovah-*Shalom,* means, "I am thy peace." We can find our peace in God. When we need soothing, He will lead us beside still waters. A second such text, Jehovah-*Rohi,* means, "I am thy shepherd." God will give us guidance throughout our lives. We don't need to strike out on our own apart from Him; He will lead us wherever we need to go. Yet another, Jehovah-*Jireh,* means, "I am the One who provides." Whatever our needs, Jehovah Himself will provide. And Jehovah-*Shammah* means, "I am the One who is there." Wherever we are, whatever we need, God is there!

Don't you feel comforted, knowing that through all the changes of life, through all the ups and downs of the economy—inflation, hyper-inflation, recession, or depression—God's ability to provide never changes? What a sense of security we have when we rest in that fact! Today, lay your needs at Jesus' feet. Ask Him to provide, then trust that He will fulfill His promise to "supply all your needs according to His riches in glory by Christ Jesus."

You can't stand on promises [from the Bible] if you don't know what they are.

CHRISTIAN SONG

October 5

THE INCREDIBLE POWER OF THE TONGUE

But no man can tame the tongue. It is an unruly evil, full of deadly poison. With it we bless our God and Father, and with it we curse men, who have been made in the similitude of God. Out of the same mouth proceed blessing and cursing. My brethren, these things ought not to be so.

JAMES 3:8–10

Do you remember the last time you said something you wished you could take back? Do you remember the consequences?

We all have said things we later regret. You'd think we'd learn, but we continue to fall into that trap. Someone once said, "The trouble with talking too fast is that we say things we have not thought of yet." Why do we persist in doing something we know will hurt us in the end? Because we have no control over our tongues.

The Bible says the tongue is a great evil. James compares it to a bridle, a fire, an untamed creature, and a double fountain, among other things. The tongue is like a bridle because even though the bit is very small, it controls the horse's movement. In the same way, a little word can change the whole direction of our lives. The tongue is also like a fire. Just as one little spark can start a raging forest fire of destruction, one little word can destroy a relationship, a hope, a life. The tongue is like a caged but untamed animal that paces restlessly back and forth, looking for any opportunity to escape. Though humans have tamed all kinds of wild beasts, they cannot tame their own tongues. When we least expect it, a harmful word escapes. As well, the tongue is like a double fountain that brings forth both fresh water and bitter water. Just as saltwater poured into fresh water makes all water salty, so bitter words absorb the sweet. If you bless God but also curse your brother or sister, your good words lose their effectiveness.

Our tongues can get us into all sorts of trouble. First, there are the sins of blasphemy, cursing, and profanity. The Third Commandment forbids these. The Ninth Commandment forbids deceit and lying. God said it is better not to make a vow than to make one and break it. We should keep our vows, even if we have to make sacrifices to do so. Backbiting is another sin of the tongue. The backbiter speaks maliciously of others, then talks behind their backs. Gossip is close kin to backbiting.

Do any of these habits hit a little close to home? If so, confess them. Ask God to show you how to better control your tongue. And today make it a goal to bless others with your words.

Many a life has been ruined by a thoughtless word.

OUR FIRST LOVE

'Nevertheless I have this against you, that you have left your first love.'

REVELATION 2:4

Many of us vividly remember the day we gave our hearts to Christ. We were awash in love and warmth. Ah, my friends, our first love! There is nothing that can replace the first time we felt saturated with unconditional love.

Sadly, though, many of us have gone adrift. Our hearts have wandered. Maybe you can relate. Perhaps you're not feeling as connected with God as you once did. Or maybe you don't have your old passion for doing God's will.

We all need to ask ourselves, "Have I remained true to my first love? Do I love Christ as when I first loved Him?" If not, Christ has a solution for those of us with diseased hearts.

There are three parts to Christ's "prescription." The first is to remember from where we have come. Christ says, "Remember from whence thou art fallen." God asks us to respond wholeheartedly to our salvation. We can give no less. Christ has loved us even to the point of enduring the pit of hell for our sake. How can we not reciprocate this love? God created and saved us to love Him forever.

The second part of Christ's prescription is repentance. Because of evil, our love for God may have become lukewarm. Satan works to cool that love and constantly pours the waters of this world and its trappings upon us to kill the flame of our love for Christ. To revive that fire, we must confess and turn away from evil.

The third part is our return. God wants us to turn back to Him fully, holding nothing back. We must get down on our knees. Once we've humbled ourselves before God, we must ask Him to light such a flame in our hearts that it shall never go out. We need to ask for His forgiveness and cleansing and the ability to move forward in His grace.

When we are in love, we can accomplish all sorts of things for the object of our affections. When we're out of love, even the smallest effort can seem burdensome! Today ask God to show you what your first love is. If you find that it isn't Him, ask Him to help you remember where you came from, repent of your lukewarm attitude, and return to that fire of your first love!

Oh, make me Thine forever, and should I fainting be, Lord,
let me never, never outlive my love for Thee.

"O SACRED HEAD" (HYMN)

THE HOLY SPIRIT: WHAT DOES HE DO?

But you are not in the flesh but in the Spirit, if indeed the Spirit of God dwells in you.
Now if anyone does not have the Spirit of Christ, he is not His.

ROMANS 8:9

Have you ever wondered about the role of the Holy Spirit in Christianity and in your life? Well, literally hundreds of verses from Genesis to Revelation describe the work of the Holy Spirit, and as you delve into them, you'll discover that the Holy Spirit has played and continues to play an active role in your faith.

Just as God the Father is in everything, so, too, is the Holy Spirit. The Holy Spirit played an important part in the creation of the world. In Genesis we read that "the Spirit of God moved upon the face of the waters" as the earth formed. As well, the Holy Spirit caused Christ to be conceived in Mary's womb. The angel told Mary, "The Holy Spirit will come upon you,…therefore, also, that Holy One who is to be born will be called the Son of God" (Luke 1:35). And the Holy Spirit, with the Father and Son, participated in Christ's resurrection.

When we allow Him to, the Holy Spirit will do mighty works within us. For example, the Spirit regenerates us, resurrecting us from spiritual death when we commit our lives to Jesus. Christ says we must be "born of the Spirit" if we want to enter God's kingdom. And so, the Spirit grants us new life in Christ. The Holy Spirit also sanctifies us, purifies us, and cultivates within us the fruit of the Spirit: love, joy, peace, long-suffering, kindness, goodness, faithfulness, gentleness, and self-control.

To experience the fullness of God's power in our lives, we must allow the Holy Spirit to work within us. Invite the Holy Spirit to do so today, then watch as He responds!

We must not be content to be cleansed from sin; we must be filled with the Spirit.

JOHN FLETCHER

SURMOUNTING THE INSURMOUNTABLE

'And it shall come to pass…that the waters of the Jordan shall be cut off,
the waters that come down from upstream, and they shall stand as a heap.'

JOSHUA 3:13

Remember the last time you faced a situation so daunting that you didn't know how to respond, a situation in which all potential solutions just produced more challenges? Perhaps you're facing this kind of situation today.

Life seems to constantly throw challenges in our paths. We overcome one challenge, and there's another one in our way. And the greater level of comfort we seek in life, the greater our consternation when hardships arise.

But if we're to grow in Christ, we must persevere. Consider what Joshua faced. As Moses' successor, Joshua had been commissioned by God to lead the Israelites into the Promised Land. After the Israelites had wandered in the desert aimlessly for years, God finally led them out of the sands and to the river's edge.

The Israelites had never come to this point before, and despite the heat and rough terrain, they'd grown familiar and comfortable with the desert. At the river's edge, the Israelites confronted a new fear. The river was not fordable, and beyond it were walled cities and hostile tribes. But consider the troubles they were leaving behind: a desert and raging sun that had consumed a generation of Israelites. If they stepped into the river, they'd leave all that behind and enter the green and pleasant land of Canaan. Joshua led them into taking a step of faith, and God miraculously opened up the Jordan River. From there, God helped the Israelites conquer one tribe after another in order to inhabit the Promised Land.

We can identify with the Israelites' situation. All at once something disrupts our usual flow: a new danger, a new fear, a new expectation, a new unknown. We get comfortable with the familiar and hesitate to engage in a new endeavor. But when we challenge new obstacles, we simultaneously leave others behind.

Are you facing a new possibility today, something unknown, unfamiliar, maybe even a bit dangerous? If God calls you to move ahead, step into the river. Don't hesitate to trust God. He anxiously waits to bestow His blessings on you as you follow His call.

There is no education like adversity.

BENJAMIN DISRAELI

TODAY NOT TOMORROW

This is the day which the Lord has made; we will rejoice and be glad in it.

PSALM 118:24

How is your day going so far? Are you enjoying it, unfettered by regrets about the past and worries about the future? Or do you find your mind focused on everything else but this day?

When I wake up each morning, I like to quote aloud Psalm 118:24—"This is the day which the Lord has made; we will rejoice and be glad in it!" We need to focus on the present moment. The psalmist encourages us to seize the day...the moment...and rejoice and be glad in it. We can't leave our happiness in the past, thinking our best days are behind us. Nor should we wait until tomorrow to rejoice. Today, at this very moment, we must be glad because this day and this moment are gifts from God.

Enjoying each day is like the art of reading aloud. When you read aloud, you must pay attention to each word you read *as* you read it, putting the appropriate emphasis and nuance on every word to impact the hearer as you desire. You cannot let your thoughts race three or four words ahead of the words you are presently saying. Doing so causes the words to lose their meaning and impact. Similarly, do not think about rejoicing tomorrow. Such thoughts cause today to lose its importance in your life. Instead, think about rejoicing *today*...and do it!

Why can we be so free to think only of today? Because, unlike the atheistic existentialist who blocks out the past and the future, the Christian can perceive and enjoy past and future events for their own value. Christians can look to the past—to the Crucifixion and the Resurrection—and rejoice in forgiveness, cleansing from sin, and spiritual renewal. Christ has disposed of sin, shame, and guilt. As Christians we can trust Christ with our past, knowing that He has erased our transgressions and made us new persons in His family. Our salvation is great cause for celebrating today!

In the same way, we can rejoice today because we trust Christ with our future. As Christians we look ahead and boldly affirm the glorious tomorrow that awaits us. We eagerly anticipate Christ's return, an event that will usher in freedom from pain, fear, and death. The sovereign Lord has tomorrow in His hands, and He works all things together for good. We can rely on that truth.

Today, lay your feelings about yesterday and your anxieties about tomorrow at Christ's feet. Trust Him with your past and with your future, and rejoice in each moment of this day, a gift from God to you.

Live in daytight compartments.

SIR WILLIAM OSLER

FORGIVENESS

Bearing with one another, and forgiving one another,
if anyone has a complaint against another; even as Christ-forgave you, so you also must do.

COLOSSIANS 3:13

Has anyone ever hurt you so deeply that you not only refrained from forgiving that person but you also waited for poetic justice to catch up with him or her, perhaps helping it along by planning a little retribution yourself? "Revenge is sweet," says the world, and we often buy into that mentality. But while revenge may offer sweet satisfaction, it sure isn't biblical! God tells us that vengeance is His; He will take unjust matters into His hands. (Besides, revenge doesn't often turn out that sweet; usually it just brings on disaster.)

God tells us to forgive those who have sinned against us, even our enemies! I believe that we can't truly forgive others until we've experienced God's forgiveness for our offenses against Him. People who don't know Christ often find it difficult to forgive people who have "done them dirt." But Christians, who have experienced God's full forgiveness, must radiate a forgiving nature.

The Bible says a great deal about forgiveness, particularly about our need for it. Jesus taught us to pray, "Forgive us our debts, as we forgive our debtors." Jesus instructs us to ask God for forgiveness. We can't experience a full relationship with God unless we regularly confess our sinfulness to Him.

But that petition has a second part: We need to forgive others. Christ underscored this by commenting that only when we forgive others will God forgive us (Matthew 6:14–15). This is the only condition God describes for our own forgiveness. Forgiving others comes hard to our fallen natures, but it's crucial to our walk with the Lord. Our forgiveness of others is the indispensable sign and seal of God's forgiveness of us. Since the ultimate Christian quality is love, we should remember that in a world of fallen creatures, where we continually sin against one another, we must show our love through forgiveness.

Since God has forgiven us, how can we not forgive others? Who do you need to forgive today?

Christians aren't perfect. Just forgiven.

BUMPER STICKER

THE BEAUTY OF HOLINESS

Give unto the Lord the glory due to His name; worship the Lord in the beauty of holiness.

PSALM 29:2

What do you expect when you go to church on Sunday mornings? Do you view Sunday morning church as a type of performance? Many people do. They listen to the choir as if they were at a concert, ready to critique the choir's performance. They sing hymns but never once as they sing do ever think of praising God. Instead, they sing hymns by rote, with their minds turned off.

But God doesn't want us to sit back as passive observers. He wants us to actively participate in worshiping Him.

Soren Kierkegaard, the Danish philosopher, thought that most people conceive of church as a drama wherein they are merely spectators. In this drama, the minister is the principal actor. God prompts the minister by whispering His lines in the minister's ear (should the minister chance to forget them), and the congregation members are the critics who pass their judgment on the performance.

The truth of the matter, says Kierkegaard, is that church is a drama of sorts. But if we view worship as God designed it, the congregation members should be the actors, the minister the prompter, and God Himself the critic. Why? Because worship is one's response to the revelation of God. When we recognize God's true nature, we *want* to worship Him in direct proportion to the clarity of our vision of Him.

So many people don't understand the true joy of worship. And God doesn't want us to miss it. This Sunday, remember to actively worship God as a participant, not as a mere spectator. When the choir sings and the minister preaches, lift their words in praise to God. "Give unto the Lord the glory due unto His name."

If absence makes the heart grow fonder, some people ought to love their churches greatly.

ANONYMOUS

WAS COLUMBUS A CHRISTIAN?

*'And this gospel of the kingdom will be preached in all the world
as a witness to all the nations...'*

MATTHEW 24:14

Today marks the annual remembrance of Christopher Columbus' discovery of the New World. Columbus was a brave and farsighted leader whose monumental discovery changed the world. But our society often questions Columbus' character. We know he was a man of flesh and blood, a sinner as we all are. And we know he made mistakes. Yet we can't hold him responsible for all the things modern critics would like to blame him for.

So what kind of person was Columbus? His son portrays him as a gracious, loving father. Columbus was a godly man who so fervently attended to Scripture reading, prayer, fasting, and all of the worship services, that if one didn't know he was a seafaring man, one would have suspected that he belonged to a holy order. In fact, when Columbus first landed in the New World, his first act was to plant a cross on the land.

The names Columbus chose for the places he discovered also indicate his dedication to Christ. He named his first landing place "San Salvador," which means "Holy Savior." He named his next landing places "Vera Cruz," which means "True Cross," and "La Navidad," which means "The Nativity" or "Christmas." Then Columbus came to an island with three hills on it, and he named it "Trinidad," meaning "The Trinity." He did this time after time in the places he landed, indicating his godly focus and nature.

Today you'll often hear people doubt the goodness of Columbus' character. Part of this is because they perceive that Columbus sailed for "gold and glory." But listen to what Columbus himself said about his reason for sailing: "It was the Lord who put it into my mind to sail to the Indies. The fact that the gospel must be preached to so many lands—that is what convinced me." Overall, I think Columbus is a model of courage, who admirably drew his life's vision from Jesus Christ.

*No one should fear to undertake any task in the name of our Savior,
if it is just and if the intention is purely for His holy service.*

CHRISTOPHER COLUMBUS

THE OLD LAMPLIGHTER

For you were once darkness, but now you are light in the Lord. Walk as children of light.

EPHESIANS 5:8

Have you ever visited a historical village where a lamplighter lights the street lamps at night? If you have, then you can relate to what Sir Henry Lauder, a famous Scotsman of the turn of the century, saw as he watched a lamplighter one evening at the Hotel Cecil: "I was sitting in the gloaming [dusk], and a man passed the window. He was the lamplighter. He pushed his pole into the lamp and lighted it. Then he went to another and another. Now I couldn't see him. But I knew where he was by the lights as they broke out down the street, until he had left a beautiful avenue of lights. You are lamplighters. They'll know where you've been by the light you have lit."

Christ said, "I am the light of the world. He who follows Me shall not walk in darkness, but have the light of life" (John 8:12) and "The light has come into the world, and men loved darkness rather than light, because their deeds were evil" (John 3:19). All of those in whom the Light of life—Jesus Christ—burns brightly must bring light to those who sit in the shadow of darkness so that upon them the wondrous light of Christ might shine. We are the lamplighters. The darkened lamps are the lives and souls of lost men and women who sit in sin's dark night, far apart from God's life and light. The flame is Jesus Christ burning within our hearts through His Spirit. The pole is the presentation of Jesus Christ.

Are you a lamplighter for Christ? Have you touched the dark world with the light of Jesus Christ, encouraging lost men and women to catch fire? The world will know where you are—what you believe—by the lights you have lit. Ask God to teach you the joy of spreading Christ's light in a dark world.

O Lord, send me to the darkest spot on earth!

PRAYER OF JOHN MACKENZIE, NINETEENTH-CENTURY
SCOTTISH MISSIONARY TO AFRICA

JUSTIFICATION

*'Knowing that a man is not justified by the works of the law but by faith in Jesus Christ,
…for by the works of the law no flesh shall be justified.'*

GALATIANS 2:16

Most people don't get it. The darkness of spiritual ignorance has pervaded people's minds, leaving vast numbers abjectly ignorant of this central doctrine of Christianity.

What am I talking about? The doctrine of justification by faith—the fact that we can have eternal life because Christ's death has cleansed us of all sin, making us worthy to live in God's presence.

Do *you* understand justification by faith? If you don't, you're not alone. So many, including Christians, can't explain it. If you were to ask people from a variety of church backgrounds how to get to heaven, I believe that most answers would include a work or act. "I go to church every Sunday." "I keep the Ten Commandments." "I try not to hurt people." But none of these answers matches what the Bible teaches us about salvation.

So how do we become "justified"? The Westminster Catechism describes it most aptly, saying that justification is an act of God's free grace wherein He pardons all our sins and accepts us as righteous because of Jesus' substitutionary death on the cross. What does that mean? Most important, it means that God sets us free from eternal punishment by His will, not our own. The only thing we can do is accept the gift by faith.

God is the only one who can justify us, and yet we continue to try to justify ourselves. Someone once said to me, "I can justify everything I have done to God." Though most people wouldn't state it that way, many people try to do just that. But the doctrine of justification condemns every person's effort to justify himself or herself. Only God can justify us. He does it once and for all, completely and perfectly, in the twinkling of an eye.

Who are you trusting for your salvation: yourself or God? Only God's free grace can save you. Accept His undeserved favor, and stop your striving. Allow Him to give you the free gift He offers, and just watch where it will take you!

Justification is the pivotal point around which all else turns.

GEERHADUS VOS

TRIALS

And Abraham stretched out his hand and took the knife to slay his son.

GENESIS 22:10

Call to mind the biggest trial you've ever faced (you might face it even today). Remember the struggle, the pain, the despair? Does it help to know that through your trials God tests and perfects your faith?

Consider Abraham trudging his way toward Mount Moriah to offer his son Isaac as a sacrifice to God. From Abraham's trial and faithful response we gain great blessing, a treasure-trove of lessons, to give us insight into what God teaches us through trials.

The first lesson we learn from Abraham's story is that God needs to test our faith to strengthen and purify it, just as gold must endure fire to gain strength and purity. God tested Abraham's faith to determine upon whom Abraham relied, and Abraham passed the test by offering his son as a sacrifice. In turn, God provided another offering, a ram, saving Isaac's life. As Abraham endured this trial, he gained even greater trust in God. Through our trials, we learn to trust less in ourselves and more in our heavenly Father.

Second, Abraham's story teaches us that we'll face trials throughout our entire lives. Even as a very old man, Abraham was called to leave his homeland and go to a place he did not know. When Abraham was ninety years old, God challenged him to believe he'd have a son. Until the end of Abraham's life, God tried and perfected Abraham's faith.

Third, we learn from Abraham's story that God prepares us for difficult trials. Only after Abraham passed the tests of so many other trials did God allow the most difficult one to occur. God teaches us to climb the lower peaks before calling us to scale the loftiest summits. He teaches us to wade in the shallows before He calls us to plunge into the depths of the oceans. At each level of our faith, God has lessons for us to learn, and by His grace He enables us to pass successfully through each trial.

Take some encouragement from these lessons today. If you're presently enduring a trial, know that God has not forgotten you. In fact, through it He wants to draw you closer to Him. Trust your heavenly Father to bring you through victoriously and with a greater faith in Him.

The brook would lose its song if we removed the rocks.

ANONYMOUS

HOW CAN WE KNOW GOD?

'And this is eternal life, that they may know You, the only true God, and Jesus Christ whom You have sent.'

JOHN 17:3

Do you yearn to know God? Do you long for a special relationship with the Father, the intimate knowing that comes from interacting with Him as His child?

The stronger we grow as Christians, the closer we grow to God. As the New Testament says, we "grow in grace, and the knowledge of our Lord and Savior Jesus Christ."

But *how* do we get to know God better? First, we spend time with Him. *Every* relationship grows with time and tender care, including a relationship with God. In the psalms we read, "Be still, and know that I am God." Yet achieving this stillness is difficult. Noise and diversion constantly bombard us; we struggle to have quiet time alone with God. But if we want to know Him better, we have to discipline ourselves to carve out quiet time and space to be with God. And as we fall silent, we can hear God speak to us about His nature.

We can also grow closer to the Father by obeying His commands. Scripture tells us that we'll know God better as we follow His instructions. We can't grow closer to Christ while knowingly living in disobedience. If you want to know Him, obey Him in everything.

We also learn more about God by loving Him. The Bible says, "Everyone who loves is born of God and knows God…for God is love" (1 John 4:7–8). Christ laid down His life on the cross for us, and in return we need to love Him sacrificially, laying down our lives for God, submitting our will for His glory. As we do this, we discover more about God's sovereignty and love.

Does your soul pant for a more intimate relationship with God? Then spend time with Him this very moment, in His word, in a quiet place. Choose to live obediently, and focus your love on Him. Do so, and you'll come to know Him who loves you with a love far beyond anything humans can offer. You'll find the fulfillment of your heart's desire.

Our hearts are restless till they rest in Thee.

ST. AUGUSTINE

WHEN TROUBLE COMES

Yet man is born to trouble, as the sparks fly upward.

JOB 5:7

"You're in trouble!"

If you're a living, breathing human being (and if you can read this, I assume you are), those words apply to you. We don't like this fact of life, but we just can't escape trouble. Because we live in a sinful world, we can expect it. But though we can't avoid trouble, we *can* determine how we'll handle it. In fact, our lives are shaped, to a large extent, by how we deal with the troubles that come our way. Some people face trouble with despair, others with hope. Some approach trials in the agony of doubt, others in faith.

But what does trouble do in our lives? Some troubles can act as *preparation*. They clear the way for God to do greater works in our lives. When God sent His Son into the world in preparation for His greatest work—our salvation—there was great trouble on the earth. Herod commanded the massive slaughter of the innocents at Bethlehem. But that pain ushered our Savior into the world. Trouble can act as the grindstone upon which God sharpens the ax of battle.

Trouble can also be *education*. We learn things when in trouble that we don't learn any other way. Many have risen from the furnace of affliction to say they've heard God's voice as never before. Dear friends, stars come out only at night. We learn lessons in the darkness that we never learn when the sun shines brightly.

In addition, trouble can be *revelation*. As we endure our troubles, we learn a great deal about our character. Shadrach's, Meshach's, and Abednego's characters were never more fully revealed than in the glow of the open door of Nebuchadnezzar's furnace! When the heat is on, the real person emerges.

Is trouble hounding you today? Instead of attempting to avoid the inevitable, seek the Lord in your trouble and allow Him to prepare you, educate you, and reveal your character according to His design.

Even a misfortune may prove useful in three years.

JAPANESE PROVERB

LIVING BY FAITH

…'The just shall live by faith.'

ROMANS 1:17

Do you want to know the secret of successful living? God wants to teach it to you. He wants you to know that you can trust Him for everything that happens in this world and in the world to come.

Do you trust God to take care of today and for that day when you shall see Him face to face?

Many people find life overwhelming. They look down the road of their lives and fear all sorts of impending disasters and tragedies, believing that nothing will work out right. As these people clearly and realistically look at the world, nothing looks encouraging, and therefore they worry.

And that's just the way Satan likes it. He doesn't want us to trust God. He wants us to fret about our lives, so he attempts to entice us into living for ourselves, in our own power. He says, "Come and do it my way. Forget about God. Try it this way. Live for the pleasures of the flesh. You only go around once; grab all the gusto you can." If we don't follow him but instead persist in following God, then what does Satan do? He screams, "Look out! Calamity! The bridge is out. Disaster ahead! Everything is going to go to pieces." Satan wants to fill our hearts with fear and despair so that if we follow God, at least we'll do it with long faces, furrowed brows, and hearts devoid of joy.

But Romans 1:17 offers the solution for troubles, despair, and hopelessness: "The just shall live by faith." This Scripture communicates the brightness of an everlasting hope in Christ. As we trust in Christ, he protects us. He takes care of our needs, our concerns. As we look to Him, the brooding mists of gray seem to dissolve, and we walk right through them.

You now know the secret of successful living. Live by it. Refuse to listen to Satan's whisperings. Instead, trust Jesus Christ for this day and for all your tomorrows.

Be not dismayed whatever betide; God will take care of you.

WELL-KNOWN HYMN

LIVING JOYOUSLY

You will show me the path of life; in Your presence is fullness of joy;
at Your right hand are pleasures forevermore.

PSALM 16:11

Do you know something that grieves me? I grieve that the world has believed the lie that God is mean and narrow, a killjoy who thwarts our happiness. And even more tragic is that many Christians have succumbed to this lie. Many walk around with sad countenances and sorrowful attitudes. What picture of Christianity does this present to the world?

Have you believed the lie? Do you worry about having "too much fun," afraid that if you enjoy yourself God will swoop down and zap you? Nothing could be further from the truth.

God originally planned for our lives to be full of joy and free from sorrow. In the beginning, God created a man and a woman, and He placed them in...the garden of sorrows?...the garden of misery? No! He placed them in the Garden of Eden. "Eden" is a Hebrew word transliterated as "a garden of delight, a garden of pleasure." At the beginning of His plan for us, God created a garden of delight and pleasure. He put Adam and Eve there so that humankind might share His joy.

Though humankind disobeyed God, bringing sin and sorrow into the world, God didn't give up on His plan. Instead, He gave us Jesus so that we might have another chance to live joyfully. Through His life, Jesus showed us the meaning of joy. While the Bible never says that Jesus laughed, we can safely surmise that He did. Furthermore, Jesus wept *in our place* because He took on our sin and our guilt, and His sorrow became our joy. The shortest verse in the Bible is "Jesus wept." The second-shortest is "Rejoice evermore." Rejoice evermore. Jesus wept on our behalf so that we might experience His joy, the joy that God bestows on us. Jesus said, "These things I have spoken to you, that My joy may remain in you, and that your joy may be full" (John 15:11).

Through His sacrifice, Jesus has made joy available to all the world. Can the people around you see Christ's joy in you? If they do, they'll want some of it. So allow God to instill a joyful attitude in you, whatever the challenges you face.

Christianity...carries in its heart the happiness of heaven.

HUGH BROWN

GOD'S POWER IN OUR LIVES

'But you shall receive power when the Holy Spirit has come upon you…'

ACTS 1:8

Have you ever looked at a challenge and thought you just didn't have the power to overcome it? Maybe you face such a challenge today. If so, do you realize that you have incredible power available to you through the Holy Spirit?

Perhaps you know this hymn: "I link my earthly feebleness to Thy almighty power." These words explain the great claim Christianity makes—that God links us feeble human beings to His divine power when we entrust our lives to Him. When Jesus ascended to Heaven, He promised that the Holy Spirit would come on us, giving us this power.

Power! In the Greek it is *dunamis,* from which our word "dynamite" comes. We have that kind of explosive power in God! Consider some of the events in the Old Testament in which men and women overcame kingdoms, stopped the mouths of lions, quenched the fury of fire, and turned aside the edge of the sword. By God's grace these people grew strong in battle and put to flight their enemies. By faith they ran through troops and leaped over walls.

The apostle Paul claimed, "I can do all things through Christ who strengthens me" (Philippians 4:13), and we can make that claim too. In fact, we need to live by it, for this world desperately needs such men and women of faith to accomplish great feats for God. God calls us to wield spiritual swords for His kingdom. And He promises to give us the power to accomplish anything He calls us to do. God wants to make the world marvel, to melt frigid indifference and startle people, to make them wide-eyed at what faith can accomplish. When the multitudes saw the boldness of Peter and John, they marveled, and many gave their lives to Christ. God wants to accomplish the same through you and me.

When you and I exhibit boldness that will run through a troop and leap over a wall, the world will indeed marvel at God's power in us. Today, be bold in God. Claim the Holy Spirit's power in you, and watch what He does through your life!

> *The battle is the Lord's! The harvest fields are white…victory is sure.*
> *We face a vanquished foe; then forward with the risen Christ to battle go!*

E. MARGARET CLARKSON

A RELATIONSHIP OF TRUST

Be anxious for nothing, but in everything by prayer and supplication,
with thanksgiving, let your requests be made known to God.

PHILIPPIANS 4:6

The whole Christian life begins with trusting God for something. It begins with trusting God for our salvation, just as the Israelites had to trust God for their deliverance from Egypt. When we believe and trust Christ, He applies His blood to our hearts, and we are redeemed.

Having received that gift of salvation through grace by faith, we have crossed the Red Sea and have entered into the life of Christ. At this point many people expect to find a bed of roses, but instead they begin to wander through a wilderness. But God doesn't expect us to wander in an endless spiritual desert, just as He never intended the Israelites to wander in the wilderness for forty years. God had originally planned for the Israelites to go directly to the mount, receive His instructions and the Ten Commandments, proceed to Kadesh Barnea, and enter and occupy the Promised Land. When the twelve spies went ahead, they saw giants and walled cities in the land. They reported that the inhabitants were greater than they could conquer. Because of the Israelites' unbelief, God said, "So, I swore in my wrath, they shall not enter into my rest." He condemned them to wander for forty years in the wilderness, apart from His perfect plan of immediate rest and security in the Promise Land.

Though you have received God's gift of grace, you may not have yet entered into God's rest. Your soul may be wandering in a vast wilderness, wandering because you haven't believed that God will conquer the "giants in the land." But only when you place your trust in Him—the only one worthy of your total trust—can you enter into the joy of His rest and the delight of a close relationship with Him.

Are you withholding your trust from God today? I encourage you to trust God with all your concerns. When you hand them to Him, one by one, He'll open to you a promised land of rest and security in Him.

On Christ the solid rock I stand…all other ground is sinking sand.

WELL-KNOWN HYMN

WILLING AND JOYFUL

*...And the people were restrained from bringing [any more], for the material
they had was sufficient for all the work to be done—indeed too much.*

EXODUS 36:6–7

Some people complain when pastors bring up the issue of money. They seem
to forget that churches need money to expand. On the other hand, have you
ever heard any pastor say, "Look, folks, we appreciate your generosity, but we
already have too much"? I doubt it, but that actually happened one time with
Moses and the Israelites.

The Israelites had come together to build the first sanctuary for the true and
living God. The Bible tells us that Moses called all the children of Israel together,
saying, "This is the thing which the Lord commanded." He wanted all of the
congregation to participate in the offering for and the building of the tabernacle.
Moses commanded them, "Take from among you an offering to the Lord." Who
should participate? "Whoever is of a willing heart." God didn't compel or pressure anyone to give. Instead, God in effect said, "If your heart leads you to do
this, then do it."

God had provided for all the Israelites' needs and given His Ten
Commandments; now the Israelites rejoiced in bringing their gifts. We read,
"Everyone came whose heart was stirred, and everyone whose spirit was willing, and they brought the Lord's offering for the work." They brought gold and
silver and brass. These people had no home of their own and no certain future,
but they trusted in the Lord, giving willingly and joyfully. In fact, so many came
forward with gifts that Moses had to command them to stop!

I wish that could be the case more often in churches today! I believe that
God blesses those who give to His work; we miss that blessing when we withhold. We should give willingly and joyfully...as Chuck Swindoll likes to
remind us, "God loves a *hilarious* giver."

Most need a goad to quicken their charity. Few need a bridle to check it.

MATTHEW HENRY

DAVID LIVINGSTONE

'...and lo, I am with you always, even to the end of the age.'

MATTHEW 28:20

Today I want to share a spiritual secret. This secret was the key to the extraordinary service of David Livingstone, one of the greatest missionaries in the Church's history.

Livingstone committed himself to living for Christ. Consider this prayer from his diary: "Lord, send me anywhere, only go with me. Lay any burden on me, only sustain me. Sever any ties but the tie that binds me to Thy service and Thy heart." And so it happened that God took Livingstone to task. "Send me anywhere..." Livingstone had learned of the villages in Africa where no missionary had ever gone before, and he felt led to go there. "Lay any burden on me..." Once in Africa, Livingstone encountered numerous trials. First, a lion attacked him, crushing his shoulder. Then, while crossing one of the vast plains of Africa, one of his children died. To add to that, when his children reached school age, he had to send them and his wife back to Scotland. The loneliness weighed heavily upon him. But Livingstone was undaunted, and he went deeper and deeper into Africa all alone. "Sever any ties..." When Livingstone went back to Scotland, he found that his beloved father had died. Later Livingstone returned to Africa, and though his wife joined him in this venture, she passed away soon after her arrival. But Livingstone pressed on despite all this. Livingstone tramped across Africa for thirty-three years. Because of his faithfulness to the Lord, two million people heard the gospel, and the light of Christ came into Africa. Livingstone set his heart on Christ and committed himself wholly to the Lord.

What was Livingstone's secret to maintaining his commitment despite all his struggles? Christ's presence! In the midst of all of his hardships and toils, he knew Christ remained with him, for He had said, "I am with you always." This day, let Livingstone's example encourage you. No matter how hectic your life may get, remember that Jesus Christ is with you wherever you go, whatever you do.

Give me, O God, this day a strong and vivid sense that Thou art by my side.

JOHN BAILLIE

HOLINESS IN AN UNHOLY WORLD

'...be holy, for I am the LORD your God.'

LEVITICUS 20:7

Have you ever noticed how many people claim to "believe in God," but on closer inspection, the "god" they believe in is merely one made up in the factory of the human mind? And rarely, it seems, does that god have any standards of holiness. I recall once sharing the gospel with a woman, and when I began talking about God's judgment, she stopped me and said, "Oh, no! My God would never do a thing like that." I said, "Madam, you are absolutely correct. Your god would never bring anyone into judgment. The fact of the matter is, your god would never do anything at all. He doesn't exist anywhere other than in the fantasies of your own mind. However, the God and Father of our Lord Jesus Christ, the God of the Scriptures, has declared explicitly what He will do; He will judge every evil thought and way." I'm afraid that many today are guilty of the same idolatry, diminishing or eliminating God's holiness, and that leads to an "anything goes" attitude.

As people have created their own images of God, our society has endured a moral decline. Pollster George M. Gallup Jr. says the United States faces "a moral and ethical crisis of the first dimension" and needs to find spiritual answers to deal with the situation. Our educators and courts have forgotten George Washington's warning in his farewell address—that we should not be so naive as to suppose that we can maintain morality in the absence of religion. All history and experience forbid us to indulge in such a vain supposition, he said. But we have been just that naive, and now having sown the wind, we reap the whirlwind. Today we indeed face a moral crisis of the first dimension.

Yes, we live in a largely immoral world. But like the white lily blossoming on a dung heap, so God calls us to purity in the midst of an impure world. The Bible tells us that God wants us to be holy, even as the Lord is holy.

Growing in holiness is like riding a bike. If you stop pedaling, you fall off.

ROB WARNER

THE WHOLE ARMOR

*Therefore take up the whole armor of God, that you may be able to withstand
in the evil day, and having done all, to stand.*

EPHESIANS 6:13

In Ephesians, Paul shows us the treasures hidden for us in Christ—redemption in our Savior resulting in eternal life. But as Paul finishes this epistle, he warns us that before we enter into heaven's gates, we shall experience great tribulation, the protracted spiritual warfare that faces every Christian. Our antagonists are not flesh and blood, but spiritual, invisible, and powerful. These principalities are the world rulers of darkness and spiritual wickedness in high places.

On our own, we can't fight and win against such foes. We need, first of all, strength beyond our own. We need Christ to strengthen us through His own might. Second, Paul exhorts us to take unto ourselves the whole armor of God that we may stand in the evil day. The watchword is "stand." Stand against the wiles of the devil, withstanding *all* of his onslaught. And having done all, when the battle has ended and our foes lie strewn in the field, we shall stand victorious as overcomers for Christ.

Are you facing a battle today? Then clothe yourself in the armor of light, every piece of which is Jesus Christ Himself. Clothed in His might and armor, you may go forth into battle, not merely to preserve your own soul from loss but also to win the multitudes of this world into Christ's kingdom, that their knees may bow before the cross and they may proclaim Him as Lord and King of all.

How many Christians are trying to fight a spiritual war with natural weapons?

NEW AGE

'…and you will be like God, knowing good and evil.'

GENESIS 3:5

Have you felt as bewildered as I at the recent proliferation of crystals, psychics, and gurus? A "new" religion has swept through our land—the New Age movement—attracting converts with the speed of a runaway train. But the only thing new about this movement is its slick Madison Avenue makeover. In reality, the New Age movement has existed since the Garden of Eden. An old serpent in a new skin, this worldview slithers around our society today, consuming people by the millions.

The term "New Age" refers to an astrological belief that every two thousand years the world moves into a new zodiac age. New Agers believe that at the beginning of the twenty-first century, we will pass out of the house of Pisces and into the age of Aquarius. (Interestingly, the fish symbol has always signified Christianity.)

Although the New Age movement has many different and loose strands, we may glean three dogmas underlying it:

1. The material world is an illusion. It's not real. Only things in the spiritual realm are authentic. Sounds like Plato.

2. Only one infinite, eternal reality exists—one force, one life energy, one spirit—and it envelops everything (including us). Sounds like pantheism—each of us is one spark from the same fire. In other words, each of us is "god."

3. Since each of us is "god" or a part of "god," we have no need for the "old-fashioned" Christian concepts of sin, guilt, and redemption. We only need enlightenment—to *recognize* that we are "god."

The New Age religion takes bits and pieces from Eastern mystical religions—Hinduism, Buddhism, and Taoism—Western neo-pagan occultism, ancient philosophy, modern psychology, and Taoist physics. When we mix all this together, what do we come up with? The original lie that Satan gave to mankind in the Garden of Eden: "For God knows that in the day you eat of it [the tree of knowledge of good and evil] your eyes will be opened, and you will be like God, knowing good and evil."

New Age thinking weasels its way into many places, even into so-called Christian organizations. As you seek to grow closer to God, test the philosophies you hear. If anything sounds suspect, seek the truth in God's Word and by His Spirit. God will never lead you into anything contrary to His being or His will.

The devil often transforms himself into an angel to tempt men.

ST. AUGUSTINE

October 27

THE OCCULT

'Give no regard to mediums and familiar spirits;
do not seek after them, to be defiled by them…'

LEVITICUS 19:31

Have you noticed the recent explosion of the occult, witchcraft, and Satanism in our society? If you pay attention, you can see it everywhere—in movies, in television programs, in many of the songs of our pop culture. Drive down Main Street, U.S.A., and you'll most likely see the storefront office of a psychic or a palm reader. The work of the devil and his demons takes many forms and has many names. It ranges from Satan worshipers to those who experiment with parapsychology and read horoscopes. And our country has embraced it all.

Why do people turn to the occult? Some people hunger for the supernatural. Ignorant of the gospel and unacquainted with Christ, these people seek a supernatural connection in the occult world. Others seek power. They don't care where they get it; they just want as much of it as they can grab. Yet others just *play* with the occult. It serves as an entertaining diversion for them, a game to play. And as the occult gains more and more popularity, many dabble in it out of curiosity.

God created us as spiritual beings for a realm beyond this world. For this reason, people hunger for spiritual things. But many don't understand that their spiritual needs can only be met in Christ. So they turn to the dark side. The occult becomes an illegitimate way to fulfill a legitimate need.

This all sounds very dark and depressing, but as Christians we can have, and share with others, hope. Jesus came into this world to defeat Satan and destroy his works. By His death, Christ accomplished this once and for all, and He set the prisoners free. You and I need to share the good news of Christ, who alone can truly satisfy the longings for the supernatural. Zig Ziglar suggests that rather than listening to the stars by following our horoscope, we should listen to the One who *made* the stars by reading the Holy Bible.

Have you allowed the occult to take hold of you? If so, you needn't feel possessed by it. Confess your involvement to Jesus Christ, and repent of it. As you do, Christ will forgive and cleanse you from all sin. And whether or not you've experienced the occult, pray today that God will break the hold the occult has on our nation, setting people free from Satan and drawing them to Christ to experience the most potent supernatural power—the power of the gospel.

Satan works best where his existence is denied.

WHO IS SATAN?

How you have fallen from heaven, O morning star, son of the dawn! You have been cast down to the earth, you who once laid low the nations! You said in your heart, 'I will ascend to heaven; I will raise my throne above the stars of God; I will sit enthroned on the mount of assembly, on the utmost heights of the sacred mountain. I will ascend above the tops of the clouds; I will make myself like the Most High.'

ISAIAH 14:12–14, NIV

If we want to achieve success as Christians, then we must be aware of him who opposes that goal—the devil. To understand Satan's plot, we must first understand his origin, and the Bible gives us several clues about that. Satan began his existence as an angel of light named Lucifer, the light bearer. Being God's most powerful, brilliant, and beautiful angel, Lucifer became puffed up with pride, believing he could reach the same status as God. When he wanted to become like God, war erupted in heaven. Michael the archangel fought against Lucifer and his angels. Michael won, and Lucifer and his angels were cast from heaven forever. Lucifer became Satan, and his angels became demons.

Satan now tries to lure as many humans as possible to his own depraved condition. He is filled with wrath and seeks to destroy all powers of God, the kingdom of God, and all who love Him. Satan hates God and Christ, and he exercises his vengeance against those whom God created. The Bible frequently warns against Satan's craft and powers, his work, and his ways. He is a seducing spirit, evil, malevolent, and deceitful. He only desires to destroy. Peter tells us that our adversary roars around like a lion, seeking to devour whom he will.

But Christ has defeated the devil. He did that on the cross. Though Satan may seem to win on earth, he is a defeated foe, and his days are numbered. If you ever feel that he has gotten the best of you, remember that greater is He (God) who is in you, than he (the devil) who is in the world (1 John 4:4).

Those who deny the existence of the devil are easy pickings for him!

THE WARFARE WITHIN

For the good that I will to do, I do not do; but the evil I will not to do, that I practice.

ROMANS 7:19

Have you ever felt the aggravation of doing the very sin you wanted to avoid? Or of not doing a good work you had intended to do?

Why do we find ourselves in this bind on such a consistent basis? When we hand our lives to Jesus, He gives us a new nature that is spotless and clean, incapable of sinning. But as fallen people we also carry within us a nature capable of vile and hideous deeds. And herein lies the battle. Our regeneration sets up a dichotomy of the new and old natures, and when the Spirit of God dwells in our hearts, we recognize just how wretched we truly are. Only when Paul identified his God-given nature was he able to comprehend his captivity, "O wretched man that I am! Who shall deliver me?" St. Augustine, poignantly aware of his sinfulness, wrote, "By these links, as it were, a chain was I held, shackled with a hard bondage. So these my two wills—the one old, the other new; the one carnal, the other spiritual—contended together, and by their discord disturbed my soul."

Does your soul cry out for deliverance from your sinful nature? Then nurture your new nature. Read God's Word daily, and spend quiet time with the Lord. My friend, I urge you to act on God's directive: "Be still, and know that I am God." If you want your new nature to conquer the old, you must allow Him to feed your soul. And no matter how tough the battles get, always remember that on the cross Jesus Christ won the war—once and for all.

I make it a rule of Christian duty never to go to a place where there is not room for my Master as well as myself.

JOHN NEWTON (AUTHOR OF "AMAZING GRACE")

TO WIN THE WARFARE WITHIN

'That which is born of the flesh is flesh, and that which is born of the Spirit is spirit.'

JOHN 3:6

When we become born again, we inherit a spiritual battle. Our old nature wars against our new one. Dr. Bill Bright of Campus Crusade used to tell a story that described these old and new natures as two dogs: a black dog and a white dog that were wont to fight viciously. Dr. Bright said, "Which dog will win is determined by which dog you feed. Feed the black dog and starve the white dog, and the black dog will win; feed the white dog and starve the black dog, and the white dog will win."

Which nature are you feeding? Much in our culture feeds the "black dog." We feed our sin-filled natures often—not always, but often—when we turn on the television set; go to a movie; read a newspaper, magazine, or novel; or listen to modern music.

But we have a bountiful feast with which to feed the "white dog"—God's Word. As we read Scripture, God prepares us for the spiritual warfare we face. To be strong warriors for Christ, we need to dwell less on things of the flesh and instead delve into the Bible. We need to write God's Word on the slates of our minds and the tablets of our hearts. "For as he thinketh in his heart, so is he." We can also feed our new nature by spending quiet time with God, especially by praying for forgiveness, guidance, and counsel. If we are ever to win the warfare within, we need to engage evil with God as our guide.

Do you need to reevaluate your spiritual "diet"? Choose to feast on God's Word and on time spent with Him. Do so, and you'll gain all the strength you need for the battles ahead.

> *Two natures beat within my breast. The one is foul, the other blest.*
> *The one I love, the other I hate. The one I feed will dominate.*

ANONYMOUS

LUTHER'S QUEST FOR GOD

For in it the righteousness of God is revealed from faith to faith;
as it is written, 'The just shall live by faith.'

ROMANS 1:17

While our culture sets this day aside as Halloween, I think a much more fitting event to celebrate happened on this day in 1517—the Reformation of the Church, when Martin Luther, a humble monk, made public ninety-five reasons the Church needed to reform. Luther knew how desperately the world and the Church needed to know we could gain grace only through faith. He dedicated his life to discovering and preaching this truth.

Luther was born November 10, 1483, into a poor family of German wood-cutters. Realizing that their son was gifted, Luther's parents scrimped and saved to send him to the university, where he studied law. Returning home from school on foot, he and a friend were caught in a thunderstorm, and his friend was struck by lightning and killed. This terrified Luther, and he vowed to enter a monastery so he could search for God. One question plagued him without ceasing: How could he, a sinful man, ever become pure enough to stand in the awesome presence of a holy God who was an all-consuming fire? Luther spent years trying every way he knew to purify his soul. He spent hours each day confessing his sins. He beat himself with a whip until he became bloody and unconscious. He prayed for six weeks, fasted, and slept very little. He stayed out all night long, naked, in the deep snows of Germany.

But one day the Lord spoke to him through the Scriptures, specifically Romans 1:17: "The just shall live by *faith*." Suddenly Luther saw the gospel! He discovered God's grace! He realized that only those justified by faith in Christ's blood will live and those who seek to justify themselves in any other way shall not live. Luther spent the rest of his life promoting and defending this truth. Even when he was on trial, faced with being burned at the stake, he clung fiercely to it. Justification by faith is still our great hope and joy.

Here I stand. I can do no other. God help me! Amen!

MARTIN LUTHER

THE FELLOWSHIP OF THE SAINTS

And they continued steadfastly in the apostles' doctrine and fellowship,
in the breaking of bread, and in prayers.

ACTS 2:42

"It is not good that man should be alone." God knows this; He said it. God also knows that few things surpass being in a group of people with whom one really belongs. He knows we need that kind of relationship, and so He created it. On Pentecost Sunday two thousand years ago, He created a new kind of fellowship that had never existed in the world before. Scripture calls it *koinonia*, the "family of God" or the "forever family." The family of God includes all those who have invited Christ to make them new creatures and have experienced the regenerating power of the Holy Spirit. Everyone in the family bears the same name, Christian, and has the same Father in heaven. This makes us all brothers and sisters in Christ. What a comforting reality to belong to such a group!

As members of God's family, the Holy Spirit has bonded us together in many ways. Let's think of some. We are equal heirs, and our inheritance is infinite and inexhaustible. We are believers; our hearts and minds share the same spiritual perception of the world. We are disciples; we all sit at the feet of one Master and learn our worldview from Him. We are witnesses; we share the special joy of leading people to Christ. We are soldiers; we share trials and triumphs and strengthen each other in faith. We are also a fellowship of slaves. Have you ever thought of that? During Roman times, a bond slave's life and death were in his or her master's hands. Paul delighted to call himself a bond slave of Christ, and we should view ourselves in the same light.

Do you realize how blessed you are to belong to such a wonderful family? Do you want God's family to grow closer, stronger, and more loving? Today ask God to show you how to play your part in the family.

Blest be the tie that binds our hearts in Christian love.
The fellowship of kindred minds is like to that above.

JOHN FAWCETT

CLOSE ENCOUNTERS OF THE FOURTH KIND

He was in the world, and the world was made through Him, and the world did not know Him.
He came to His own, and His own did not receive Him. But as many as received Him, to them
He gave the right to become children of God, even to those who believe in His name.

JOHN 1:10–12

You've probably never had an encounter with a UFO (unidentified flying object), but thousands of people claim to have had such strange experiences. The reports of UFOs have been divided into three types: close encounters of the first kind—the sighting of UFOs, close encounters of the second kind—physical evidence for the presence of UFOs, and close encounters of the third kind—being kidnapped for short periods of time by beings who operate UFOs. You may doubt people who have claimed to have experienced such encounters, but there is another encounter about which you could have no question.

I'm talking about a close encounter of the fourth kind. It, like the others, began with a brilliant light in the sky that people followed until it finally stood still. The light drew attention to a Visitor from outer space who came to a small village on the other side of the planet two thousand years ago. This Being had a wisdom far beyond anything that we know. He had a power greater than any creature. But He was no alien. He came unto His own, and thousands of His own saw Him.

In fact, many of them claimed that He rose from the dead. Over five hundred people saw Him alive after His public crucifixion. The people who claimed to have this final earthly encounter did something which gives a credibility to their testimony not found in the testimony of modern close encounters. God, in His wisdom, saw to it that a persecution arose, and the people who encountered this Being suffered hardships, torture, and death specifically for claiming they had seen Him after His resurrection.

The mysterious thing about the close encounter of the fourth kind is that although it was an historical event, we can *still* experience it. Have you met with Jesus Christ today? Daily communion with the Lord of the universe is our close encounter of the fourth kind, the most precious part of our life.

[Ours is] the visited planet.

C. S. LEWIS

FAITHFUL SERVANT

'Who then is a faithful and wise servant…?'

MATTHEW 24:45

How do we serve God? We serve God by serving each other. Jesus said that what we do for our fellow humans, we do for Him. He encourages us to visit the sick, feed the hungry, clothe the naked, and house the homeless. He asks us to be hospitable and generous and to proclaim the gospel.

Have you faithfully served the Lord by serving those around you?

To learn more about serving God, consider one of God's servants—Billy Graham. God has used Billy Graham so mightily in our time. Why? Because Graham is the most brilliant theologian of our day? Probably not. Because he is the best speaker in America? Probably not. What is it about him, then? God uses Billy Graham because Billy Graham is the kind of person God can trust to do His work!

Can God trust *us*? If He entrusts us with a task, will we do it? When God puts people in our way who need Him, do we minister to them faithfully?

In all areas of our lives, God wants us to be faithful. He wants us to faithfully serve our spouses, our children, and our parents. God wants us to be faithful to our Church and to the ministry He has given us to do. The Lord may ask us to accomplish a task of private or public nature, to one person or to many. But whatever we do for Him, let us do it steadfastly. Jesus said of the faithful servant in the parable of the two servants: "Blessed is that servant whom his master, when he comes, will find [him working faithfully]" (Matthew 24:46). Ask God to show you how you can serve Him faithfully today.

The task Thy wisdom hath assigned, O let me cheerfully fulfill;
In all my works Thy presence find, And prove Thy good and perfect will.

CHARLES WESLEY

A CHRISTIAN OFFENSIVE

'Go therefore and make disciples of all the nations, baptizing them in the name of the Father and of the Son and of the Holy Spirit, teaching them to observe all things that I have commanded you; and lo, I am with you always, even to the end of the age.'

MATTHEW 28:19–20

Are you aware that we're at war? But ours is a war of beliefs, not bullets. The spiritual conflict between Christ and the devil is intensifying at home and abroad. We don't necessarily fight against other nations so much as we battle against ourselves. America is engaged in a spiritual civil war. With all the evangelical radio and television ministries, you'd think that more Christians would join in the fight, but many Christians haven't committed to do their parts to change our land. Others have heard that Christians shouldn't concern themselves with political and social issues, so they don't even register to vote! We read in Genesis 1:26 that God gave humans dominion over everything in the world. This has become known as the Cultural Mandate. To properly fulfill that mandate, we must participate in our local and national elections. (Let me say that I believe it's a sin not to vote.) Have you registered to vote and exercised that avenue to make a difference for Christ?

We also need to stand up and speak about the truth God has given us. Jesus has called us to be salt and light in the world. We can't fulfill that call if we stay within the walls of our churches. We need to touch the world around us. Jesus said that the well do not need a doctor; the sick do. He came to seek and save the lost and has called us to do the same. We can do this by praying for our nation. (Two men I know meet at 6:30 every morning to pray for the revival of our nation.) We also need to witness. We should hold as our first concern Christ's last command—the Great Commission. We can change the direction of this country if we change ourselves and put forth the energy and dedication required to obey Christ's commands. We all have a post in the great battle!

Onward Christian soldiers! marching as to war!
With the cross of Jesus going on before.

SABINE BARING-GOULD

CHRISTIAN CITIZENSHIP

… 'Render therefore to Caesar the things that are Caesar's,
and to God the things that are God's.'

MATTHEW 22:21

Do you ever wonder how much you should involve yourself in political matters? At this time of year, this issue is particularly pertinent. So today I want to address the Christian's obligation as a citizen.

Jesus declared, "Render therefore to Caesar the things that are Caesar's, and to God the things that are God's." In this comment, Jesus identifies two spheres in which we must render our due responsibilities: the spiritual and eternal realm of the kingdom of God, and the kingdom of this world where we must render the things due to Caesar. For a long time, some quarters of the Church have held to a false piety that has resulted in refraining from all political involvement. As Christians have avoided the political realm, unbelievers have taken over the various spheres of influence in our society, such as education, the courts, and the legislatures. Thus, by abandoning the public spheres, Christians have effectively removed salt and light from our culture.

Although many Christians have recently involved themselves in the public sphere, we still have much ground to regain. And we still must confront a wrong attitude some Christians hold toward citizenship. A lady who works in one of our voting precincts said that the average voter turnout in her precinct is ten percent. I'm sure that quite a few Christians make up that ninety percent who don't vote. I believe it's a sin not to vote; voting is one way we can make a difference in our society, and we need to use it.

I encourage you to practice good Christian citizenship. Use the opportunities that come your way to make a difference in your town or city, in your state, and in your country. Be active as a citizen, rendering to Caesar what is Caesar's, and do so in the name of the Lord.

He who converts his neighbour has performed the most practical Christian-political act of all.

C. S. LEWIS

REVIVAL IN THE BIBLE

After two days He will revive us; on the third day He will raise us up.

HOSEA 6:2

Have you ever watched the news or observed the people around you and wished that God's almighty hand would sweep across this land, bringing everyone to Him? Many Christians today pray fervently for national revival. It can happen—the Bible gives us great examples of national revival from which we can learn…

Following the prosperity that Israelites enjoyed during Solomon's reign, spiritual apathy set in. King Solomon died, and his rebellious son took over the throne. Hearkening to the council of his foolish compatriots, Solomon's son brought disaster upon the land of Israel. Civil war ensued. The country divided into two lands—Israel, which included the ten tribes in the north, and Judah, which included the two tribes in the south.

In the land of Judah, national revival stopped the descent into apostasy five different times. These revivals stayed the hand of God's discipline and prolonged the life of the country. In Israel, on the other hand, not one single national revival took place. Consequently, the Assyrian hordes attacked and led the Israelites into captivity with fishhooks in their lips; the Assyrians killed thousands of others in cruel ways. God's wrath fell upon the disobedient people of Israel. But because of its revivals, Judah's life extended about a hundred and fifty years.

Judah's national revivals always consisted of three elements. First, the revivals were prompted by a crisis, generally a threat from some outside power such as Syria, Egypt, or Babylon. Second, in the midst of this crisis a prophet arose who spoke boldly to the issue at hand. Third, a godly king hearkened unto God's Word and understood God's reasons for the national crisis. The king then led the people in repentance and renewed godliness. These three elements never existed in the northern kingdom, so it was swept away into oblivion.

We need to pray for revival in our land. Today will you ask God to renew our country, drawing all people to Him?

A true repentance shuns the evil itself more than the external suffering or the shame.

WILLIAM SHAKESPEARE

A FORM OF GODLINESS

Having a form of godliness, but denying its power…

2 TIMOTHY 3:5

Have you ever done well in some big contest only to lose because you were disqualified on some seemingly minor point? During one of the most exciting baseball games of all time—the seventh game of the 1924 World Series between Washington and New York—something like this happened. In the bottom of the ninth with two outs and two strikes, Goose Goslin, batting for Washington, hit a home run—or so it seemed. Goslin made it safely to home plate, but Washington lost the entire World Series because as Goslin ran around the bases, he failed to touch first base. What a shock! And what a shame to lose a championship game because of a failure to follow a fundamental rule.

Sometimes this same sort of thing happens in churches. Some people who have been church members for years have never gotten to first base when it comes to Christianity. They've never been born anew. Somehow they thought they could skip that base and proceed to join a church, be baptized, be confirmed, participate in all the outward practices of religion, then make their way around the infield and head for home with a great welcome to follow. Instead, these people will hear these words from the Great Umpire, "I never knew you; depart from me" (Matthew 7:23). These people have a form of godliness, but they don't have true godliness because they don't know God. They don't experience His power. They don't allow Him to transform their lives. They find worshiping God a great burden, struggling to sit through church, to pray, or to read their Bibles. Sometimes these people continue practicing these forms of godliness to quiet the outward clamor of spouses, parents, or grandparents. Sometimes they do these things to quiet the inward clamor of their own consciences.

We all have to touch first base so that we might hear the Lord say to us: "Come you blessed of My Father, inherit the kingdom prepared for you." Do you know God? Have you accepted Jesus Christ as your Lord and Savior, and do you enjoy an intimate relationship with Him? If not, touch that base today so that you might win the game and receive the prize—eternal life.

A hypocrite is a fellow who isn't himself on Sunday.

ANONYMOUS

THE ARK OF SAFETY

So God looked upon the earth, and indeed it was corrupt; for all flesh had corrupted their way on the earth. And God said to Noah, 'The end of all flesh has come before Me, for the earth is filled with violence through them; and behold, I will destroy them with the earth.'

GENESIS 6:12–13

Have you ever been caught in a storm, terrified by the cracking of thunder and the flash of lightning? Imagine how the people of Noah's day felt when the thunder crashed, the winds howled, and the water poured for days. The Flood was such a terrifying experience that it has remained forever etched in the memory of humankind. People all around the globe—from the Indians of Mexico to the inhabitants of the South Seas to the Eskimos of the Arctic—have included the story of this worldwide catastrophe in their oral and written histories.

We know that God decided to destroy the earth because the people were evil, but why did He decide to do it through a flood? Why did He decide to save Noah in an ark? God put these things in place as symbols. God wanted to preserve humankind and His truth from a *flood of sin* which covered the earth. He used a flood of water to wash away the flood of sin—the profanity, blasphemy, pornography, divorce, fornication, adultery, homosexuality, and perversion of every sort that covered the earth. God wanted to keep Noah safe from His wrath against sin, so He told Noah to build the ark. The ark was the only safe place in the world during this catastrophe.

Today the world is just as wicked as it was before the Flood, and God has told us He will destroy it again. God has promised that this time He will destroy it by fire. But in His mercy, He has provided another ark. This one isn't made with human hands, but by God Himself. This ark is His only Son, Christ Jesus, whom He sent into the world. Christ is our ark of safety. He is the only place where we will stay safe when God releases the raging fire of His wrath. Once it starts, we'll have no time to tell others to "come aboard." So let us work as long as we can so that others might know that they can have safe passage to heaven through Jesus Christ.

There is only one ark of safety, and it has only one door. That ark is Jesus Christ.

THE MAGIC OF A TOUCH

Then He put out His hand and touched him, saying, 'I am willing; be cleansed.'
And immediately the leprosy left him.

LUKE 5:13

Have you ever felt lonely or low on energy, aching for some rejuvenation, then someone came to you and patted you on the back or gave you a hug? If so, how did that simple touch affect you?

A touch can work magic. Touch is like a rainbow arcing up and over the distance between two people, drawing them nearer emotionally and spiritually. This happens in friendships; as we hug or shake hands, we feel a deeper connection and intimacy with our friends. Touching between married people rekindles love and stokes the fire of romance. God commanded man and woman to cleave to each other and become "one flesh," knowing that oneness of mind and spirit begins with a touch.

Unfortunately, our society doesn't allow much touching these days. We talk about staying in touch, about being in touch, about getting in touch, but these are figurative phrases, not physical realities. Children learn touching at a young age in their families, but as they grow, the rules of society teach them to keep their hands to themselves.

This is such a shame, because a touch can minister to the soul. Dr. Frederick Treves brought a young man to London who was suffering from a disease so hideous he was called "the elephant man." One day a beautiful lady smiled at the elephant man and shook his hand. Because of this simple gesture, the elephant man burst into tears. No one had touched him or smiled at him since his mother's death many years before.

Jesus touched people regularly, in many cases to minister healing. In the Gospels there are thirty-one occurrences of the term "touch," as well as other terms indicating that Jesus held or touched people. He placed His hands upon blind eyes and dumb tongues; He placed his fingers on deaf ears; He touched the dead; He even touched a leper. And because of Jesus' touch, people's lives were forever changed.

Do you know someone who needs a simple touch today? All it takes is a simple handshake or a pat on the shoulder. Let us reach out, as Christ did, to touch and heal and restore.

Nothing can build or rebuild an intense feeling of love in a marriage as responsive touching, reaching out to a responding partner.

DR. ED WHEAT

HOW I KNOW JESUS IS GOD

When Jesus came into the region of Caesarea Philippi, He asked His disciples, saying, 'Who do men say that I, the Son of Man, am?' So they said, 'Some say John the Baptist, some Elijah, and others Jeremiah or one of the prophets.' He said to them, 'But who do you say that I am?' And Simon Peter answered and said, 'You are the Christ, the Son of the living God.' Jesus answered and said to him, 'Blessed are you, Simon Bar-Jonah, for flesh and blood has not revealed this to you, but My Father who is in heaven.'

MATTHEW 16:13–17

The central tenet of Christianity is that Jesus Christ is God. However, some doubt this truth. If you run into someone who questions Jesus Christ's divinity, Scriptures can help you prove it. First, let's consider some Scriptures which tell us plainly that Jesus Christ is God. In Matthew 1:23 we read that Mary and Joseph were to call Him Immanuel, which means "God with us." John 1:1, 3, and 14 tell us that Jesus existed in the beginning, that He cocreated the world, and that He is God. Colossians 2:9 says, "For in Him dwells all the fullness of the Godhead bodily." Isaiah 9:6 says "And His name will be called Wonderful, Counselor, Mighty God, Everlasting Father, Prince of Peace." Another group of Scriptures ascribes all of God's attributes to Jesus (except "invisibility" because Jesus came in the flesh): He is unchangeable (Hebrews 13:8), almighty (Colossians 1:17), all-knowing (John 21:17), searcher of hearts (Revelation 2:23), and judge of all (2 Corinthians 5:10).

Also, the New Testament indicates many times that Jesus fulfilled prophecies about Himself from the Old Testament, proving His deity. Isaiah 40:3 was fulfilled in Matthew 3:3—"a voice crying in the wilderness." Zechariah 12:10 was fulfilled in John 19:37—"they will look on Me, whom they have pierced." The Bible also says repeatedly that we must worship God only, and Jesus openly received worship. The shepherds, the Magi, the rich young ruler, and the disciples all worshiped Jesus.

As we read these passages, I think that our response to Jesus should echo that of Thomas when he acknowledged Christ's deity: "My Lord and my God" (John 20:28).

We know what God is like because we know the character of Jesus Christ.

GEORGE HODGES

A TIME TO REMEMBER

*'The instant I speak concerning a nation and concerning a kingdom, to pluck up, to pull down,
and to destroy it, if that nation against whom I have spoken turns from its evil,
I will relent of the disaster that I thought to bring upon it.'*

JEREMIAH 18:7–8

Do you ever stop and think about the freedom you enjoy in this country? Have you ever thanked someone who has fought for that freedom? We owe a tremendous debt to those men and women who have served in our armed forces so that we might remain free in this country. And yet we so often forget their sacrifices. All have sacrificed time. Some have sacrificed limbs or eyesight or hearing. Just walk around a veterans' hospital one day, and look at the permanent wounds of those who have made some kind of sacrifice for this country.

But we so often take those sacrifices—and the reason they were made—for granted. Tragically, our country has forsaken, bit by bit, its original calling. Consequently, those who have served—including those who died in battle— might be dismayed at how far we've drifted from being one nation under God. One writer asked a disturbing question in a letter to the editor: "What would the veterans who died in World War I, World War II, Vietnam, and Korea [and the Gulf, we might add]—by the hundreds of thousands—say if they could see the lifestyle in the United States today? Would they say, 'Is *this* what I gave my life for? Was it worth it?'" So many in our country have taken liberty too far, using the term to justify whatever they want to do.

Today on Veterans Day, let's remember those who served this country. Telephone or jot a note to a veteran, thanking that person for serving our country. Also, I ask you today to pray earnestly for our nation, that we would turn around and repent so that we may not lose our freedom, so that all those who have fought will not have done so in vain. God promises clemency for the nation that repents.

No people ever lost their liberties unless they themselves first became corrupt.

ANDREW JACKSON

A LONG AND HAPPY LIFE

My son, do not forget my law, but let your heart keep my commands;
for length of days and long life and peace they will add to you.

PROVERBS 3:1–2

Solomon admonishes us to never forget God's law and to keep it safely in our hearts. However, so many of us, creatures of the divine Creator, brashly ignore God's commandments. Do you know that half of the people in this country cannot name even five of the Ten Commandments?

Are you one of those people?

God wants us to know His law, but He doesn't want us just to memorize it so we can recite it by rote. He wants us to have it in our hearts. "Let your heart keep my commands." God wants us to love His law so much that we keep it in the treasure chest of our hearts where we store everything most dear to us. If we love God, we will treasure His Word in this way.

If, like David, we delight ourselves in the law of the Lord, God promises us "long life and peace." Not only is this promise a spiritual law, it's a principle with natural consequences. If a person lives according to God's commandments, that person will live longer because he or she takes fewer life-threatening risks. Even insurance companies know this. A person of good moral character, who does not indulge in many worldly habits and sins, gets preferred rates. Why? Because statistics show that a moral person tends to live longer. By acknowledging this, insurance companies endorse the Word of God.

Today, ask God to hide His law in your heart. Choose a few special verses, and commit them to memory. Then meditate on them throughout the day. As you keep God's Word close to your heart, God will grant you peace and length of days.

Live blameless; God is near.

CARL VON LINNE

THE TRINITY

'...baptizing them in the name of the Father and of the Son and of the Holy Spirit.'

MATTHEW 28:19

Have you ever tried to explain the Trinity to someone unfamiliar with the idea? If you have, then you probably know how difficult it is to define. Not even a rocket scientist could plumb its depths and comprehend it. In fact, we humans won't fully understand it until we meet God in heaven.

Recently, a lady said to me, "We really shouldn't talk about Jesus being God, because when He was on earth, God was in heaven, don't you know?" As a matter of fact, I did know that. But her statement reminded me that we need to develop a clear understanding of the Trinity, the foundation of all Christian doctrine. Many have denied the concept of the Trinity and rejected it as absurd. The Jehovah's Witnesses will remind us that $1 + 1 + 1 = 3$, and by such an argument, they discount the Trinity. But $1 \times 1 \times 1 = 1$, not 3. Three persons in one is just a concept beyond our comprehension.

But we can understand a few things about the Trinity. We know the Father is the first person, the Son the second, the Holy Spirit the third. And in many Bible texts, we see how the Trinity works. When Christ was baptized, the Father spoke from heaven, and the Spirit as a dove descended upon Jesus (Matthew 3:16–17). When Jesus set forth the Great Commission, He told the disciples to baptize in the name (one name) of the Father, Son, and Holy Spirit (Matthew 28:19). In the upper-room discourse (John 13–17), Jesus foretold the coming of the Spirit that He and His Father would send.

The Trinity is a critical doctrine because it lies at the heart of the gospel. If there is no Trinity, then Christ is not God. And if Christ is not divine, then we have no hope of salvation, for only a divine Savior could accomplish that monumental task.

Bring me a worm that can comprehend a man, and then I will show you a man that can comprehend the triune God!

JOHN WESLEY

ATTEMPT GREAT THINGS FOR GOD

'Call to Me, and I will answer you, and show you great and mighty things, which you do not know.'

JEREMIAH 33:3

God is a great and wondrous God who delights in great and marvelous things. He wants to do great and mighty things through you and through me. However, many of us never quite grasp God's glory and greatness; thus, we miss spiritual growth and tremendous adventures.

Do you know that God can and wants to do great things, using you as His instrument?

God tells us to attempt great things for Him by faith. And only through faith can we accomplish what He calls us to do—not in our own strength, not by our own power, but by God's might. Most of the great accomplishments of this world are done by faith. The great missionary William Carey initiated the modern world missionary movement by faith. His motto? "Attempt great things for God. Expect great things from God." We need to trust God if we're to make any difference in the world for His kingdom.

Even though God will give us all we need to accomplish His goals, He won't necessarily make our missions easy. We'll have to make sacrifices if we're to achieve great things for God's sake. Reflect on what the Pilgrims did in the settling of this great nation. Nearly half of them lost their lives during their first winter in this land.

And as we pursue great accomplishments for Christ's kingdom, we must keep in mind our motives. Everything we undertake, big or small, we must do for God's glory and not for our own. Whether we do something for our glory or for Christ's ultimately determines the value of anything that we do. Generally, the great doers of history have been great because they kept their sights on God. They trusted in Him rather than in themselves. They realized their own limitations, but understood that "with God, all things are possible."

Are you ready to do great things for God? Then trust Him to come through for you, even as you make the sacrifices, and give the glory to Him for the results.

We can never have too big a conception of God.

J. B. PHILLIPS

TAKING THE FEAR OUT OF DEATH

Precious in the sight of the Lord is the death of his saints.

PSALM 116:15

Have you ever considered the great contrast between how the unbeliever faces death and how the Christian does? Read these last words of several unbelievers, and contrast them with those of Christians.

Marabeua, unbeliever: "Give me laudanum [a narcotic painkiller used in past centuries] that I may not think of eternity."

David Brainerd, missionary: "I am going into eternity, and it is sweet to me to think of eternity."

Voltaire, caustic unbeliever: "I am abandoned by God and man! I shall go to hell!"

William Pitt, British statesman and Christian: "I throw myself on the mercy of God through the merits of Jesus Christ."

William Randolph Hearst, newspaper magnate: "Death is not to be discussed in my presence." (Though he could forbid the discussion, he could not forbid the reality.)

Michelangelo, Christian artist: "I die in the faith of Jesus Christ, and in the firm hope of a better life."

Talleyrand, leader during the French Revolution: "I am suffering the pangs of the damned."

Dwight L. Moody, evangelist: "Earth is receding, and heaven is opening, and this is my coronation day."

Why does the Christian not fear death? Because Jesus says that we who believe in Him should live, even though we die. Through Him, we can have the assurance that we shall join Him forever in Paradise after we leave this earth. He tasted death for us so that we don't have to!

Will you pray with me today for the world to know Jesus Christ? Will you do your part to share the good news with those around you? No one need fear death. Let's spread the wealth of eternal life in heaven!

We go to the grave of a friend, saying, 'A man is dead.'
But angels throng about him saying, 'A man is born.'

ANONYMOUS

November 16

TAKE HEED

And He said to them, 'Take heed and beware of covetousness…'

LUKE 12:15

Have you ever wanted something so badly that you put yourself in too much debt? Or have you ever fudged a little on your taxes so you could squirrel away some money to buy something for yourself?

Think for a moment: What desire fuels these actions? Could it be covetousness?

Jesus says, "Beware of covetousness," which is defined as an *"inordinate* desire to have something." It's an easy sin to hide, but it's sin just the same. The Pharisees put on an outward show of righteousness, yet Christ saw their hearts when he called them "whited sepulchers [graves]." Though outwardly respectable, they were inwardly full of dead men's bones because of their covetousness.

God requires a total transformation of what, to the fallen world, seems so natural that it never even comes under question. Thousands of books will tell you how you can obtain the things of this world. But the authors and readers of these books set their affections on things, and never question whether their lives are misdirected.

At this point you may be wondering, "If God commands us not to covet things, can I not desire *anything* or have *any* ambition?" Let me give you a word picture that might help you answer that question. Abraham Kuyper compares our lives to a magnificent sailing vessel. He says a ship may have beautiful masts and billowing sails filled with ocean breezes. Its banners may flutter in the wind, and its hull may be loaded with all manner of wonderful cargo. Yet the entire destiny of that ship rests on something tiny and unseen: the rudder. That small rudder, beneath the surface of the ocean, determines whether that great ship ends up resting peacefully in the harbor or lying scattered among rocks on some barren shore.

The same is true of our lives. We may have tremendous ambitions and the power to make them realities. Our lives may be laden with treasures, talents, and successes. Yet the final destination of our lives, whether in the glorious harbor of heaven or scattered among the rocks of hell, is determined by an unseen rudder—our motives—that turns us toward ourselves or toward God. When we do everything solely for God's glory, it does not matter how rich or accomplished we are. We can be fulfilled and obedient with much or with little.

Today, assess the direction of your rudder. Are your aspirations pointing you toward the harbor or toward the rocks? Remember Christ's admonishment— "Beware of covetousness"—and pursue possessions and ambitions only when they draw you in His direction.

Let my world be centered not in myself but in Thee.

JOHN BAILLIE

THE SPARKLE OF THE SOUL

Restore to me the joy of Your salvation, and uphold me with Your generous spirit.

PSALM 51:12

Have you ever noticed how difficult it is to maintain eye contact with someone, especially someone you don't know? Perhaps we find this so difficult because it feels so intimate. Some have said that the eye is the window of the soul, so perhaps when someone gazes into our eyes, we feel vulnerable, as if that person can see all our deepest secrets. And perhaps that's why, when we fall into sin, we can't maintain eye contact with others, fearing they can see the sin in our eyes. Sin clouds our souls, and we lose our inner sparkle.

Now consider King David when he had been derelict in his duty. He had failed to go with his army into battle. In his idleness, he walked atop his palace and happened across Bathsheba as she was bathing. Enticed by her beauty, he lured her to the palace and committed adultery with her. In an attempt to cover his sin, he compounded it by having her husband murdered. David had now committed two grievous sins for which the Old Testament provided no forgiveness. The king was crushed by his sinfulness. For one year, all of the joy went out of him. All of the light left him. All of the sparkle disappeared from his soul and his eyes. The sweet singer of Israel sang nothing but doleful laments. He felt as though the very bones of his body were crushed under the weight of his guilt.

No doubt about it, David was great in his sinning. But he was also great in his repenting, and for that reason Scripture calls him "a man after God's own heart." When God convicted David of his transgressions, David said, "Have mercy upon me, O God, according to thy lovingkindness: according unto the multitude of thy tender mercies blot out my transgressions." David wouldn't let sinfulness keep him away from his Lord any longer.

Are you a great repenter? Do you truly sorrow for your sins and turn from them as David did? I encourage you to confess and repent of anything that comes between you and God so that He may restore the sparkle to your soul and grant you the joy of your salvation.

What can wash away my sin? Nothing but the blood of Jesus.

WELL-KNOWN HYMN

GRACE

…that in the ages to come He might show the exceeding riches of His grace…

EPHESIANS 2:7

The more I reflect upon it, the more convinced I am that we can encapsulate the whole essence of the Christian gospel in one single word—grace. What is this "amazing grace"? I have asked many people, and I have yet to meet an unconverted person who understands the concept! Only those who have experienced God's grace know what it is, and yet many still don't have words to describe it. Grace is beyond comprehension; it is, I am sure, the *greatest* thing in all the world.

So, what *is* grace?

Grace is not justice, because it is above fair. Grace is infinitely higher, more exalted, and more noble than fairness could ever be.

Grace isn't the same as love. Even though grace has love within it, not all love has grace in it.

Is grace not the same as mercy? Now, we're getting closer to the target. But grace still goes beyond extending love to someone who does not deserve it.

Grace *is* totally unmerited favor given to those who deserve disfavor. Grace is receiving everything good when we deserve everything bad.

We will never appreciate grace until we see our need for it…when we see ourselves as rebels against God, as breakers of His laws, as capable of all manner of evil…when we know that our hearts hold depravity…when we see ourselves as sinners in the deepest, darkest parts of our being. *Then* we will begin to appreciate the meaning of grace.

When the God of all grace freely and willingly forgives and accepts us on the basis of what Jesus Christ has done, then we experience grace. And after experiencing it, we want to share it freely with others. If you were a beggar and found an endless supply of bread, wouldn't you share it with your fellow beggars? That picture gives us just a small glimpse of what it's like when we share God's amazing grace with others.

Can you share God's grace with someone today?

Grace is spelled 'God's Riches At Christ's Expense.'

ANONYMOUS

THE TEN COMMANDMENTS FOR TODAY

Therefore we conclude that a man is justified by faith apart from the deeds of the law…Do we then make void the law through faith? Certainly not! On the contrary, we establish the law.

ROMANS 3:28, 31

Have you noticed that the Ten Commandments seem to have fallen on hard times lately? This growing rejection of the Commandments comes from anti-Christian groups who want to remove them from public view and even from the churches that falsely teach that the Commandments don't apply to us today because "we're under grace."

But consider this. The Creator of the universe descended upon Mount Sinai and gave to us a reflection of His own nature, a revelation of His will: the Ten Commandments. The more I've studied them over the years, the more I've come to realize that they cover all things pertaining to the conduct of a person's life and his or her relationships with others and with God. Contrary to what some churches and some cults teach, Christ did not render the Ten Commandments null and void when He died. No one could possibly void them. Jesus said that the one who loves Him *keeps* His commandments, not to gain heaven but to show love for Him.

The Law brings us death and damnation because we can never fulfill it except through Christ's death on the cross. Only when we see our sinfulness, do we realize our need for forgiveness, and only then can we find salvation. After we're cleansed by Christ's blood, then the law of God becomes a guide for the Christian's life. Martin Luther gave us three pictures of the role of the Law in a Christian's life: a hammer that smashes our self-righteousness, a mirror that shows us our uncleanness and guilt, and a whip that drives us to the cross of Christ for redemption. Even though we've been saved, we still need the Law as a tool for our sanctification, to draw us nearer to Christ while we are still on this earth.

Have you allowed the Ten Commandments their appropriate place in your life? Ask God to use them to draw you nearer to Him each day.

If we should repeal all the regulatory laws on our statute books, and enforce only the Ten Commandments, in ten years we would become the most law-abiding nation on earth.

JAMES R. PAGE

THE MEMORY OF THE HEART

Oh, give thanks to the Lord, for He is good!...

PSALM 107:1

Thanksgiving will soon be upon us, and it's the perfect time for evaluating how often we offer thanks to God. Thanksgiving is "the memory of the heart," the way we show God that we know Who takes care of us every day of the year.

How are you doing in the gratitude department? Have you counted your blessings lately and thanked God for each one?

In Luke 17, we read of ten lepers whom Jesus healed. Despite this tremendous miracle in their lives, only one leper returned to thank Jesus. This story shows how even the most spiritual people often forget to thank God. We can see from the story that the lepers were *praying* men. They cried out, "Jesus, Master, have mercy on us." They asked the Lord to help them. The ten lepers were also *obedient* men. When Jesus told them to show themselves to the priest to prove that they were clean, they didn't say, "We can't go. Look at us. We have no fingers or toes. We need to talk about this." Instead, they went immediately. Also they were *believing* men, otherwise they wouldn't have obeyed Jesus' command. Jesus hadn't healed them yet, but they believed in Him enough to do whatever He said, knowing He would come through for them.

Yet despite their obvious spirituality, only *one* of them returned to thank the Lord. Jesus was shocked by their ingratitude. When the one leper thanked Him, He didn't say, "It was nothing. Forget it. You don't have to thank me." Instead, He said, "Where are the other nine? Were not ten lepers cleansed?" The lepers were praying men, obeying men, and believing men—but they weren't thankful men. Their faith was incomplete because they didn't praise God. Jesus healed them, but they didn't receive the full blessing which the tenth leper received. After all, Jesus told him, "Your faith has made you whole."

There once was a man who praised God so much that people called him "Hallelujah Smith." We should all strive to earn that same first name. The Bible says God works all things for our good. Therefore, in every situation, let us give thanks, especially on Thanksgiving.

Today, think of something you haven't thanked God for yet, then lift up a prayer of thanksgiving. And this year, make Thanksgiving a real "memory of the heart."

You can pray and grumble, you can obey and grumble, you can believe and grumble,
but you cannot praise and grumble.

THE CHRISTIAN'S MAGIC WAND

Let us come before His presence with thanksgiving...

PSALM 95:2

Have you ever wished for a magic wand that could change all the unpleasantness of life into something good? Wouldn't you love a way to instantly sweep away all the trivial things that accumulate until they drag you down?

I believe the Lord has offered us something similar to a magic wand. It can change our outlook on the circumstances surrounding us. What is it? Gratitude. When we feel grateful, our perspectives toward things change. We see our circumstances in a new, more positive light. And when we have grateful hearts, we want to express our gratitude outwardly through thanksgiving. This can work in reverse, too. If we give thanks even when we don't feel very grateful, we often feel our attitudes change in a more grateful direction, just as if we passed a magic wand over ourselves.

Thanksgiving transforms the secular or commonplace into the sacred. When we give thanks to God, suddenly we see God everywhere! We find ourselves living in an enchanted land, a land in the presence of our great Creator and Redeemer. With our spiritual eyes open, we can see that it is God who gives us everything, from our daily bread to the money we need. Our faith grows stronger as we express gratitude. All things become suffused with the divine presence.

And as we recognize God's blessings, our thankfulness gives us victory over temptation and sin. How can we commit adultery when we are grateful for our spouses? How can we steal when we are grateful for and content with what we have? How can we envy others' talents and abilities when we feel thankful for the way God has made us? How can we grumble or complain when we're thankful for God's blessings?

We should thank God, and we should also show gratitude for the ways others have blessed our lives. Everyone needs the kind of lift that gratitude brings.

What are you grateful for today? Thank God for all the blessings He has given you, and see how it changes your perspective on life. And don't forget to express thanks to someone who has enhanced your life. I hope that in your thanksgiving you'll experience joy.

When you drink from the stream remember the spring.

CHINESE PROVERB

THE SECOND MILE

'And whoever compels you to go one mile, go with him two.'

MATTHEW 5:41

How do you deal with people who "do you dirty"? We all have people in our lives who stab us in the back, say cruel things about us, or do mean things to us. But the Bible has a secret, one we often overlook, for dealing with those who mistreat us. It's the secret of "the second mile." To understand it, we need a quick history lesson.

The Medes and the Persians, and later the Romans, had a law that stated that a government official could, at any time, force a citizen to carry any burden for one mile. When Jesus told His followers to walk the second mile, he referred to this law. Jesus wanted people to return good for evil—to, out of their free will, go far beyond what others expected of them.

Christ's urging is like a timid flower within the Sermon on the Mount, but the fragrance it gives can transform your whole life and work wonders of reconciliation with those who anger you. People who fail in relationships and in business are often those who, when asked to go a mile, try to make it a half-mile. The mediocre people are those who go the one mile, doing what people expect of them but not an inch more. But when you look at a successful person, you'll find someone who has gone the second and the third mile a thousand times over. A person who habitually does more than expected, who find ways to please, will succeed.

So how does this work? It's simple. If someone does you wrong, you do them right. I'll be the first to agree that this goes against human nature as does much of applied Christianity. But the second mile allows us to transform any slight or injury into a blessing, and it gives us a tool to knock down barriers in school, in business, in our marriages, and in our homes. See today if you can't find some opportunity to go the second mile for someone in your life.

Forgiveness is the fragrance the violet sheds on the heel that has crushed it.

MARK TWAIN

ABSOLUTES IN A RELATIVISTIC AGE

I have no greater joy than to hear that my children walk in truth.

3 JOHN 4

Today many people try to live as if no absolute truths govern their existence. They say, "Truth is relative." But imagine if these people declared that the law of gravity was not "their truth." If they jumped from the top of a skyscraper, they'd soon discover the error of their philosophy! Gravity, like all other absolutes, exists whether or not we choose to believe in it.

Relativism may seem like a wonderful philosophy, but life without absolutes is meaningless. The philosopher Nietzsche promoted moral relativism, and he exerted a strong influence in the lives of Hitler and others, but we can sum up Nietzsche's life in two graffiti messages once found on a building. The first message: "God is dead.—Nietzsche." The second message: "Nietzsche is dead.—God." Whatever "truth" humans profess, God's truth always prevails in the end. (By the way, Nietzsche was insane during the last several years of his life.)

Jesus proclaimed the existence of absolute truth, and we learn of it through God's Word, our source for defining absolute rights and wrongs. Jesus said, "You shall know the truth, and the truth shall make you free" (John 8:32). Jesus didn't say, "You will know *a* truth." He didn't say, "You will know *your* truth." He said, "You shall know *the* truth." God's truth stands for everyone. We cannot reject God's truth as just "somebody else's truth, but not mine." Jesus said, "I am the way, the truth, and the life. No one comes to the Father except through Me" (John 14:6). Jesus is not *a* truth, *part* of the truth, or *somebody else's* truth. He is *the* truth. How ironic that Jesus, the incarnation of absolute truth, had to stand trial before Pilate, a coward whose truth changed to please the crowd, and to hear Pilate sneer, "What is truth?"

God's absolute truths give us joyful purpose in this relativistic age. How wonderful to know that our faith is built on truth! I'm a Christian not because I need to be or because it feels right (although both are true). I'm a Christian because Christ is the *truth*.

In regard to this great book [the Bible], I have but to say, it is the best gift God has given to men.
All the good the Savior gave to the world was communicated through this book.
But for it we could not know right from wrong.

ABRAHAM LINCOLN

A SONG OF FAITH

And you will seek Me and find Me, when you search for Me with all your heart.

JEREMIAH 29:13

Felix Mendelssohn was one of the greatest musical geniuses of all time. (If you've ever attended a wedding, you're probably familiar with his famous "Wedding March.") Mendelssohn was born in 1809 to a wealthy family, unlike most other composers of his time. He was happy, although one blotch marred the perfect picture of his life. Because they were Jewish, the Mendelssohns often received unfair treatment and were denied basic rights by those around them. It is shameful that everything the Mendelssohns owned could be snatched up at a moment's notice. To avoid mockery and persecution, Felix's father, Abraham, took his children to the Lutheran state church and had them baptized. The Mendelssohns put on the cloak of state respectability and became "Christians"…at least in name.

Though Felix was outwardly a Christian, his heart was empty. He sought to fill this vacuum until his grandmother shared with him a manuscript that was written by an obscure composer who had died seventy-five years earlier. The composer was Johann Sebastian Bach, and the manuscript was *St. Matthew's Passion.* The music moved Mendelssohn, but the words captivated him. As Mendelssohn considered the meaning of these words in *St. Matthew's Passion*— "He hath borne our griefs and carried our sorrows…God hath made Him to be sin for us"—he came to realize that indeed a Savior had come into the world and His name was Jesus. Mendelssohn discovered that being a Christian was not about religion, but about a relationship with Jesus Christ. This discovery changed his life.

Because of his exposure to Bach's work, Mendelssohn made a great contribution to music, reviving interest in Bach's work, which had fallen into neglect. Later Mendelssohn, like Bach, wrote music that glorified the Lord. In doing so, Mendelssohn shared with the world the treasure he had found—the gospel of Christ—a musical testimony that continues to affect people's lives.

Music is one of the fairest and most glorious gifts of God.

MARTIN LUTHER

THE LEGACY OF THE PILGRIMS

*Beloved, I beg you as sojourners and pilgrims,
abstain from fleshly lusts which war against the soul.*

1 PETER 2:11

Thanksgiving is a uniquely American holiday. Its origins, of course, go back to the Pilgrims. But who exactly were they? The Pilgrims were a group of Christians who secretly formed in 1606 in Scrooby, England, at a time when it was forbidden to read the Bible in public. When the Pilgrims formed their secret church, they made a covenant with each other. Fourteen years later, in 1620, that spiritual covenant was echoed in a political covenant, the Mayflower Compact. Historians, believers and nonbelievers alike, agree that the Mayflower Compact was a very important step in the formation of our constitutional republic and that it served as the cornerstone of our Constitution. This charter for self-government was essentially the first compact between people and God to form a nation in three thousand years, since the Israelites demanded a king! In the Mayflower Compact, the Pilgrims declared their purpose: "…having undertaken a voyage for the glory of God and the advancement of the Christian faith…" The Christian origins of this nation clearly shine through when we brush away the cobwebs of revisionist history.

During their first years in America, the Pilgrims struggled to survive, in great part because of their communistic economy. About half of them died; the rest neared starvation. Later, as the Pilgrims turned to a system of free enterprise, God blessed them with a tremendous bounty. On the thanksgiving days in their bountiful times, the Pilgrims put five grains of corn on their plates to remind them of the time five kernels of corn was each person's daily ration. But in both good times and in bad, the Pilgrims celebrated days of thanksgiving.

Let us, too, give thanks to the Lord, in good times and in bad, for He is good. What blessings can you thank God for today?

*By this time harvest was come, and instead of famine, now God gave them plentie and
ye face of things was changed, to ye rejoyceing of ye harts of many, for which they blessed
God…so as any general want or famine hath not been amongst them since to this day.*

GOVERNOR WILLIAM BRADFORD

THE BIBLE AND POLITICS

The wicked shall be turned into hell, and all the nations that forget God.

PSALM 9:17

Until about fifty years ago, legislators tried to create laws based on biblical prin-ciples. Nowadays, whenever someone proposes legislation that might defend a Christian cause, naysayers often oppose it, arguing that no one can impose his or her values on others. Yet every time our legislators pass a law, they impose somebody's morality on someone else. And these days, legislators often allow secular humanism to be that morality. By its own definition, as stated in the Humanist Manifesto of 1933, secular humanism is a "religion," and people who believe in it want to make it the religion of the future, replacing all others. Secular humanism denies that God exists and that any being, other than our-selves, can save us. It replaces God's Ten Commandments with human ideas of ethics and morality. To achieve its agenda, secular humanism has declared a full-scale war on Christianity, its battleground being the schools, the legislatures, and the courts of our land.

Secular humanists would have us believe that our founding fathers did not form America on Christian principles. But our founding fathers gave their *lives* to establish a Christian government, and we should do our best to keep it so. In 1828, Supreme Court Justice Joseph Story wrote his opinion of the First Amendment. He said its intent was not to approve or advance Mohammedanism or Judaism or unbelief, but to prevent the government from establishing one Christian denomination as more important than others. We need to do what we can to keep our nation on its original path by voting for Christian leaders and making sure they pass legislation based on biblical prin-ciples.

Do you keep up with critical issues in our society? Have you registered to vote, and do you regularly hit the polls on election days, casting your votes based on biblical truths? As you do these things, you can make a difference in our country. And today please pray for all those in leadership positions: our president, congressmen and congresswomen, governors, and state and local officials. Ask God to give them wisdom as they create laws for us to live by.

It is the duty of nations as well as of men to own their dependence
upon the overruling power of God.

ABRAHAM LINCOLN

SAMSON

So he told her everything…

JUDGES 16:17, NIV

Have you ever relied on your own abilities to accomplish something, only to fall flat on your face? One of the dangers of self-reliance is our tendency to flirt with temptation. Samson's trouble began this way. Samson was the strongest man who ever lived, but as he trusted in his own strength, he was weak when it came to resisting temptation.

One day Samson was in enemy territory, a place he should not have gone, when he met Delilah, the woman who caused his downfall. When the Philistine lords realized that Samson loved Delilah, they asked Delilah to lure Samson into telling her the secret of his strength. The Philistines wanted this secret so that they might subdue Samson. So she pursued his secret. On three separate occasions, Delilah tried to extract from Samson his secret, and each time he revealed a secret, she had the Philistines act on it. But he had deceived her each time, and the Philistines couldn't overwhelm him. After the third attempt, Delilah was very upset, and she said to him, "You have mocked me these three times." At length, because of her persistence, Samson told her the truth: "If I am shaven, then my strength will leave me." So as he slept, the Philistines cut off his hair, and Samson awoke weak and helpless. The Philistines gouged out his eyes and forced him to do the work of a beast of burden. His life, which began with great promise, had come to tragedy. However, God answered one more prayer for him. Samson's hair grew back, and he gained enough strength to destroy the Philistine temple and all the lords within it. He died in this last heroic act, but in his death he killed more Philistines, who had oppressed Israel, than he had in his entire life up to that point.

We see that in spite of his great strength, Samson lacked moral discernment. He had never shown strong moral character. He fell into a trap that even a schoolboy might have enough sense to avoid. When we have faith in ourselves, we lean against a broken reed. But when we trust in the Lord and flee temptation, we won't be an easy target for Satan, as Samson was.

Are you leaning on faith in yourself for anything? If so, give it to God. Trust in His strength alone to help you resist temptation and to achieve all He has designed you to accomplish.

Character is destiny.

HENRY LUCE

THE VALUE OF A NEGATIVE EXAMPLE

*Now all these things happened to them as examples, and they were written
for our admonition, on whom the ends of the ages have come.*

1 CORINTHIANS 10:11

Out in his yard, a minister was building a trellis to support a vine that he was
going to plant. As he worked, the minister noticed a young boy, about twelve
years old, standing nearby watching him. The minister nodded at the young lad
as he continued to work, thinking the boy would go away. After a while, however, he noticed that the boy still stood there. Finally, the minister asked the lad,
"Getting a lesson in horticulture?" "No," came the response, "I just wanted to
hear what a preacher said when he hit his thumb with a hammer."

Do you realize that nonbelievers often study your life, watching to see if
your actions and reactions corroborate what you profess? They not only watch
preachers; they watch all Christians. Some of them watch hopefully, wanting
confirmation of the life-changing potential of Christianity. Others watch hate-
fully, looking for an opportunity to blaspheme God. In either case, the world is
watching.

While we all want to serve as good examples, as humans we can't help failing. Yet, as humbling as it is for us, God can still use our mistakes as opportunities to show His greatness. Note the candor of Scripture concerning the sins
of those who professed faith in the living God. Even the greatest saints have
their portraits drawn with all warts present. Consider Abraham and his lie about
his wife. Or Moses and his anger and disobedience to God. Remember David's
adultery and his attempt to cover it up with murder. As we turn to the New
Testament, let's not forget the cowardly denials of Peter or the failure of Mark,
who turned tail and ran during his first missionary trip. Yet despite their failures, God used these people to accomplish mighty things.

The next time you make a mistake, especially if you know someone has
observed it, ask God to forgive you and to use you despite your sinfulness. And
today pray that God will enable you to be a good example for the cause of Jesus
Christ.

You may be the only Bible that some people ever read.

ANONYMOUS

HOW I KNOW THERE IS A GOD

The fool has said in his heart, 'There is no God.' They are corrupt,
they have done abominable works, there is none who does good.

PSALM 14:1

Do you get into conversations with people who don't believe in God? If so, then you've probably encountered one or two people who give no credence to your own personal experience or to the truth of Scripture. These people want hard and fast proof that God exists.

Such proof does exist. Let me give you a few bits of information I use when people want proof of God's existence. First of all, I ask these people to consider the universe. (This is called the cosmological argument. Cosmology means "the study of the universe.") I point out that the universe is the biggest thing there is, and it had to come from somewhere (every effect has a cause). The universe could not have created itself, because according to the First Law of Thermodynamics, you cannot create nothing out of nothing. Therefore, Someone eternal must have created it. And those are the Bible's first words: "In the beginning God." The second proof is the presence of life itself. Life could not have come from non-life, nor could it have happened by chance. It also had to be created. Who else could have created it but God, who *is* life? The third proof comes from examining the intricate design of the universe. (This is called the teleological argument. "Teleo" means "end" or "design.") Because the universe is so intricately designed, Someone all-knowing must have designed it. The fourth proof is God's loving care. If the earth orbited ten percent closer to the sun, we would burn up. If it orbited ten percent farther away, we would freeze and die. Instead, the earth orbits around the sun at just the right distance to sustain life. The fifth proof is the soul's transformation. This happens so mysteriously that no one can explain it. We know only that Someone changed Paul from a killer of Christians into the world's greatest missionary, and this Someone has changed our hearts as well.

God is the One who touches people's lives and brings them into fellowship with Him. But He can use you to accomplish that purpose. So as you speak with those who challenge God's existence, ask Him to show you when to present any or all of the information I've shared with you. And pray that God will ultimately reveal Himself to them.

The beauty, order, and harmony of the universe is an expression of the will of God;
the structure of the universe is the work of a great intelligence.

ARISTOTLE

GRIEVING THE HOLY SPIRIT

And do not grieve the Holy Spirit of God, by whom you were sealed for the day of redemption.

EPHESIANS 4:30

Did you know that the Holy Spirit is a person? The Bible makes it very clear that the Holy Spirit is not just a force, like electricity. Rather, He is a person who knows, loves, speaks, leads, guides, intercedes, teaches, cries, testifies, and approves or disapproves of what we do. And when we love a person very much, we don't want to do anything that will make him or her sad. In the same way, we need to know that we can grieve the Holy Spirit, just as we can grieve any other person whom we care about.

The Holy Spirit lives in our hearts. When God calls us as Christians, He sends the Spirit to live inside us. This indwelling is called "being sealed" by the Holy Spirit. (John 6:27 tells us that Christ was also sealed by the Holy Spirit: "God the Father has set His seal on Him.") Being sealed by the Holy Spirit brings us many blessings. It indicates that God has accepted us and that we're precious in His sight. It testifies to a finished transaction: Jesus has paid for all our sins. It verifies our security: God has sealed our sins in a bag and buried them in the depths of the sea. It attests to ownership: We are His, and He is ours. It indicates authority: Anyone who tries to break the seal will incur God's wrath. It verifies that we have a personal destiny: Heaven will be our home—the Holy Spirit has sealed us for the day of redemption.

Because the Spirit lives in us and loves us so much, how we live becomes much more than whether we obey certain laws. We must act in ways so as not to grieve Him. We grieve the Holy Spirit when we do not listen to His voice or seek His guidance, or when, having heard His guidance, we choose to disobey.

Do you listen for the Holy Spirit's guidance? Do you willingly follow His directions? Or have you done something that would grieve Him? The Holy Spirit wants to guide you, to show you the way you should live your life. And He'll forgive you when you confess going down your own sinful path. Ask Him to show you how you can live to please Him and bring Him joy, not grief, through your life.

A Christian is a person who is led by the Spirit of God.

HOME FOR CHRISTMAS

'And if I go and prepare a place for you, I will come again and receive you to Myself;
that where I am, there you may be also.'

JOHN 14:3

Have you ever felt deeply homesick, wishing with all your heart to return to home and family? Well, as Christians, we are far away from our true home—heaven—and we should feel "homesick" for it, anxiously waiting for the time that Christ will take us there.

Advent is upon us, and this time of year is a little bit about feeling homesick for heaven. At this time of year, we celebrate Christ's first coming and eagerly anticipate His return to take us to our true home. Advent means "to come," taken from the Latin "ad venio." At the first Advent, Christ came with much humility. He laid aside His robes of glory and came to earth in a humble stable, in a manger, as a baby, seen only by a few people: the shepherds, the Magi, and His immediate family. But when Christ comes again, every eye will see Him. We wait fervently for that day when Christ will come in glory with all of His angels and ten thousand times ten thousand of His saints, to receive His own to Himself and to destroy all wickedness and evil forever. For Christians, Christ's second coming brings the greatest excitement and joy. We lift our heads and pray the final prayer of the Bible: "'Surely I am coming quickly.' Amen. Even so, come, Lord Jesus!" (Revelation 22:20).

As Christmas works its annual enchantment around us and the songs of the kingdom float on the airwaves, the Christian longs for even more. "I'll be home for Christmas" sounds so right. It sounds like belonging and peace. For a child of God, the most wonderful Christmas will not take place on this earth. Our climactic Christmas is the one we shall celebrate anew, home in heaven…when we will forever be truly home for Christmas. Today dwell on that truth, and pray that the Lord will quickly come.

I do not think that in the last forty years I have lived one conscious hour
that was not influenced by the thought of our Lord's return.

LORD SHAFTESBURY

December 2

BESIDE THE STILL WATERS

He makes me to lie down in green pastures; he leads me beside the still waters.

PSALM 23:2

What is the pace of your life these days? Do you feel as if you speed from one event to the next with barely enough time to catch your breath? Or do you regularly allow yourself time to rest and rejuvenate, to ponder life's mysteries, to reconnect with God?

These days, our lives run at almost terrifying speeds. With the advent of the automobile, then the airplane, and later the jet plane—not to mention the telephone, computer, and many other technological discoveries—life races along like a motion picture played at ten times its normal speed.

Our mobility has offered us great opportunities, but it has also cost us dearly. One-third of Americans move every year. People change jobs frequently. Because of our pick-up-and-move mentality, we lack the roots our parents and grandparents once had.

We pay for our busy ways in our relationships, and we pay for them physically as well. Stress takes a major toll on our bodies. Today, over one million people die each year from stress-related illnesses such as heart attacks, some forms of cancer, and a multitude of other diseases. Did you know that stress destroys the walls of your arteries? Once the walls begin to deteriorate, your body must respond. So what does it do? It lays down plaque inside the arteries. The plaque builds up until it finally blocks the arteries, and once that happens, you're in for a stroke.

All this talk about the effects of stress can add even more stress to our lives! But the Bible has a time-honored solution to all this. God's Word calls us to *stillness*. In Psalm 23 David wrote that God leads us "beside the still waters." In this hectic, frenetic, busy, noisy world, we need to find a calm, quiet place to spend time alone with the Lord. Studies have shown that a regular time of prayer or meditation does, perhaps more than anything else, remove stress and its effects.

God wants to lead *you* beside still waters today. Will you let Him take you there? I urge you drop your responsibilities at God's feet, come away to a quiet place, and just be still and know that He is God.

To overcome stress:
Rule #1: Don't sweat the small stuff.
Rule #2: Everything is small stuff.

DR. ROBERT ELIOT, PROFESSOR OF CARDIOLOGY

THE FIRST AND SECOND COMING OF OUR LORD

…'In the future you will see the Son of Man sitting at the right hand of the Mighty One and coming on the clouds of heaven.'

MATTHEW 26:64, NIV

Have you ever heard the voice of someone you've never met, such as a radio personality, and created a mental image of that person, and then when you saw the person, were you surprised that his or her appearance was completely different from your expectations? I think when it comes to the second coming of Jesus, some people have in their minds a very different picture from that which will actually come to pass. I have this opinion because I think many people anticipate Christ's second coming to be a carbon copy of His first.

But consider this:

The first time He came, He was despised and rejected; the second time He will be glorified and admired by all who believe.

He came to hang upon a cross; He will come to sit upon a throne.

He came in dim obscurity; He will come in bright splendor.

He came to be seen by only a few; He will come to be seen by all, for every eye shall see Him; many shall rejoice at His coming, and many will weep because of Him.

He came to be judged for us; He will come as judge over all of us.

Instead of anticipating Christ as the suffering servant He was on earth, we must expect the majestic, triumphant Christ, who will return in power and glory! Because we expect His victorious return, we have a glorious hope. As you walk with Christ each and every day, ask Him to prepare you for that great and magnificent day when you shall finally see Him face to face!

For every prophecy on the first coming of Christ, there are eight on Christ's second coming.

PAUL LEE TAN

SELF-EXAMINATION

Examine yourselves as to whether you are in the faith. Prove yourselves.
Do you not know yourselves, that Jesus Christ is in you?—unless indeed you are disqualified.

2 CORINTHIANS 13:5

Did you like taking tests when you were in school? If you didn't, you're in good company. Most of us dreaded tests, unlike the blessed few with natural smarts and good study habits.

I hate to say this, but today is test day. Are you ready? In today's passage, Paul commands us to take a test—an open-book test comparing our lives with God's Word. We must administer the test to ourselves, for this test is a self-examination, a test for Christ's presence within us...a test with eternal consequences.

When it comes to making moral and spiritual judgments, we're often prone to examining everyone *but* ourselves. All of us have something of the critic within us, always willing to point the finger at others. The Corinthians had the same tendency. In fact, they were the hypercritics of the ancient world. They criticized Paul's apostleship, and in reaction to their criticism, Paul urged them to examine the reality of their own faith.

We still have Corinthians with us today. In fact, we so often *are* the Corinthians. How many of us have left church saying such things as "Well, what did you think of that sermon?" or "How did you like that preacher?" Sounds like Corinth, doesn't it? But we shouldn't judge God's servants. Instead, we need to place ourselves at Christ's feet and submit ourselves to the judgment of God's Word.

The Word of God explains that one day we shall give account of ourselves before Christ. On that day you won't criticize your spouse, your parents, your neighbors, your church members, or your pastors. You'll give an account of your own life. No other statements or input will be allowed. That's a sobering thought.

As hard as it is, take that test today. Use the psalmist's prayer to aid in this process: "Search me, O God, and know my heart. Try me and know my anxious thoughts. And see if there be any hurtful way in me. And lead me in the everlasting way." Amen. Make sure your heart is right with God. Let's get our own act together before we try to direct everyone else's.

I have had more trouble with myself than with any other man.

DWIGHT L. MOODY

THE JOY OF THE FATHER

'…"Rejoice with me, for I have found my sheep, which was lost." '

LUKE 15:6

Have you ever had the thrilling experience of participating in something bigger than yourself, bigger than your town, bigger than your world? If you and I attend to it, we can have that privilege every day. How can we participate in such an exciting venture? By finding the Good Shepherd's lost sheep and returning them to His fold.

In Luke 15, Jesus tells the story of a shepherd who, upon losing one sheep, went out to search for it. The shepherd traveled everywhere looking for that lost sheep. He trudged high and low, far and wide. He peered down precipitous ravines. He traveled into the valleys of darkness where the wild beasts had their dens. Finally the shepherd found the sheep trapped in tangled briars, and after freeing the sheep, he joyfully placed it upon his shoulders and brought it home.

When the shepherd returned to his home, he called together his neighbors and said to them, "I have found my sheep that was lost. Rejoice with me. Enter into my joy." But could his neighbors really do it? Oh, they could come to the party that he provided and enjoy the delicious food he served, but could they rejoice with him? Perhaps they could if they had searched with him on the rain-swept, storm-driven moors. If they had dared to face the dangers of the wild animals and the cold night, if in those circumstances they had found the sheep, then they would have truly rejoiced with him.

Christ's joy is to find His lost sheep. Heaven rejoices over one sinner who repents and comes to Christ. And we experience that joy when we witness a lost sheep return to the Shepherd. Today, be on God's search party, and reach out to a lost soul. If you live your life searching for lost sheep, caring for them, and feeding them, then you will one day hear the Good Shepherd say to you, "Well done, thou good and faithful servant…enter thou into the joy of the Lord."

To enter into the joy of finding, we must have entered into the pain of seeking.

THE SINLESS SAVIOR

'[Christ] committed no sin, nor was guile found in His mouth.'

1 PETER 2:22

A man able to walk through this life yet never sin—doesn't that seem an impossibility? Only one human has ever accomplished this feat: Jesus Christ. In our society, we raise up many as heroes, but upon closer inspection, we find they have feet of clay. Yet Jesus could say, "Which of you convicts Me of sin?" (John 8:46).

Holy men and women confess their sins. They keep short accounts with God. As holy people grow closer to God, they recognize their own sinfulness more and more. One of the greatest Christians in the history of the Church, the apostle Paul, called himself "the chief of sinners." Conversely, people guilty of heinous crimes often claim innocence. (Visit a prison, and you'll be amazed at how many prisoners claim they've been falsely accused!) But Jesus Christ towers above all people, sinners and saints, in the perfection of His character.

Through the centuries people have tried and failed to find any blemish in Jesus Christ's flawless life. One time a Hindu Brahmin, alarmed at the spread of Christianity in India, set out to write a tract to expose Christ's weaknesses. But the Brahmin abandoned this task because he could find no weak points or sins in Jesus. There aren't any. Even skeptics have shown their respect for the Savior. Listen to what one of them, Ernest Renan of France, said about Christ: "Whatever may be the surprises of the future, Jesus will never be surpassed." He is the perfect one!

Today praise Jesus Christ for His sinlessness. Thank Him that because He lived a sinless life, you can live for eternity.

Jesus, good paragon, thou crystal Christ.

POEM

WHO AM I?

*'I am the Alpha and the Omega, the Beginning and the End,' says the Lord,
'who is and who was and who is to come, the Almighty.'*

REVELATION 1:8

"Who am I?" "Why am I here?" "Where am I going?" Sometimes these are called "college questions." But by no means are they restricted to the college campus. I cannot imagine anyone in this world who has not at some time asked these penetrating questions.

Unfortunately, most people who ask these questions never seem to find satisfactory answers. I don't believe they ever will unless they look outside of themselves and direct these same questions to another—to the One who holds in His hands the key to all things—Jesus Christ. We can ask the same "college questions" about Jesus, and as we discover the answers, we find answers to those questions for our own lives. So let's ask them!

Who is Jesus? He says He is the eternal One, the Almighty, the Beginning and the End. Jesus is God the Son. In believing and affirming these truths about Christ, we can realize that we're God's creation, placed on earth by His will and His design. We're His children.

Why did Jesus come here? He came to reconcile us to God. In our natural state, we are separated from God. God's holiness and purity cannot coexist with our impurity and the filth in our hearts. And we can do nothing to bridge the distance between us and God. So Jesus Christ made a way, spanning the distance by His death on the cross. Whenever we go to Jesus Christ for cleansing and forgiveness, whether we come for the first time or for the billionth time, His death sufficiently atones for all. When we know why He came, we also know why we are here—to glorify Him and spread His kingdom.

Where was Jesus going? Jesus said, "I go to prepare a place for you...that where I am you may be also." When we know where Christ has gone, we discover our final destination: heaven, where we will live with Him for eternity. He's already preparing it for us and will receive us to Himself as soon as our time on earth is done.

In Christ, we have the answers to all our questions about our purpose and our destiny! We know who we are, why we're here, and where we're going. Today thank Christ for providing those answers for you.

Life is filled with meaning as soon as Jesus Christ enters into it.

STEPHEN NEILL

December 8

THE ONE TO COME

...'Go and tell John the things which you hear and see: The blind receive their sight and the lame walk; the lepers are cleansed and the deaf hear; the dead are raised up...'

MATTHEW 11:4–5

Do you ever wonder whether Jesus is all He claimed to be? whether He'll fulfill all the promises He made to us? Well, even John the Baptist, the one sent to prepare Christ's way, had his moments of doubt. And when we wonder if Jesus is really the one, the answer He gave John should suffice for any of us. John was very familiar with the prophet Isaiah, and he knew the ancient prophecies concerning the Messiah (Isaiah 29:18, 35:4–6). So when Jesus wanted to prove to John His true identity, He told John, in Isaiah's words, how He had fulfilled prophecies.

In the same way, when we have doubts, we can look to how Jesus fulfilled biblical prophecy, proving that He is the Messiah. According to just a few of the 333 concrete prophecies in the Old Testament, the Messiah would

- be Abraham's descendant;
- be of the lineage of Judah and of David;
- be born in Bethlehem;
- be born of a virgin;
- come 483 years after the decree to rebuild Jerusalem;
- exercise a benevolent ministry;
- open the eyes of the blind, heal the lame, and cure the deaf;
- be betrayed by His friends;
- be sold for thirty pieces of silver which would be cast down for a potter's field;
- give His body as a ransom for others;
- endure the piercing of His hands and His feet;
- die amid transgressors;
- lie in a rich man's grave; and
- rise from the dead.

And the list goes on! My friends, God has given us enormous evidence of Jesus' identity as the Christ. We need have no question about the granite foundation upon which our faith rests. We may know that just as these prophecies of the Old Testament came to pass, so will the promises of the New Testament come to pass. We can trust in Jesus, come what may.

The next time you find yourself doubting Jesus Christ, remember how He has fulfilled every promise He made. Then dwell on the truth that in the same way He'll fulfill the promises He has made to you.

I came to believe that Christ was the One predicted by the prophets of my people.

JEWISH BELIEVER IN JESUS

PROPHECIES CONCERNING THE MESSIAH

*'But you, Bethlehem Ephrathah, though you are little among the thousands of Judah, yet
out of you shall come forth to Me the One to be ruler in Israel, whose
goings forth have been from of old, from everlasting.'*

MICAH 5:2

One January my wife and I listed fifty-five separate prophecies made by today's leading seers and psychics. As that year unfolded, we watched to see which of those prophecies would come true. Not a single one came to pass! Worldly prophets rarely predict events accurately. The worldly prophet Nostradamus became famous because he made one single and obscure prophecy which some believed Hitler fulfilled, but that prophecy could have applied just as easily to a number of other people at various times in Europe's history. Worldly prophecy leaves room for many interpretations.

While worldly prophecy is weak, we can bank our lives on biblical prophecy. The prophecy about the Messiah in Micah 5:2 states two things about Him: (1) He would be born in Bethlehem, and (2) He would be eternal. Some may say that this prophecy is weak and unsatisfactory. And it is, just as one single thread is weak and easily snapped. But if you take 333 such threads (some of which we discussed in yesterday's devotion) and wind them together, no one could break the cord produced! In the same way, no one can break the prophecies made about Jesus Christ. The Old Testament contains an incredible 333 prophecies that describe in detail virtually every aspect of the life and ministry of Jesus Christ. Nothing remotely like this exists anywhere else in all of the annals of history or all the other religious books of the world.

These biblical prophecies show us not only that Jesus of Nazareth is the Messiah but that the Word of God is divinely inspired and that we can trust in what it says. The fulfillment of these prophecies demonstrates God's existence—in no way could all these prophets have made these prophecies if God hadn't inspired them to know these things long before they took place. We have seen the utter failure of secular prophets. Only in the Bible and by God's inspiration do we find prophecies fulfilled.

*God the Holy Spirit moved the prophets to write, and put into their minds the very thoughts
which they expressed and the very words which they wrote.*

MARTIN LUTHER

O LITTLE TOWN OF BETHLEHEM

'For there is born to you this day in the city of David [Bethlehem] a Savior, who is Christ the Lord.'

LUKE 2:11

Do you know the story behind one of the most beloved Christmas carols, "O Little Town of Bethlehem"? Let me tell it to you. A young Episcopalian minister arrived in Jerusalem on December 24, 1865. He made his way on horseback about six miles south, to the little town of Bethlehem. He stood at the bottom of a hill and was struck by the vision of the town. With very little light around it, the town seemed so dark. How still and silent was the sight! So unlike the flaming metropolises of America, blackness hovered over the little town of Bethlehem.

Three years later, the minister, Phillips Brooks, wrote a poem about Bethlehem. During the week before Christmas, Brooks' music director, Lewis Redner, wrote a melody for that poem, finishing it just in time for Christmas Sunday, when it was first sung by six Sunday school teachers and thirty-six children. And every Christmas since, that song has touched our hearts, for it speaks of the deepest needs and greatest longings of the human heart and soul.

For centuries the human soul has longed for something more than death. "Is life no more than this?" people ask as they watch their loved ones descend into the tomb to return no more. "There must be more than this." The hopes of all the world rested with that little Babe in Bethlehem.

Also, the fears of all the world were met there with Him—the fears that life has no ultimate meaning and no significant purpose, that humanity has no future, that we must go down into the pit of oblivion never to live again. But Christ's birth gives humankind new hope to combat those fears.

Today as you anticipate Christmas, think of Bethlehem and the event that occurred in that humble little town. Allow Christ to meet all your hopes and fears, for He came to do just that.

Yet in the dark street shineth the everlasting Light;
The hopes and fears of all the years are met in Thee tonight.

PHILLIPS BROOKS

LIGHT IN DARKNESS

Those who dwelt in the land of the shadow of death, upon them a light has shined.

ISAIAH 9:2

"Why are there so many lights, Daddy?" Have you ever wondered the same thing at Christmastime, when you see hundreds of houses decked with colorful, twinkling lights? The question about the Christmas lights came on a dark December night from a four-year-old girl. Her father perceptively answered, "Because Jesus is the light of the world."

Before the Light of the world came to earth, the world was very dark. The Golden Age of Greek philosophy had passed, and an intellectual barrenness had covered the landscape of the mind. The faith in the Homeric gods had all but vanished completely, and skepticism had paled the souls of many. The moral structure of society had collapsed everywhere, and humanity had sunk deep into the mire of depravity and vice. When there was nothing but discouragement, disillusion and despair—when everything was the bleakest and darkest and grimmest—Jesus came.

By no mere coincidence does Christmas come in December. Christmas comes after the season when the dead leaves have flown across the ground with every gust of wind. Christ did not arrive in the time of blooming flowers and balmy breezes. Christ did not arrive in the time of fields ripe for harvest. He arrived when frost lay sheeted over the earth. He came in the midst of a bleak and dark December under a glittering star. This reminds us that Christ came for those who feel frostbitten by life. He came for those who are snowed under. He came for those overwhelmed by the cold realities of life. He came to soothe and rock and cradle and kiss and lullaby a cold, hurt, crying world.

Christmas makes December beautiful and bright. Christ makes His birthday a time of joy, miracles, and light. Thank Him today for the light He brought to the world at Christmastime, for the light He brings daily to your life.

Before Christ came, the devil made it 'always winter and never Christmas.'

PARAPHRASE OF C. S. LEWIS

FEAR NOT

There is no fear in love; but perfect love casts out fear, because fear involves torment.
But he who fears has not been made perfect in love.

1 JOHN 4:18

When was the last time you felt your heart pounding, your stomach tying itself into knots, your hands shaking like leaves in the wind? Was it last year? last month? yesterday?

Maybe you feel those things this very minute.

Fear runs deep in the human race, a legacy passed down from the very first of God's creation. It's the natural response of a sinful people to impending judgment. After Adam and Eve had tasted forbidden fruit in the Garden of Eden, what was their immediate response to hearing God's voice? They were afraid and ran to hide themselves among the trees of the garden.

Do you remember the three angels who visited Abraham and then went to Sodom to talk to Lot? One of them was none other than God Himself appearing briefly in angelic form. But He came not as a savior; he came to spy out the wickedness of the land. He came as a destroyer, bidding the red-hot sulfur to fall upon Sodom and Gomorrah to end the wickedness of their people.

God also came in judgment of the world during the time of Noah. In the face of the flood that eventually wiped wickedness from the face of the earth, the people cried out in fear before they cried out no more.

Do you ever feel that fear?

People truly had every reason to fear God and the supernatural, just as a criminal fears a police car's blinking lights and wailing sirens. But the angel that announced Christ's birth said, "Do not be afraid." During his lifetime, Jesus repeated those words often. Jesus didn't quote them from the angel. Jesus *gave* those words to the angel when He commissioned the angel to communicate His birth to the world. This message and Jesus' life, death, and resurrection, ushered in a new relationship with God: "Fear not." "Be not afraid." "It is I, be of good courage." "Fear not, little flock."

We don't have to be afraid. Perfect love drives out fear, and God loves us— loves you—perfectly. You and I need not fear God's punishment, for Jesus has taken it for us.

Will you accept God's perfect love today?

Hear the angel's words—God's message to you: "Be not afraid, for I bring you good tidings of great joy."

Now we need not fear the grave; Jesus Christ was born to save.

LATIN CHRISTMAS CAROL

NO MORE CURSE

'...Cursed is the ground for your sake;...In the sweat of your face you shall eat bread...'

GENESIS 3:17, 19

Do you remember the last time you blew it with God? Do you remember what that did inside of you?

You're not alone. People have experienced those feelings since the beginning of time.

What happened to Adam and Eve when they sinned? They died spiritually. Their minds were darkened. They stubbornly followed their own wills, their spirits out of tune with God. Through their sin, Adam and Eve allowed sorrow, separation, guilt, fear, and self-centeredness into Paradise—into the lives of all humankind—bringing hatred, crime, violence, war, death, and hell in their wake.

The curse resulting from Adam and Eve's sin has not only spiritual implications but also physical ones. God pronounced the curse first upon Satan for deceiving and tempting the woman, condemning the serpent to crawl on its belly and eat dust. Then God cursed the woman, increasing her suffering in childbirth and subjecting her to her husband. For the man, God took the delight from work, relegating the man to a life of labor and toil in the midst of thorns and thistles. All of the animals came under the curse, and what had been kindly and loving pets became dangerous, wild, and poisonous creatures. Finally, all creatures would eventually succumb to physical death most often preceded by disease, illness, pain, and weakness.

Maybe you'd rather not dwell on such depressing issues at this time of year. And, fortunately, you don't have to. Why? Because Christmas is all about Christ's coming to take away the effects of this horrible curse. Christ came to earth as a baby to absorb the curse for us. Through His death and resurrection, Jesus destroyed the devil's works and created a way for us to be restored, perfect in God's sight.

God begins that work in you and me when we surrender to Him and become *His* children, born of the Spirit. That work continues throughout our lives in the process of sanctification. Fully and perfectly, we will be restored when we reach heaven; Christ will have completed His work in us and eliminated the curse. In a perfect world and in perfect bodies, we shall dwell forever with Christ.

This is the message of Christmas, the reason Jesus came to earth as a babe. As you and I anticipate Christmas this year, let's rejoice that all curses are reversed in Jesus Christ.

So God imparts to human hearts the blessings of His heav'n.

PHILLIPS BROOKS

"FAR AS THE CURSE IS FOUND"

And there shall be no more curse…'for the former things have passed away.'

REVELATION 22:3, 21:4

When Christ came to earth, he began reversing the effects of the curse that resulted from Adam and Eve's sin in the Garden of Eden. This restoration process, which will only be complete in heaven, includes the development of science.

Have you ever thought of it that way? Most people don't. After all, the tenets of science and those of Christianity often seem at odds in today's world. But modern science has *Christian* origins. Not only did science arise in a Christian culture, but all of the major founders of the different branches of science were Christians, some of them very devout. Great scientists who were committed Christians include Isaac Newton, Robert Boyle, Louis Pasteur, Blaise Pascal, Joseph Lister, Michael Faraday, and Lord Kelvin, to name just a few. We need to recognize the link between their Christian worldview and their pioneering discoveries. Science, said Kepler, the great astronomer, was "thinking God's thoughts after Him."

Science has proved to be a great blessing to all of humankind, saving the lives of millions and lengthening the life spans of virtually all it has touched. And science was born from the Christian faith! When we experience the benefits of modern science—driving to an antiseptic hospital, receiving anesthesia, and having pure, germ-free surgery—we owe all this to Christ and His devoted people of faith.

Let's remember that science's breakthroughs are Christ's blessings to us. As Isaac Watt's great Christmas carol, "Joy to the World!" declares, "He comes to make His blessings flow, far as the curse is found." What's one blessing from science that has further removed the curse from your life? I encourage you to thank God for that scientific development during this Christmas season.

There are two books laid before us to study, to prevent our falling into error;
first, the volume of the Scriptures, which reveal the will of God;
then the volume of the Creatures, which express His power.

FRANCIS BACON, FATHER OF THE SCIENTIFIC METHOD

THE INCREDIBLE INCARNATION

And the Word became flesh and dwelt among us, and we beheld His glory,
the glory as of the only begotten of the Father, full of grace and truth.

JOHN 1:14

Do you remember the fairy tale about the toad that, when kissed by a princess, became a handsome prince? Well, Christmas is the story about a prince who became a toad—about the *Creator* of the universe who became a *creature* to redeem the creatures in bondage. How would you feel about becoming an animal—a donkey, an ostrich, or a toad? I submit to you that the distance between Christ, the eternal Son of God, and a human being is infinitely greater than the distance between a human and any part of the animal creation. Christ is immortal; death was alien and foreign to His nature. Yet He tasted death for us.

Through the centuries, the hymn writers, theologians, and heralds of Christ have told us that this Babe in Bethlehem is none other than God Himself, the same One who enwrapped Himself with the starry clouds of the Milky Way and flung from His fingertips the vast myriad of galaxies that light the night sky. He is none other than the eternal, omnipotent, omniscient Creator of all things. He is our God, the Almighty One, God the Son. He left heaven so we could gain heaven. He came into the valley of sorrows so we could have a way out of it. He became poor to give us His riches. He suffered to free us from pain and death.

Christ's life on earth was absolutely unique. He never learned because He knew all things. He never apologized because He never did anything wrong. He never corrected His teachings; He never sought advice. Never before or since has such a Man as this lived, who invariably evoked from the hearts and minds of those who beheld Him the startled question, "What manner of man is this?" The baby asleep on Mary's lap was Christ our King, Lord of the universe. What a privilege to know Him!

Veiled in flesh, the Godhead see; hail the incarnate Deity.
Pleased as man with men to dwell, Jesus our Emmanuel.

CHARLES WESLEY

THE VIRGIN BIRTH

'...the virgin shall conceive...'

ISAIAH 7:14

Have you ever heard of a *white* crow? I sure haven't seen one, but that doesn't mean that one doesn't or couldn't exist.

Many people view the Virgin Birth as a white crow. They say that Jesus couldn't possibly have been born of a virgin, just because that type of birth had never happened before and hasn't happened since. But the Bible teaches that Jesus was conceived in a miraculous and supernatural manner; the Holy Spirit overshadowed Mary, conceiving within her Jesus Christ, making Him both God and human.

We can understand that unbelievers would attack and ridicule this doctrine. With no biblical knowledge, they can dismiss this assertion as mythical and not historical. But sometimes the attacks come from within the Church, and when this happens, we have a much more serious problem. In this case, wolves in sheep's clothing attempt to deceive the masses.

What would happen to our faith if the Virgin Birth were a myth or hoax? What consequences must follow? To begin with, Jesus would have been an illegitimate child. If this were the case, then the angel lied to Mary when he said, "The holy one to be born will be called the Son of God." Mary would not be blessed among women, but rather unchaste and immoral, despised and outcast by her culture.

If Jesus had been born of humans, He Himself would have been only human, not divine. And without His divinity, He could never be our redeemer. He couldn't save anyone. He would have no power to forgive sin, and Christianity would be a fraud. Even God Himself would be a liar, for He said, "This is My beloved Son, in whom I am well pleased" (Matthew 3:17).

The issue of the Virgin Birth is no fine point of theology; it lies at the very heart of our faith, because it asserts Jesus' true nature. He is indeed the virgin-born Son of God!

If there is a God, a God who has created the universe, who spoke the world into existence, and has created a vast expanse of galaxies, is it any great thing for Him to simply reach down and place a microscopic cell in the womb of a woman that He made?

PARAPHRASE OF DR. MANFORD GUTZKE

JESUS CHRIST: MYTH OR MESSIAH?

That which was from the beginning, which we have heard, which we have seen with our eyes, which we have looked upon, and our hands have handled, concerning the Word of Life...that which we have seen and heard we declare to you...

1 JOHN 1:1, 3

Do you know how much proof we have that Jesus really lived? If you put together both biblical and secular sources, we have an enormous amount of information about Christ's life. While today we have only one or two copies of ancient secular manuscripts, fifteen thousand biblical manuscripts have survived. And down the years, Bible translators haven't just copied the Bible from one modern language to another. Instead, they've consulted the original Greek and Hebrew sources. Because the stories of Christ's life have been communicated in this way, we can trust their accuracy. Unlike the stories of mythical heroes, which grow more exaggerated with time, the number of miracles Jesus performed, as reported in the Gospels, diminished over time. The book of Mark, written first, describes twenty, and the books of Matthew and Luke, written later, describe twenty-two and twenty-one, respectively. But the book of John, written much later, describes only eight.

The two most important historians of the first century—the Jewish historian Josephus, and the Roman historian Tacitus—also confirm every basic fact of the Gospel narratives. As well, about twenty other early secular historians speak factually of Jesus. Some even wrote whole works against Him. The Jews wrote of Him in the second part of the Jewish Talmud, called the Gemara. Though they wrote this work to discredit Jesus, the Gemara gives an ancient confirmation of the basic facts of Christ's life: His unusual birth to Mary, His ministry in Palestine, His miracles, the divisions He caused among the Israelites, His crucifixion on the day before Passover.

Modern skeptics, who have sought to prove Christ was just a myth, have been convinced by their own research that He not only lived but was the most extraordinary person who ever inhabited the earth. Jesus is the greatest fact of history. Today, thank God that we do not follow "cunningly devised fables" (2 Peter 1:16); rather, we follow the Word made flesh so that we might have abundant life!

The historicity of Jesus is no longer questioned seriously by anyone, whether Christian or unbeliever. The main facts about Him seem to be beyond dispute.

H. L. MENCKEN

O COME, O COME, EMMANUEL

' ...and they shall call His name Immanuel,' which is translated, 'God with us.'

MATTHEW 1:23

Christmas weaves its own magic spell with twinkling lights and silver bells, wonderful music and special memories. And as we let nostalgia flood us with warm feelings, we find ourselves hoping for a perfect Christmas. We long in our hearts for something to make everything right in our world. I believe that at this time of year, whether people recognize it or not, everyone longs for God.

Some have said that next to the Bible, we should know best the hymnal. The Scriptures contain doctrine and ethics. Our hymns, which have been called "three minute sermons," consist of great truths set to music. This is certainly true concerning most Christmas hymns and carols. Some of the most beautiful music in the world belongs to the Christmas season, and these songs clearly communicate the message of Christ's coming and of His redemptive work.

Consider the ancient hymn, "O Come, O Come, Emmanuel." This hymn begins with the shortest lyric in the history of songwriting: one letter—"O." Not even "Oh," it was simply "O." The Latin Church of the eighth century called this syllable the antiphon, and they sang it as the deep-seated plea of the human heart after God. The Bible tells us, "As the heart pants after the water brooks, so pants my soul after Thee, O God." This is the personal longing communicated in "O Come, O Come, Emmanuel."

Just as the godly Jews waited for the Messiah to come, so now the Church waits and longs for Him to come again. As you sing "O Come, O Come, Emmanuel" this Christmas season, thank God that Christ will return to make everything perfect and whole again.

It has been said by scholars that the second coming of Christ is mentioned no less than 1,200 times in the Old Testament and 300 times in the New Testament.

FRANCIS W. DIXON

FOLLOWING THE STAR

...the star which they had seen in the East went before them, till it came and stood over where the young Child was. When they saw the star, they rejoiced with exceedingly great joy.

MATTHEW 2:9–10

Have you ever gazed at the stars in the sky and wondered what Christ's star—the star of Bethlehem—looked like? What a magnificent star it must have been for the wise men to pack up and take off after it. They left everything to follow that star.

Many people have speculated about the exact physical nature of that star, but in the end, all speculations are merely guesses. But we *do* know that this star heralded Christ's coming, and as it did so, it communicated His nature to us.

The star of Bethlehem was a star of love that pointed to the incarnate yet divine love of Jesus Christ, God's perfect love that had come to earth in human form.

The star of Bethlehem was a star of hope that led the wise men to the fulfillment of their expectations, the success of their expedition. Nothing in this world is more fundamental for success in life than hope, and this star pointed to our only source for true hope: Jesus Christ.

The star of Bethlehem was a star of joy. "When they saw the star, they rejoiced with exceedingly great joy." All true joy comes from Him. From deep within the well of our souls, Christ's joy bubbles up and overflows. Those who know Jesus the best rejoice the most.

The star of Bethlehem was also a star of witness. It witnessed about the one true King and Messiah Who came to the Jews first and then to the Gentiles.

But most of all, the star of Bethlehem was a star of guidance. The star guided the wise men through the desert and across great distances. It guided them to the Lord Jesus Christ. We also are guided by our Star—God's Word—a lamp to our feet and a light to our path. As pilgrims through this barren land, God's Word guides us to Jesus Christ, the light of the world.

Today thank God for the love, hope, joy, witness, and guidance we gained when Jesus Christ was born under that star. May the light of His star guide you this day and every day until together we bow down and worship Jesus with the wise men in Heaven.

Wise men still seek Him.

CHRISTIAN BUMPER STICKER

IN THE FULLNESS OF TIME

But when the fullness of the time had come, God sent forth His Son,
born of a woman, born under the law.

GALATIANS 4:4

Have you ever noticed that God has perfect timing? Sometimes we have to look back to discover how God worked things out for us, but when we do, we can always find His hand moving just at the right time.

Just as God uses perfect timing in our lives, He carefully planned the timing of Christ's birth. According to Scripture, Jesus came "in the fullness of time." We can see that, before Christ came, the entire history of humankind had been a preparation for His advent. God even used pagans to prepare the world for Christ. For example, when Jesus came, the whole civilized world spoke one language. Why? When Alexander the Great conquered the world, he conquered it linguistically as well as physically. The world was unified by the koine Greek language, and the apostles wrote the New Testament and preached the gospel in this language.

As well, the entire world had come under the one government of Rome—a single citizenship—prior to Christ's coming. Paul and the early Christians could thus travel the length and breadth of the Roman Empire, from North Africa to South Brittany, from Palestine to Spain, to share the gospel. This would never have been physically possible if the Romans had not constructed their roads, an incredible accomplishment for that period. Not until the latter part of the nineteenth century did modern civilization equal that achievement!

So with a single language, a single citizenship, and roads connecting every part of the empire, the physical world was prepared for the coming of Christ, and Caesar Augustus could order a census of the entire Roman world. And so Mary and Joseph went to Bethlehem where, as prophesied, the virgin would give birth to the Messiah in the city of David.

As you wait for Christmas this season, and as you wait for God to work in your life, remember God's perfect timing in sending His Son. Thank Him for His wisdom and His ability to perfectly order the events of your life, including the most important event: Christ's coming.

When the Christian religion first appeared upon earth, Providence, by whom the world was
doubtless prepared for its coming, had gathered a large portion of the human race, like an
immense flock, under the scepter of the Caesars.

ALEXIS DE TOCQUEVILLE

THE IMAGE OF THE INVISIBLE GOD

He is the image of the invisible God, the firstborn over all creation. For by Him all things were created that are in heaven and that are on earth, visible and invisible, whether thrones or dominions or principalities or powers. All things were created through Him and for Him.

COLOSSIANS 1:15–16

One day, a little boy was drawing a picture. When his Sunday school teacher asked him what he was drawing, he replied that he was making a picture of God. The Sunday school teacher objected, "But, Billy, nobody knows what God looks like." "They will now!" he confidently replied.

Like Billy's Sunday school teacher, we may believe that we won't know what God looks like until we get to heaven. But if we want to know what God is like, we can just look at Jesus for, as the Scripture says, He is the visible image of the invisible God. No one has seen God, but those who have seen Jesus have seen the Father!

Just about everything that Scripture says about the Father, it also says about the Son. Note the following verses that draw the parallels between them (in each set, the first passage refers to the Father, and the second passage refers to the Son):

"I am the First, and I am the Last; besides Me there is no God" (Isaiah 44:6).
"I am the First and the Last. I am He who lives, and was dead" (Revelation 1:17–18).

"Fear not, for I am with you" (Isaiah 41:10).
"Lo, I am with you always, even to the end of the age" (Matthew 28:20).

"For I am the Lord, I do not change" (Malachi 3:6).
"Jesus Christ is the same yesterday, today, and forever" (Hebrews 13:8).

"The King of kings, and the Lord of lords" (1 Timothy 6:15).
"King of kings and Lord of lords." (Revelation 19:16).

Many other passages draw similar parallels. At Christmastime, we can dwell on this truth: God the Almighty Himself became one of us. Offer a praise to God today for coming to earth in human form so that we might live with Him in heaven for eternity.

Pleased as man with men to dwell, Jesus our Immanuel.

CHARLES WESLEY

THERE'S GOOD NEWS TONIGHT!

'...behold, I bring you good tidings of great joy which will be to all people.'

LUKE 2:10

When I was a boy, a radio network news announcer named Gabriel Heater began his program every night with the same words: "There's good news tonight." I have always remembered those words. I don't remember what good news he shared, but don't those words themselves communicate a sense of hope?

I can't think of any news commentator today who would have the nerve to begin his or her program that way. Watching the news the other day, I saw one disaster after another in unremitting repetition. It seems we rarely have good news anymore.

But thank God that we as Christians celebrate the greatest news the world has ever heard. God predicted this good news when He said that the seed of the woman would bruise the head of the serpent (Genesis 3:15). He promised this good news to the patriarchs, "And in thy seed shall all nations of the earth be blessed" (Genesis 28:14).

And at long last, God fulfilled His promise. He came to earth. From His palace of crystal and gold, God rose from His golden throne and stepped into the world, born as a baby. What a wondrous day that was. And the angel declared the good news.

To appreciate the significance of this good news, we need to go back to the Garden of Eden when Satan first conquered the human will and brought humankind into bondage to himself. Through that devilish deceit, sin entered the world, and it has blighted the earth ever since. Sin extinguished God's light in the human soul.

The devil still tells us lies. He tells us that Christianity is some sort of wet blanket thrown over what the world offers. But the fun of the world is fleeting and passing at best. In contrast, Christ gives an everlasting joy that wells up within the hearts of believers. Christianity is not only good news, it's the greatest news the world will ever hear.

Today, thank God for the good news we celebrate at this time of year, and share it with those around you who need to hear it.

It [the gospel] can and will correct everything needing correction.

WILLIAM GLADSTONE

THE GOSPEL ACCORDING TO MARY

'...Behold the virgin shall conceive and bear a son, and shall call his name Immanuel.'

ISAIAH 7:14

Do you sometimes face what may seem like impossible obstacles? Perhaps you're facing one even now. In these times, take heart because God can do the impossible. He did the impossible in the life of one of His humble servants, Mary, the mother of our Lord, the most famous woman in the world.

The promise of Isaiah 7:14 had been made long ago. All Jews knew about it. In all the godly homes, mothers would tell their daughters about that promise, and a thrill would go through the young girls' hearts. It seemed an inspired dream that had blossomed only to fade with each passing century.

Mary knew the Scriptures; she had hidden God's Word in her heart. And when the time came and the angel of the Lord spoke to her, she recognized the words of the prophet Isaiah. She, Mary, would give birth to the Son of the Most High, who would rule over the house of Jacob! Mary heard and believed. She placed her will and her dreams of a life with Joseph under God's will, under the awesome fulfillment of the prophesies of the Messiah.

The mystery of Mary is a paradox—adored by some, ignored by others. What is the truth about this one chosen by God, who in her own life experienced the paradox of God's blessing? To be chosen by God involved not only a crown of joy, but also a cross of sorrow. She knew the wonder, the tremendous joy of bringing the Messiah into the world, but she also knew the heartbreak as she stood before the cross at Golgotha.

At the beginning and at the end of Jesus' life, we find that the light shone brightly upon Mary, and we see her at her greatest moments. We see that, truly, she was blessed among women. We should all aspire to be like Mary, who answered God with humility and resigned herself joyfully to His will no matter the cost. As you consider impossible obstacles in your life, follow Mary's example, trusting your life to God and submitting your will to His.

Next to her son, Mary is the most touching figure in the narrative.

WILL DURANT

THE JOY OF CHRISTMAS

'…I bring you good tidings of great joy…'

LUKE 2:10

Imagine yourself in the shepherds' sandals. You're minding your own business, tending to the evening duties all shepherds attend to, when an angel shows up and the glory of God shines all around you. You not only behold such a magnificent sight, but you also hear the angel proclaim, "I bring you good tidings of great joy."

That angel was the first preacher of the gospel—glad tidings, wonderful news, the glorious message of great hope and joy for all people!

The joy of Christmas is the joy of reconciliation. If you're like the rest of us, you know the sadness and pain of being at odds with someone—especially with someone you love—because an argument or harsh, cruel words have divided you. When those times come, you can feel a cold, thick wall separating you from your spouse, child, friend, or relative. You believe you'll never experience joy again until the moment you reconcile. And when you finally knit your hearts together again and your tears of sorrow have turned into laughter and hugs, you can feel joyful once more.

How much more do we feel that joy when we've reconciled with God!

Our sin and rebellion have built a wall between us and God. Ever since that fateful day in Eden, humankind and God have been estranged. But Jesus was born to break down that wall by atoning for our sins. Because of Jesus' sacrifice on the cross, we can be reconciled with God. At last we can rest in His arms and receive the robe of righteousness and the ring of kinship. Now the joy bells start ringing in our hearts, and a song bursts forth from our lips—a song of praise unto Jesus Christ, who has made it all possible, who has joined the hand of the sinner with the hand of the Father.

What a joy is that reconciliation! Today, join with me in celebrating the wellspring of joy that comes from a heart reconciled with God.

Peace on earth and mercy mild, God and sinners reconciled!
Joyful all ye nations rise, join the triumph of the skies.

CHARLES WESLEY

GOD'S CHRISTMAS GIFT

…the gift of God is eternal life in Christ Jesus our Lord.

ROMANS 6:23

Well, have you opened yours yet? I'm talking about your Christmas gift from God! It's what people have always wanted. For centuries people have searched for the fountain of youth, wondering if something somewhere can stop aging and give life anew. The search for immortality…has this been your quest?

Once we open God's Christmas gift, our search is over. What is this incredible gift that satisfies our deepest longings? *Eternal life*. God gives it to us as a Christmas gift, totally free because it's priceless. If it weren't a gift, who could buy it? How could anyone pay for a hundred billion eons of centuries in Paradise…in a new body that never aches…in a new world without sorrow, weeping, or death? Nobody could pay even one billionth of one percent of the value of this gift.

If you had received all the presents you ever dreamed of and even a thousandfold more, but you lay in your bed with your hands cold and your heart stopped, then it doesn't matter what's under the Christmas tree. But God's gift is eternal life. It can't be snatched away by death. But, of course, you have to open your gift, which you can do by trusting in Jesus for your salvation.

And unlike many gifts we buy for those we love, God's Christmas gift has been paid for already. Despite the incredible expense of the gift, He hasn't charged it—Jesus paid the full price once and for all. Upon that cross of agony, Christ endured in body and soul the wrath of God, which is the wages of sin. Christ paid the price, not with silver or gold or precious stones, but with His own blood.

If you have already opened your Christmas gift from God, then point someone else to the gift this Christmas. Someone near you might not know the true joy of Christmas, unwrapping material gifts while the most beautiful gift in all of heaven and earth lies unopened. God loves us so much that He gave us His Son. That's why we give gifts to each other. That's why we celebrate Christmas.

Merry Christmas!

God's gifts put men's best dreams to shame.

ELIZABETH BROWNING

WISE MEN STILL SEEK HIM

'...For the Gentiles shall seek Him...'

ISAIAH 11:10

Through the ages Israelites as well as people of other nations have waited for the promised Messiah. Many Gentiles had heard of the Messiah from the Jews in captivity. In Babylon, in Persia, in every place the Jews were taken, the message spread of the long-expected one, the Savior to come.

The wise men who followed the star of Bethlehem had heard the news in this way. Who exactly were these men? Contrary to some accounts, they probably were not kings. Most likely they were ancient scientists, perhaps astrologers or philosophers from Persia or Babylonia. These men traveled a great distance to find the Christ. They had received some sign of His birth, some clue, some message from that strange and singular occurrence in the sky. Why would these men set out on such a hard and hazardous journey? Why would they travel so far to find a new king?

I think the answer these men would give us is the very epitome of wisdom: Truly wise men will ever seek after Christ.

Did the wise men find what they sought? Yes, indeed! They not only found *a* way to God, they found *the* way. They not only found *some* truth, they found *the* truth. They not only found life, they found *the* life. And they fell down and worshiped Him.

This beautiful saga has enshrined itself in the hearts of humankind as a permanent part of the Christmas story. The wise men were the very first of a vast host of Gentiles who would seek and find the Messiah. Most of us are like that...Gentiles privileged enough to come and worship at His cradle! Enjoy that privilege today; come and worship our Lord the Messiah!

They followed what little light they had, and it brought them at last
into the presence of the living, incarnate God.

LIFE EVERLASTING

*'And God will wipe away every tear from their eyes; there shall be no more death, nor sorrow,
nor crying; and there shall be no more pain…'*

REVELATION 21:4

When did you last think about how incredible heaven will be? Often we take heaven for granted. In fact, our culture—even our cartoons—trivialize it, and we buy into the watered-down images. But heaven will be a truly glorious place. What a great promise we have in knowing we'll spend eternity there!

Can you imagine a place where every house is a mansion or a palace? every step a triumph? every covering of the head a coronation? every year a jubilee? every month an enchantment? every week a transport of delight? every hour a paradise? every moment an ecstasy? That is what heaven will be like! Who can imagine it, and who can understand what God has prepared?

In heaven, there shall be no entropy, where everything breaks down. For indeed, the curse will have been lifted, and sin will be gone forever. We'll have perfect bodies that shall never age nor grow sick, never weary nor grow weak, and never need sleep. We will know no grief or loss. We'll experience the full love of others. We'll all gather in fellowship; no one will feel rejected or snubbed.

Above all, we'll see our Savior face to face! We will know Him, love Him, and enjoy full fellowship with Him. Our relationship with Him will go beyond anything we could ever imagine here on earth.

As you walk through your day, especially when circumstances get you down, turn your thoughts toward heaven. Let the hope of heaven buoy you up this day!

*The reward for serving the Lord might not be much in this life, but
the retirement benefits are out of this world!*

ANONYMOUS

THE LORD'S DAY

'The Sabbath was made for man...'

MARK 2:27

At the end of a given week, do you often find yourself tired and weary from the toils of work? Are you ready to relax and give praise to the Lord? That is exactly what the Sabbath is for! We should reserve it as a day of rest and rejoicing. In fact, do you know why many churches (including the one I pastor) choose not to have kneeling benches? Because in the early church, Christians were forbidden to kneel on Sunday. They instead observed Sunday as a day of *rejoicing* in God for His mighty deeds.

The Sabbath is a blessed day, and so it should be, for even the Lord rested on the Sabbath after creating the universe. On this day of the week, we remember that God made us as special creatures, designed to lift our heads toward God, honoring Him for who He is and for what He has done. The Sabbath is a pledge of that eternal rest which is ours. Not only should we rest on the Sabbath, we should take advantage of it as family time. For those of us with children, we can take that day to spend time with our kids, to model rejoicing for them, and to teach them spiritual truths.

But we so often compromise the Sabbath. Amos castigated the ungodly people in Israel who eagerly awaited the end of the Sabbath so that they might sell their crops. In the same spirit as these sinful Israelites, many people today don't even wait for the Sabbath to end before they engage in work. Some people may *have* to work on this day, but many without Sunday work obligations choose to work anyway. In doing so, these people demonstrate how far their hearts are from God! They dishonor God by not keeping His day holy.

This week, plan to set the Sabbath aside as a day to rest and rejoice in the Lord. Give your responsibilities to God, and allow Him to hold them while you enjoy Him and the day He has made.

The stops of a good man are ordered by the Lord as well as his steps.

GEORGE MUELLER

A LOOK AT THE HEREAFTER

*And I saw a new heaven and a new earth, for the first heaven and
the first earth had passed away…*

REVELATION 21:1

Many years ago I heard a man derisively described as someone who was "so
heavenly minded that he was no earthly good." We may hear that from time to
time, but for every one person who fits that description, ten thousand people
are so *worldly* minded that they are no *heavenly* good at all!

Where do your thoughts dwell: on the concerns of this world or in anticipation of eternity spent in heaven?

Once I was in an unfamiliar building. When I was ready to leave, I opened
a door, thinking it was an exit, but instead I had stepped into a tiny broom
closet! Of course, I stepped out instantly and closed the door. I was probably
in there only one or two seconds at the most. Now, wouldn't you think it extra-
ordinarily odd if I spent the rest of my life thinking about that little closet when
I had spent such a short time in it? In the same way, why do we spend all of our
time thinking about this "little closet" of earth that is but a fleeting moment in
the framework of eternity? Many people spend more time preparing for a two-
week vacation than they do preparing for eternity!

The more we dwell on our final destination, the more we'll be prepared to
live eternally in heaven, thanks to Jesus Christ, who has experienced and conquered hell on our behalf. And in anticipating our eternal destination, we'll
experience a foretaste of heaven in *this* life as we seek to know the Lord more
every day.

I pray that you and I will live each day with eternity in mind. As you go
through your day today, remember that there are eternal consequences to your
choices. Dwell on heaven today, and allow those thoughts to guide your actions.
Thanks to Jesus Christ's free offer of salvation, we can become both heavenly
minded and earthly good at the same time!

The created world is but a small parenthesis in eternity.

SIR THOMAS BROWNE

A MATTER OF PROFIT AND LOSS

'For what will it profit a man if he gains the whole world, and loses his own soul?'

MARK 8:36

"Show me the numbers." This motto typifies our society's attitude and focus. We're driven by the financial "bottom line." How much money can we make? How will our choices impact our bank accounts? But the true bottom line is the end of our lives, and when we get there, the amount of money we have won't matter at all. Instead, the ledger either will or will not have our names in the "life given to Christ" column.

Will your name be there?

A little girl once asked her father, "Daddy, is your soul insured?" Puzzled, he responded, "No, darling, why do you ask?" She answered, "Well, you were just saying that your car is insured and our house is insured, and last week I heard Uncle George say that he was afraid you would lose your soul. Daddy, is your soul insured?"

Some people don't think about their souls until they come to the end of their lives. Edward Gibbon, the author of *The Rise and Fall of the Roman Empire* and a great skeptic, often attacked Christianity. But at the end of his life, he said, "All is now lost, irrecoverably lost. All is dark and doubtful."

How can you lose your soul? You can lose it through rejecting Christ outright, or you can lose it by simply neglecting Him. Scripture asks, "How shall we escape if we neglect so great a salvation?" (Hebrews 2:3). I believe more people lose their souls this way than by outright denial—by simple neglect, by merely putting it off. To "insure" our souls, we must receive Jesus Christ as the Savior and Lord of our lives.

If we do, we'll experience a great reward in the bottom line of life. When Phillip Jenks, a humble Christian, was asked, "How hard is it to die?" he answer "I have experienced more happiness today when dying than in all my life."

Don't neglect your soul. If you haven't already, give it to Christ. V you're saved or not is the ultimate bottom line.

He is no fool who gives up that which he cannot keep
in order to gain that which he cannot lose.

JIM ELLIOTT

A REMEMBRANCE OF DEATH

What man can live and not see death? Can he deliver his life from the power of the grave?

PSALM 89:48

Tonight we say goodbye to the old year and usher in the new. It's a special time of reflection and tradition, and perhaps tonight you'll engage in your own celebration as this year passes into the next. Perhaps you'll look back on favorite memories of the past year and anticipate some new adventures in the year to come.

But many will spend their New Year's Eve getting drunk. Have you ever wondered why so many people feel the need to do that? Think about it. Is it just a tradition? Or is it something more?

Perhaps the Romans of old knew. They had a phrase for it: *momento mori,* a "remembrance of death." The old year is frequently pictured in art as a doddering old man staggering his way into oblivion.

If you think about it, the picture is quite fitting. The Bible tells us that Satan has held the whole world in bondage through the fear of death. With that truth in mind, I can realize why the unregenerate, who have never been delivered from that fear, who do not have the blessed assurance of eternal life, feel the need to get drunk. If another year's passing brings them that much closer to death, it's no wonder they want to obliterate that reality with alcohol. It is really ironic, for the whole world prides itself on its realism and chides Christians for believing in "fairy tales." Some realists! These people can't face the greatest reality that every human being must inevitably face: the fact of death.

But that doesn't stop some people from trying. If we go back to 300 B.C., we find the hedonist philosopher, Epicurus, who said that death doesn't concern us, for as long as we exist, death is not here, and when death comes, we no longer exist. But that isn't so. We cannot remove death through philosophy, science, or medicine.

It is only in Christ that our mortality ceases to be frightening. For only in Him do we know what awaits us after death or, more accurately, *Who* awaits us after death. Christians can echo the apostle Paul: "To live is Christ; to die is gain!"

Tonight, as you say goodbye to an old year and usher in a new one, rejoice you're one year closer to meeting our Father in heaven. Death's door holds ar for you; you're on your way to eternal life united with Christ. Now that's hing to celebrate!

Not what we call death, but what [is] beyond death is…[what]…we fear.

T. S. ELIOT